Vietnam:
The War at Home

Vietnam:
The War at Home

Vietnam and the American People
1964—1968

by Thomas Powers

G.K.HALL &CO.
Boston, Massachusetts
1984

This G. K. Hall paperback edition is published by
arrangement with the author.

First published in paperback by G. K. Hall in 1984.

Library of Congress Cataloging in Publication Data

Powers, Thomas, 1940 Dec. 12-
  The war at home.

  Reprint. Originally published: New York : Grossman,
1973.
  Bibliography: p.
  Includes index.
  1. Vietnamese Conflict, 1961-1975 — Public opinion —
United States. 2. United States — Politics and
government — 1963-1969. 3. Public opinion — United
States. I. Title.
DS559.5.P69 1984   959.704'33'73   84-15678
ISBN 0-8398-2855-1 (pbk.)

For Candace

Vietnam:
The War at Home

Contents

Preface

Histories of the American involvement in Vietnam have so far tended to focus on the men who held positions of power, as if their struggles, hidden from the public eye, were solely responsible for what this country did or did not do. As a result it sometimes seems that the opposition to the war is in danger of being written out of history. The many accounts of the election in 1968 and of President Johnson's decision to halt the bombing of North Vietnam are alike in neglecting the larger public forces that persuaded Eugene McCarthy to challenge the President in the primaries and convinced Clark Clifford that the cost of the war was too high, the chances of success too remote, to justify a huge new commitment of men and money following the Tet offensive. The private meetings and memorandums which led to the decision to halt the bombing at a critical moment, ending a long history of escalation and turning the United States toward a policy of disengagement, were of course important. But it is also important to remember that the President and his administration were equally the victims of things beyond their control. It was Lyndon Johnson's fate neither to start nor to end the war in Vietnam, but rather to preside during the period when the nation, in its broadest sense, changed its mind about the war.

The revolutionary upheaval in Southeast Asia is one of the major events of the twentieth century, involving all the great powers of the last two generations, with the sole exception of Germany, in a long and bitter struggle whose final outcome is still in doubt. In one way or another the United States has been involved in that struggle since the Second World War, the American role slowly but inexorably expanding until the moment in 1968 when American politics pivoted on the fighting in Vietnam and the fate of Southeast Asia seemed to hang on the outcome of an American election. This book is not about that struggle, still unfolding, or even about the American role in it, not yet ended. Instead, it is a partial and preliminary history of what went through the public mind during the period when the war in Vietnam became an American war and sometimes threatened to slip so entirely out of control that even an ultimate nuclear catastrophe could not be ruled out with confidence. Specifically, it is about events within the United States during the nearly four-year period from the Tonkin Gulf incidents of 1964 to the decisions of early 1968. There is a good deal of evidence that Johnson did not at first recognize the partial bombing halt that he announced in March, 1968, for the irreversible step that it was, but that decision nevertheless established a new direction in policy which would be no easier to reverse than the policy of escalation had been earlier.

The question this book attempts to answer is, Why did President Johnson turn from escalation toward disengagement? The book's thesis is that he was forced to do so by political realities within the United States, that the people, ordinary citizens with no authority but the force of their belief and their commitment, simply refused to tolerate the war or the official assumption that there was no alternative to war. The rebellion Johnson faced within his own administration, and the challenge raised by Eugene McCarthy and Robert Kennedy, were the result of a broad-based popular opposition to the war which brought the United States to a point of profound political crisis in late 1967 and early 1968.

The crisis that forced Johnson to do what he had said he would never do was not the result of some vague "concern" over the war, of "doubts" and "reservations" and "reassessments," of a disembodied public opinion as detected by poll takers. It was the result of an irreconcilable collision between those who supported the war for whatever reasons of national policy or pride or simple inertia, and those who considered it stupid, cruel, and vile. McCarthy, Kennedy, Clark Clifford, and all the other major public figures who turned against the war did not lead the opposition; they were led by it.

The purpose of this book is not to argue again the merits of the various points raised by those for and against the war, but rather to show why and how those arguments were accepted or rejected by the public. There is little here that was not available at the time to those who knew where to look. It would be interesting to know something of Dean Rusk's private feelings as he prepared to testify before the Senate Foreign Relations Committee in February, 1966, or again two years later, but what concerns us here is what he actually said, and how the country reacted to what he said. The struggle over the war was carried out in the open, each side appealing directly to the public at large. A number of peace activists have been indicted for "conspiracy" in recent years, but in fact they did very little in secret. Every step in the struggle was debated openly and at length. The attempt here is to show what opponents of the war did and why they did it.

The efforts of the opposition ranged widely, from petitions and rallies and teach-ins and electoral campaigns, to public fasting, intellectual assault on every facet of American life and politics, draft resistance, and even, toward the end, rudimentary forms of insurrection. The opposition was often in a state of bitter internal war about how best to proceed, but its deeply felt, sometimes contradictory, always determined efforts steadily sharpened debate on the war. The opposition simply would not let the issue die, escalating its efforts in intensity as the administration escalated the war. What kinds of opposition worked? The answer seems to be that every kind worked, but in general those worked best that cost the most in a personal sense, and they worked best the first time or two, before the national consciousness learned to accept and then to ignore them.

The opposition had no power in the conventional sense. David Harris, a leader of the Resistance in California, once said those opposed to the war had only "the tool of a life," and, ultimately, it was that tool which was used. Young men who refused to submit to the draft left the government with a painful choice between ignoring them (out of the question, since in that event there quickly would *be* no draft) or jailing them. It is one thing to jail a few dozen, or even a few hundred young men, quite another when their numbers become thousands and potentially tens of thousands, as they did. The tool of a life was also used by the young men and women who took to the streets in such a way as to invite violence or arrest, and by their elders who technically broke the law by counseling young men to resist the draft, or by refusing to pay their taxes.

In a broader sense the tool of a life was used by the hundreds of thousands who turned against their country in their hearts. They imposed a price on the war by their own bitter disillusion, by their belief that the war was not just senseless but cruel, by their conclusion that American democracy was a sham if it offered no alternative to a policy so widely opposed, by their growing sense that the United States was a brutal *imperium*, interested only in money and power, and supported only by military violence. In 1967 Martin Luther King, Jr. said the United States was "the greatest purveyor of violence in the world today." His statement was attacked as exaggerated, but huge numbers of people agreed with him. The crisis of late 1967 was not only a political crisis, a conventional conflict of opposing factions, but a deep crisis of the spirit that divided the country passionately and bitterly. There were plenty of crude jingos who easily dismissed moral objection to the war and were willing to jail the opposition no matter how large it became, but they did not include McCarthy, Kennedy, or, in the end, the President himself. In one sense the very bitterness of the struggle over the war created the political conditions that forced Johnson to back away from escalation.

During the period when American military involvement in Vietnam and the opposition were both mounting, a great many things were happening at once in the United States: sharp and sudden changes between the races; the passage of progressive legislation that had been pending since the 1930s, followed by a frustrating failure to put it into effect and make it work; a new readiness to question the most accepted institutions and principles; a spontaneous movement among the young to change society, then to reject it, and finally, on the part of a passionate few, literally to destroy it; a heightening of passions on all sides to the point where charges of treason and of genocide were not only casually made but widely believed; a growing atmosphere of violence culminating in urban riots, street battles between police and protestors, and, finally, the murders of Martin Luther King and Robert Kennedy. All of these things played a part in public attitudes toward the war and, in varying degrees, were even consequences of the war. A history of that period must be a history of the passions it aroused and the manner in which they finally forced a deeply reluctant nation to recognize the fact of the war, to face the doubts it had raised, and finally to reject it.

One final matter ought to be mentioned. Attempts have been made, and more will be made, to blame the failure of the American military in Vietnam on the opposition at home. In fact, however, the development of the opposition followed rather than preceded events in Vietnam. Strong as the opposition became, it was not strong enough to prevent the commitment of more than half a million American troops, to prevent the most concentrated bombing campaign in the history of warfare, to prevent the use of weapons widely considered to be outlawed by the Geneva and other conventions, or to prevent the expenditure of more than $100 billion. Hanoi and the National Liberation Front, it seems clear, were encouraged to continue the war because of the way the United States chose to fight it, not from any illusions about the political potential of the American antiwar movement. When things began to go badly for the French in the early 1950s, they were repeatedly warned that the struggle was political in nature and could never be settled by military means. That warning was to the point then and remains so. The attitude of Hanoi seems to have been that American failure in Vietnam would inevitably create an opposition within the United States; not the other way around. The experience of the French in both Indochina and Algeria seems to bear this out. Serious public division over a war is likely only when it is going badly, and the American effort in Vietnam went badly from the start. Furthermore, it has been a source of continuing despair among those in the opposition that Johnson's policy in Vietnam was abandoned not because it was wrong, but because it failed.

This point is an important one: the opposition to the war did not *cause* the failure; it forced the government to *recognize* the failure. It is impossible to say what would have happened if there had been no opposition and the American government had been free to fight in any way it liked for as long as it liked. A number of government officials insisted then, and still insist now, that Hanoi would have abandoned its efforts if there had been no division within the United States over the war. Maybe so, but a thousand years of Vietnamese history would seem to controvert that hopeful assumption. It is more likely that frustration in Washington would have caused the war to spread even further than it did, with terrible consequences.

The war did not end in 1968, of course, and neither did the struggle over the war, but the decisive turn in American policy from escalation to disengagement occurred in that year. The aftermath has been a kind of endgame, bloody, bitter, and costly, but also inexorable.

It is only fair, on a subject that has aroused such strong feelings, to declare my bias. I suspect it is obvious from the preceding pages that I have been, and am, opposed to the war. For those who take the trouble to read further, however, this will not really cast much light on why I have written as I have. The point of view that infuses this book is a more complicated thing than simple opposition, growing out of the way the war touched me personally. Looking back on it now, it is obvious that my reaction to the war between 1964 and 1968 was decidedly chaotic, or rather that it consisted of a series of very clear, positive, and vehement attitudes which changed daily, although tending to drift in a single direction.

In November, 1963, I went to Mississippi with a group of students from Yale who had volunteered to help the Student Non-Violent Coordinating Committee run a mock election. I was plunged immediately into another world, fearing the police cars which waited on side streets at night with their lights off; fearing the white, thin-faced farmers in pickup trucks who followed us along dusty country roads; fearing the approach of strangers. Once in that world, the senses of oppression, injustice, and physical danger were overpowering. I remember thinking, at the end of eight days, that I knew how the world appeared to the Vietcong. There was no middle ground; your only loyalty was to your friends; every attempt to understand your enemies was affected by their fierce hostility and their very real power to injure you. Compared to the immediacy of Mississippi, however, Vietnam seemed distant and insignificant.

Like everyone else who read the newspapers, I was reminded periodically of Vietnam during the next fifteen months, frightened by Barry Goldwater's suggestions for winning the war and reassured by Johnson's promise to keep out of it. The war did not really force itself upon me until February 7, 1965, when Johnson ordered the second bombing raid on North Vietnam following a Vietcong attack on American military barracks at Pleiku. Two days earlier I had been inducted into the army for National Guard training and had been transported to the snowy, windy, frigid flatland of Fort Dix, New Jersey. The lights went out at ten o'clock that night, but we all remained awake in the dark, covered by green army blankets, lying on metal army bunks, staring in the dim light at the ceiling of an army barracks, listening to transistor radios report the raids and half-believing (since anything seems possible in the army) that we would be on an early plane to South Vietnam.

The army, of course, made maximum use of the heightened situation during our eight weeks of basic training. "This is important," sergeants snapped. "What are you going to do if your M-14 jams in Veet-nam?" Since they jammed only too frequently on the Fort Dix firing ranges, we took this more or less seriously. We lay on the cold ground, looking out at the devastated areas where every living thing had long since been shot to pieces, the trunks of trees frayed even twenty and thirty feet above the ground, the very ground itself literally poisoned by millions of copper-jacketed bullets. A sergeant in a wooden tower shouted over a loudspeaker system: "Ready on the right. Ready on the left. Firers, lock and load one fourteen-round magazine and commence firing."

When the stiff, olive-green silhouettes popped up behind sand dunes and next to shattered tree stumps, it was not too hard to believe this was leading toward the dark and steaming jungles we imagined in Southeast Asia. I was "against" the war in an abstract way, but its impact on me personally was more confusing: it seemed possible the National Guard might be called up and that I might go. I was not altogether certain if I feared this would happen, or wanted it to happen.

Later, during a second eight weeks of training as a switchboard operator at Fort Gordon, Georgia, I calmed down somewhat, although not entirely. (For awhile I thought about joining the Special Forces. This is so far from what I would be likely to do now that it is hard for me to remember why I considered it then. I think it was a combination of boredom in switchboard class and curiosity about war.) I spent a lot of time in the base library, which was air-conditioned, and read Franklin Mark Osaka's anthology on guerrilla warfare and other books. What I read convinced me the United States was in serious trouble in Vietnam, since we were apparently breaking all the rules of guerrilla war, and I began to argue about the war during smoke breaks between classes.

The air of official crisis persisted through the summer, but was generally in the back of my mind, with the exception of one bad week in July when it looked as though Johnson would call up the reserves. I was out of the army by this time and was not at all eager to go back in. In September I went to Italy to work on the Rome *Daily American*, a small English-language paper published there since the end of the Second World War. In a curious way it was not until I had left the United States that I became truly conscious of the war, my awareness fed by the vast number of news stories about Vietnam and the American reaction to it, which I read daily. For two years I read the entire file of the United Press International and Associated Press European wires at least five times a week, as well as the Paris editions of the *Herald Tribune* and the *New York Times* (until the latter was absorbed by the former).

In spite of the fact that I experienced the war entirely at second hand, it became something of an obsession. The American community in Rome was a microcosm of the larger public at home, split along pretty much the same lines for the same reasons, with the same results. Arguments were frequent and often bitter and always inconclusive. People who were "for" the war became visibly ill with anger when they read about kids burning their draft cards or the flag; those "against" it were sickened by Washington's bland insistence that all the violence was in the cause of peace. The anger and frustration were unbearable, as real and immediate as if the war had been an argument in the family. It was a terrible time that seemed to go on forever, and I am sometimes surprised that people have been so quick to forget what it was like to live through.

In the late fall of 1967 I returned to this country and went to work for United Press International as a reporter in New York. The following year I covered the conflict at Columbia University and stayed with the story, eventually traveling to Harvard, Cornell, Yale, the University of California at Berkeley, the University of Wisconsin, the University of Michigan, and other schools. In the course of talking to dozens of students, as well as activists in the antiwar movement, it became apparent that what I had felt in Rome was by no means unique. Consciousness of the war amounted to a kind of pathology, with a pattern like that of a fever, throwing the victim into an intense agitation mounting to a crisis.

The pattern was the same, but not the ways in which those I talked to specifically thought and felt. The positions they held reflected the degree to which their personal lives had been actually touched by the war. Those who took the most extreme positions were often—not always—those who had worked the hardest to end the war. I had been touched only at a distance, by the simple fact of the war. Many of the students I talked to had been working for *years* to end the war. They had picketed military recruiters, organized demonstrations, been beaten by police, were often planning to refuse induction or go into exile in Canada. It was not hard to see why so many young peace activists, embittered by their long struggle, had become revolutionaries. We talked about politics, but no amount of simple reasoning could have reconciled our opposing views. Our experiences separated us too completely. It became increasingly clear to me that politics is only partly a rational matter; the rest is existential.

I remember sitting in the sun on the steps of Harvard's Memorial Church one morning a day or two after police had violently cleared an administration building in April, 1969. I was talking with a couple of students, one of them with a lacerated scalp, gaudy with Mercurochrome. "The reason you feel free," he told me, "is that no one has ever tried to make you do something you really don't want to do. Try refusing to go into the army and see what happens." He was right, of course. I remembered the way I had felt in Mississippi six years earlier; if I had remained in the movement I am sure much the same things would have happened to me that happened to so many others.

And yet, if my own views were inevitably those of one who had been touched only indirectly by the war, theirs had sometimes been distorted by the very passion of their opposition. Their anger gave them the strength to resist when resistance seemed hopeless, but their failure to achieve everything they had hoped sometimes blinded them to what they *had* achieved. I found a widespread belief, for example, that the opposition to the war had failed completely, that Johnson's defeat in 1968 had been meaningless and empty, that Nixon was simply pursuing the war with equal determination by other means. This seemed to me a misunderstanding no less basic than the error of those who feel the issue was decided entirely in Washington.

The war in Vietnam is a huge event, the central fact in the life of an entire generation, and it is not likely to be understood fully until long after it is over. This book is a preliminary attempt to recount the history of the struggle over the war, to show how the opposition created and then organized itself, and to demonstrate the ways in which it finally forced Lyndon Johnson to abandon his chosen policy. The political process is a much broader thing than sometimes recognized. The "system" includes both those who run the government and those who oppose it in the streets. A formal statement by the President may have less impact on the national consciousness than one young man burning his draft card and then going to jail for that act of defiance. The opposition often seemed pitifully weak compared to the power of the presidency, but in the end it prevailed.

Vietnam:
The War at Home

ONE

"No Wider War"

War and the fear of war dominated the presidential campaign of 1964 from its beginning. Indochina and then Vietnam had been in the background of American politics since the end of the Second World War, occasionally coming forward as a public issue, but more often a potential problem in a world filled with all-too-many immediate problems. A handful of congressmen, journalists, liberal intellectuals, and tiny radical or pacifist groups knew what was going on in Vietnam and wrote or spoke about the alarming drift of events, but their warnings had been heard only by that fragment of the public interested in public things, and heeded by few. The broad mass of the people did not really become conscious of Vietnam, even as the name of a place, until Barry Goldwater began referring to the fighting there as a war and speculated in public about the various weapons that might be used to win it.

Goldwater, a plain-speaking Republican senator from Arizona, had emerged as a national leader and presidential candidate through years of speaking before audiences made up largely of conservative Republicans. He had mastered an almost evangelical oratorical style consisting of approximately equal parts of faith in God, love of country, anticommunism, and hostility to modernism in art, religion, and economic theory. He was a man of considerable charm and rectitude, but narrow political appeal. When he spoke about standing up to the Communists, about victory in Vietnam, about having the courage to die if that's the way it had to be, his audiences understood him to be speaking in praise of stern and traditional virtues, not daring the world to fight. They were used to his style. The country, however, was not.

1

Goldwater had none of the instinctive caution that lets most politicians know when they are pursuing an unpopular issue. He went on talking about Vietnam as a war and how the war could be won long after it was apparent to everyone else that the country was being frightened rather than convinced. As a general in the Air Force Reserve, fascinated by mechanical things, Goldwater was used to musing about military matters. On one occasion early in his 1964 presidential campaign he suggested the United States could isolate the Vietcong in South Vietnam by bombing the supply routes connecting China and North Vietnam. On another he wondered aloud, while millions of people were watching him on television, if nuclear weapons might not be used to clear the jungles where the Vietcong were presumably hiding. The public reaction to these notions was one of horrified alarm. In an abstract way Goldwater understood this. "You mention the word nuclear," he said, "and all they can think of is the big mushroom cloud, the red blast and twenty million dead."[1] At the same time, however, Goldwater knew that the nuclear arsenal included weapons that were only a kind of gigantic artillery, that respected civilian strategists had recommended their use in situations far short of total war, and that the military itself had all but formally proposed the use of nuclear weapons on a number of occasions in the past.[2] He refused to moderate his position simply because less sophisticated people insisted on misunderstanding him. His staff, sensing the damage he was doing to his chances in November, first tried to quiet him and finally began isolating him from reporters altogether.

Goldwater's casual asides were only part of the problem, however. His formal statements often had a certain crude belligerence which made him appear a more bellicose man than in fact he was. The main thrust of his campaign was directed at a slackening of the nation's moral fiber, an obsession of conservatives for more than a generation, but the public seemed to hear nothing except his clarion calls for resolution in the face of Communist provocations. At a fund-raising dinner in Los Angeles on March 18, he struck a note which conservative Republicans interpreted as an altogether appropriate manliness, but which a larger public heard as a naked challenge to the Communist nations:

Where is the leadership in an administration that stands cross-eyed with our friends, wide-eyed with our enemies, wall-eyed in Berlin, glassy-eyed in Southeast Asia and downright blind in Cuba? Today it is Soviet brinksmanship that commands the field and it is American backdownsmanship that is losing the field. There is only one way for this, the mightiest nation in history, to deter war and to keep the peace. That way is to make sure the enemy knows he cannot and will not win any war that he might be tempted to start. But our enemy will never know that —our enemy will never respect that so long as the architects of defeat are in power in Washington.[3]

Although Goldwater was finally persuaded to stop talking about nuclear weapons, he refused to abandon the issue of Vietnam. At rallies across the country he challenged President Johnson to explain what was at stake in Vietnam, why the war was going badly for our side, and what he intended to do about it. Goldwater's opponents in the Republican primaries naturally emphasized his loose talk about bombs, implying that they were more pacific men since they did not propose to defeat the Vietcong by obliterating Vietnam. They generally side-stepped the more difficult question of what, exactly, they did plan to do about the very real setbacks that the United States was facing in Southeast Asia. Once the differences in rhetorical style had been cleared away, Goldwater and his Republican opponents basically felt much the same way: the American commitment in Vietnam was too important to abandon; things were not going well; something would have to be done. A few days after his defeat by Goldwater in the bitterly fought California primary, New York's Governor Nelson Rockefeller told a reporter that being out of the race was not all bad. "There are things you don't have to worry about anymore," he said, "like do you have to take the country into war over Vietnam."[4]

After his nomination at the Republican convention in San Francisco in July, Goldwater made it clear he would not pass over the hard questions being raised by the situation in Vietnam. Isolated in the television lights above the cheering crowd, he defined the issue sharply:

Yesterday it was Korea, tonight it is Vietnam. Make no bones of this. Don't try to sweep this under the rug. We are at war in Vietnam. And yet the President, who is commander-in-chief of our forces, refuses to say —refuses to say, mind you—whether or not the objective there is victory, and his Secretary of Defense continues to mislead and misinform the American people, and enough of this has gone by.[5]

The country did not want to hear what Goldwater had to say, but in fact his case was a strong one. The United States *was* at war in Vietnam, a fatal confusion *did* infect our policy there, the administration *had* consistently misled the press and the public about the nature and extent of American involvement. In the summer of 1964 Johnson himself did not really know what he was going to do about the war, and his previous involvement on two critical occasions had pointed in sharply differing directions.

Ten years earlier, in the spring of 1954, the French had requested American intervention to save their besieged forces at Dien Bien Phu, and Secretary of State John Foster Dulles had been strongly inclined to meet their request. A variety of plans were proposed and rejected for one reason or another until April 3, 1954, when Dulles called eight key members of the Senate and the House of Representatives to a secret meeting in the State Department as the first step toward securing congressional approval for an American attempt to save Dien Bien Phu. Johnson, then minority leader of the Senate, was decidedly cool to Dulles's proposal. He pointed out that the United States had just extricated itself from a war in Korea where 90 percent of the troops and funds had been provided by the United States. He, and eventually the other members of Congress present at the meeting, opposed getting into a similar situation without clear commitments from Britain and other allies. When Dulles was unable to persuade the British to join an American effort, the plan fell through.

Seven years later, however, after Johnson's election to the vice presidency, he found himself on the other side of the argument. Early in the administration of John F. Kennedy it became apparent that Ngo Dinh Diem, the Catholic president of South Vietnam, was gradually losing the war against the Vietcong despite American military and financial aid. In May, 1961, Kennedy sent Johnson on a tour of Southeast Asia as part of an attempt to find out what was happening there and what the United States ought to do about it. During his visit Johnson publicly enthused about Diem as "the Churchill of Asia," but he apparently realized Diem's very real limits as an ally. When, on the flight out of Saigon, a reporter began to criticize the austere, remote, and suspicious

South Vietnamese president, Johnson abruptly cut him off. "Don't tell me about Diem," he said. "He's all we've got out there."[6]

Despite his doubts, when Johnson returned to Washington he submitted a report to Kennedy arguing that South Vietnam could still be saved, but only if the United States was prepared to increase its commitment significantly. Kennedy sent a second delegation to Saigon shortly after Johnson's return and then, in October, a third, headed by General Maxwell Taylor and Walt Rostow. By the end of 1961, persuaded that Diem's decline could still be halted and that U.S. interests in South Vietnam justified the attempt, as well as keenly aware that domestic politics demanded he avoid anything that looked like a Communist victory, Kennedy approved a broad plan for an enlarged U.S. effort, including a limited combat role for the American military. Rostow's suggestion for the bombing of North Vietnam was set aside, but it remained in the background of all future discussion of the war, periodically emerging in high-level debate whenever things were going badly, which was often.

For a brief period the new military equipment, and especially the introduction of helicopters in large numbers, appeared to be stemming the Vietcong tide. By the end of the next year, however, Diem's political failings, the inherent weaknesses of the South Vietnamese army, and Vietcong resilience had combined to neutralize the American effort.

The political situation in Saigon, where Diem listened only to the members of his immediate family, and the military situation both continued to erode throughout 1963. The disparity between the reports of newsmen and official estimates handed up the chain of command became a source of embarrassment in Washington but did not appear to darken the air of optimism that surrounded U.S. policy in Vietnam. The U.S. military commander in Vietnam, General Paul D. Harkins, the U.S. ambassador to Saigon, Frederick Nolting, and the Kennedy administration, their illusions reinforced by a steady stream of sunny progress reports, sometimes sounded as if they felt the only problem was the willful pessimism of journalists. Nolting, for example, bitterly resented the skepticism of reporters who argued that whatever official statistics might say, Saigon's authority was evaporating in the countryside. "You're always looking for the hole in the doughnut, Mr. Halberstam," he once told the *New York Times* correspondent in Saigon.[7]

It is important to remember that the difference between journalists and the Kennedy administration was not over the wisdom of U.S. policy, but over whether or not it was working. The criticism their stories evoked in Washington centered on the failure of U.S. assistance to Saigon, not on its goal. Harkins's optimism collided with reality on November 1, 1963, when long-standing political grievances in South Vietnam and realization by the Kennedy administration that the existing regime could never respond to them finally brought a military coup and the murder of Diem and his hated brother, Ngo Dinh Nhu. The military newspaper *Stars and Stripes* carried a story on its front page that day which quoted Harkins as saying that "victory in the sense that would apply to this kind of war" was less than a year away.[8]

When Kennedy was assassinated in Dallas three weeks later, he left Lyndon Johnson a commitment to success in Vietnam all the more difficult to abandon for being undefined. On Sunday, November 24, two days after Kennedy's death, Johnson met with Henry Cabot Lodge, appointed to replace Nolting shortly before the coup, General Taylor, Secretary of State Dean Rusk, Ambassador-at-Large W. Averell Harriman, Central Intelligence Agency (CIA) chief John McCone, and others to discuss the situation in Vietnam. Johnson was told that Saigon's collapse was only a matter of time unless the United States took action to prevent it. The President assured them he did not plan to abandon Kennedy's policy of support for an independent, pro-Western South Vietnam. The following month he set up a White House working group to study the problem under the leadership of Walter Sullivan, a young State Department protégé of Harriman. Sullivan's report, submitted to the President six weeks later, accepted the premise that the war in South Vietnam was under the control of North Vietnam and could be ended by pressure on Hanoi. Like Rostow in 1961, Sullivan argued that the right kind of pressure would be military, and he recommended a series of graduated steps which would, if necessary, include the blockade of Haiphong harbor, bombing raids on the North, and the introduction of up to 100,000 U.S. troops in the South. Johnson read the report but postponed a decision.

The official American position continued to be one of steadfast support for Vietnam. Financial aid was increased, clandestine operations of various kinds were mounted against the North, and limited bombing of Communist supply-lines in Laos was begun, but Johnson refused to approve anything that would be apparent as a sharp departure. He

resisted military pleas for escalation as well as a suggestion for recon-
vening the Geneva Convention put forth by the French president,
Charles de Gaulle, and supported by a number of senators, especially
Mike Mansfield, a Democrat of Montana. While Washington anxiously
maintained the status quo, the Vietcong made steady progress.
Throughout 1964 they increased terrorism against the Saigon government and American forces, strengthened their hold on large areas of
the countryside, and began to initiate battalion-size actions, a clear sign
they felt the war was entering its final stages. On May 14 Secretary of
Defense Robert McNamara met with the President for ninety minutes
to report on his recent visit to Saigon and then talked with White House
reporters. He dismissed the importance of rumors that bombing raids
might be launched against the North, said the United States was prepared to extend Saigon additional aid, and insisted he was still convinced victory could be achieved in the end:

> But I want to emphasize that it is not going to come soon. This is not
> that kind of war. This is a war for the confidence of the people, and the
> security of those people, and that kind of war is a long, hard war.[9]

American caution in 1964 was partly the result of unsteady political
conditions in Saigon, where a second coup on January 30 had placed
General Nguyen Khanh in power. The main reason for Washington's
relatively subdued response to an obviously critical situation, however,
was Johnson's sense that hard decisions were coming. It was clear that
minor increases in the level of American aid were not going to prevent
disaster; eventually the United States would have to expand dramatically its own role in the war, or abandon Saigon's cause as lost. Each
small step deeper into the war only limited Johnson's freedom to deal
with the much larger decision that would have to be made later.

Johnson's public attitude toward the war remained somewhat vague
until Goldwater began to attack him for his lack of resolution. As
politically adept as Goldwater was clumsy, Johnson went after him
with a sure sense of where he was weakest. With the help of Rusk and
McNamara, both quiet and serious men, Johnson emphasized his sol-
idly presidential qualities, his restraint, his sense of responsibility, his
concern for *all* the people, his comprehension of the dangers inherent
in a world where the Great Powers had the ability to annihilate each
other.

Inevitably, Johnson began to misrepresent his true position. In criticizing Goldwater's talk about getting tough in Vietnam, Johnson naturally cast himself in the role of peacemaker. He emphasized that the American role in the fighting was to help the South Vietnamese win the war for themselves. At the same time, however, without defining what the rules of the war were, he repeatedly warned the North Vietnamese against breaking them. At the University of California at Los Angeles on February 21, Johnson stated both attitudes succinctly:

> The contest in which South Vietnam is now engaged is first and foremost a contest to be won by the government and people of that country for themselves. But those engaged in external direction and supply would do well to be reminded and to remember that this type of aggression is a deeply dangerous game.[10]

People naturally wondered just exactly what this meant, but when reporters asked the President to elaborate at a press conference a week later, Johnson testily answered that,

> In my California speech I intended to say just what I did, that aggressors who intend to envelop peaceful, liberty-loving, free people, and attempt to do so through aggressive means, are playing a very dangerous game. That's what I said and that's what I meant.[11]

What everyone wanted to know, of course, was just how dangerous, to whom, in what way, but Johnson refused to make himself clearer, limiting himself to the vaguest of threats, which neither silenced domestic critics like Goldwater nor intimidated North Vietnam. As the military situation in the South slowly deteriorated during the spring and summer, Johnson shifted uneasily between pledges of increased aid for Saigon and hazy warnings to the North not to push things too far. In June he replaced the sunny but ineffective American commander, General Harkins, with General William Westmoreland, and then, three days later, named General Taylor to replace Henry Cabot Lodge as the U.S. ambassador to Saigon. In July, less than two weeks after the Republican convention, where Goldwater publicly promised to make the war an issue, Johnson tacitly admitted the gravity of the situation by sending another five thousand American troops to join the sixteen thousand already in Vietnam.

Americans did not really feel they were at war, exactly, and yet this act was in fact the clearest possible promise of wider war to come. The question, as Goldwater well knew, was whether or not the United States would win the war for Saigon if Saigon could not win for itself. Goldwater was close enough to the military to know the true military situation, which was not encouraging. Eventually an American president, almost certainly the winner of the election in November, would be faced with a choice between failure or a major American land war in Vietnam. When Johnson committed another five thousand men he indicated how he would decide that ultimate question. Goldwater did not attack Johnson's apparent policy but his fundamentally dishonest attempt to hide the decisions which that policy implied. Truth in government would later become a major political issue, but in 1964 Goldwater's honesty gained him nothing but abuse.

Despite Johnson's steady lead in the opinion polls, his position contained certain contradictions which limited his freedom of action. He had been convinced that Hanoi's plans depended on what it saw to be American intentions, and yet the clear unpopularity of Goldwater's position on the war seemed to preclude strong action, or even language, by the President if the situation in Vietnam took a sudden turn for the worse. He knew the country did not want to go to war over Vietnam, but he also knew that what George Orwell used to call "the Big Public" —the broad mass of the people—was changeable. What looked like restraint on Johnson's part one day might appear to be weakness the next. In its heart the public probably wanted it both ways: they didn't want to fight, but they wanted to win. People were frightened by Goldwater's offhand remarks about nuclear weapons, but at the same time something thrilled within many of them when Goldwater talked about hammer blows that would force the other side to back down. The country would vote for Johnson in the end, less beguiled than frightened by the sort of gunboat diplomacy that Goldwater's pugnacious language seemed to promise, but it might withhold the mandate Johnson wanted for both practical and personal reasons. The only way to get that mandate was to deny Goldwater room to maneuver on the Vietnam issue. Johnson wanted to run on the peace issue, but not as a pacifist. As in so many things, he sought a middle position: tough in defense of the national honor, and yet cautious to avoid unnecessary war. In a word, responsible.

At 10:15 Sunday morning, August 2, the Pentagon released a 110-word statement tersely describing an attack on an American destroyer off the coast of North Vietnam by patrol boats which the statement did not identify, but which were clearly understood to have been North Vietnamese. Three of the attacking craft had been damaged in the encounter, one of them badly, and the U.S. had suffered no casualties. In fact, only a single machine gun bullet had struck the destroyer, the *Maddox*. The initial reaction of the American government was calm. Rusk went to New York, gave a scheduled speech to the American Field Service, and told reporters who pressed him for a comment, "The other side got a sting out of this. If they do it again, they'll get another sting."[12]

Senator Mike Mansfield, an expert on Asia who had long been worried by the steadily growing involvement of the United States in Vietnam, tentatively suggested that the attack had not been entirely gratuitous. "We have got to remember," he told reporters seeking the customary reactions, "that we are rather heavily committed out there and that in view of our involvement such occasions will arise from time to time. We hope they do not, but we should not be surprised if they do."[13] Barry Goldwater, resting before the campaign in Newport Beach, California, did not respond until the following day, when his press secretary released a statement:

> I think the American people are entitled to ask some questions of their own in regard to this event: Does the presence of American destroyers in the area signify the possible landing of larger American ground forces? Does it mean medium bombers are going to be used to interdict supply lines? Does it mean a change is taking place in foreign policy at the White House and State Department levels?[14]

A comment in similar vein by Senator Everett Dirksen, the influential Republican minority leader who had made Goldwater's nominating speech in San Francisco, made it clear to Johnson that his conduct of the war would be pressed hard during the campaign. On the same day, August 3, he called reporters into the White House Oval Office and read them a statement threatening strong retaliatory action if there were any more attacks on American ships in international waters.

Then, at 6 P.M. on Tuesday, August 4, the Pentagon announced that a second attack had taken place. This time Washington plunged immediately into a crisis atmosphere. At 6:45 P.M. sixteen congressional leaders met with the President, who told them what he planned to do, and then were briefed on the attack and the planned response in somewhat greater detail by McNamara, CIA Chief John McCone, and General Earle Wheeler, the new Chairman of the Joint Chiefs of Staff. At 8:25 P.M. presidential press secretary George Reedy told White House reporters the President would go on national television later in the evening. He warned them it was not safe to go to dinner, the semiofficial way of saying the President's statement would be important and that it might come at any moment.

The White House contacted Goldwater, who responded with a statement of support which reached reporters before Johnson had announced publicly what he planned to do:

> I am sure that every American will subscribe to the action outlined in the President's statement. I believe it is the only thing that he can do under the circumstances. We cannot allow the American flag to be shot at anywhere on earth if we are to retain our respect and prestige.[15]

At 11:37 P.M. Johnson appeared before the television cameras set up in the White House Fish Room, described the attack, and announced a retaliatory air strike, which he said was under way at that very moment. At 12:02 A.M. Wednesday, August 5, the television cameras cut to McNamara in the Pentagon, where he described the retaliatory strike in greater detail and added that military reinforcements were being moved into the general area. At the same time, Rusk briefed newsmen at the State Department, making it clear the next move was up to Hanoi.

The reaction of the public, the press, and Congress was almost unanimous: the attacks on American destroyers were intolerable and Johnson's response had been altogether suitable to the provocation. During those brief days in August between the second and seventh the issue seemed clear-cut: the United States had been attacked gratuitously while exercising its right to send its ships anywhere it pleased so long as they remained in international waters. Rusk and McNamara confessed bewilderment about Hanoi's true purpose in carrying out such a dangerous operation. The response of almost the entire country was one of anger and a feeling of satisfaction at the sharp blow in response, which had destroyed twenty-five North Vietnamese PT boats and 90 percent of the oil storage facilities at Vinh.

Johnson moved quickly to take advantage of the crisis atmosphere. By noon on Wednesday his staff had drawn up a final draft resolution supporting his actions and granting him authority "to take all necessary measures to repel any armed attack against the forces of the United States and to prevent further aggression."[16] The text of the Southeast Asia Resolution, as it was formally called, was taken to the Capitol where it was immediately read by the clerk of the Senate. Hearings of the Senate Foreign Relations and Armed Services committees were scheduled for the following morning.

Many members of the Senate were privately critical of what history has dubbed the Tonkin Gulf Resolution, feeling it would give the President the right to make war at his own discretion, a power that the Constitution placed under the control of Congress. Only Senator Wayne Morse, however, actively challenged the administration's version of what had happened on the night of August 4, when the second attack was said to have taken place. Morse began his solitary campaign against the resolution on the afternoon of August 5 with a long, somewhat rambling speech based on doubts about what had happened that had been brought to his attention by a civilian employee in the Department of Defense. Morse stated that the *Maddox* had penetrated the twelve-mile territorial limit claimed by North Vietnam (but not recognized by the United States), challenged the administration's description of the patrol as routine, and charged that the *Maddox* had been supporting South Vietnamese naval raids on North Vietnamese territory, in appearance if not in strict fact. He repeated his charges during the closed hearings held jointly the following morning by the Foreign Relations and Armed Services committees, but they were either denied outright or explained away by McNamara, Rusk, and Wheeler. Senator J. William Fulbright, chairman of the Foreign Relations Committee, asked no questions during the one-hour-and-forty-minute hearing. The two committees voted twenty-four to one in favor of the resolution as submitted by the President. House hearings held immediately afterward lasted less than an hour.

Nevertheless, Morse did not give up. Johnson wanted the resolution passed the same day, but Morse insisted a vote be postponed until Friday, August 7, and that he be allowed to speak for two hours on both Thursday and Friday. Fulbright, floor manager of the resolution, was forced to agree in order to avoid a filibuster threatened by Morse if he were not granted the delay.

When formal debate on the resolution began Friday morning, a number of senators expressed an uneasy fear that the resolution they were about to pass would allow President Johnson to commit American forces to the war. Senator Daniel Brewster of Maryland, who had been in the Far East during the Second World War, warned against getting more involved than we already were:

> I have had the opportunity to see warfare not so very far from this area, and it was very mean. I would look with great dismay on a situation involving the landing of large land armies on the continent of Asia. So my question is whether there is anything in the resolution which would authorize or recommend or approve the landing of large American armies in Vietnam or in China.[17]

Fulbright said he sympathized with Brewster's position and that the resolution would not specifically approve such a move on the part of the United States. "However," he added, "the language of the resolution would not prevent it."[18]

Other senators expressed similar reservations, and each time Fulbright answered that he shared their concern, that he opposed widening the war, that as far as he knew the administration did not plan to widen it, but that the resolution as written would not actually prevent it. Finally Senator Gaylord Nelson of Wisconsin, unconvinced by Fulbright's attempts at reassurance, moved to amend the resolution specifically to rule out "a direct military involvement in the Southeast Asia conflict."[19] Fulbright had conferred with the White House, which wanted the resolution passed without amendments since they might limit the strength of the endorsement sought by the President, as well as encourage amendments in the House, which was also considering the resolution. Fulbright told Nelson he would not accept the amendment. Morse issued a final warning that the resolution would prove to be a "historic mistake,"[20] and then the Senate voted eighty-eight to two (only Morse and Ernest Gruening of Alaska dissenting) in favor of the resolution.

Under the circumstances the only surprise was that the vote was not unanimous in both the Senate and the House, where Adam Clayton Powell registered a degree of protest by voting present. President Johnson's position was, of course, difficult to attack. Since he had asked Congress to approve an action he had already taken, they were forced to go along. The vote in the Congress also reflected the feeling of the country as a whole, however. People confused about what was happening in South Vietnam found the PT-boat attacks satisfyingly clear; they had been angered by Hanoi's audacity and pleased by the President's response.

From that point on, Goldwater's chances of election virtually ceased to exist. The President had proved he was tough and as a result felt free during the rest of the campaign to prove that he was a peacemaker, too. In planning his campaign strategy Johnson was in a uniquely favorable position. Since he was almost certain to win, he could design his campaign to obtain a large mandate, or he could focus it to win a narrower but more specific mandate for some sharply defined course of action. He chose the first, for both personal and practical reasons. In the first place he still felt overshadowed by the example and memory of President Kennedy, who had captured the hearts of most of the men who wrote about presidents, but whose plurality had been tiny. Kennedy had, in fact, been elected with less than half the total vote. Second, Johnson knew that his chances of enacting controversial legislation depended largely on the extent to which members of Congress felt they were in his debt. Kennedy's legislative program had been crippled by his narrow victory, since many Democratic congressmen had run ahead of him in the 1960 election and naturally felt they owed him nothing.

The most important reason Johnson sought a broad mandate, however, had to do with his character. As a senator and as President he always sought to preserve his "options"—that is, the freedom to change his mind—until the probable effect of his decision was clear. He bitterly resented speculation about what he was thinking or planning to do and often changed his mind simply to confound those who presumed to predict his actions. He wanted a decisive victory above all because it would be a kind of readily negotiable political currency, which he could then spend as he saw fit. The result was that Johnson's campaign focused less on what he planned to do with a term of his own than on the ways in which he was not like Goldwater. Since the public saw Goldwater as a warmaker, Johnson inevitably cast himself in the role of a responsible man of peace. At moments his exploitation of the peace issue verged on the politically scurrilous. One particularly harsh television commercial, broadcast only once, showed a child picking petals from a daisy and counting one, two, three, four. Then a voice came in counting backwards: four, three, two, one, and a nuclear blast. Whom did the people want to have the ultimate power to press that final button? The man who talked about nuclear weapons as just another tool of power? Or President Johnson, so painfully conscious of their awesome horror? The impact of the ad went far beyond its single showing, expressing a deep fear of war that Goldwater would never be able to reason away. Every time Goldwater mentioned Vietnam he evoked fears of spreading war, but he nevertheless continued to press the issue, insisting it was a war like any other and ought to be conducted like any other. Johnson found this opening irresistible. Again and again, in stronger terms each time, he emphasized that "the United States seeks no wider war," that he wanted to keep American boys home where they belonged, that wild talk of bombing and blockading offered no solution to a struggle that would be decided in the end by the people of South Vietnam. In Manchester, New Hampshire, on September 28, referring obliquely to yet another political upheaval in South Vietnam just two weeks earlier, Johnson spoke at length about the dangers in widening the conflict:

Some of our people—Mr. Nixon, Mr. Rockefeller, Mr. Scranton and Mr. Goldwater—have all, at some time or other, suggested the possible wisdom of going North in Vietnam. Well, now, before you start attacking someone and you launch a big offensive, you better give some consideration to how you are going to protect what you have. And when a brigadier general can walk down the streets of Saigon, as they did the other day, and take over the police station, the radio station and the government without firing a shot, I don't know how much offensive we are prepared to launch.

As far as I am concerned, I want to be very cautious and careful and use it only as a last resort, when I start dropping bombs around that are likely to involve American boys in a war in Asia with 700 million Chinese. So just for the moment I have not thought we were ready for American boys to do the fighting for Asian boys. . . . We are not going North and drop bombs at this stage of the game, and we are not going South and run out and leave it for the Communists to take over.

Now we have lost 190 American lives, and to each one of those 190 families this is a major war. . . . I often wake up in the night and think about how many I could lose if I made a misstep. When we retaliated in the Tonkin Gulf, we dropped bombs on their nests where they had their PT boats housed, and we dropped them within 35 miles of the

Chinese border. I don't know what you would think if they started dropping them 35 miles from your border, but I think it is something you have to take into consideration. . . .

It is not any problem to start a war. . . . I know some folks that I think could start one mighty easy. But it is a pretty difficult problem for us to prevent one, and that is what we are trying to do.[21]

On October 21, only two weeks before the election, Johnson left little doubt where he stood on the subject of the war: "We are not about to send American boys nine or ten thousand miles away from home to do what Asian boys ought to be doing for themselves."[22]

Things that might have seriously threatened any other candidate, such as the discovery that an important presidential aide had been arrested on a morals charge, hardly interrupted Johnson's momentum. Goldwater later admitted he had known his situation was hopeless as early as August, but it is in the nature of a political campaign for the issue to seem increasingly in doubt as election day approaches. A dramatic event at the last moment has the power to change everything, and such an event occurred in Vietnam two days before the campaign ended. On the night of November 1, mortar shells suddenly began to explode among a fleet of forty B-57 bombers parked on the tarmac of Bien Hoa airport, just outside Saigon and supposedly guarded by South Vietnamese forces. Five of the planes, which had been brought to Vietnam as a gesture of strength following the second Tonkin Gulf incident, were completely destroyed, and another fifteen were damaged, a loss estimated at $25 million. Four Americans were killed and twenty injured in the barrage, dramatically illustrating the Vietcong's ability to maneuver freely even in the vicinity of the capital. (Bien Hoa was, in fact, in the middle of Vietcong territory. Three months earlier a B-57 had crashed after takeoff and rescue teams had been unable to fight their way to the scene of the crash, only ten miles away.)

Compared with the single bullet hole in the *Maddox,* the raid on Bien Hoa might logically have been presented as a provocation of some magnitude, but instead the White House hurriedly moved to play down the incident and to calm fears that it might trigger an expansion of the war. White House spokesmen specifically emphasized to newsmen that the attack was of the sort to be expected in a guerrilla war, that the United States had knowingly risked such attacks in deciding to support the South Vietnamese, and that it was by no means serious enough to justify retaliation against North Vietnam. During a Saigon news conference the next day, General Westmoreland went out of his way to point out that the mortar shells used in the attack were actually American-made and had probably been left behind in Vietnam by the French, who had been supplied with such shells before their departure in 1954. In this way an attack that might have triggered a crisis was allowed to pass quietly as a minor incident.

When the campaign was finally over, Johnson, his wife, and his daughters went back home to Texas. The night before the election he flew into Austin for a party with old friends. There was no doubt who was going to win the following day, only doubt about the size of Johnson's victory. The President told a friend, "It seems to me tonight that I have spent my whole life getting ready for this moment."[23]

The following day Johnson was elected with the widest margin—61.1 percent—and the greatest plurality—16.9 million votes—of any president in the nation's history. Goldwater had aroused all the vague fears of nuclear holocaust which had been building for a generation. He had called on the country to steel itself, to face the harsh reality of war in Southeast Asia, to prepare to send its sons to die, and the country had rejected him. Johnson had promised to contain the war, to keep American boys at home, to preserve the peace, and the people believed him. They had not read the small print, listened to the qualifying clauses and parenthetical remarks, the careful insistence things might change, the warning that he was speaking only for the moment. Johnson would later react in aggrieved disbelief when he was charged with having fundamentally misled the public. Hadn't he said there would be no bombing of the North "at this stage of the game"? That "when" the bombing began he would be "very cautious and careful"? That "just for the moment I have not thought we were ready for American boys to do the fighting for Asian boys"?

These lawyerly provisos had been lost in the heat of the campaign, however. They had been intended for historians, not the people, and the people had failed to hear them. They had heard only the promise of peace, of "no wider war," of restraint by a president who had pledged not to send American boys nine thousand miles to fight another country's war. If any American president had ever promised anything to the American people, then Lyndon Johnson had promised to keep the United States out of the war in Vietnam.

TWO

Mississippi and Berkeley

In the weeks following the election it naturally seemed as if Johnson, with Goldwater's considerable help, had created his consensus. The choice that Goldwater had offered the people had not been an easy one. He had described the world as a place of bitter struggle abroad and a subtle, velvet tyranny at home. He had asked the country to renounce foreign and domestic policies that had slowly evolved over a period of thirty years and to return to the stern virtues of an earlier time, when those who could not help themselves were expected to suffer in silence. The voters had overwhelmingly chosen Johnson's softer vision of gradual reconciliation between the nations of the world and the orderly redress of grievances at home. The size of Johnson's victory seemed to indicate a broad agreement on the nature of the problems the country faced and how it ought to solve them. Beneath the surface of that apparent consensus, however, there were profound discontents which had failed to emerge, or had been ignored, during the campaign.

In the fall of 1964 American society was, in fact, fragile. Goldwater's success in the Deep South,[1] where race had been an obsession for well over a century, only hinted at the true extent of the passions that threatened consensus. When Goldwater had been nominated in July it was still widely assumed that the racial problem was fundamentally a Southern problem. In the ten years following the Supreme Court's 1954 decision outlawing segregation of the races in Southern schools, black discontent had created a broad and powerful movement, but so far it had remained in the states of the old Confederacy. The confrontations between white and black and between federal and state authorities had all occurred in the South; the civil rights legislation proposed in Congress had all been aimed at ending Southern injustice; the voices of hate and resistance had all seemed to speak in Southern accents. On July 18, 1964, however, two days after Goldwater had accepted the Republican nomination in San Francisco, black anger suddenly erupted in the North. A Harlem rally originally called to protest the apparent murder of three civil rights workers in Mississippi shifted its focus to the killing of a black teenager by a white policeman in New York. The crowd turned into a mob and marched to a nearby police station, where angry shouts quickly escalated into rock and bottle throwing, precipitating four days of bloody rioting. Negroes had long warned of the rage building in Northern ghettos, but the country had preferred to focus its attention on the South, ignoring the discontented only a bus ride away. When a police captain urged the crowd to go home that night, a shout came back through the darkness of the Harlem streets: "We are home, baby."[2]

The riots spread to the Bedford-Stuyvesant section of Brooklyn and then to other cities in New York, New Jersey, and Pennsylvania, giving sudden force to the argument that white "backlash" might swing the election in Goldwater's favor. On Sunday, July 19, George Wallace, the aggressively white supremacist governor of Alabama who had been waging a third-party campaign for the presidency, dropped out of the race without explanation. The handful of states in the Deep South that Wallace had been expected to win would now almost certainly end up in Goldwater's column. In the wake of the riots and Wallace's decision to leave the field, Negro leaders met and agreed to call off all demonstrations until after the election in order to avoid the risk of a white reaction.[3] President Johnson, experienced in capturing the middle ground for himself, acted quickly to ensure that Goldwater would be unable to use the race issue during the campaign. He scheduled a meeting with Goldwater at the White House for Friday afternoon, July 24, and then announced a press conference to take place immediately before Goldwater's arrival. At the same time he quietly arranged for a reporter to ask if he planned an agreement with Goldwater to avoid exploiting the race issue during the campaign, making it difficult if not impossible for Goldwater to resist such an agreement when Johnson proposed it. After the sixteen-minute meeting the two men issued a terse, three-sentence statement on the importance of avoiding anything that might further sharpen already dangerous racial tensions. Throughout the rest of the campaign Goldwater occasionally referred to the race issue indirectly, but he never attempted to exploit it and, in the end, backlash won him few votes outside of the South. The effect of this paper unity was, of course, superficial. The racial divisions that went largely unmentioned during the campaign were deep and serious, touching every aspect of American life. Once they were closely examined they would reveal contradictions that went far beyond the relatively simple oppression of one race by another in the South.

Racial hostility was not the only result of a decade of increasingly sharp Negro demands for an end to their position of inferiority within the United States. The justice of their cause and the violent nature of Southern resistance had created a political climate in which moral considerations began to play an important part, eventually arousing whole sections of the American public that had been traditionally indifferent to politics. Probably a majority of the country had been surprised and then horrified in September and October, 1962, when the state of Mississippi seemed to be flirting with insurrection in a desperate attempt to keep a former U.S. Air Force sergeant named James Meredith from becoming the first Negro at the University of Mississippi. The violent passions behind this conflict were completely outside the experience of most Americans. The public was equally surprised and shocked the following spring when blacks demonstrating in Birmingham, Alabama, were met by police dogs, fire hoses, and night sticks. On June 11, 1963, President Kennedy gave a nationally televised speech in which he stressed at length, for the first time, the moral aspects of the black drive for equality. What Kennedy said took on greater weight the following night when Medgar Evers, the leader of the Mississippi chapter of the National Association for the Advancement of Colored People (NAACP), was shot to death in front of his home in Jackson. On June 19 Kennedy proposed a sweeping civil rights act, the broadest since the Civil War, which would put the federal government behind black demands for justice "not merely for reasons of economic efficiency, world diplomacy and domestic tranquility, but above all because it is right."[4]

Most people lead insular lives; they hardly notice what happens three blocks away, let alone events that touch people they have never known, in places they have never been. Americans were accustomed to thinking of themselves as a peaceful people with an honest commitment to justice and fair play. They knew nothing of the routine violence which was a daily presence in the lives of most black people. The crisis at the University of Mississippi in which two men were killed; the brutality of the Birmingham police; the murder of Medgar Evers; the bombing of a Birmingham church on September 15, 1963, killing four Negro girls in a Sunday school class; all forced Americans to take notice of things they had ignored since Reconstruction. When Byron de la Beckwith went on trial in Mississippi in January, 1964, charged with the murder of Evers, the country was watching almost in spite of itself. The local prosecutor, William Waller, made a genuine, but ultimately unsuccess- ful, effort to obtain a conviction and he chose the jury with care:

> "Do you think it is a crime for a white man to kill a nigger in Mississippi?" Waller asked a prospective juror.
> "What was his answer?" inquired the judge.
> "He's thinking it over," Waller said.[5]

Southern racism was brutal and straightforward; once people began to pay attention there was no denying it existed and that it was wrong. This fact only sharpened the conflict, however. The rage of white Southerners, caught in a painful contradiction between their conventionally decent beliefs and their practice, had its Northern counterpart. In unions, in suburban communities, on the fringes of black ghettos, in small towns and executive board rooms and private clubs, a fear and resentment of black people existed which had a dangerous potential for shifting the direction of the entire nation. Because few Northerners were prepared to identify themselves with the crude and violent racism of the South, this potential failed to come alive during the election of 1964, but it continued to threaten the tranquil surface of American life. So long as racism had remained hidden, Americans were free to think of themselves in traditional ways, but once black people, the long-unwilling partners in this mutual deception, refused to tolerate it any longer, new questions were raised filled with ugly potentiality. Kennedy had clearly sided with black demands because they were right, but what if the country refused to follow his lead, or if federal efforts proved inadequate? What would Americans think of themselves then? The problem was made infinitely more complex by the fact that black oppression was not limited solely to dramatically unfair Jim Crow laws.

The Swedish economist and sociologist Gunnar Myrdal had described the full range of black oppression in *The American Dilemma* in 1944. Now a whole generation of Americans, their sympathy quickly captured by the relatively clear and simple early confrontations, was about to learn what a few had always known.

When the civil rights movement began in Montgomery, Alabama, at the end of 1955, its principal source of strength was the church, the oldest, strongest, and most independent of all black institutions. Churchgoers organized the bus boycott in Montgomery; they brought the lawsuit that eventually ended segregated seating on buses; they inspired the Negro community to walk to work for a year by themselves walking; and they were the ones arrested, tried, convicted, and jailed. As the movement began to spread throughout the South, it remained a movement of churchgoers, of the respectably middle-aged and middle-class segments of the black communities, tired of the indignities they had suffered.

Early in 1960, however, the movement suddenly expanded to include the young. On February 1 that year, four students at the all-Negro North Carolina Agricultural and Technical College in Greensboro walked into the local Woolworth's, sat down at the segregated lunch counter, and asked to be served. When they returned the following day and the day after that, whites began to respond violently, national attention was captured, students at other black schools in other Southern towns began to follow the Greensboro example, and the sit-in movement was born. The involvement of black students had an immediate effect on white students in the North, harshly criticized during the last years of the 1950s as a "silent generation" more interested in personal security than social justice, or anything else. As the movement spread through the Upper South in the spring of 1960, white demonstrators from Northern colleges organized picket lines outside local Woolworth's stores and other chain stores as a gesture of support.

The creation of the Student Non-Violent Coordinating Committee (SNCC) by black leaders of the sit-in movement was followed by the creation of two loosely organized support organizations, the Friends of SNCC and the Northern Student Movement, both overwhelmingly white. White students also joined the Congress of Racial Equality (CORE) in sending integrated buses on "freedom rides" into Alabama and Mississippi in the spring of 1961, and they joined the voter registration projects which SNCC began organizing in the rural, almost feudal counties of Mississippi and Alabama in the same year.

Even before the civil rights movement had captured the imagination of white students, there had been faint political stirrings on Northern college campuses. Discontent with a cautious and feeble student government at the University of California at Berkeley led to the creation of an insurgent political party called SLATE, elected in 1958 on a pledge to abolish student government altogether. At Harvard a group called Tocsin took a passionate and meticulous interest in nuclear disarmament, and at the University of Wisconsin students and faculty founded a radical magazine, *Studies on the Left*. In May, 1960, students in the San Francisco Bay area, consciously imitating the example of young black activists in the South, demonstrated outside a hearing of the House Un-American Activities Committee (HUAC) being held in the San Francisco City Hall. When the demonstrators failed to clear a lobby quickly enough following a police order, the police suddenly turned a fire hose on them and then waded into the crowd with night sticks. HUAC later pieced together a film of the demonstrations called *Operation Abolition*, which suggested, crudely and inaccurately, that the demonstration and the violence by police had both been organized by the Communist Party. During the following three years the film was shown on dozens of campuses, usually providing the occasion for a debate on HUAC by a supporter of the committee, typically a retired military officer, and an opponent. The net effect was to thoroughly discredit HUAC's fundamentalist anticommunism, at least in the eyes of a small group of students who were beginning to think of themselves as not only activists, but in some sense radicals as well. When Cuban exiles organized by the CIA attempted to invade Cuba at the Bay of Pigs in April, 1961, an important handful of politically sophisticated students who had supported Kennedy the year before turned against him in anger. Most students, however, continued to focus their attention on conditions in the United States, deliberately ignoring the Cold War struggles which obsessed their elders.

During the first few years of the 1960s, concern with civil rights issues was paralleled by interest in disarmament and proposals to end nuclear testing. The Committee for a Sane Nuclear Policy (SANE), founded in 1957, began to set up campus chapters and in 1959 the Student Peace Union (SPU) was organized by several members of the Socialist Party active in Chicago. In February, 1962, these groups and others joined to organize a demonstration in Washington. Some four thousand students spent the weekend meeting with presidential advisers (one of whom suggested they ought to picket the Pentagon), government officials, and representatives of the Russian embassy. It was the largest peace demonstration in the capital's recent history, but it was also the last on relatively neutral issues like disarmament. By the end of the year the peace groups had been completely overshadowed by civil rights organizations, which demanded moral qualities like courage and self-sacrifice rather than the intellectual discipline involved in the necessarily painstaking study of weapons policy.

The most important of the new white groups, the Students for a Democratic Society (SDS), was founded in Port Huron, Michigan, in June, 1962, primarily by students at the University of Michigan active in a campus group called Voice. The SDS emphasis on absolute democracy and on working at the very roots of society reflected the anti-ideological, existential spirit emerging in the movement. Despite its loose organization and the comparative lack of drama in its early projects, SDS's yearly conventions provided an important forum for the ideas that were fermenting within the student movement. Like the movement itself, SDS quickly severed its ties to the old left. There were other issues and organizations, some of which survived a season or two on individual campuses and then died, but the single most important influence on white students remained the example of black students in the South.

Pacing the spread of the civil rights movement was a growing interest in the cultural style of the beat generation, a small but passionately alienated group of loosely related writers and poets active in New York and San Francisco and almost nowhere in between. The beats, born near Columbia University in the late 1940s but invisible for a decade until the publication of Jack Kerouac's *On the Road,* rejected the upward-striving, cautious mentality of the young men who sought lives in the huge corporations in favor of existential intensity. Allen Ginsberg, who wrote the long poem *Howl* which was almost the national anthem of the beat movement, talked about the 1950s as a time of mental and emotional shutdown, of narrowness in art, religion, and life itself. Two new styles were beginning to appear among white students in the North in the early 1960s: the SNCC style of levis, denim jackets, dark glasses, and work boots; and the beat style of army fatigue jackets, long hair, beards, mattresses on the floor, and marijuana. The cultural alienation of the beats complemented the inevitable political alienation of the civil rights groups who quickly learned just how few were their allies. Both styles were distinctly isolated on most campuses before 1964, but they had a vitality lacking in the conservative political groups, the traditional literary magazines, and the weekending fraternities which had long been the focus of student life. In New York's Greenwich Village, in Cambridge, Massachusetts, and in San Francisco, marginal student communities came into existence which would expand steadily throughout the sixties. More important, they provided a concrete image of a way of life which touched the imagination of students throughout the country.

The civil rights movement brought these various strands of discontent together and created a new political atmosphere on Northern campuses, populist in spirit and activist in mood. Although relatively few students actually went South, the principal battleground remained there and the experience of the few who went touched the many who stayed behind. In the fall of 1963 a number of white students from Yale and Stanford universities, recruited by a liberal political activist named Allard Lowenstein, drove to Mississippi to help SNCC canvass votes in a mock election held to dramatize the number of blacks who wanted but had been denied the right to vote. The national attention attracted by the white students persuaded Bob Moses, a twenty-eight-year-old Negro with degrees from Hamilton College and Harvard University who had gone into Mississippi almost alone in 1961, to organize a major voter registration effort the following summer. His proposal met some opposition from black members of SNCC and other organizations working together in the Council of Federated Organizations (COFO), but it was eventually adopted.

On June 19, 1964, while most of the country was paying attention to presidential politics, the first of an eventual one thousand white volunteers left the training center in Oxford, Ohio, and headed South for the Mississippi Summer Project. The attention of the country was fully captured two days later, however, when three civil rights workers, two of them white, disappeared in Philadelphia, Mississippi, where they had gone to investigate the burning of a church. On June 23 their burned car was found in a swamp.

In the days immediately following, a profound reaction set in among the white students still training in Ohio. For the first time in their lives they found themselves on the side of people who felt the government was at best indifferent, and perhaps downright hostile. John Doar, a member of the Justice Department's Civil Rights Division who had repeatedly risked his own life in the South, was sharply questioned by white students at the training center on the federal government's failure to protect the civil rights workers:

"How is it that the government can protect the Vietnamese from the Vietcong and the same government will not accept the moral responsibility of protecting the people in Mississippi?"

"Maintaining law and order is a state responsibility," Doar said.

"But how is it"—the questioner persisted—"that the government can accept this responsibility in Vietnam?"

"I would rather confine myself to Mississippi."[6]

The Mississippi Summer Project marked a turning point in the civil rights movement little noticed at the time by the rest of the country. During the summer relations soured between white college students who sometimes seemed to think they should be running everything and black activists who resented the whites as late arrivals who could always go home again when the going got rough, as it inevitably would. When President Johnson ordered the military to join in the search for the three missing civil rights workers, black members of SNCC bitterly noted the contrast with the official indifference that had followed murders of black activists in the past. This feeling deepened when the bodies of two Negroes turned up in a river the first day but were ignored, and when reporters and federal officials paid little attention to beatings and church burnings unless white students were involved. At the same time the white students, many of them coming face to face with violence for the first time, were deeply affected by the obvious injustice they saw all around them and by the reluctance or inability of the federal government to do anything about it. While the rest of the country felt a lingering sentimental attachment to the dead President's brother, Attorney General Robert F. Kennedy, the white volunteers in Mississippi saw him as a cold, ambitious figure, angling for the vice presidential nomination while they were risking their lives.

White volunteers were shocked at the cynical openness with which

Mississippi voting registrars simply refused to approve or even accept the applications of Negroes. They were angered by the casual lawlessness of the Mississippi police, who harassed activists with arrests for crimes they had not committed and who refused to intervene when volunteers were physically attacked. They were depressed by the grinding poverty in which most Mississippi Negroes lived, by the fear that dominated Negro lives, by the violent hate expressed by Mississippi whites, and above all by the fact that such things could exist without arousing indignation outside the state. At times the Mississippians almost seemed to be taunting the rest of the country with their shouts of "Never!" and their mocking abuse of "Martin Lucifer Coon." One ancient white farmer told a *Newsweek* reporter, "Hell, we treat our niggers good. We let 'em put new crocus sacks in their windows every year."[7] The rest of the country seemed deaf to the challenge, much less ready to meet it.

The apparent murder of the three civil rights workers cast a dark presence over the project in a state where every pickup truck carried a gun rack. Beatings occurred regularly, shots were fired at cars, and buildings were bombed. Project directors kept a close eye on volunteers, who were asked to let someone know where they were going and when they expected to get there. If a volunteer failed to arrive on time, the nearest FBI office was called, but in fact the FBI provided little protection. This indifference by federal authorities angered Summer Project volunteers more than anything else. They gradually began to feel that J. Edgar Hoover, the FBI's aging director, had accurately summed up the nation's attitude when he testily remarked in Jackson on July 10:

> We most certainly do not and will not give protection to civil rights workers. The FBI is not a police organization. It is purely an investigative organization. The protection of individual citizens, either natives of this state or coming into the state, is a matter for local authorities.[8]

By the time the bodies of the missing workers were finally found on August 5, buried in an earthen dam, suspicions had begun to center on local authorities in Philadelphia, where the three had been arrested on a minor traffic charge and then released, apparently into the arms of a lynch mob, the night they disappeared. Leaving protection to the "local authorities," who routinely arrested the victims of attack, in effect left activists without any protection at all. Violence infected the

Summer Project, transforming a desire to help black people into bitter suspicion and resentment of the society that allowed their oppression to continue. Bob Moses was not alone when he noted at the funeral of one of the three that their bodies had been found on the same day American planes bombed North Vietnam in retaliation for the second Tonkin Gulf incident. Speaking in his soft, measured voice, Moses said that what was happening in Mississippi was part of a larger pattern, that the killing could not end in the American South until it ended everywhere.

As the summer progressed many of the white volunteers were transformed. Beginning with a faith in the importance of civil rights, especially the right to vote, they ended the summer with a belief that American failings went far deeper than the question of civil rights. After returning to the United States from Vietnam early in 1964, David Halberstam was startled by the bitterness he found in one of the Mississippi civil rights workers, who told him, "I enjoyed your coverage of America's other colonial war."[9] White volunteers began to see the United States as a façade of official piety about equal rights hiding the violence used to keep Negroes in their place. Their faith in traditional liberal solutions was weakened by the magnitude of the problems they found in Mississippi, by the superficiality of federal efforts to solve them, and, finally, at the Democratic convention in Atlantic City in August, by the shallowness of the liberal commitment to what was right.

The Freedom Schools and voter registration efforts of the Summer Project had been aimed at creating a Mississippi Freedom Democratic Party (MFDP), which could challenge the regular Democratic Party's right to sit at the convention on the ground that it had systematically excluded Negroes. When the convention opened on August 24, MFDP members appeared before the Credentials Committee and described in painful detail the violence and economic reprisals taken against Negroes who tried to vote in Mississippi. The attorney managing their challenge was Joseph L. Rauh, a long-time liberal and leader of Americans for Democratic Action (ADA). The MFDP was seeking all sixty-four seats allotted to Mississippi, but President Johnson, anxious to avoid a Southern walkout, which would weaken his chances in the South, was said to have made it clear he wanted the MFDP challenge to end in a compromise, not a revolution.

The Credentials Committee finally proposed that the MFDP be given two seats as "honored guests" and that no delegation be seated in 1968 that had excluded Negroes from political activity. Liberals considered the compromise a solid victory for the MFDP, but Moses and other leaders felt they had an overwhelming moral right to all the regular party's seats. In a closed meeting Senator Hubert Humphrey, whose chances for the vice presidential nomination were widely believed to hinge on his success in coming up with a compromise solution to the MFDP challenge, urged the group to sacrifice its principles for a limited but nonetheless significant victory. He was joined by other moderate leaders, including Martin Luther King, whom Moses had expected to support the MFDP all the way. At one point the leader of the United Auto Workers union, Walter Reuther, who had provided King with both moral and financial support in the past, crudely insisted that King back the compromise. Clearly visible in his argument was a threat to end UAW support of King's organization, the Southern Christian Leadership Conference (SCLC), if King did not go along. The threat was clumsily gratuitous because King had been prepared to accept the compromise anyway, but Moses, unaware of this, was stunned and sickened by the threat and King's apparent acquiescence. Many of the MFDP members, so politically unsophisticated that they did not really know who Humphrey was, looked to the agonized Moses for a decision on what to do. Finally, unwilling to compromise a moral right for which people had suffered and died, Moses simply ran from the room, leaving the meeting to end in confusion.

Few in the country paid much attention to the details of what had happened in the Credentials Committee, but the bitterness of the MFDP quickly spread through activist circles. Almost exactly a year before, during a demonstration by 250,000 blacks and whites in Washington, John Lewis, the leader of SNCC, had expressed the doubts beginning to be felt throughout the movement. "I want to know," he had asked, "which side is the Federal government on?"[10] The rejection of the MFDP's challenge at Atlantic City seemed to answer Lewis's question. Stokely Carmichael, a charismatic SNCC leader who had begun to attract attention as chief of the Summer Project's voter registration drive in Greenwood, Mississippi, remarked after the convention that the MFDP's failure proved there was no difference between liberals and Goldwaterites. The remark accurately reflected a new mood in the movement and it was widely quoted by SNCC members and allies around the country. During the election the SDS formally issued a button which read, "Part of the way with LBJ," specifically that part which promised no wider war. For the rest, they sought solutions to the problems of poverty and racism far broader and deeper than those offered by Johnson's war on poverty. The SDS position was in keeping with the feelings of white Summer Project volunteers who returned to college campuses across the country in September, bringing with them sharp memories of poverty in the South and the air of violence which had surrounded even their orthodox and limited efforts to change the Southern way of life.

The political passions aroused by the civil rights movement and the 1964 election campaign found a focus in Berkeley, where students at the University of California had responded quickly to the student awakening of the 1960s. The struggle within the Republican Party in the weeks between Rockefeller's defeat in the California primary in June and the party's convention in July naturally spread to students at Berkeley. Groups backing Pennsylvania Governor William Scranton and Goldwater solicited student support, and volunteers set up tables along the so-called Bancroft Strip, a twenty-five-foot-wide stretch of sidewalk between Sproul Plaza and Bancroft Way which was the traditional center of political activity on the campus since the university's Board of Regents prohibited it on university property. A reporter for the conservative Oakland *Tribune*, owned by former senator William F. Knowland, a Goldwater supporter, discovered that the strip was actually owned by the university and not by the city of Berkeley, as had long been assumed. No action was taken, however, until September, when the university formally began to study the situation on the same day that the Ad Hoc Committee to End Discrimination organized a picket line to protest racial discrimination at the *Tribune*. On September 14, Dean of Students Katherine A. Towle sent a letter to officers of student organizations announcing that political activity along the Bancroft Strip would be banned as of September 21.

The reaction of Berkeley students from left to right was immediate and passionate: they considered the ban a denial of basic political rights and, more important, they were determined to resist it. The position of the university, never seriously questioned while the Bancroft Strip had offered a sanctuary, was that education and political activity were somehow incompatible. Berkeley's chancellor, Edward W. Strong, made the administration's position clear on September 23 in reaction to sharp student protests against the closing of the strip:

> The university, rightly, as an educational institution, maintains an open forum for the free discussion of ideas and issues. Its facilities are not to be used for the mounting of social and political action directed at the surrounding community.[11]

The official rationale for the policy was that the process of learning and political activity would inevitably get in each other's way, a position taken by no other major college or university in the United States. In effect the ban suspended much of the Bill of Rights, creating an enclave where the Constitution did not obtain. In spite of this theoretical weakness, the Berkeley policy had been defended at length the previous May 5 by University of California President Clark Kerr. On September 25, when it was apparent Strong's statement had satisfied no one, Kerr defended the ban again during an interview:

> I don't think you have to have action to have intellectual opportunity. Their actions—collecting money and picketing—aren't high intellectual activity. . . . These actions are not necessary for the intellectual development of the students. If that were so, why teach history? We can't live in ancient Greece . . .[12]

Kerr's casual dismissal of "collecting money and picketing" angered students who felt the United States was in the middle of a racial crisis largely caused by the fact that too many people had done too little for too long about social conditions that were indisputably *wrong*. Already sophisticated about the forces within society that resisted change, students suspected that Kerr's ban on political activity was based less on an academic ideal than on local political pressures. During the preceding ten months students at Berkeley and other schools in the Bay area had made a number of powerful enemies with aggressive campaigns to end discrimination in hiring. Students had played the dominant role in a picketing campaign aimed at a chain of drive-in restaurants during November, 1963, which eventually brought III arrests; in picketing Berkeley stores that Christmas and a supermarket chain in February, 1964; in a prolonged campaign against discrimination by San Francisco's Sheraton-Palace Hotel in March (nearly 1,000 arrests); in picketing of the Cadillac and other automobile agencies beginning that same month (326 arrests); and in a sit-in at the office of the U.S. Attorney in San Francisco following the disappearance of the three civil rights workers in Mississippi in June.[13] When Kerr banned the political activity that had allowed these local campaigns to take place, picking the very moment of a new campaign against the Oakland *Tribune,* students did not hesitate to conclude he was surrendering to pressure. The practical effect of the ban, certainly, would have been an end to the local activism which had aroused so much local resentment.

The struggle at Berkeley quickly escalated. On the night of September 30–October 1, more than 500 students marched into Sproul Hall, the university's administration building, to protest disciplinary action initiated against 8 students for breaking the ban by setting up tables at Sather Gate. Before leaving the building at 3 A.M., the students formally created the Free Speech Movement (FSM) to coordinate resistance to the ban and elected Mario Savio, a leader of Friends of SNCC who had spent the summer in Mississippi, to lead the new organization. Later on October 1 university police arrested Jack Weinberg for again defying the ban, but when the police attempted to drive him away about 100 students sat down around the police car and prevented it from moving. Savio took off his shoes and climbed to the top of the car to urge students to support Weinberg. By 11:15 that night more than 2,500 students were blockading the car and singing civil rights songs. California Governor Edmund G. Brown issued a statement supporting Kerr and defining the issue as one of "law and order." The following day 500 police were called to the campus to prepare for action against the demonstrators. At 5 P.M. on the afternoon of October 2, while 7,000 students surrounded the police car with Weinberg still inside, Savio and other FSM leaders met with the university's administration. An agreement was finally reached two and a half hours later, and the demonstration ended. The effect of the confrontation on students throughout the country was electric: for the first time students had confronted university and civilian authorities on a plainly political question with the direct action techniques developed during the civil rights movement. The FSM continued to seek an end to the ban on political activity, but the issue for the administration had changed radically. Unable to find legitimate fault with a plea for free speech, theoretically a legal right of every citizen, the administration resisted the FSM on the ground that it was challenging the rule of law and that reversing the ban would legitimize the use of force. The contest became one of crude power, the university insisting its rules be maintained even if unjust for the sole reason that it embodied established authority. The effect was to turn bitter a struggle already passionate.

The conflict continued to intensify throughout the fall, becoming immeasurably more complicated as charges were made and answered, meetings were held to counter meetings, and statements issued to confute statements, leading to dozens of side disputes about who had said what, who had promised what, who had threatened what. At the heart of the conflict was a contest of wills over the political ban. Things had gone too far for either side to back down gracefully: either Clark Kerr was going to lose his job, or the students would abandon the struggle in bitter disillusion. On December 1 the FSM issued an ultimatum which was predictably ignored by the administration. The following day one thousand students gathered in Sproul Plaza, where Savio gave an impassioned defense of the movement and its aims:

Last summer I went to Mississippi to join the struggle there for civil rights. This fall I am engaged in another phase of the same struggle, this time in Berkeley. The two battlefields may seem quite different to some observers, but this is not the case. The same rights are at stake in both places—the right to participate as citizens in democratic society and the right to due process of law. Further, it is a struggle against the same enemy. In Mississippi an autocratic and powerful minority rules, through organized violence, to suppress the vast, virtually powerless majority. In California, the privileged minority manipulates the university bureaucracy to suppress the students' political expression. That "respectable" bureaucracy is the efficient enemy in a "Brave New World". . . .

After a long period of apathy during the Fifties, students have begun not only to question, but, having arrived at answers, to act on those answers. This is part of a growing understanding among many people in America that history has not yet ended, that a better society is possible, and that it is worth dying for. . . .

There is a time when the operation of the machine becomes so odious, makes you so sick at heart, that you can't take part; you can't even tacitly take part, and you've got to put your bodies upon the gears and upon the wheels, upon the levers, upon all the apparatus and you've got to make it stop. And you've got to indicate to the people who run it, to the people who own it, that unless you're free, the machines will be prevented from working at all.[14]

When Savio finished speaking Joan Baez began to sing "We Shall Overcome," and the crowd, picking up the song, filed into Sproul Hall. At 3:45 A.M. on the morning of December 3, a force of more than six hundred police began clearing the building, leading out the students who refused to leave and carrying them out, none too gently, when they refused to walk. The building was finally cleared twelve hours later.

Technically, perhaps, the university had maintained its authority, but within a week Kerr and the administration capitulated, one day before the university's academic senate voted, 824 to 115, to grant the essence of the FSM's demands for free political activity on the campus. The controversy lingered for another few weeks with new attempts by the regents to amend the settlement, but it was clear the students had won.

Despite the intense political passions aroused during the four-month-long struggle at Berkeley, and despite the students' feeling that a lot more was wrong with American society than Clark Kerr's notion of political freedom, students at Berkeley were slow to take up other issues. After eighty-three days of confrontation with the administration, and indirectly with the state of California, the students were emotionally exhausted. Equally important, however, was the fact that broad political movements like the FSM respond to events rather than create them. The anti-discrimination campaigns in the San Francisco Bay area which indirectly led to the upheaval had been a response to obvious injustice and the example of blacks in the South. By the time Berkeley students had won an undisputed right to carry on civil rights activity, the movement as a whole had passed to another stage. The Civil Rights Act signed into law by President Johnson on July 2, 1964, canceled the vast majority of the Jim Crow laws which had been the original impetus behind the movement. The Mississippi Summer Project had already established the conditions that would lead to a major federal voting rights statute the following year. As the FSM crisis gradually faded in December, the mood of SNCC and other activist organizations in the South was changing. On November 16, for example, a coalition of groups integrated a bus station, a theater, and a motel in McComb, Mississippi, a considerable victory in light of the violent and unsuccessful attempt to integrate the bus station alone in 1961. A white member of SNCC made it clear, however, that the aims of the movement were expanding.

> So a Negro eats in a motel. So what? Will he come back tomorrow? Can he afford to? The problem is getting people determined to force the issue on better jobs, and voting rights that will establish them as first class citizens, not to waste energies with this frosting on the cake of a room at the Holiday [Inn] while people are living in shacks and starving.[15]

During its first four years the American student movement, beginning to be referred to as the New Left by those who hoped it would transform the nation, had concerned itself almost exclusively with racial questions. Only in those sections of the movement closest to the old left had some interest centered on foreign policy issues, particularly after the Bay of Pigs. The anger on the part of many in the Democratic Party's left wing was intense, but it touched students only briefly. Groups like the Fair Play for Cuba Committee, which protested the invasion at rallies in New York and San Francisco, remained relatively weak. There was plenty of opposition to Kennedy's decision to expand the American role in Vietnam, especially on the part of liberal magazines like *The Nation* and the *New Republic* and among the few senators who knew something about the area, but outside of official circles opposition either centered on doubts that the Kennedy policy would work or was limited to radical and pacifist groups with little popular following.

As the American commitment in Vietnam gradually expanded, the student movement slowly began to take notice. In the fall of 1963, when Madame Nhu toured the United States in a last-minute attempt to reverse American disenchantment with the regime of her brother-in-law, Ngo Dinh Diem, she was picketed in San Francisco by students who were also involved in the antidiscrimination campaigns. The following June the raucous founding convention of the W.E.B. DuBois Clubs, attended largely by members of groups on the old left and eventually dominated by the Communist Party, was interrupted so that convention delegates could demonstrate against President Johnson while he was in the city. A few weeks earlier a handful of radical students at a Yale University conference organized the May Second

Movement (M2M) to protest the war. It issued a petition which claimed that the "war is for the suppression of the Vietnamese struggle for national independence"[16] and committed its few signers to refuse to fight in Vietnam. M2M, however, was under the control of the Progressive Labor Party, a small but militant group founded by former members of the Communist Party who sided with Mao Tse Tung in the Moscow-Peking struggle, and it never attracted much of a following. Later that summer, on August 28, 1964, a small group of faculty members and graduate students at Berkeley, alarmed by the Tonkin Gulf incidents, placed an ad in the San Francisco *Chronicle* protesting American policy in Southeast Asia. That fall seventy faculty members and two hundred students at the University of Pennsylvania signed a letter urging the United States to adopt a policy of negotiations as a way to end the war.

In November the War Resisters League (WRL) publicly called for the "immediate withdrawal of all U.S. military forces and military aid" from Vietnam and a month later it joined with other pacifist groups to demonstrate in New York against the war. WRL's clear position would eventually have an important intellectual effect on the opposition, but for the moment, like most other efforts of the long-established groups in the peace movement, it reached only the convinced. There were other ads, rallies, petitions, and letters protesting the war in late 1964, but they remained frail and isolated efforts, partly as a result of the illusion that the issue had been settled during the presidential campaign. The attention of students was firmly fixed on the Free Speech Movement in Berkeley and on the continuing civil rights issues. The war was far away, as President Johnson had said, and the question of sending American troops to fight it had apparently been decided. The first stages of a cultural revolution were taking place among the young; charismatic groups like SNCC and the FSM were moved to action by conditions that actually touched their lives; the things that captured the interest of the young were those closest to home.

By the end of 1964 the civil rights movement of the early 1960s had separated into three distinct strands: the broad, church-centered movement headed by the Southern Christian Leadership Conference and Martin Luther King; the increasingly militant black student movement led by SNCC; and the white student movement, beginning to be cut off from civil rights issues by the resentment of blacks and therefore shifting its attention to new grievances. The Free Speech Movement had discredited the notion that education was somehow separated from the rest of life and that students could be restricted to their formal studies. When Berkeley students won the right to engage in political activity without interference by the administration, they won it on behalf of students throughout the country. In the process they developed a sense of their movement as not merely seeking changes in society, but as an alternative to society.

The three strands of discontent in American society were deep and self-sustaining. The idealism of the early 1960s had been touched with anger. The desire for reform had been supplanted by an insistence on fundamental change which went beyond the willingness, and perhaps even the ability, of established society to grant. A critical spirit had been aroused, and people once willing to give national leaders the benefit of the doubt had lost all patience. Lines had been drawn which were invisible to those looking down from positions of authority, but which mapped vast potential fissures in society. The movement had proved itself doubly by the end of the year, in Mississippi and Berkeley. Students had developed a confidence in their own ideas and in their ability to confront evils directly, without flinching or compromise. They were no longer willing to confine themselves to cloistered academic pursuits, or even to Mississippi. Like Mario Savio, they had begun to see the entire country as a battleground.

THREE

The Way the Game Is Played

By the end of 1964 it was apparent that the hard decisions on Vietnam so long avoided by President Johnson could not be put off much longer. The additional five thousand American troops Johnson had sent to Vietnam in July had been no more successful than the sixteen thousand already there in the attempt to improve the fighting capacity of Saigon's army, and the Vietcong continued to initiate battalion-size operations with something close to impunity. General Maxwell Taylor, the former Chairman of the Joint Chiefs of Staff who had replaced Henry Cabot Lodge as the ambassador to Saigon earlier in the year, was increasingly open about his pessimism. Long an advocate of a sharply increased military commitment, he felt the moment was approaching when nothing less could prevent a complete collapse of Saigon's ability to go on fighting. In November, Taylor, scheduled to return to Washington for conversations with the President, told a team of reporters from *Life* magazine, "Let us say, generally, that the issue is still very much in doubt."[1] Following years of official optimism, Taylor's remark had considerable impact.

Back in Washington on December 1, a Tuesday, Taylor met for two and a half hours with President Johnson, McNamara, Rusk, McCone, the Bundy brothers, Vice President Humphrey, and others. An official statement given to newsmen following the meeting admitted there had been reverses in South Vietnam but, as always, insisted there was still ample room for hope. The President planned to allow General Taylor to answer the questions of reporters, but McNamara dissuaded him as newsmen filed into the cabinet room following the meeting. "It would be impossible," McNamara was overheard to say to the President, "for Max to talk to these people without leaving the impression the situation is going to hell."[2] Before leaving Washington for Saigon the following day, Taylor made it clear that a bombing campaign against North Vietnam had been one of the proposals discussed at Tuesday's meeting.

Speculation that the United States would attempt to change the terms of the war by carrying it to Hanoi had been periodic since Walt Rostow had forcefully recommended a bombing campaign following the trip he made to South Vietnam with General Taylor in the fall of 1961. His enthusiasm for the plan gave it the semiofficial title of "Rostow's Plan 6." Despite its rejection by President Kennedy, Rostow's plan inevitably surfaced whenever the problem of Vietnam reached one of its frequent turning points. The Vietnam working group headed by Walter Sullivan had given new life to the proposal in early 1964 by its detailed contingency plans for an escalation of the war against Hanoi, beginning with "sonic boom" raids over the city and proceeding step by step toward a full-scale bombing campaign. Throughout the year there was continuing speculation, fed by the quiet remarks of administration officials who favored escalation, that bombing the North was being seriously considered. The raids following the second Tonkin Gulf incident only increased the speculation.

Perhaps more important was the fact that over the years the *idea* of a bombing campaign had slowly begun to exercise a fascination for many members of Congress and of the administration, as well as for military men. The basic premise of a bombing campaign, that Hanoi was the cause of all the trouble, and the solution a bombing campaign implied, that an attack on the North could end the war in the South, naturally had considerable appeal for those impatient with the complexity and ambiguity of the struggle. Years of air force lobbying in Congress had convinced many legislators that the air force offered a clean, relatively inexpensive way of using force to solve international problems. It was no secret that the air force felt the Bay of Pigs invasion in 1961 could have been a success if only President Kennedy had allowed the use of American aircraft.

In early 1965 the Air Force Chief of Staff was General Curtis LeMay, an experienced pilot whose years with the Strategic Air Command had nurtured a crude but passionate conviction that air power could solve almost any kind of military problem. He had absorbed a simplified version of Dulles's "massive retaliation" strategy, based on the notion that international relations have two forms, war and not-war. In war one went for the jugular. Shortly before LeMay's retirement on February 2, he was quoted in White House circles with two unofficial suggestions for ending the war in Vietnam. Convinced, with Rusk, that Hanoi was behind the Vietcong, and that Peking was behind Hanoi, LeMay said, "We ought to nuke the chinks."[3] His explanation was equally forthright: "We are swatting flies when we should be going after the manure pile."[4] Few in the White House or in the air force were comfortable with LeMay's way of explaining himself, but more than a few shared his conviction that toughness would work and that the air force offered the cheapest way of getting tough.

Pressure for a bombing campaign was largely the result of the official explanation of the war. The administration's insistence that the war was led and supplied by the North supported the notion that bombing the "supply lines" could have a decisive effect. The force of the idea of a bombing campaign lay in its swiftness, its cheapness in terms of casualties, and in the undisputed capacity of the air force to drop bombs in staggering quantities. Official Washington believed in the air force without any clear idea of just what an air force can actually do. Constant references to the Ho Chi Minh trail connecting North and South Vietnam through Laos allowed the notion to spread that Hanoi's supply line was a literal *line*, something like a mountain road, easily severed. In fact, an air force is effective in terms of space and time. Aircraft can make it impossible for anyone to enter the Yale Bowl and live at two o'clock on the afternoon of a given day, but the situation in Vietnam was more like trying to stop someone from driving a pickup truck through Connecticut between April and October, by any of a thousand routes, at any hour of the day or night, in any kind of weather. Nevertheless the air force tacitly suggested, and official Washington believed, that Hanoi could be simply swept aside. Even experts on Vietnam like Bernard B. Fall were inclined to think North Vietnam, with a small but highly prized industrial base, vulnerable to bombing.

One thing, certainly, was clear; Congress's faith in air power was such that it would never stand for the use of troops in the South without a bombing campaign in the North. Congress remembered vividly the public discontent with casualties during the Korean War. Using American lives would be the final step and would be supported only when it was clear that nothing else, including the bombing of the North, would be sufficient.

During November and December of 1964 the air force began to plan for a bombing campaign. Military planners generally prepare contingency plans for all sorts of possibilities, likely and unlikely, but in this case the President himself took an interest, poring over aerial reconnaissance photos spread out on a large table in the cabinet room. Despite his growing preoccupation with Vietnam, however, Johnson brushed over the war lightly in his State of the Union speech on January 4, 1965. "Our goal is peace in Vietnam," he said, as he had said dozens of times previously. "That will come only when aggressors leave their neighbors in peace."[5]

The quickening efforts of the administration to come up with a plan for preventing the collapse of Saigon created little stir in Washington. A survey of eighty-three senators two days after Johnson's State of the Union message found no clear consensus on what the problem was or what the President ought to do about it. Three senators wanted to start bombing the North, three favored pulling out altogether, and the rest fell into various positions in the middle.[6] The Council on Foreign Relations, an unofficial but prestigious group centered in New York, found a similar lack of consensus when it polled six hundred of its members, all of them accustomed to thinking in terms of national interests and world strategy. Not quite half wanted to pull out, slightly fewer to extend the fighting. Eighty percent favored the U.S. policy of support for Saigon; 90 percent felt the policy was failing.[7] These two surveys revealed a far broader range of opinion on the war than was to be the case again for years. The reason was that the President had not yet taken a firm public position on the question of escalating the war. Once he did, senators and Council members would fall into line behind him; there would be no more talk of pulling out, once the President had decided to fight. Very few would suggest military action was not the way to settle the war. Until he made that decision, however, there was agreement on nothing concerning the problems of Vietnam except their intractability.

Into this atmosphere of pessimism, fatalism, and even indifference, former Vice President Richard Nixon, long a supporter of resolute action, including war, to back U.S. interests in Southeast Asia, tried to inject a sense of crisis. "We are losing the war in Vietnam," he told a group at New York's Hotel Roosevelt on January 26. "If our strategy is not changed we will be thrown out in a matter of months—certainly within the year."[8] Nixon's prediction was not widely quoted. His failure to have his "availability" for the Republican presidential nomination taken seriously during 1964 had dimmed his already faint presence on the American political scene. Few seemed to hear his altogether accurate warning. Outside the administration, even fewer were inclined to heed it.

Early Sunday morning, Saigon time, February 7, 1965, only two hours after the end of a seven-day cease-fire declared by the Vietcong in honor of Tet, the Vietnamese new year, 81-millimeter mortar shells suddenly began to land on the American military base at Pleiku. Eight Americans were killed and 126 wounded. Within twelve hours, the United States retaliated with air raids against North Vietnamese military installations near the De-Militarized Zone (DMZ) which had divided the two halves of Vietnam since the Geneva Convention in 1954. In announcing the raids in Washington, McNamara said American intelligence indicated that the attack on Pleiku "was ordered and directed and masterminded directly from Hanoi." Under the circumstances, he said, a sharp U.S. response was unavoidable if American support for Saigon were to be taken seriously. "I think it's quite clear," he said, "that this was a test of the will, a clear challenge of the political purpose of both the U.S. and the South Vietnamese governments."[9]

On February 8 and again on the eleventh, U.S. and South Vietnamese aircraft raided North Vietnam. When one White House official was asked why Pleiku had provoked such a sharp response when the attack on the Bien Hoa air base the previous November had been dismissed as one of the inevitable risks of a guerrilla war, the official answered, "There is a limit to America's patience."[10]

Without any official statement, the raids on the North came to an abrupt halt following the attacks of February 11. For nearly three weeks the administration hesitated, apparently waiting to see what the reaction would be to its escalation of the war. On the day after the first raid the *New York Times* published a short but highly skeptical analysis of the Pleiku incident by Charles Mohr, who had spent several years in Vietnam for both *Time* magazine and the *Times* before he was assigned to Washington by the latter. Disputing McNamara's insistence that the raid was initiated directly by Hanoi and that it differed markedly from other Vietcong operations, Mohr pointed out that the principal weapon used had been American-made 8I-millimeter mortars (as had been the case the previous November at Bien Hoa), that only a single Vietcong company of perhaps two to three hundred men had been involved, that much larger and more costly attacks on South Vietnamese units had taken place, and, most telling of all, that the retaliatory raids had been launched from three aircraft carriers conveniently located off the Vietnamese coast in the South China Sea, a highly unusual circumstance.

The American reaction to the Pleiku incident is only one of the many still murky turning points in American involvement in Vietnam. It now seems almost certain that the administration had already decided to initiate a bombing campaign against North Vietnam and that Pleiku was simply a convenient pretext, as Mohr strongly implied. A broader case can also be made persuasively that the only question in the minds of top government officials, including the President, was how to justify plausibly to the public a policy of wider war which had been adopted privately months before. There is not much doubt, at any rate, that the American government realized by the turn of the year that Saigon would not survive unless the United States fully entered the war on its behalf, or at the very least convinced Hanoi it was about to do so. Did Johnson really believe that the bombing would scare Hanoi out of the war? Was the decision to begin bombing truly separate from the decision to send troops, reached immediately afterwards? It is not yet possible to answer those questions. None of those involved in the decision to widen the war has yet indicated what they truly *expected* to be the result of the bombing. It is even possible the question never occurred to them. They certainly give every sign of having just blundered ahead, blindly confident that there would always be something left to try, that eventually something would work, that they would never be called on to explain themselves.

There were a number of minor demonstrations protesting the bombing, but in general the public supported the President. In spite of Mohr's doubts, for example, the *Times* accepted the official version on its editorial page, supported the decision to retaliate directly against the North, and limited its doubts to a muted request for an explanation by the President of "where we go from here."[11] This, of course, was the last thing he was ready to confide to the public.

During the lull following the first three raids against the North, the most significant criticism of the American escalation of the war came from the Secretary-General of the United Nations. On February 24, U Thant expressed his disappointment with the failure of the United States to negotiate a settlement of the war, warned that the bombing had complicated the situation, and then, in a comment that was not to be fully explained for nearly a year, indirectly accused the United States of lying about the war:

> I am sure the great American people, if only they know the true facts and the background to the developments in South Vietnam, will agree with me that further bloodshed is unnecessary. And also that the political and diplomatic method of discussions and negotiations alone can create conditions which will enable the United States to withdraw gracefully from that part of the world. As you know, in times of war and of hostilities, the first casualty is truth.[12]

Incensed by U Thant's attack, and by his suggestion that the United States should "withdraw gracefully" when it now fully intended to stand and fight, President Johnson acted to tamp down criticism in the press and to ensure that it did not spread to Congress. The columnist William S. White, a close friend of the President, attacked U Thant as "an apologist and propagandist for Communist aggression in Southeast Asia." When the New York *Post* columnist James A. Wechsler criticized both White and the President a couple of days later, the President responded by calling Wechsler shortly before 9 A.M. on March 4. "I know you don't want me to bomb Peking or Hanoi and I certainly don't want to either," the President told the startled Wechsler. Johnson insisted he had nothing to do with White's column and then expanded into a defense of his policies in Vietnam. "I don't want to escalate this war," Johnson said. "I want nothing more than to get our boys home. But I can't run and pull a Chamberlain at Munich."[13]

In the Senate, the February air raids were denounced by Morse, who called them "a black page in American history," and by Gruening, who recommended negotiations "the sooner the better,"[14] but both men had long since been dismissed by the majority of the press, and of their fellow senators, as Cassandras on the subject of Vietnam who failed to appreciate the exigencies of America's world role. A number of senators had long been worried by the drift of events in Vietnam, but with the exception of Morse and Gruening none had been willing to oppose the President openly. Johnson, who had always loyally supported Eisenhower in public, took quiet but effective steps to ensure that doubts about Vietnam would be expressed privately, or not at all. McGeorge Bundy had been in Vietnam at the time of the Pleiku incident and shortly after he returned to Washington, Johnson arranged to have him meet with five Democratic senators who formed a potential nucleus of opposition, Eugene McCarthy of Minnesota, Gaylord Nelson of Wisconsin, Stephen Young of Ohio, George McGovern of South Dakota, and Frank Church of Idaho. Bundy's arguments, presented with his usual debater's skill during a meeting with the five held in the office of Vice President Humphrey, did not exactly silence, but muted, the doubts of the five.

Johnson himself undertook to retain the public support of J. William Fulbright, the widely respected chairman of the Senate's Foreign Relations Committee. Fulbright's position, abilities, and well-known concern with the excesses of Cold War anticommunism made him a keystone in the united front on Vietnam which Johnson hoped to retain. On the question of Vietnam Fulbright had an equivocal record. In June, 1961, when the Kennedy administration was reconsidering the nature of the American commitment to Diem, Fulbright publicly warned that the French had spent eight years, $7 billion, and 100,000 lives in a futile attempt to achieve what the United States was now proposing to do. Vietnam wasn't worth it, he implied. Three years later, however, in perhaps his most famous speech attacking Cold War truisms in foreign policy, Fulbright approached Vietnam from an altogether different point of view. He doubted that negotiations could achieve anything while the military situation was so dismal:

> It is extremely difficult for a party to a negotiation to achieve by diplomacy objectives which it has conspicuously failed to win by warfare. . . . The hard fact of the matter is that our bargaining position is at present a weak one; and until the equation of advantages between the two sides has been substantially altered in our favor, there can be little prospect of a negotiated setttlement which would secure the independence of a non-Communist South Vietnam.[15]

This, of course, was the view of the White House in the spring of 1965, and the bombing campaign was specifically designed to achieve just such a change in "the equation of advantages." In the weeks after the full-scale bombing campaign began, administration officials often described it as a bargaining chip to be used in negotiations with North Vietnam, a kind of currency we could use to buy concessions from the other side.

For a number of reasons, Fulbright remained silent following the Pleiku incident and maintained his silence in early March after the United States openly adopted a policy of continuous bombing of North Vietnam. He did not speak when a major contingent of marines landed at Danang on March 10 and did not even mention Vietnam in a foreign policy speech at Johns Hopkins University two days later. Behind this silence, Fulbright was worried about Vietnam, but his close personal friendship with President Johnson was as important to him as his own doubts about the war. In 1960 Fulbright had openly supported Johnson's campaign for the Democratic nomination, and Johnson had indicated Fulbright would be his choice for Secretary of State. When Johnson returned to his office in the Executive Office Building on the night of Kennedy's assassination, the first person he called was Fulbright.

It was also in Fulbright's character to wait before taking a position, and then to move privately before speaking publicly. Fifteen years earlier, for example, he had failed to mention the Korean War in public until January 18, 1951, more than six months after it began and two months after the Chinese joined the North Koreans. During early 1965 he was seeing the President fairly regularly but felt Johnson failed to listen during the rare moments when he was not talking. In late March, 1965, however, Fulbright met with Johnson at Johnson's request and for the first time in months felt he was having a real effect. On April 5, he sent Johnson a policy memorandum on Vietnam in which he argued that U.S. policy in Southeast Asia ought to favor anti-Chinese rather than anti-Communist governments. He also suggested a bombing halt to test the possibility that Hanoi would be willing to negotiate. On April 6, Johnson asked Fulbright and Mansfield to come by for a look at the speech he planned to give at Johns Hopkins the following day. The President's offer of "unconditional negotiations" in the speech pleased Fulbright and, like other senators, he felt the next move was up to the other side.

When Fulbright returned from a trip to Europe in June the President invited him to the White House, and the following day, while the two men walked in the Rose Garden, Johnson said he planned to announce commitment of another six battalions of American troops to the war, along with the logistical support to maintain them. He asked Fulbright to give a speech emphasizing the President's hope that the conflict could be shifted from the battlefield to the negotiating table. On June 15, Fulbright delivered the speech Johnson had asked for, repeating almost verbatim the White House view of the war:

> I am opposed to an unconditional American withdrawal from South Vietnam because such action would betray our obligation to people we have promised to defend, because it would weaken or destroy the credibility of American guarantees to other countries and because such a withdrawal would encourage the view in Peking and elsewhere that guerrilla wars supported from outside are relatively safe and inexpensive ways of expanding Communist power.[16]

Throughout the spring and summer Fulbright continued to worry about American foreign policy, especially after Johnson's decision to intervene in the Dominican Republic in April, but he was far from ready to break openly with the President. Eventually Fulbright would become a strong, effective opponent of the war, but for the time being he acquiesced in what he saw as inevitable.

The dilemma that faced Fulbright and other senators with doubts about the expanding war was a real one, not easy to solve. Every additional death in Vietnam, every wounded soldier, and every downed plane added to the President's stake in his gamble for a decisive gain through military action. If American bombing and American troops failed to win anything of value, then the President would have to answer for every casualty. Equally important, he was acting not only as Lyndon Johnson the man but as President of the United States, the leader of the country: a defeat for Johnson was a defeat for the entire nation, and for every American who cared whether or not Saigon fell to the Communists, there were ten who would react strongly to a failure of American arms. They were less moved by thought of the casualties that U.S. forces must inevitably suffer in the future than by the 356 who had already died by January, 1965, and whose deaths had to be justified. Once the President had acted it was futile to warn of the consequences. Having decided on a military solution, the President could be deflected only by military failure. American history, American pride, and above all American politics demanded support for the President once he had committed American troops to battle. Those who opposed the decision knew it was both too late and too early for effective opposition: too late to prevent the decision in the first place, too early for its futility to be apparent. Not everyone in Washington was happy with the war, but in the rest of the country opposition to Johnson appeared as only the faintest sort of demurring whisper.

Moreover, Johnson made it clear that the price would be heavy for any political figure who decided to abandon caution and oppose him publicly. Morse and Gruening, whose warnings then seem like transparent common sense now, had already been dismissed as unbalanced extremists. The President knew better than anyone where senators and representatives were vulnerable, and as President had the power to act on what he knew. After the Eighty-ninth Congress convened in 1965, Vice President Humphrey gave new members a welcoming speech which included some pointed advice. "If you feel an urge to stand up and make a speech attacking Vietnam policy, don't make it," he warned them. "After you've been here a few years you can afford to be independent. But if you want to come back in 1967, don't do it now."[17]

On another occasion, the President himself was even more direct. At a congressional briefing where Senator Frank Church criticized Vietnam policy, the President snapped, "Okay, Frank, next time you need a dam in Idaho, ask Walter Lippmann for one."[18] During the summer of 1965 the President's control of Congress extended even to the junior senator from New York, Robert F. Kennedy. At the request of the White House in July, Kennedy toned down a speech only mildly critical of the President's handling of the war, even agreeing to delete the phrase "victory in a revolutionary war is not won by escalation, but by de-escalation."[19]

The President's tactics did not win the hearts of dissidents in Congress, but it kept them largely in line. He failed to persuade his critics he was right, but he denied them room for effective opposition. Most criticism was expressed privately and when it leaked to the press, Johnson was quick to distract the public's attention. On the night of July 27, 1965, for example, during another of the periodic Vietnam "crises," Johnson held a private meeting with congressional leaders to let them know what he would say about Vietnam in a speech to be televised nationally the following morning. Senator Mansfield insisted on reading a statement at the briefing in which he told the President he would go along publicly, but that privately he profoundly disapproved of Johnson's plan to send another fifty thousand troops to Vietnam, of the bombing, and of the U.S. decision to avoid negotiations in favor of military action. "Well, Mike," Johnson was reported to have said, "what would *you* do?"[20] Reports of Mansfield's highly unusual act and the President's lame response quickly leaked to reporters, but on August 1, asked about the reports during a press conference in Texas, Johnson adroitly shifted attention by angrily blaming the leak on the newly elected House Republican leader, Gerald Ford. In Washington, Mansfield's opposition was a strong indication of the shallowness of the President's support on the war. In the rest of the country, however, he seemed firmly in control.

Johnson's ability to silence public officials extended well beyond the limits of Washington. One of the few to express tentative doubts about the war in July, 1965, was Governor George Romney of Michigan, a Republican moderate who had refused to support Goldwater the year before. Johnson's meeting with Mansfield and other congressional leaders had happened to coincide with the National Governors' Conference being held in Minneapolis. On Monday, July 25, Republican governors at the conference had refused to grant Johnson advance approval for a dramatic increase in the American military effort, which at that time was expected to include a call-up of the reserves. Romney and Mark Hatfield, the Republican governor of Oregon, were both fairly outspoken in their criticism of the President, but Romney left himself room for maneuver. "I am reserving judgment," he said. "I don't consider myself in any position to say whether we have done what we should have done in Vietnam or not."[21]

On Wednesday, July 28, Johnson announced over nationwide television that he was sending another fifty thousand troops to Vietnam immediately and more later, as they were requested. He did not call up the reserves. With the exception of Hatfield and Romney, the governors at the conference all voted for a loosely worded, oral resolution backing the President's action. Hatfield's opposition was clear and principled: he considered the war a foolish, tragic mistake. Romney was more elusive. He was unwilling to give the President a "blank check" but said his reluctance to do so was based on a lack of understanding as to what was really going on. "I hope it [Johnson's decision] is right, but the lack of information is disturbing," he said. "He told us nothing new that would indicate to me why he has taken the course he has."[22]

When the Governors' Conference ended the next day, Johnson flew all of them to Washington aboard the presidential plane for a special White House briefing on the war, very much like the one given congressional leaders a few days earlier. At the end of the briefing Hatfield said he was "more satisfied" and Romney unequivocally reversed himself. "Based upon the additional information received today," he said, "I support the President's actions taken yesterday and I urge all Americans to do the same."[23] One might wonder what Johnson could have said to convince Romney and Hatfield so quickly. The answer is apparently twofold: first, that without American troops the war would be lost, and second, anyone who refused to support our boys was going to find himself feeling mighty lonely. Romney, already entertaining presidential ambitions, had no desire to join Morse and Gruening in their principled isolation. Romney supported the war, in short, because no major political figures were prepared to join him in opposing it.

The techniques that quickly snuffed out opposition in the Congress and state capitals were not so effective, however, with ordinary people. Thousands of Americans who had supported Johnson in 1964 on the peace issue were furious at the escalations of early 1965. They were less interested in the practical realities of political life than in finding an effective way to oppose expansion of the war. They did not get much encouragement. Everywhere, those who might have led were silent or discreet. The churches said nothing, the unions were firmly anticommunist, and even many leading spokesmen for peace and disarmament were more inclined to talk about a vague world peace in the future than the war at hand. At the end of February the Center for the Study of Democratic Institutions held a huge meeting at the United Nations to discuss Pope John XXIII's encyclical, *Pacem in Terris*. More than 2,500 statesmen and scholars spent three days discussing peace, but they did not formally recognize the war in Vietnam. A. J. Muste, a peace activist since 1914 and leader of the Committee for Non-Violent Action in New York, had been invited but withdrew at the last moment because of a more pressing engagement: he was demonstrating against the war in Vietnam.

Muste was not alone in feeling that it was more important to protest the war in Vietnam than to discuss peace in the abstract, but he was typical in his isolation from the established political institutions of American society. Johnson's escalation of the war brought protests from a wide range of groups in the spring of 1965, but none of them received support from mainstream political leaders. When students held a teach-in at the University of Michigan in March, and the SDS sponsored a demonstration in Washington the following month, they were filling the vacuum created when the loyal opposition, embracing the old rule that "politics stops at the water's edge," fell into line behind the President. Much of the antiwar movement would eventually acquire a bitter contempt for the liberals who were silent when the war began, but early in 1965 they were ready to enlist allies wherever they could find them. In a typical attempt, a group of seven writers and intellectuals in New York arranged to meet with Adlai Stevenson, the U.S. ambassador to the United Nations, to urge him to resign in protest against the war.

Despite Stevenson's relative impotence and a certain dimming of his reputation following his defense of the United States during the Bay of Pigs invasion, the Tonkin Gulf incidents, the beginning of the bombing in February, and the landing of marines in the Dominican Republic in April, Stevenson remained a figure of considerable influence with the liberal wing of the Democratic Party. His insistence on the importance of reason and decency in international affairs, his willingness to criticize Senator Joseph McCarthy during the height of McCarthy's power in the early 1950s, his support for an end to nuclear testing when that was considered little short of treason, his wit, his intelligence, and his humanity had created an aura about him of selflessness and integrity. He was, or had been, one of the few genuinely inspiring figures of American politics. The members of the New York group which met with Stevenson at the U.S. mission to the United Nations on June 21, 1965, were consciously making one last effort, with varying degrees of hope for success, to create an opposition to the war within established political institutions. All of the group were opposed to the war. All had been disappointed by the silence of liberal congressmen, liberal magazines, and the editorial boards of liberal newspapers. All felt the time had come to stop expressing "doubt" and "concern" and to begin saying no. All felt that if Stevenson failed them, altogether new political forces would have to be created throughout the country to oppose the war.

The seven—David McReynolds, Paul Goodman, Dwight Mac-Donald, Harvey Swados, Kay Boyle, Nat Hentoff, and William H. Meyer—accurately reflected the small class of dissidents who seriously opposed the war. They agreed on few things, probably not even on their exact purpose in asking Stevenson to resign, but all refused to accept the war as inevitable or necessary. During the hour and a half while the group urged Stevenson to resign, he remained courteous and even grateful that they still took him with sufficient seriousness to make the request. He made it clear he was worried by the situation in Vietnam, that he doubted the wisdom of American intervention in the first place ("But how the hell are we going to get out of there?"[24] he asked), and was all but openly critical of the American intervention in the Dominican Republic.

At the same time, however, Stevenson made it clear he intended to remain at the United Nations. "No, I will not resign," he said. "I would never take advantage of my political position to resign for political reasons. That's not the way we play the game."[25]

Most of those at the meeting had supported Stevenson during his campaigns against Eisenhower. They had considered him a force for progress in the United States and peace in the world, and his refusal to speak for them on the war came as a deep disappointment. Like thousands of other people throughout the country, they felt Johnson was heading into a quicksand where spreading war might lead to conflict with China or the Soviet Union. It was not so much Stevenson's refusal to resign that disturbed them as his failure to accept what they saw as the gravity of the situation. Throughout most of the meeting, Meyer, a former Democratic congressman from Vermont and a friend of Stevenson, remained silent while others implored Stevenson to resign. "Adlai," he said after listening for nearly an hour, "I fought for you through three campaigns. I believed in you. I would have given anything I owned to see you win. But now you've let us down."

"What do you mean by that, Bill, by 'I let you down'?"

"I'm a farmer," Meyer said. "I'm a plain-speaking man. You know what I mean by 'let us down,' Adlai. You betrayed us."[26]

The meeting continued for another forty-five minutes but achieved nothing. The seven left feeling that Stevenson had allowed himself to be trapped. If Fulbright or Stevenson or even a group of lesser-known senators and representatives had been willing to create a position from which to oppose Johnson's conduct of the war, those opposed to it, a small but growing number throughout the country, would probably have turned to him or them. When they found nothing but private reservations discreetly expressed, the opposition turned elsewhere.

FOUR

The Appeal to Reason

Two days after the election in November, 1964, President Johnson called Dr. Benjamin Spock in New York to thank him for the work he had done on the Doctors for Johnson Committee during the campaign. "I hope I will be worthy of your trust," the President said. "I'm sure you will," the doctor answered.[1] When the United States began to bomb North Vietnam on February 7, 1965, Dr. Spock was hopping mad. He sent the President a series of letters, some of them stinging. The first was answered vaguely by the President, the rest by McGeorge Bundy, Walt Rostow, and other White House aides. When Spock saw that letter-writing was not going to have any effect, he, like thousands of others who felt personally betrayed by the escalation of the war, began casting about for other means of protest.

At the University of Michigan a group of faculty members who had strongly supported Johnson against Barry Goldwater began discussing the idea of some sort of academic strike as a way of protesting the war. On Thursday, March 11, the day after three thousand U.S. Marines had landed at Danang to protect the U.S. air base there, about twenty-five people met in the living room of a faculty member and agreed to issue a formal appeal for a one-day "moratorium" so that students could study the war. Immediate opposition by university officials and state legislators blocked the original idea, and it was decided to hold the special study session at night instead. This reassured the legislators and university administrators, who quickly granted special permission for women students to stay out all night and for the use of four large auditoriums and several classrooms. When the teach-in (as it quickly

54

came to be called) began at 8 P.M. on March 24, 1965, more than three thousand students and faculty members had packed the auditorium, three times the number organizers had been hoping for. It was a freezing night, the temperature dropping at one point to twenty degrees. A handful of students picketed the teach-in with signs supporting U.S. policy in Vietnam. One large banner had a large black silhouette of a bomb and the legend, "All the way with LBJ." Another sign read, "Get the *Daily* out of Vietnam, Defoliate the Arb, Deflower the Thetas, Stop the senseless waste of human beings, Close the Union Pool."[2] The dominant mood, however, was one of seriousness, even earnestness, as students soberly discussed the war. Bulletin boards were covered with clippings about Vietnam and students carried copies of I. F. Stone's *Weekly,* Bernard B. Fall's *The Two Viet-Nams,* and books on guerrilla warfare. The majority of the three thousand students remained for the midnight rally, held outside, and more than six hundred were still talking when the teach-in formally ended at 8 A.M. on the morning of March 25.

The tone of the discussion was less one of anger than sadness, a reasoned, almost scholarly concern that the United States was making a terrible mistake. One of the few to take a sharper view was Carl Oglesby, then a national officer of SDS, who described the war as a revolution and the American intervention as an attempt at counterrevolution, both with classical economic causes. The main speaker at the teach-in was Arthur Waskow of the Institute for Policy Studies in Washington. He was more conciliatory in his analysis, suggesting that the war was an aberration, a departure from traditional American policies, an error to be corrected. At one point during his speech a helmeted policeman came up to him and handed him a note. He read it in silence, then turned to the audience. "I should not think this would happen in the United States," he said, "but there has been a bomb threat. We must clear the building."[3]

The entire audience trooped outside, where Waskow finished his speech in the snow. While police searched the building, finding nothing, Waskow said the most disturbing thing about the war was a new sense of arrogance emanating from officials in Washington. He urged the government to abandon its attempt to impose a military solution and instead to pursue a political settlement which would recognize the legitimate aspirations of all sides.

If we took the course I have suggested, then the United States might make itself again what Jefferson once called it—the last, best hope of earth. But if we take the course of arrogance—either the arrogance of America as a world policeman or the arrogance of neo-isolationism—then we will find our arrogance suffocating and corrupting not only others but also ourselves. I fear the new arrogance is increasing among us. . . . When I meet it in *our* country, when I hear it in *our* country, I can only remember something else that Jefferson told us. He was talking, 150 years ago, of a remarkably similar arrogance that afflicted our domestic life, the arrogance of slavery, and he said, "Indeed, I tremble for my country when I reflect that God is just." Tonight, my fellow Americans, I tremble—I tremble for my country when I reflect that God is just.[4]

The success of the March 24–25 teach-in at the University of Michigan created a kind of euphoria among its organizers. The idea spread rapidly, and other teach-ins were held, at Columbia University on March 25, organized as soon as plans for the Michigan teach-in became known; at the University of Wisconsin on April 1; New York University on April 14; Rutgers University and the University of Oregon on April 23; in Washington on May 15; at Berkeley on May 21 and 22. There were scores across the country in the five or six weeks following the Michigan teach-in, convincing the original organizers that a way had been found to educate the public about the war and simultaneously to put pressure on Washington to end it. In their initial burst of enthusiasm, the teach-in organizers felt that the antiadministration weight of informed argument might change the situation overnight.

A group of eighty-five professors was organized which traveled to Washington for two days of meetings with officials beginning on April 8. One of the officials was John Bailey, the Johnson-appointed chairman of the Democratic National Committee, who admitted there was a lot of sentiment against the war and promised to pass the professors' views on to the President. Senators Jacob Javits and Robert F. Kennedy assured them that Johnson could be counted on to "listen to the votes"[5] and said the President's Johns Hopkins speech on April 7, in which he offered Hanoi unconditional negotiations, was the result of pressure brought by opponents of the war.

In mid-April plans for a national teach-in began to take form. Criticized for the one-sided nature of the first teach-in, the organizers planned a confrontation with the White House as a way of dramatically revealing the weakness of the administration's justification of the war. The Inter-University Committee for a Public Hearing on Vietnam, in charge of plans for the national teach-in, de__ _led that the ideal government spokesman would be McGeorge Bundy, a former Harvard dean with a reputation as an intellectual. Bundy, a rigid and aloof Cold War ideologue, led them a confusing, infuriating chase in which he was coy, conciliatory, and insulting by turns. On April 10, 1965, Robert Buckhout, secretary of the Ad Hoc Committee on Foreign Policy at Washington University in St. Louis, wrote to Bundy proposing a debate on a date of his choosing. Bundy replied on April 16, rejecting Buckhout's invitation on the grounds of prior commitments and the general press of official business, and contemptuously dismissing Buckhout's letter "either as a piece of propaganda or as a serious effort to engage in discussion." With characteristic disdain, Bundy concluded:

> There are other distortions in your letter, and other assumptions in its questions which are contrary to fact, but I have written enough to suggest that if your letter came to me for grading as a professor of government, I would not be able to give it high marks.[6]

Bundy's attitude, not surprisingly, only whetted the professors' appetite for a confrontation. A group of four hundred University of Michigan faculty members jointly sent him another invitation, which he responded to somewhat more gently, accepting the idea of a debate in principle. The Inter-University Committee quickly pursued the apparent opening. During negotiations Bundy refused to appear opposite Professor Hans Morgenthau, citing personal reasons, or Senator Wayne Morse, to whom the administration was not anxious to draw attention. Finally, he agreed to debate Professor George M. Kahin of Cornell University. Once the committee had what appeared to be a firm commitment from Bundy, it began organizing a national teach-in to be held in Washington on Saturday, May 15.

The administration, meanwhile, had been searching for a way to silence academic opponents of the war who could not be persuaded with the direct and simple methods so effective with governors and congressmen. The first step was the publication of a State Department white paper on Vietnam intended to prove once and for all that the war had been forced on the United States and that Saigon could not be abandoned in good conscience. The paper, *Aggression from the North*, was a long, detailed argument, supported by appendices heavy with statistics, that the National Liberation Front (NLF) of South Vietnam was a creation of the Lao Dong (Communist) Party ruling North Vietnam; that twenty thousand men had been infiltrated into South Vietnam between 1959 and 1964; that the infiltrees were increasingly North Vietnamese in origin, rather than southerners who had gone North in 1954; that Hanoi was supplying the Vietcong with arms and ammunition made in China, Russia, and Eastern Europe; that the fighting in the South was under the direct control of the North through a Central Office for South Vietnam; that Hanoi had decided on aggression because of the "economic miracle" under Diem in South Vietnam; and that southerners were recruited into the Vietcong by terrorism, not idealism. Literally hundreds of speeches had been given by American officials about the war since 1961, but the white paper was the single most coherent defense of the official claim that this was not a civil war, but simple aggression. Under the close scrutiny that it received by both scholars and polemicists the white paper fell apart. In the end it was more of an embarrassment than a help to the government that produced it.

One of the first, and probably the most influential, of the critiques of *Aggression from the North* was I. F. Stone's "A Reply to the White Paper," published in his *Weekly* of March 8, 1965. With characteristic wit, logic, and recourse to the public record, Stone demonstrated that the white paper was incomplete where it was not inaccurate, misleading where it was not dishonest, and contrary in its broad argument to every informed history of the war. He granted the government's claim that Hanoi was supporting the NLF, pointing out that we made no secret of our own, much greater support for Saigon, but denied that this meant the war was a case of aggression. Far from supplying the Vietcong heavily with Communist-made munitions, Stone said, Hanoi actually provided only a tiny percentage of the material used by the Vietcong. He cited American military estimates that 80 percent of the Vietcong's weapons had been captured from U.S. or Saigon forces, and he pointed out that the Pentagon's own figures showed only 179 Communist-made weapons among the total of 15,100 captured by Saigon between 1962 and 1964. Stone wondered why the United States included only six North Vietnamese among the twenty-three infiltrees named in the report if in fact northerners predominated in the forces sent South. He was scornful of the white paper's failure to mention the elections on Vietnam's reunification, to have been held in 1956. He pointed out that an International Control Commission report criticizing North Vietnam for breaking the Geneva accords was only half the story; the same report also attacked the United States for its military buildup in the South, a fact left out of the white paper. Finally, Stone rejected the white paper's argument that the "economic miracle" in the South was the cause of the war, saying this would have been "the first time in history a guerrilla war spread not because the people were discontented but because their lot was improving."

The effect of the white paper, and of Stone's reply, was to destroy the government's claim that it understood the war because it alone had the facts. Added up, the facts showed a civil war between the two halves of Vietnam, with only the United States trying to prevent a purely Vietnamese solution. By the time the teach-in movement began to spread, the argument over the war had shifted its focus. Administration apologists abandoned detailed attempts to prove aggression, instead pressing parallel arguments about U.S. "credibility" and the difficulty in deciding what else to do. The chief effect of the white paper was to convince people the war was *not* a classic case of aggression, however difficult it might be for the United States to get out, once in. In the following years government officials offered other explanations of the war, but the fact that the first had been abandoned did nothing to recommend those that followed.

More immediately, the administration authorized the creation of an Inter-Departmental Speaking Team on Vietnam Policy under the direction of William Jorden in the Department of State. The four-man team, which visited six midwestern campuses during May, included Thomas F. Conlon of the Agency for International Development (AID), the team's chairman; another AID official; and two lieutenant colonels. The reception of the "truth team," so named by *Time* magazine, was chilly where it was not downright hostile, and the confrontations with students tended toward niggling debates on the exact terms of the 1954 Geneva agreements, who was in the National Liberation Front, the role of U.S. troops, what Eisenhower *really* said about Ho Chi Minh and the 1956 elections, what Secretary of Defense McNamara *really* meant when he said in 1963 that U.S. troops would be coming home at the end

of 1965, and similar questions. On May 6 the team visited the University
of Wisconsin in Madison at the invitation of the Committee to Support
the People of South Vietnam. While Conlon and two other team members had coffee and cookies with their hosts before the meeting, they
were loudly heckled from outside by members of the Student Committee to End the War in Vietnam.

Later, when the main meeting was held in the hot and humid auditorium of the Social Science Building, about two hundred students wearing black armbands stood against the rear wall. The team's attempt to
present the official view of the war was a fiasco. Before Conlon set out
on the tour he had privately admitted in Washington that academic
objections to the war had already been considered by the administration
and rejected. His attitude was quickly detected in Madison, and Conlon's attempt to retain control by telling students to shut up and sit
down and send him their objections by mail only increased the number
and passion of heckling questions from the floor. A typical exchange
went like this:

Student: "Why do prisoners we take confess to infiltration only after
a month of interrogation?"

Conlon: "Have you ever had anything to do with interrogation?"

Student: "No, and I don't want to."

Conlon: "Sometimes it takes a long time before a prisoner wants to
talk."

Another student, shouting: "Torture!"

Conlon: "Do you also charge the North Vietnamese with torture?"

Student: "I condemn torture whoever does it!"

Conlon: "The Americans do not torture."

Third student: "But we run the show."

Conlon: "We do not run it."

Shouts from throughout the room: "Aw c'mon. Let's be honest."[7]

The principal effect of this bickering was to demonstrate the gulf that
separated students not only from the government, but also from those
professors whose tightly reasoned arguments against the war were a
tacit admission that other arguments could presumably bring them to
support it. Like Conlon, the students wearing black armbands at the
University of Wisconsin had decided the basic issues of the war before
the State Department team arrived. The moral intensity that infused
their questions about napalm, tear gas, and torture could never be

quieted by reference to Eisenhower's letter to Diem or President Johnson's offer of unconditional negotiations.

The largest and in some ways most important of the teach-ins was held simultaneously in Washington and on 122 college and university campuses connected by telephone lines on Saturday, May 15. The intensity of the long-awaited confrontation was only slightly mitigated by the fact that it fell in the middle of a five-day halt in the bombing of North Vietnam, Johnson's attempt to prove the bombing was not, in fact, the only obstacle to peace, as the North Vietnamese claimed. The administration took the teach-in seriously, picking its spokesmen for the weight of their academic credentials, demanding three hundred tickets to ensure that administration arguments would be applauded, and renting a room in the Sheraton Hotel for State Department researchers who might be called on to deal with awkward facts at a moment's notice. Before the teach-in Jorden held a number of strategy sessions in his office to prepare a coherent response to the dozens of separate attacks that had been launched at the White House since the bombing had begun three months earlier. Shortly after 10 A.M. on the fifteenth, Professor Ernest Nagel of Columbia University, who was to moderate the debate between Bundy and Kahin, was summoned from a meeting and taken to the White House, where he was handed a message from Bundy by a member of Bundy's staff. Bundy, it appeared, would not be able to take part in the teach-in. His message of apology reflected a characteristic disdain for the whole event as interesting, perhaps, but peripheral to the real business of running the government.

The rest of the teach-in took place as scheduled but was clouded by Bundy's absence, since the entire event had been conceived and promoted as a climactic confrontation between critics of the war and the administration's most able apologist. The only other surprise was the response to the speech given by Arthur Schlesinger, Jr., a pungent analysis of the war which poked witty fun at members of the administration while accepting their basic arguments for continuation of U.S. policy. Schlesinger, who disliked Johnson and was disliked equally in return, had nevertheless been listed as a representative of official views, which added significance to his small deviations from the White House line. His only genuinely sharp attack centered on the bombing of North Vietnam. He cited the official Strategic Bombing Survey made by the United States following World War II, which had indicated that strategic bombing strengthens, not weakens, an enemy's will to resist. He argued that more troops, not more bombs, would enhance the prospects of negotiation by discouraging the hopes of the Vietcong, who understood the limitations of bombing better than the administration. "Indeed," he said, "if we took the Marines now in the Dominican Republic and sent them to South Vietnam we would be a good deal better off in both countries."[8]

When Schlesinger doubted the moral purity of the Vietcong or the disinterest of Peking, many in the audience booed, hissed, and hooted, and later asked hostile questions which frequently turned out to be miniature speeches, strong on declaration and weak on interrogation. "When I hear questions like that," Schlesinger said instead of answering one, "I begin to wonder whether Mac Bundy might not be right."[9]

The majority of the audience, however, responded eagerly to Schlesinger's refusal to take hard moral positions. They were uneasy with vilification of the U.S. government or uncritical support for Hanoi. Schlesinger's obvious, and entertaining, disenchantment with Rusk and other spokesmen for the administration, combined with his defense of a policy of negotiation, brought a spontaneous burst of applause near the end of his speech.

> My own conclusion is that we must persevere in developing the combination of military, political, economic and diplomatic action most likely to bring us closer to a negotiated settlement. This may not be very satisfactory. It doesn't promise a perfect solution. But life is not very satisfactory. [Applause.] I welcome this existential endorsement.[10]

Examined carefully, Schlesinger's speech was in effect a point-by-point defense of official White House policy, but most of the audience remembered, newsmen reported, and columnists remarked upon his critical tone. When another teach-in was held at the University of California at Berkeley the following weekend, Schlesinger's speech was singled out for attack by the Yale history professor Staughton Lynd, who had helped organize the national teach-in. Lynd, long active in the civil rights movement and director of the Freedom Schools of the Mississippi Summer Project in 1964, scorned the idea that anything Schlesinger had said in Washington justified referring to him as a critic of the war.

> Now, Professor Schlesinger at Washington presented himself as a supporter of this policy with a difference, with certain infinitesimal differ-

ences, designed to indicate that he was a supporter of presidential candidate Robert Kennedy rather than Presidential incumbent Lyndon Johnson.[11]

Lynd's speech, rejecting the premises of American foreign policy and the elitist background of the secretaries of state who had formed it, reflected the movement atmosphere of the Berkeley teach-in. The Washington teach-in, organized largely by members of the faculty at the University of Michigan, had been rigorously academic in tone. Speakers at the Berkeley teach-in, attended by twelve thousand people at its peak, ranged from Dr. Spock to Mario Savio, leader of the Free Speech Movement, the success of which had made Berkeley's "Vietnam Day" possible. Charles Cobb and Bob Moses of the Student Non-Violent Coordinating Committee related the civil rights struggle in the United States to the war in Vietnam, arguing that favoring the one necessarily involved opposing the other.

The difference between the two teach-ins reflected the difference between intellectual opposition to a policy and an instinctive opposition to a whole way of life. Where speakers at the Washington teach-in had subjected administration arguments to close scholarly scrutiny, Vietnam Day speakers expressed a profound moral horror at not only the violence, but the very purpose of American intervention. Where Schlesinger had emphasized the importance of respecting opposing points of view, Lynd rejected the possibility of compromise, saying that coalition with liberal critics of the war like Schlesinger would amount to a "coalition with the Marines."[12] The Washington teach-in focused on the war alone; at Berkeley Vietnam was described as a symptom of deeper things wrong with America. In Washington, academicians argued that a mistake had been made and should be corrected. At Berkeley, activists said a new movement was rising up all over the country which would not only end the war, but replace the system that had created it. Paul Potter, a former national officer of SDS, described that movement as a new humanism, a resurgence of the spirit, a reawakening of brotherly feeling in a country that had grown callous in its obsession with producing, consuming, and getting ahead. In words that would seem embarrassingly sentimental, and frustratingly vague, in less than two years, Potter concluded his speech with a passionate exhortation to overcome the barriers that isolate people in a mass society:

When I say we're inarticulate I mean we don't know how to say very basic things about ourselves. We don't know how to say that we're alone. We don't know how to say that we are afraid—afraid to change our lives and do what we know we should do with our lives. . . . You see, there's a caption on the sign in that SNCC poster that says, "Come, let us build a new world together," and that's what we have to learn to say to one another. I can't say that to you from here because I don't know your names and I can't see your faces and I don't know the expressions in your eyes. There's no way for you to talk back to me, and I can't say what I want to say to you—and I would if I could—"Come, let us build a new world together."[13]

When the thirty-six-hour teach-in finally ended on Saturday, May 22, it was clear that Paul Potter and Arthur Schlesinger would never be able to agree on a common strategy for opposing the war. McGeorge Bundy would probably find difficulty in seeing just how Potter's speech represented an attack on the war; he would certainly be unable to refute the argument it made. The idealistic yearning of Potter and other members of the New Left was the result of their experiences in the civil rights movement early in the decade. Facing violence in the South they had needed, and had learned to value, courage, honesty, and the intense communal feeling naturally evoked by a common cause and common danger. By the spring of 1965 the specific reforms originally sought by the New Left had been superseded by a broader commitment to a reworking of the world which would resemble, emotionally and socially, the movement in its first flush of moral fervor in the South. Gradually closed out of black organizations, white radicals began to think of the movement in a broader way, less interested in correctives than alternatives.

The tone of the speeches at Berkeley marked an important change in the opposition to the war. Opponents felt the exhaustive discussion of the war at scores of teach-ins between March 24 and May 22 had settled the argument. The lame explanations of the State Department's truth team, the critiques of the white paper, the refusal of McGeorge Bundy to argue the issue in public, and the growing tendency of Vietnam apologists to admit mistakes in the past while challenging the opposition to come up with an alternative now all seemed to indicate that reason, or at least scholarly expertise, was on the side of the opposition. At the height of the teach-ins Rusk once referred slightingly to "academic gullibility," the sort of *argumentum ad hominem* one instinctively uses when he feels he is getting the worst of the argument. There was never much chance the teach-in movement would reverse official policy, of course; the bombing of North Vietnam and the dispatch of American troops were a kind of earnest money not easily recalled. The teach-in movement was, in fact, about a year too late to do any good. In 1964 it might conceivably have headed off the massive American intervention of 1965, but no mere argument could affect that intervention once begun. The significance of the movement, then, was not its influence on official policy, which was nil, but the fact that it served to focus discontent with the war. The teach-ins ended but the movement remained.

By the late spring of 1965 the arguments for and against the war had been made repeatedly and the dispute inevitably began to acquire a certain note of shrill abuse. Rusk's insulting reference to "academic gullibility" began to elicit insults in returns. The widening breach between the White House and American artists, academics and intellectuals burst open at the White House Festival of the Arts held on Monday, June 14. The festival, originally conceived in February before opposition to the war had begun to organize, was planned as a celebration of American creativity. Eric Goldman, a Princeton University professor quietly recruited by the White House shortly after the death of John F. Kennedy, proposed the festival in a memo to the President on February 25 but failed to win a final acceptance until May 23, the day after the Berkeley teach-in ended.

The ill feeling over the war which had been growing since the beginning of the bombing was suddenly and forcefully revealed after invitations to the festival were sent out by the White House. The poet Robert Lowell at first accepted the invitation but then hesitated, reconsidered, and finally sent Goldman a letter of pointed rejection which he said he wanted to be passed on to the President. Goldman called Lowell and tried to persuade him to withdraw the letter, knowing how the President would react to it. Lowell said it was too late; he had already given the text of the letter to the *New York Times*, which reported it in a front-page story the following day, Thursday, June 3. In his letter Lowell said he reacted to Johnson's foreign policy "with the greatest dismay and distrust" and he concluded, "At this anguished, delicate and perhaps determining moment, I feel I'm serving you and our country best by not taking part in the White House Festival of the Arts."[14]

On Sunday, May 30, while Lowell was still preparing his letter, his wife, the writer Elizabeth Hardwick, had been called by the editor of the *New York Review of Books*, perhaps the most influential literary periodical in America. The editor, Robert Silvers, who had been calling about another matter, was intrigued by Lowell's plan and dropped by later in the day to read the letter. On Monday Silvers and Stanley J. Kunitz, a poet, drafted and sent a telegram to the President supporting Lowell's action and pledging the twenty signers to refuse to attend the festival. Among the signers were some of the most distinguished writers and artists in the country. Other guests who had already accepted invitations to the festival were thus tacitly asked to join Lowell or repudiate him, or somehow justify a decision to attend the festival in spite of their feelings about the war. The novelist Saul Bellow told the *Times* he felt this would be a ceremonial occasion without political overtones, but John Hersey told reporters he had decided to read a selection from *Hiroshima*, his short, brutal book about the dropping of the first atomic bomb on August 6, 1945. Hersey said he hoped the President would attend the reading and heed the implied warning that nuclear disaster could lie at the end of the road of escalation in Vietnam. The President, not surprisingly, was furious, and his wife tried to talk Goldman into blocking Hersey from doing as he had promised. "The President and I do not want this man to read these passages in the White House,"[15] she said. Goldman refused to intervene, saying it would only make things worse.

As the furor mounted so did Johnson's anger. He blamed hostility toward his policies on the fact he was a Southerner; the intellectuals would never give him a chance no matter what he did. "Some of them insult me by staying away and some of them insult me by coming,"[16] he said one day within earshot of reporters.

On the day of the festival, Dwight MacDonald, one of the signers of the Silvers-Kunitz telegram, changed his mind and flew to Washington where he spent most of the day buttonholing guests for signatures on a petition expressing further support for Lowell, who dominated the gathering by his absence, as Bundy had dominated the national teach-in a month earlier. The atmosphere was bitter. A brief argument flared between MacDonald and Charlton Heston, the actor, who denounced the petition as boorish. Saul Maloff, the *Newsweek* book reviewer and himself an aspiring novelist, attacked Bellow for supporting the President, even going so far as to say that reviewers had made Bellow's reputation, and reviewers could break it.

The President appeared at the festival despite threats he might stay away, and his presence diluted the attacks on his Vietnam policy. He made a point of engaging Fulbright in a long conversation and then touring the White House grounds with him, looking at the art. A photo that appeared in papers across the country showed Johnson and Fulbright studying a sculpture by Alexander Calder, one of four guests who had changed their minds about coming after publication of Lowell's letter.

The effect of the festival, and of the attitude expressed by Lowell, Silvers, Hersey, MacDonald, and others, was to carry public argument over the war beyond the limits of good manners. It was no longer enough to oppose the war publicly in an abstract, reasoned way; one was called on to disown it, and to repudiate those responsible for it. The entire issue was now infused with a certain moral urgency; to favor, or even to tolerate, the war was not simply mistaken, but wrong. The President had been right on one point, at least: these people did intend to insult him. Once insult became a weapon in the argument over the war, there could be no middle ground. This fact did not enhance the prospects for victory by the opposition, exactly, but it did promise a good deal of bitterness, and that bitterness, in the end, would have much to do with deciding the issue.

The final confrontation between the Johnson administration and opponents of the war in 1965 came on June 21, when McGeorge Bundy debated Professor Hans Morgenthau on a special CBS television program. The professors had kept after Bundy following his failure to appear at the national teach-in May 15, but Bundy, far more sophisticated than they, independently reached an agreement with CBS for a televised debate in which he would have control of the ground rules. In return, he agreed to debate Morgenthau, although he had once rejected him as an opponent.

The moderator of the program, Eric Sevareid, asked four questions basic to the administration's view of the war. Bundy, quoting heavily from official documents, said that we had intervened to fulfill sacred commitments, that the war was a case of aggression from the North, that a primary purpose of our intervention was to contain the Chinese, and that only two alternatives existed to the current policy: further escalation, or withdrawal. In answering Bundy, Morgenthau was the victim of his own unwillingness to embrace Bundy's second alternative, withdrawal. On that rock Johnson's policy abided. Like other critics of the war asked what *they* would do, Morgenthau found himself arguing that surely the President was smart enough, or had advisers who were smart enough, to figure a way out of the Vietnam impasse short of surrender:

> I have, indeed, always believed that it is impossible for a great power which must take care of its prestige to admit, in so many words, that its policy has been mistaken during the last 10 years and leave the theater of operations. But there are all kinds of face-saving devices by which a nation or a government which has made a series of mistakes can rectify the situation, and I think President DeGaulle has shown how to go about this, with regard to Algeria. And, if you look at the prestige of France today, it is certainly higher than it was when France fought in Indochina.[17]

Morgenthau went on to cite reports by European journalists contradicting the administration's view of events in Vietnam but was suddenly interrupted by Bundy, who charged him with "giving vent to his congenital pessimism with regard to these matters."[18] Bundy then read two passages obviously culled in advance from the vast quantity of political analysis written by Morgenthau over a long career. The first passage suggested that the American-financed Marshall Plan at the end of World War II was going to be a failure, and the second predicted, in 1961, that "Communist domination of Laos is virtually a foregone conclusion."[19]

Morgenthau: "I may have been dead wrong on Laos, but it doesn't prove that I am dead wrong on Vietnam."

Sevareid: "Since this has become something of a personal confrontation I think Professor Morgenthau should have a small chance at least to answer Mr. Bundy."

Morgenthau: "I admire the efficiency of Mr. Bundy's office. . . ."

Bundy: "I do my own [work]."

Morgenthau: "Oh, well, I am honored by the selected quotations from my writings. As I have said before, nobody who deals with foreign policy professionally can always be right. Obviously, one makes mistakes. And I probably was too pessimistic about Laos. But not terribly more pessimistic than the situation warranted. . . .

"So, I think no useful purpose is served by pointing to one mistake, and I admit freely that I have made mistakes, I have made many more than Mr. Bundy has found—but I have not *always* been wrong."[20]

After two full months of pursuing Bundy, the organizers of the original teach-in movement were profoundly disappointed by the debate that finally took place. Bundy's sudden personal attack might have been predicted and some personal *riposte* prepared, but the debate still would have faded out of focus. All the arguments had been made before, and if Bundy did not demolish Morgenthau's critique, neither did Morgenthau discredit Bundy's. Official advocates, like lawyers, are never at a loss for arguments, and thus argument becomes self-defeating, wasting energies that might be used for other attacks from different directions. The Bundy-Morgenthau confrontation was especially frustrating and inconclusive, the sharp words an indication of the bitter potential of the issue. Gradually, it had become clear that the question was one of failure or success for a policy already adopted. If American troops won in Vietnam, no argument could diminish their success. If they lost, no *apologia* could dilute their failure. The administration had committed itself to a contest in the field and was not about to be talked into a confession of failure.

The professors had tried to maintain a kind of fairness ever since they were criticized for the one-sided nature of the first teach-in. After the Bundy-Morgenthau debate this commitment to fair play began to diminish, since fair play only seemed to mean giving the government a platform to attack its opponents. The professors, with a certain lack of realism, had hoped that a face-to-face debate would reveal the true nature of the dispute, perhaps even leave the administration speechless and defenseless. It did not work. Stanley Diamond, a professor of anthropology at the University of Michigan, felt the final debate had only further confused the issue, to the probable benefit of the administration. "After viewing the program," he wrote in a newsletter published by the Inter-University Committee, "I am forced to conclude that we pursued McGeorge Bundy until he caught us."[21] The idea, he said, was not to argue with the administration, but to oppose it.

Few great questions of policy had ever been debated at such length, in such detail, with so little effect. There were other teach-ins after the spring of 1965, but they never again became the focus of the opposition to the war. For the opposition the time for words was passing. They knew where they stood; the question was what to do about it.

FIVE

Into the Streets

Despite all the rallies, teach-ins, symposia, lectures, discussions, petitions, and protests, the war continued to grow. By June it was evident that the administration could not be talked into abandoning its military policies, but it was by no means clear what might work in argument's place. Those who felt the teach-in movement had been a success cited President Johnson's speech on April 7 and the five-day bombing halt in May. The pessimists argued that the bombing halt ended before Hanoi had a chance to respond and that a willingness to "talk" with the other side was not the same as a willingness to compromise. The President's true intentions, they said, were better revealed by the quiet announcement early in June that American troops were taking on a combat role, and by the decision in July to send another fifty thousand troops to Vietnam, with more later. A broad strategy for the opposition was proposed on the night of June 8 when eighteen thousand people attended an antiwar rally held in Madison Square Garden in New York, where they heard Senator Wayne Morse, Dr. Spock, Norman Thomas, and Mrs. Martin Luther King all attack the war. Bayard Rustin, a long-time pacifist and civil rights activist who had organized the 1963 March on Washington, told the crowd that argument must give way to direct action:

> We know that the Wagner Act which gave labor the right to organize and bargain collectively was empty until workers went into the streets. The civil rights movement has learned this lesson. This is a lesson that must be applied now to the peace movement as well. We must stop meeting indoors and go into the streets.[1]

Critics of the war had been going into the streets, of course, since the visit to the United States by Madame Nhu in the fall of 1963, but they had generally been few in number or had belonged to traditional pacifist or radical groups too burdened by theory and history for most of the country to comprehend, much less follow. When Rustin referred to the peace movement he was speaking more of a state of mind and a condition of social ferment, an inchoate possibility, still in a process of becoming. Before the peace movement could go into the streets it had to exist, and that meant creating not only a literal organization, with phones, desks, and mimeographs to run off leaflets, but more importantly a sense of common purpose. The movement could not grow beyond the limits of a letterhead, or even a coalition of letterheads, until it had at least some theoretical notion of what it was against, what it was for, and how to proceed. The inevitable struggles over strategy and purpose were never fully resolved. Some factions within the movement attacked each other more fiercely than they attacked the war itself. Most of this infighting went unnoticed by the public, but it was always important, strengthening the movement at some moments, near to crippling it at others. If we spend a good deal of space following some of these arguments and counterarguments, it is because they were central to the growth of the movement that was the first and most important locus of opposition to the war. If the opposition had remained only a state of mind, a condition of the public not unlike atmospheric pressure, rising and falling in keeping with a logic of its own, detectable only by the barometers of opinion pollsters, then Johnson's policy of escalation would not have ended as and when it did. The movement created itself in order to make its opposition to the war effective. If it never attained the order and clarity of say, the League of Women Voters, it also attempted more and achieved more.

The peace movement came into existence slowly, by fits and starts, as the result of deliberate intitiatives by small groups of people. One of the first of the critical early decisions to act came in December, 1964, when the largest of the new student activist organizations, the Students for a Democratic Society, issued a call for a Vietnam protest march to be held in Washington the following April 17. When the plans for the march were first announced by Clark Kissinger, the SDS national secretary, almost no one was paying attention, including a probable majority of SDS members themselves, who had taken no part in the decision and felt only the loosest sort of fealty to the national headquarters in New York. When the United States began bombing North Vietnam in February, 1965, however, interest in the SDS march quickly grew among civil rights and peace groups.

The SDS asked the long-established pacifist groups to forgo their traditional Easter demonstrations so the energies of the peace movement could be concentrated in Washington for the march. In quiet meetings with pacifist groups in New York they insisted on retaining complete control over administration of the march, and they refused to exclude groups like the May Second Movement, secretly controlled by the Progressive Labor Movement (later Party), or the W.E.B. DuBois Clubs, the Communist Party's instrument for attempting to capture the student movement. Long-established pacifist leaders like A. J. Muste, Dave Dellinger, and David McReynolds were disappointed by SDS's obvious attempt to gain all the credit for a march that would in fact be sponsored by a number of organizations, but they nevertheless agreed to the SDS conditions. In order to understand their reluctance, it is important to know that demonstrations are to activist groups what football games are to colleges: major sources of publicity and money. The question of openness was more complex. Every group on the left was bitterly hostile to red-baiting, the attempt to discredit a group and its aims simply by claiming that Communists were involved in it. The left was divided on the best way to respond to red-baiting, however. Some groups felt excluding Communists would solve the problem; others felt this was a surrender of democratic principle and a sign of defensiveness. McReynolds and others, for example, felt that M2M, Youth Against War and Fascism (YAWF), and PL might, in fact, attempt to spark a riot, but that the principle of openness was worth the risk. Despite SDS's refusal to "screen" the march, a reflex action on the part of many activist groups that remembered the 1950s, its analysis of the war was thoroughly moderate in tone and free of traditional leftist jargon. Most, but not all, of the members of SDS favored an immediate withdrawal of troops from South Vietnam, but the organization decided against using that as one of the slogans of the march, fearing that "extreme" positions might split the movement and alienate the public. The call for the demonstration, a full-page ad in the March, 1965, issue of *Liberation*, was a tightly reasoned attack on the conflict in Vietnam as "a civil war . . . a losing war . . . a self-defeating war . . . a dangerous war . . . an undeclared war . . . an immoral war":

What kind of America is it whose response to poverty and oppression in South Vietnam is napalm and defoliation, whose response to poverty and oppression in Mississippi is . . . silence?

The SDS march was the center of much bitter dissension on the left. Moderate peace groups feared that the inclusion of Communists would discredit the antiwar movement. At the same time there was an element of jealousy and resentment of SDS's sudden rise to a central position in the peace movement, and its sole control of what would clearly be the most important demonstration in years. A counterattack was led by Bayard Rustin, whose militance in Madison Square Garden did not extend to revolutionary groups like M2M, PL, and the Communist Party. On the night of Friday, April 16, Rustin called a meeting of fifteen leaders of the peace movement and proposed that a statement be issued disavowing the support of M2M, YAWF, and the W.E.B. DuBois Clubs despite SDS's refusal to screen them out of the march. A. J. Muste and Norman Thomas refused to sign Rustin's proposed statement but, after hours of debate, agreed on a much milder compromise document welcoming all who were "not committed to any form of totalitarianism nor drawing inspiration or direction from the foreign policy of any government."[2] Dellinger and McReynolds insisted that even this was nothing more than a veiled concession to anticommunism and refused to sign.

A similar effort was made on the West Coast where Robert Pickus, western regional director of Turn Toward Peace, held a press conference before the march to protest leftist infiltration. He charged that leadership of the West Coast march was divided entirely between M2M and the DuBois Clubs and said, "It is time that someone within the peace movement challenged activity which is in fact more hostile to America than to war."[3] He said he opposed the slogan, "Get out of Vietnam":

> That is not the way to end war in Southeast Asia or to help change America's mind about the use of national military power there. . . . America is involved in Vietnam. It should stay involved. The question is how. . . . [4]

Dellinger, McReynolds, Staughton Lynd, and others argued that Rustin's and Pickus's red-baiting would only tend to discredit the movement by suggesting that it was Communist-inspired. Their apprehensions proved justified when the New York *Post* on the day of the march cited the Rustin-Muste-Thomas compromise statement issued in New York and said:

> In the aftermath of Mr. Johnson's call for "unconditional negotiations" there is no justification for transforming the march into a frenzied, one-sided, anti-American show. Some of the banners advertised in advance are being carried to the wrong place at the wrong time.[5]

It is not easy to explain the complexity of this issue or the strong feelings it aroused. Coalition with the Communists did not win friends, and the Communists, Trotskyists, and Maoists like PL were not easy to work with. SDS eventually wrecked itself trying to expel PL, and a number of peace organizations spent more time fighting Trotskyist takeover attempts than they did organizing against the war. For other reasons, however, it was important that peace groups welcome everyone, Communists included, despite the risk of dissension, partly because democratic principle demanded it, more importantly because the question of Communism was at the heart of American foreign policy. When all the official rhetoric had been pared to its core, the United States was fighting in Vietnam to stop Communism, or it was fighting for nothing at all. Nothing else could make sense of the origins of the war or the frequent decisions to continue it. Our credibility was allegedly at stake not in some abstract way, but concretely: we had promised to defend the Free World against Communism, and if the South Vietnamese could not trust us, neither could the Germans, the Indians, the Turks, the Greeks, or the Guatemalans. If the element of Communism were excised from every official document, every official argument based on national interest or world peace would evaporate. The Munich analogy would collapse, because it was Communism, not North Vietnam, we feared. Resisting Hanoi could no longer be construed as containing Peking, since a China and a North Vietnam without Communism in common would have nothing in common. If opponents of the war granted the administration's basic premise, that Communism was dangerous enough to justify war, then the dispute over the war became one of detail. The movement's first task was to exorcise the fear of Communism, and thus to deny its validity as a basis for policy. To be effective, the movement had to oppose the war, not quibble over its proper conduct. To have excluded Communists from its own ranks would have fatally weakened their argument that fear of Communism was not a proper justification for the devastation of Vietnam. The movement faced this dispute again and again, of course, but the openness of the SDS march in April, 1965, set a precedent which was widely followed.

In San Francisco on Saturday, April 17, only two hundred people showed up at the Federal Building to protest the war, but twenty thousand marched in Washington, far more than SDS or anyone else had anticipated. Senator Ernest Gruening, I. F. Stone, Staughton Lynd, Bob Parris, and Paul Potter all spoke at a rally held near the Washington monument. Gruening proposed a halt in the bombing, Stone urged the opposition to think of the administration as mistaken rather than vicious, Lynd insisted the war could not be supported morally, Parris said Mississippi was a mirror of America, and Paul Potter, twenty-four years old, said that Vietnam must provide the occasion for a complete reexamination of American society. His attitude verged on the moral rigidity against which Stone had warned, and on the sort of fundamental break with America against which Bayard Rustin and Robert Pickus had been maneuvering when they had sought to exclude the totalitarian left from the march. Said Potter:

> The further we explore the reality of what this country is doing . . . in Vietnam, the more we are driven toward the conclusion of Senator Morse that the United States may well be the greatest threat to peace in the world today. That is a terrible and bitter insight for people who grew up as we did, and our revulsion at that insight, our refusal to accept it as inevitable . . . is one of the reasons that so many people have come here today . . . .
>
> We must name the system [which led to the war]. We must name it, describe it, analyze it, understand it and change it. For it is only when that system is changed and brought under control that there can be any hope for stopping the forces that create a war in South Vietnam.[6]

Potter's hesitation to name the system was not simply coyness. Like the vast majority of the young, white, middle-class activists who had come of age during the civil rights movement in the early 1960s, he felt that things were profoundly wrong with America, but he also felt a deep reluctance to embrace the analysis of the old left as to just what the problem was. The movement already thought of itself as radical, but not yet as socialist. When the New Left attacked the system, they were referring to cold, elitist bureaucracies and the powerlessness of ordinary people, not just private property. They were collectivist almost by instinct but at the same time feared that the old, sterile disputes of the left were simply waiting to be revived. In one sense, the civil rights movement had attacked injustice in the South because its sight was short; it saw the evil and looked no further. Once activists began to blame the evil on the system, and to fight the system rather than its evil, the movement would meet greater resistance with fewer allies. It was tough enough to fight Southern sheriffs, just as it had been tough enough in the 1930s to win the right to a living wage, without having to remake the entire country. Nevertheless, many of those in the crowd listening to Potter were old Socialists, Trotskyists, Marxists, and they all felt the answer to his question bursting from their lips: *Say the word!* they wanted to shout. *Say the word! Capitalism!*

The old left in America was a chaos of splinter groups fighting each other with violent rhetoric in tiny publications, but they all felt in common that capitalism was the system that Potter hesitated to name, and they all planned to turn the struggle against the war into a struggle against capitalism (not from any inherent viciousness, one hastens to say, but because they felt that that way peace lay). The old left was quick to see that the war in Vietnam was the first issue with a potentially mass appeal since the 1930s. Every aging group fully intended to capture the opposition to the war, so that a victory of the antiwar movement would also mean the triumph of their own. The mass of Americans reading about the march on Washington, and even the mass of the marchers themselves, had no idea how many of these groups there were, how violently they opposed each other, or how completely they were willing to subordinate any issue to their internecine struggles, since each inclined to see itself as the sole salvation of the country. Rustin and Pickus did understand this, which was one reason they had risked the success of the demonstration in a vain attempt to purge the opposition of the traditional totalitarian left. It was not to be. In the following years the movement would divide between those like Martin Luther King, who could hate the sin and love the sinner, and the revolutionaries, who rejected American society and government along with the war.

While the crowd rallied at the Washington monument, and then marched down the grassy slope toward the White House, President Johnson in Texas, and Rusk in Washington, both issued statements rejecting a bombing halt as a way to open negotiations with Hanoi but reaffirming American readiness to begin unconditional talks with "any government,'" a phrase clearly intended to exclude the National Liberation Front.

Lynd and Dellinger were elated by the success of the march and infuriated by Rustin's attempts to purge it. In the June-July issue of *Liberation,* Lynd attacked Rustin with a venom which seemed, on the surface, more suitable to life-or-death enemies than near allies. In effect, Lynd accused Rustin of selling out the movement, not only in Washington, but at Atlantic City the previous summer, where he had supported the compromise offered the Mississippi Freedom Democratic Party. Rustin's article in the February, 1965, issue of *Commentary,* "From Protest to Politics," Lynd said, proposed a kind of latter-day liberal-activist united front which meant, in fact, "coalition with the Marines." The differences between Rustin and Lynd ran deeper than the disputes Lynd cited and reflected an ambivalence that was dividing the entire movement. Rustin felt that the civil rights movement to which he had devoted his life was finally coming to fruition, that the voting rights bill proposed by President Johnson in a speech before a joint session of Congress on March 15, 1965, marked a major turning point in American history. For Rustin, the war was a dangerous diversion from the true thrust of events, not fundamentally a new direction. Lynd, on the other hand, embittered by his experience in Mississippi and horrified by the war, felt that Johnson's sudden conversion to civil rights was a perversion of the movement, that the war was a moral issue transcending tactical political considerations in the United States, and that the American system was beginning to break down, not reform itself.

> If Vietnam is permissible, can anything be forbidden? And how many more secret, undebated Presidential decisions will it take to convince us that a constitutional crisis exists in America, that we have moved into a twilight zone between democratically delegated authority and something accurately called "fascism"?

Lynd said that the aim of the movement should not be the creation of new coalitions within the American political system seeking further reforms, but a "nonviolent revolution." He proposed that the movement seek to create new institutions, police departments for example, which would supplant the old ones because they would command the allegiance of the people. In a final paragraph Lynd expressed a vision of peaceful upheaval which created a strong and lasting impression on the growing civil rights–peace movement, but alarmed men like Rustin, who sensed within it an explosive potential for violence:

> At the April 17th march in Washington it was unbearably moving to watch the sea of banners and signs move out from the Sylvan Theater toward the Capitol as Joan Baez, Judy Collins and others sang "We Shall Overcome." Still more poignant was the perception—and I checked my reaction with many others who felt as I did—that as the crowd moved down the mall toward the seat of government, its path delimited on each side by rows of chartered buses so that there was nowhere to go but forward, toward the waiting policemen, it seemed that the great mass of people would simply flow on through and over the marble buildings, that our forward movement was irresistibly strong, and that even had some been shot or arrested nothing could have stopped that crowd from taking possession of its government. Perhaps next time we should keep going, occupying for a time the rooms from which orders issue and sending to the people of Vietnam and the Dominican Republic the profound apologies which are due; or quietly waiting on the Capitol steps until those who make policy for us, and who like ourselves are trapped by fear and pride, consent to enter into dialog with us and mankind.

When Rustin read this paragraph, it appeared in his mind's eye, and was often quoted elsewhere, with only the opening clause of the final sentence, thus: "Perhaps next time we should keep going. . . ." Lynd's qualifications were less important than the general idea. A new stage in the movement had been reached: politics would no longer mean ending segregation at lunch counters, as it had during the sit-in movement; or ending segregation on buses, as it had during the freedom rides; or registering the unregistered, as it had during the Mississippi Summer Project. The movement would no longer fight for justice in concrete things, but justice in the abstract. Politics for the movement had become total: the essence of Lynd's "nonviolent revolution" was not the nonviolence, but the revolution. At most a few thousand people read Lynd's article in *Liberation,* or Rustin's response in *Partisan Review* later that year, and yet their dispute marked an important turning point. The war was not to be just another issue within the broad consensus of American politics, a point to be argued and compromised, but rather "the incredibly sharp razor,"[8] in Paul Potter's words, which would divide the country into camps whose enmity, not yet fully expressed, was to be bitter and complete.

Rustin's position was echoed on the West Coast by twenty-six faculty members of the University of California at Berkeley, who wrote an open letter to the Vietnam Day Committee (VDC) arguing that civil disobedience in protests against the war would only weaken the opposition:

> The university can best serve the cause of peace and morality by serving first the cause of rationality. In this perspective, the good your committee can do for peace in Vietnam is, at best, doubtful; but the harm it can do the values of the university is quite certain.[9]

Behind the rationalizations of the professors was a clear understanding that Vietnam was an issue that could wreck the country. The signers of the letter naturally did not say so, but, given the choice, they would rather have the war than the social animosities that would inevitably arise from a really determined effort to end it. They did not want to force the issue. The VDC, on the other hand, felt an irresistible moral impulse to oppose the war not only intellectually and morally, but, in the end, even physically:

> What basically divides us on this question is the position we each take on the war. While you have "grave reservations" about the war, we are convinced that the United States government is committing a major moral crime in Vietnam. You are preoccupied with concern for the "dilemma of the President. . . ." We are preoccupied with the million Vietnamese who died in the war against the French which the United States paid for, and the hundreds of thousands who have died since then because of the United States' decision that the Geneva Accords should not be observed. We are more than "deeply concerned" about the war. We are rife with shame and anger that this blood-bath is made in our name.[10]

While this dispute was unfolding, the SDS, brought to national attention by the march on Washington, was having serious doubts about shifting its efforts from community organizing to the issue of the war. Following the march the organization moved its national headquarters from New York City to Chicago, where it rented a storefront in the run-down, racially mixed Woodlawn district not far from the University of Chicago. At its annual convention, held in Kewadin, Michigan, June 9 to 14, the SDS debated whether or not to continue an antiwar program. Clark Kissinger, the outgoing national secretary, proposed a program against the draft which would include deliberate violations of the Espionage Act of 1917 in an attempt to force political trials that would center on the moral issues behind the war. The organization failed to reach a final decision on Kissinger's proposal because it was split almost evenly between two fundamental thrusts. One half of SDS wanted to pursue attempts to organize the white working poor like that of the Newark Community Union Project (NCUP) in New Jersey. This broader movement might not stop the war in Vietnam, they conceded, but it would halt "the seventh war from now."[11] The other half of SDS agreed with Kissinger, who felt that the war was a pressing moral issue and offered a way of organizing a mass radical movement. The Oakland, California, SDS, for example, had begun with a community organizing project like that in Newark but, influenced by and influencing the VDC, had gradually shifted its activities to the war. SDS's inability to make up its mind on this issue left leadership of the antiwar movement open to all comers, and a variety of radical, civil rights, and peace groups attempted to fill the gap. SDS continued to be active on campuses across the country, focusing protests on the draft, military research, and the use of napalm, but it did not again sponsor a national action until its last, in October, 1969.

The first attempt to fill the gap left by SDS's indecision was made by a coalition of traditional peace organizations, led by A. J. Muste, which called for a four-day series of demonstrations and discussions in Washington between August 6 and 9, the twentieth anniversaries of the atom bombs dropped on Hiroshima and Nagasaki. Calling itself the Assembly of Unrepresented People, the coalition planned civil disobedience of the sort developed during the civil rights movement, culminating in a march on the Capitol like that musingly proposed by Lynd in his attack on Rustin. On August 6 about a thousand people held a thirty-minute vigil outside the White House and then attended a two-hour rally in Lafayette Park. On Saturday and Sunday, the seventh and eighth, discussions on the future of the antiwar movement led to the creation of a broad organization called the National Coordinating Committee to End the War in Vietnam (NCC) with thirty-three separate groups as members. On Monday, again, about a thousand people gathered at the Washington Monument and then, shortly after noon, marched down the mall toward the Capitol, David Dellinger, Staughton Lynd, and Bob Parris linking arms in the front rank. Two members of the American Nazi Party splashed the group with a bucket of red paint. When the marchers reached a line of police, Lynd and Parris insisted on pressing forward and were arrested. The rest of the marchers then sat down for ninety minutes and argued about what they should do. Dellinger finally convinced them that civil disobedience was necessary, and more than 350 were arrested, not altogether gently, after they ignored repeated police commands to leave the area.

On August 6, the day President Johnson signed the new voting rights bill during a White House ceremony, the protest had attracted little attention. The arrests of 350 people on Monday brought it far greater publicity, as did Dellinger's decision to serve a thirty-day jail sentence rather than pay his $300 fine. Both were classic examples of civil disobedience forcing a fundamentally indifferent public to recognize serious differences of opinion outside an official consensus. On the same day, President Johnson held a prolonged briefing on the war for members of the Senate. Between two sessions of the briefing he told reporters, "There is no substantial division in this country, in my judgment, and no substantial division in the Congress."[12] The President was whistling in the dark.

The Assembly of Unrepresented People was essentially a civil rights demonstration which happened to focus on the issue of the war. Those who took part were largely confirmed activists in the civil rights and peace movements. Their willingness to commit civil disobedience distinguished them from the large numbers who had attended the April march, since the majority of those concerned about and opposed to the war were not yet convinced that the issue was moral in nature, or that more moderate forms of protest would not eventually prevail.

Similar demonstrations were held on the West Coast that summer, where the Vietnam Day Committee and the Oakland SDS sponsored a series of attempts to block troop trains on August 5 and 6 and then again the following week on August 12. The Oakland Army Terminal was only seven and a half miles from the Berkeley campus of the University of California; the fact that it served as an embarkation point for troops being shipped to Vietnam made it an inevitable target for antiwar demonstrations. When the VDC learned that troop trains would be passing through Berkeley on the way to Oakland, the group sent several members up the tracks to call when the trains were spotted. When the trains reached Berkeley, passing at one point within a few blocks of VDC headquarters, an attempt was made to block the tracks. On the first day the engineer ignored them, plowing slowly but steadily ahead through the demonstrators, who jumped out of the way at the last moment. On the final two attempts, local sheriff's deputies cleared the tracks. Ranging between two and three hundred in number, the demonstrators passed out leaflets to the troops hanging from train windows, and carried signs reading, "Peace Corps—not Marine Corps," "Why are they sending you there?" and "You haven't killed yet—don't."[13]

The demonstrations, like those held in Washington by the Assembly of Unrepresented People, were dictated more by a desire for militant action than by a reasoned sense that the public, or even an appreciable segment of it, could best be turned against the war by militance. In fact, the majority of the public found such actions simply incomprehensible. Nevertheless, the Assembly in Washington and the troop train demonstrations in Berkeley established important precedents. The bombing campaign proposed by Rostow in 1961 was not actually adopted until 1965, after all. In much the same way, the early militance of the peace movement was only premature.

The first actions called by the National Coordinating Committee had been set for the weekend of October 15–16, 1965. At Berkeley, planning for the demonstrations led to a split between soft-liners, who wanted to march down Telegraph Avenue to the Oakland Army Terminal and then hold a rally in a vacant lot across the street, and hard-liners, who wanted to block access to the base and perhaps even invade it. A meeting on the night of September 21, organized by the FSM leaders Jack Weinberg and Steve Weissman and the VDC's Jerry Rubin, finally decided on a peaceful march.

The weekend began with a teach-in on Friday evening, October 15. Organizers had hoped for perhaps five thousand people. Their hearts sank as they looked out over the small initial crowd, but then, as dusk fell, it began to grow. When the final speakers took the stand about 8 P.M., more than fifteen thousand people were listening to them. The novelist Ken Kesey, famous for his novel *One Flew Over the Cuckoo's*

Nest but for the previous eighteen months involved almost exclusively in a prolonged experiment with drugs, threw march leaders into a nervous fit with a long, rambling speech. Stopping from time to time to play passages from "Home on the Range" on his harmonica, Kesey urged people to turn their backs on the war and the antiwar movement alike. "There's only one thing to do," said Kesey finally, speaking slowly and deliberately. "There's only one thing's gonna do any good at all. . . . And that's everybody just look at it, look at the war, and turn your backs and say . . . fuck it. . . ."

"Who the hell invited this bastard?"[14] one of the VDC leaders on the stand demanded of the others. Nobody owned up. Kesey was followed by a final speaker, and then the crowd suddenly spilled down Telegraph Avenue, forcing the ad hoc committee nominally in charge of the march to hurry around through side streets in order to recapture their assigned place at the head of the people.

When the fifteen-thousand-man river of marchers reached the Oakland-Berkeley town line, it was met by a solid line of helmeted Oakland police. The crowd hesitated but then turned right down a side street and finally, at the next corner, halted altogether. The nine-man ad hoc committee at the head of the column argued heatedly whether to turn left, toward Oakland and an inevitable collision with the police, or right, back toward Berkeley. Jack Weinberg argued that a battle with the police in the dark might turn into a massacre. The result could be the death of the movement. Jerry Rubin and mathematics Professor Stephen Smale insisted the mood of the crowd was overwhelmingly in favor of forcing the issue. As if backing them up, dozens of marchers just behind the leaders were shouting, "Left! Left!" Others were shouting "Martin Luther King!" referring to King's decision to turn back a crowd facing state police at the Edmund Pettus Bridge in Selma the previous March. Weinberg argued that people in the rear of the crowd had no idea what was happening and would be plunged into a street battle without having anything to say about it.

During those few passionate minutes, ad hoc committee members became enduring enemies. They sensed that the future of the student movement might be decided by what they did in the next moment or two. Weinberg finally prevailed: the committee voted five to four to turn right and head back to Berkeley.

The following afternoon, Saturday, October 16, another march was held which again ran up against a wall of Oakland police, as well as a group of Hell's Angels who crashed into the protestors' ranks, tore down banners, and began beating up demonstrators before police managed to separate the two groups. A Berkeley policeman's leg was broken and one of the Angels, 6-foot, 7-inch, 270-pound Michael ("Tiny") Walker, was clubbed unconscious and then dragged away, bleeding. This time the crowd sat down in the middle of the street and held an hour-long spontaneous teach-in which centered on the refusal of the police to let them proceed to the Oakland Army Terminal.

On the East Coast, the International Days of Protest were organized almost entirely by traditional pacifist and civil rights groups, coordinated by the Fifth Avenue Peace Parade Committee. On Saturday about twenty thousand people marched a little over a mile down Fifth Avenue from Ninety-fourth to Sixty-ninth streets. Along the way more than a thousand hecklers shouted insults and threw eggs, tomatoes, and a can of red paint at the marchers. One World War II veteran carried a sign reading, "Support our men in Vietnam—Don't stab them in the back."[15] At the end of the march a rally was held on Sixty-ninth Street between Lexington and Park avenues, a site settled on after the committee was denied permission to use Central Park by Parks Commissioner Newbold Morris. (Although he did not know it, Morris had been stricken from the list of guests to the White House Festival of the Arts after the FBI decided he was a dangerous leftist.) The march itself captured little attention.

On Friday, however, the antiwar movement had entered a new stage when David J. Miller, a twenty-two-year-old pacifist and member of the Catholic Worker Movement, burned his draft card outside the Whitehall Street Army Induction Center in lower Manhattan. His simple act, which was to cost him more than two years in jail, began a movement of personal, almost existential protest against the war which was to spread quickly and evoke an agonized response from students facing the draft across the country.

Miller was by no means the first American to burn his draft card as a protest against the American military. A small group including Dwight MacDonald had burned theirs in the 1940s as a protest against the Cold War. In July, 1965, the Committee for Non-Violent Action and the Workshop in Non-Violence (WIN), both long-established organizations with offices at 5 Beekman Street in New York, held an anti-draft demonstration outside the Whitehall Street Induction Center. One of the demonstrators, Christopher Kearns, wanted to burn a draft card as a symbolic protest but had forgotten to bring his own. He borrowed one from one of the WIN people. A *Life* photographer took a picture of the burning card which appeared in the August 16 issue of the magazine next to a picture of the paint-bespattered Dellinger and Lynd at the head of the Washington protest march held on August 9. On August 10 the House of Representatives had passed, 392 to 1,[16] a harsh bill providing for a five-year jail sentence and a $10,000 fine for burning a draft card. Publication of the picture of Kearns burning his card helped a similar bill through the Senate in record time, and President Johnson signed the measure into law on August 30. Representative L. Mendel Rivers, the white-haired Democratic congressman from South Carolina who was chairman of the House Armed Services Committee, made it clear that the law was intended to halt even purely symbolic attacks on the Selective Service System:

> It is a straightforward clear answer to those who would make a mockery of our efforts in South Vietnam by engaging in the mass destruction of draft cards. . . . If it can be proved that a person knowingly destroyed or mutilated his draft card, then . . . he can be sent to prison, where he belongs. This is the least we can do for our men in South Vietnam fighting to preserve freedom, while a vocal minority in this country thumb their noses at their own government.[17]

Angered by quick passage of the law, and anxious that it not be allowed to cow opponents of the war, Tom Cornell, an editor of the *Catholic Worker,* proposed that he, Miller, and several others publicly burn their cards outside the White House on the day President Johnson signed the anti-draft-card-burning bill into law. The plan was abandoned when they were unable to find out when the bill would be signed, but they continued to talk about the possibility of a group card burning. Miller, meanwhile, was invited to speak at the Whitehall Street demonstration being planned for October 15. After thinking about it awhile he decided to burn his draft card instead, partly because he was not much of a speaker, and partly because the action, carrying with it the possibility of five years in jail, would express his opposition with a force far beyond the power of any words he might say.

On the day of the demonstration he climbed to the top of a sound truck, tried to light his card with a match, then hunched over to shield the card with his body and managed to light it with a cigarette lighter which someone handed up to him from the crowd. After a moment he held the burning card up over his head in the dusk. The tiny light, Miller watching it, the silent crowd around him were all picked up by television cameramen and broadcast across the country, a gesture of personal and total opposition. Miller was not simply refusing to fight, as other pacifists did. He was defying the government's very authority to judge his pacifism, refusing to apply for or carry the slip of paper that would exempt him from war. By his action he was insisting that the war end, or consume him, too, thus setting a hard example not only for young men facing the draft, but for conscientious objectors who would now know there was still one more step they could take.[18]

Cornell and four other pacifists, including David McReynolds, planned to demonstrate their support for Miller's action at his arraignment on October 28, but a dense crowd of reporters and hecklers blocked their action. A. J. Muste ("Who's that old man?"[19] shouted a heckler wearing a black and orange button backing William F. Buckley for mayor) had to be removed from the scene in a police car because of the dense, threatening crowd. On November 6 the five succeeded in burning their cards at another demonstration, held in Union Square, despite the fact a heckler managed to douse them with a bucket of water. During the demonstration other hostile spectators shouted, "Burn yourselves, not your cards!"[20] They were referring to a thirty-two-year-old Baltimore Quaker, Norman Morrison, who had emptied a gallon jug of gasoline over himself on the steps of the Pentagon on November 2, struck a match, and was burned alive. Three days after the Union Square demonstration, on November 9, another pacifist, Roger La Porte, burned himself to death at the United Nations. The two immolations and the two draft card burnings, like the militant troop train protests of the VDC in August, demonstrated the passion of those opposed to the war. It was no longer a question of signing petitions or not signing them, marching or not marching, writing letters or not writing: the war had become, potentially, an issue of life and death. Very few, obviously, were ready for immolation or even jail, but the example of those who were made complacency difficult for the rest. To oppose the war without sacrifice or danger or inconvenience was to be a kind of accomplice. For thousands of Americans, and especially for students at a stage in their lives when moral passion seems to come naturally, the choice of what to do was an agonizing one. Those who risked or even destroyed themselves inevitably made it harder for others to do nothing.

The demonstrations on the weekend of October 15–16, by far the largest until that time, were nevertheless dismissed by official Washington, where the State Department spokesman, Robert McCloskey, told reporters on Friday:

> We are naturally aware of various noisy demonstrations that have taken place and are scheduled to take place but I would like to point out that these groups constitute an infinitesimal fraction of the American people, the vast majority of whom have indicated their strong support of President Johnson's policies in Vietnam.[21]

In Chicago on the same day, General Taylor, who had been replaced as ambassador to South Vietnam by Henry Cabot Lodge in July, told reporters that the demonstrators were only making things worse. He said the leaders in Hanoi might conclude "there is a real division of strength in this country and that may tempt them to prolong the war." The North Vietnamese, Taylor said, "are on a sharp hook. They're looking for something to get them off and they may think this is it."[22] This attitude, the closest thing to an official position on the demonstrations, was echoed in the *New York Times* of Sunday, October 17, by James Reston, who wrote that "lawless" demonstrations would only spark political repression in the United States:

> They are not promoting peace but postponing it. They are not persuading the President or the Congress to end the war but deceiving Ho Chi Minh and General [Vo Nguyen] Giap into prolonging [it]. . . . The problem of peace now lies not in Washington but in Hanoi. . . .

Reston's position was characteristic of those who had not faced up to the hard political problems involved in a serious attempt to stop the war. Before a major decision has been made, a columnist's word of advice might have some effect, but once the presidential mind is made up, no columnist can talk him out of it. The movement already understood that the question was ultimately one of power. If the opposition were ever to prevail, a moment would have to arrive when it was politically stronger than the President. Reston's position was a good deal like that of the twenty-six Berkeley professors who attacked the Vietnam Day Committee. The war worried them, but not as much as the social costs of any serious attempt to stop it. The movement seemed weak in the fall of 1965, but its leaders understood better than the rest of the country that this would be a long war, that the United States could not win it in any traditional sense, and that the opposition had to pursue a strategy that might take years to work.

It was not yet clear how hopeless the war truly was, however, and the demonstrations sparked a general outrage among state and local politicians around the country. In New York on October 28 the City Council voted twenty-eight to two to make Veterans Day (November 11) an official Support American Vietnam Effort Day. The two councilmen who opposed the resolution were thought to have destroyed their political careers. On November 1 in Washington, the director of the FBI, J. Edgar Hoover, attacked the sincerity, the loyalty, and the competence of those opposed to the war:

> Anti-Vietnam demonstrators in the U.S. represent a minority for the most part composed of halfway citizens who are neither morally, mentally nor emotionally mature. This is true whether the demonstrator be the college professor or the beatnik.[23]

This sort of name-calling had an initial shock effect but was to wear off quickly. In a curious, negative way, it even helped the movement to identify itself.

Even before the International Days of Protest, a third major demonstration had been announced by the Committee for a Sane Nuclear Policy for Saturday, November 27. Convinced that the antiwar movement was antagonizing much of its potential support by its strong language and occasionally belligerent tone, SANE was planning a thoroughly moderate demonstration of concern about, rather than unalterable opposition to, the war. Like the SDS in April, SANE kept tight control over the organization of the march, the list of speakers, and the seventeen approved slogans professionally printed on placards to be carried during the march. Among the slogans: "Stop the bombings," "Respect 1954 Geneva Accords," "War erodes the Great Society" and "Self-determination—Vietnam for the Vietnamese."[24] To avoid criticism that they were being one-sided in their protest, SANE's cochairman, Dr. Benjamin Spock, and Harvard Professor H. Stuart Hughes cabled Ho Chi Minh from Washington on October 28:

> Our organization helping provide leadership for Nov 27 demonstration in support of ceasefire and negotiated settlement based on 1954 Geneva Accords. Again urge you respond favorably to immediate peace talks. Demonstrations will continue but will not lead to a U.S. pullout.[25]

In Madison, Wisconsin, the National Coordinating Committee to End the War in Vietnam decided to hold its national convention in Washington so the 1,500 delegates and alternates expected to attend could take part in the protest march on Saturday, November 27.

In the aftermath of the International Days of Protest, it first appeared that the energies of the antiwar movement had been temporarily sapped. President Johnson and his administration appeared to be unreachable by those opposed to the war. At best, the President seemed blandly indifferent to the opposition, and at the worst, fully capable of escalating the war to prove his resolve, both to the American people and to the leaders of North Vietnam. In the middle of November, however, the nature of the war was suddenly forced into bold relief by a prolonged battle between American and North Vietnamese troops in the heavily forested Ia Drang Valley. The battle, bloody and inconclusive, brought an end to administration hopes for a quick turn in the tide of the war. American casualties, which had been slowly increasing during the summer as more American troops arrived, suddenly soared. During the week that ended on Monday, November 22, 240 U.S. soldiers were killed in Vietnam, more than three times the highest previous weekly total. The effect on the antiwar movement was electric. When delegates to the NCC convention met in Washington on Wednesday, November 24, they were in an angry, determined mood.

Despite SANE's care to avoid anything that looked like extremism, the divisions in the antiwar movement were immediately apparent. The U.S. Committee to Aid the National Liberation Front of South Vietnam, a tiny group headed by a young man named Walter Teague, began selling NLF flags and buttons and announced it would carry the flags in the march on Saturday. SANE's Sanford Gottlieb, who had gone to great lengths to avoid just such provocations, said the three-hundred monitors of the march would try to discourage the NLF flag carriers, but would not use force. A far deeper source of division was the sharpening, but until then little noticed, contest between the New Left and the old left for control of the NCC and the antiwar movement. During the first week in November the New York Committee to End the War in Vietnam, one of the original groups which joined to create the National Coordinating Committee, disbanded as the result of conflict between the Socialist Workers Party, an old-line Trotskyist group, and the SDS over what was called the "single issue" question. The Trotskyists wanted to build a mass movement around the single issue of the war, while the SDS, and the New Left in general, favored an attempt to create a broad radical movement which would emphasize other issues along with the war.

When the NCC held its first plenary session shortly after noon on Thursday, November 25, in Washington's Lincoln Memorial Congregational Temple, it was quickly apparent to those familiar with the techniques of parliamentary maneuver that the Young Socialist Alliance (Trotskyist) was attempting to take over the NCC, initially with the unwitting aid of the Berkeley Vietnam Day Committee. On Friday the YSA tried again with a complicated proposal on credentials intended to leave them with a majority of accredited delegates. When that was voted down they proposed that the NCC adopt three "official" antiwar slogans: "Let's Bring the Troops Home Now," "Self-Determination in Mississippi and Vietnam," and "Freedom Now, Withdrawal Now."[26] A call for immediate withdrawal, the YSA knew, would split the antiwar movement between moderates and radicals; the YSA hoped to dominate the second group, and through them the antiwar movement itself.

The majority of delegates at the convention, young idealists who had little experience with radical politics, which were generally as self-serving as any other kind of politics, were largely bewildered by the YSA's maneuvering. When they finally understood what was going on, they were less angry than disillusioned. They had believed that people in favor of "peace" and "justice" and "civil rights" were afflicted by none of the secrecy and power-hunger of conventional politicians. During the summer the SDS's vice president, a University of Texas dropout named Jeff Shero, had told a magazine writer, "There's practically nobody in the movement that I don't have a great deal of trust in."[27] At the NCC, the YSA proved there were in fact a great many people in the movement who could not be trusted.

On Saturday, while the majority of the NCC delegates joined SANE's march and rally, the YSA continued to caucus secretly in the basement of the Harrington Hotel in a last-minute attempt to come up with a strategy for capturing the NCC. When one delegate tried to enter, three YSA members guarding the door grabbed him and dragged him away. At the final plenary session held on Sunday, however, the YSA was defeated on the question of how to organize the national committee. The weekend proved a bitter foretaste of the factional fighting that was to plague, and finally cripple, the radical movement in the following years. It is worth emphasizing that there were no villains in this struggle. The Trotskyists were among the most tireless opponents of the war, and groups in the New Left, disillusioned with this or that tactic, would often simply retire from the field. Nevertheless, the Trotskyists were rigid in their politics and were thoroughly out of sympathy with the broader discontent of the student and civil rights movements which, in the beginning, were reluctant to accept socialism as the answer to all problems. The Trotskyists were certain they knew how to organize an end to the war and drove many of their allies half-crazy with takeover attempts. They rarely succeeded but even their failures enjoyed a kind of success. Their ideological rigor set the terms of debate within the movement, and one reason the SDS, for example, eventually declared itself Marxist-Leninist was that old left groups like the Trotskyists and the Progressive Labor Party took a hard revolutionary position. To prove its commitment, the New Left felt itself forced to do the same.

At the demonstration on Saturday, November 27, a cold and windy day, nearly 25,000 people marched around the White House and then gathered at the Washington Monument, as they had in April and August, and would many times again, to listen to speeches on the war. Dr. Spock sternly deplored "the virtual absence of debate in Congress" and proposed that the peace movement support candidates in the 1966 elections "who will refuse to be silenced."[28] Norman Thomas, nearly blind but still a powerful speaker, told the crowd, "I'd rather see America save her soul than her face."[29]

The crowd's strongest response, however, was won by Carl Oglesby, a thirty-year-old former technical writer for a defense contractor in Ann Arbor, Michigan, who had been elected president of SDS in June. Oglesby had once planned to be a novelist but politics had interrupted his life, as it had the life of his generation. In his speech he expressed the sense of spreading disenchantment that had accompanied each escalation of the war by Johnson. The crowd in Washington had long favored the sort of social measures that Johnson made law in 1965, the year of his legislative triumphs, but the war had canceled out each domestic victory. Vietnam not only absorbed the energies of the administration, but cast doubt on everything else it did. Oglesby focused the confused ambivalence of people who favored Johnson's domestic program and hated his war:

> The original commitment in Vietnam was made by President Truman, a mainstream liberal. It was seconded by President Eisenhower, a moderate liberal. It was intensified by the late President Kennedy, a flaming liberal. Think of the men who now engineer that war—those who study the maps, give the commands, push the buttons and tally the dead: Bundy, McNamara, Lodge, Goldberg, the President himself.
> They are not moral monsters.
> They are all honorable men.
> They are all liberals.
> We . . . are convinced by a few pretty photos in the Sunday supplement that things are getting better, that the world is coming our way, that change from disorder can be orderly, that our benevolence will pacify the distressed, that our might will intimidate the angry. . . .
> We have become a nation of young, bright-eyed, hard-hearted, slim-waisted, bullet-headed make-out artists. A nation—may I say it?—of beardless liberals.[30]

When Oglesby finished the crowd broke into strong and sustained applause while Oglesby, in confusion, turned and started to walk off the stage. Dr. Spock and Sanford Gottlieb both retrieved him and brought him back to the lectern, where Gottlieb raised Oglesby's right arm in a kind of proxy gesture of triumph. Despite the cold and the snapping wind, which had kept those in the back of the crowd from hearing long sections of the speech, the 25,000 people at the Washington Monument reacted as if their deepest doubts about America had finally been put into words. There was a dimension of moral horror to a war conducted with such cold impunity by a handful of men in Washington. It was impossible not to feel that what those men did in Vietnam discredited them everywhere.

Oglesby's speech was widely reprinted and debated, constituting, as it did, a sharp departure from the traditional liberal belief that if only the right men were elected to public office everything would be well with the Republic. The crowd did not immediately apprehend the sharpness of the break that Oglesby's speech implied and portended; they did not see that it would mean an end to the identification of idealism and liberalism in American politics, at least for a time. They did not realize the despair which would inevitably follow such a break, since only the Democratic-liberals and the Republican-conservatives had a real chance to achieve power in the United States. To reject the major parties was, in some sense, to embrace impotence. The crowd in Washington was not thinking of these things; it only felt that what Oglesby said was true.

SIX

Deadlock

When President Johnson began to escalate the war early in 1965 he cautiously avoided predictions of when to expect success, but he, his staff, and his principal advisers apparently felt it would not be long in coming. One official was quoted as saying, "We'll be at the conference table by September."[1] The source of official confidence was the belief that no nation, and especially not one as small as North Vietnam, would deliberately accept the punishment that the U.S. Air Force could deliver. The Cuban missile crisis in October, 1962, had convinced American officials that power should be used gradually, in slowly mounting steps, rather than all at once. When the United States began to bomb North Vietnam, that lesson was put into effect: raids began with military targets just north of the DMZ at the seventeenth parallel and were gradually extended throughout the country. What began as a limited action eventually became the most sustained bombing campaign in history. The idea was that North Vietnam would see what was coming, weigh its chances, and back down.

In June the air force began dispatching B-52 bombers from the island of Guam to raid Vietcong-controlled areas of South Vietnam. The planes flew so high they could not be heard from the ground. Each 30-ton bomb load, consisting of 500- and 750-pound bombs, hit the ground totally without warning. Between February and the end of the year the air force conducted 117,000 sorties (one raid by one plane) over Vietnam, 18,000 of them over the North. More than 250,000 tons of bombs were dropped. The air force claimed it had destroyed 315 North Vietnamese bridges and cut roads in 2,050 different places. The bombing was unrelenting; its effect was negligible. During the summer of 1965, when the United States began its rapid buildup of ground troops, the infiltration rate from the North was estimated by U.S. intelligence officials at 800 per month; by late fall the figure was up to 1,500; in early 1966 it reached 4,500.

In October, 1965, a U.S. Special Forces camp near Pleime in the Central Highlands of South Vietnam came under siege and additional U.S. combat units were sent into the area. On Sunday, November 14, in the narrow valley of the Ia Drang River only seven miles from the Cambodian border, U.S. forces were attacked by regular units of the North Vietnamese army. Bitter fighting, the bloodiest of the war, continued through the middle of the next week. One 29-man platoon from the Second Battalion of the 7th Cavalry, cut off on Sunday and rescued the following day, suffered 23 casualties, 8 of them killed. During the week that ended on Saturday, November 13, U.S. forces in South Vietnam lost 86 men killed, the heaviest one-week toll of the war. During the following week the number of dead jumped to 240. U.S. officials claimed that more than 1,100 North Vietnamese also died during the battle of Ia Drang Valley, and General William Westmoreland told reporters, "I consider this an unprecedented victory."[2]

Looked at from one point of view, it was, but it was also a sign of hard fighting to come. McNamara drew the inescapable conclusion during his seventh trip to Vietnam at the end of November. Following his thirty-hour visit he stated, "We have stopped losing the war," but admitted the North Vietnamese and Vietcong were far from being defeated in the field. The enemy, he said, had "expressed a determination to carry on the conflict which can lead to only one conclusion—that it will be a long war."[3]

The bombing campaign directed against North Vietnam and the search-and-destroy strategy being developed by Westmoreland in the South were both designed to force the enemy to change its mind. This may sound obvious, but it is not the usual goal of military operations, which classically are aimed at destroying the enemy's ability to wage war. For political reasons an invasion of North Vietnam was ruled out, which meant the United States could hope only to make the war so painful and expensive that Hanoi would, in effect, choose to give up.

From its beginning critics of the bombing campaign had cited the Strategic Bombing Survey conducted after World War II, which indicated that bombing alone could not halt industrial production, stop the flow of goods, or destroy the will of a people to fight. These lessons had been confirmed in Korea, where a heavy American bombing campaign destroyed every fixed enemy target in a matter of weeks without halting the flow of supplies to North Korean and Chinese troops, or shortening the war by a day. By the end of his trip to Vietnam on November 28 and 29, McNamara apparently realized that Hanoi was not going to be scared out of the war easily. The inevitable result would be a war of attrition, with patience and determination the deciding factors.

By November, then, it was clear the war was not going well, if by going well one meant, as the public did, soon to be over. President Johnson had always refused to say when the struggle would end. It was up to Hanoi; the fighting would go on until Hanoi decided to negotiate. When Johnson or Rusk said the other side was not "serious" about negotiation they meant it wasn't ready to give up the war, which was correct but hardly encouraging to those who sought an early end to the fighting. Confusion about American war aims and how the conflict might end was never dispelled by the administration. If the war would end only when one side got tired, and both sides insisted they would *never* get tired, then the war would just go on and on. An early end to the war therefore meant compromise. But the minimum American goal was a categorical end to North Vietnamese–Vietcong attempts to overthrow the government in Saigon by military force; in short, surrender. Johnson insisted the United States was ready to be reasonable; the only problem was intransigence in Hanoi. On July 13 the President told a press conference:

> I must say that candor compels me to tell you that there has not been the slightest indication that the other side is interested in negotiation or in unconditional discussions, although the United States has made some dozen separate attempts to bring that about.[4]

On November 15, 1965, the President's claim was flatly contradicted in an article published by Eric Sevareid in *Look* magazine. Sevareid's article described a long conversation with Adlai Stevenson in London the previous July 13, two days before Stevenson died. Sevareid said Stevenson told him he was deeply upset by his role in the Johnson administration, that he was thinking of resigning as ambassador to the

United Nations, and that the Johnson administration had turned down a proposal for talks with North Vietnam which had been arranged by U Thant in late 1964.[5] Adding weight to Sevareid's charge was the fact that news of the proposal for talks in Rangoon, Burma, had leaked out during early 1965 but had been categorically denied by George Reedy, Johnson's press secretary, in a statement on February 24:

> There are no authorized negotiations underway with Mr. Thant or any other government. I am not going into any diplomatic chitchat that may be going forth, or way-out feelers. But authorized or meaningful negotiations—no.[6]

The immediate result of Sevareid's article was embarrassment and confusion on the part of officials. Bill Moyers, the new press secretary, testily dismissed the importance of the article: "I follow the President's advice a long time ago on not commenting on what dead men might have said or might not have said."[7] At the State Department, however, Robert McCloskey, the official spokesman, admitted there had been a North Vietnamese offer in late 1964 to meet with U.S. representatives in Rangoon, but he denied it had really amounted to anything.

> On the basis of the total evidence available to us, we did not believe at any time that North Vietnam was prepared for serious peace talks. . . . We saw nothing to indicate that Hanoi was prepared for peace talks and the Secretary of State said he would recognize it when it came. His antenna is sensitive.[8]

Not everyone was so confident of the sensitivity of Rusk's antenna, however. All the talk about the other side's lack of "seriousness" could not disguise the fact that Johnson had been caught in what amounted to a bald lie, one made worse by the fact that he had repeatedly justified American military action by Hanoi's alleged refusal to negotiate. Sevareid's article was followed by the usual flood of backgrounders and official leaks in an attempt to explain away the inexplicable. One unidentified official said the President had not been lying because he had, in fact, never known of the proposal: Dean Rusk, who learned of it from Stevenson, had considered and rejected it on his own. Arthur Krock of the *New York Times* reported this explanation in tones of shocked disbelief on November 18, assuming the "explanation" was an even more audacious lie than Johnson's earlier denials, and more alarming than the lie if true. The administration quickly dropped that line of argument, but it was apparently true.[9]

The inescapable implication of the Sevareid story was that the war was quite possibly unnecessary. By a kind of unspoken agreement, however, established columnists and editorial writers dismissed that possibility, instead concentrating their "worry" and "concern" on the President's mendacity. They were witty at the expense of Rusk's antenna, but did not publicly doubt he had been right about Hanoi's "seriousness." The alternative was simply too disturbing. In Washington it was generally assumed Johnson's error had been technical in nature; he really *ought* to have checked out the Rangoon proposal, if only for the record. In circles farther from the center of power, however, there were many who felt Hanoi's interest may well have been serious, that a chance for compromise had been lost irretrievably, and that President Johnson could not be trusted to tell the truth. Already doubtful of America's good intentions, opponents of the war began to see America as a country that *preferred* military force to negotiation. Their vision of America was darkening.

As Christmas approached in 1965, argument over the war began to focus on the bombing of North Vietnam, which did not seem to be winning the war and which Hanoi insisted was an obstacle to negotiations. The five-day halt in the bombing the previous May had been criticized as too short, and Johnson was urged by a wide range of people, publicly and privately, to test Hanoi's interest in peace with a longer halt. On Tuesday, December 21, the State Department said the United States was considering a proposal for a twelve-hour Christmas truce made by the Vietcong two weeks earlier. On the following day it was announced the United States would observe a thirty-hour truce extending from 6 P.M. Friday, Christmas Eve, through Christmas Day.

The result of the announcement was a surge of activity by opponents of the war. On Thursday, December 23, Senator Mansfield proposed that the truce be extended through January 21, the Vietnamese New Year. On Friday, Senator Robert F. Kennedy's Washington office released a statement suggesting an open-ended extension of the truce so long as it was observed by the Vietcong. A group of 286 clergymen supported the idea of a truce extension, and other organizations began to add their voices.

The day after Christmas, however, the fighting in South Vietnam was resumed, although reporters noted that bombing raids against the North were not. Officials in Washington and in Texas, where President Johnson was spending the weekend, were vague about the reason why. As the bombing suspension continued during the following days, speculation about its intent rapidly mounted. Finally, on December 30, Bill Moyers admitted that a major peace probe was under way. To dramatize the fact that he was leaving no stone unturned, Johnson sent personal emissaries around the world to discuss peace. Averell Harriman went to Warsaw and points east; Arthur Goldberg to France, England, and the Vatican; McGeorge Bundy to Canada; Thomas Mann to Mexico; G. Mennen Williams to fourteen countries in Africa; and Hubert Humphrey to the Far East. The response was disappointing; Hanoi made no move to initiate peace talks.

As the "peace offensive" continued through January, criticism began to mount from those who had long sought a more vigorous prosecution of the war, by which they meant heavier bombing. They argued that Hanoi was not interested in peace and was only taking advantage of the halt to repair damage and increase the flow of supplies to the South. If the United States were to resume the bombing and extend it to both Hanoi and the port city of Haiphong, the North would be forced to back out of the war.

At the same time, those who favored a negotiated solution to the war urged the President to continue the bombing halt indefinitely. On January 21, seventy-seven members of the House of Representatives sent President Johnson a letter urging extension of the halt. On January 24, Senator Fulbright suggested that the President should consult the Senate Foreign Relations Committee before deciding whether or not to resume the bombing. "I have never seen any issue of significance which caused such uncertainty and questioning of policy,"[10] he said during a long news conference following a three-hour, closed meeting of the Committee with Secretaries Rusk and McNamara.

On Tuesday afternoon, January 25, four senators opposed to a resumption of the bombing visited Senator Fulbright in his office to discuss ways of strengthening their position.[11] At 5:30 that evening Fulbright and nineteen other congressional leaders were invited to the White House for a two-and-a-half-hour briefing on the situation in Vietnam. Besides the President, those meeting with the congressional leaders were Rusk, McNamara, McGeorge Bundy, Averell Harriman,

George Ball, Generals Earle Wheeler and Maxwell Taylor, and CIA chief Admiral William F. Raborn. The congressional leaders were briefed on the lack of response to the peace offensive and on the heightened supply activity along the Ho Chi Minh trail. Captured Vietcong documents and a telegram from Ambassador Lodge were read to the group. Enlarged photos of North Vietnamese supply routes were shown.

After the briefing President Johnson asked for comments, calling on Speaker of the House John McCormack, House minority leader Gerald Ford, Senate majority leader Mansfield, and Senate minority leader Everett Dirksen, in that order. Mansfield read a four-page statement repeating his old concerns about the direction of the war. When Fulbright began to speak at one point, Johnson ostentatiously turned to Secretary Rusk and began an earnest conversation. At the end of the meeting the President told the congressional leaders he had been reading Bruce Catton's book about the Civil War, *Never Call Retreat.*[12] He then read a long passage about President Lincoln's lonely agonies of decision during the Civil War, which was, his listeners were reminded, an extremely unpopular war.

The drift of the meeting was perfectly clear: the bombing of North Vietnam was about to be resumed. In an appearance before the House Foreign Affairs Committee on Wednesday, January 26, Rusk expressed puzzlement at "this curious double standard" on the part of those opposed to the bombing: "A bomb carried by a boy on a bicycle or mortar shells fired at the Danang base just three days ago are just as much bombs as those carried by planes to the North."[13] A number of senators found Rusk's equation of "a boy on a bicycle" with American Phantom jets carrying six-ton bomb loads to North Vietnam evidence of a chilling human insensitivity. On Thursday afternoon, January 27, fifteen senators signed a letter expressing their general agreement with objections to the bombing already expressed by Senators Mansfield, Fulbright, and George Aiken, but also acknowledging the difficulty of the President's position as the man burdened with the final decision. The letter was critical without being hostile, an expression of concern rather than outrage. The following day the President responded in a note, stinging in its cold brevity, which referred the senators to his earlier reply to a similar letter by seventy-seven members of the House. He also cited the Tonkin Gulf resolution, which had so clearly granted him the right to do everything that the senators now viewed with such alarm. Angry at their curt dismissal, the senators met in the office of Vance Hartke Friday afternoon, January 28, to decide what to do next.

On the same day Rusk testified at a public hearing of the Senate Foreign Relations Committee, where he was met by open hostility from a number of senators who knew the bombing would shortly resume, bringing with it the certainty of indefinite war. The core of their disagreement with Rusk was the question whether South Vietnam really mattered. Rusk insisted that Vietnam was two distinct countries, that North Vietnam was trying to conquer the South, that Peking's theory of world revolution by wars of "national liberation" constituted a threat to the international peace as great as that of Hitler between the wars, that the United States was firmly committed to the successful defense of South Vietnam and could not abandon that commitment without disastrous consequences for world peace.

Rusk repeatedly insisted that North Vietnam was literally invading the South, that the war was completely under the direction of Hanoi. He insisted that every American step deeper into the war had been a response to escalation by Hanoi. He ignored American violations of the 1954 Geneva Agreement while citing those of North Vietnam, ignored the South Vietnamese character of the NLF, and ignored the fact that American allies under SEATO (the Southeast Asia Treaty Organization) largely refused to join in the defense of South Vietnam. It was a frustrating confrontation on both sides, centering less on matters of fact than of judgment. Rusk would cite SEATO, approved by the very senators questioning him now. Didn't SEATO commit the United States to resist aggression? Wasn't South Vietnam a protocol state included within the terms of the treaty? Were the senators now proposing the treaty be scrapped? The answer was well, not exactly. Of course they were opposed to the spread of Communism, but the administration, they felt, had blown the situation entirely out of proportion; it really did not much matter who controlled South Vietnam. The senators were equally aware, however, that 200,000 American troops had already been committed to the war and could not simply be shipped home again without some painful explanations.

There was a frightening single-mindedness to Secretary Rusk's insistence that all the trouble was being caused by Hanoi, and that the United States, 200 million strong, simply had to force its will upon

North Vietnam or face disaster. At one point he told a senator on the committee:

> It is tragic that this problem could arise. It could end literally in twenty-four hours, Senator, if these people in Hanoi should come to the conclusion that they are not going to try to seize Vietnam and Laos by force. If they are determined to try to do so, then we and others have some very fundamental decisions to make, and in making them, it seems to me, sir, that we have to reflect upon how one builds peace. Do we build it by standing aside when aggression occurs or do we build it by meeting our commitments.[14]

There was a vagueness to Rusk's position which made it frustratingly difficult to counter. Did he mean that North Vietnam would sweep on to conquer the world? No, the secretary would answer, the real danger is China. "Senator, let me say that the doctrines and policies espoused by Peking today constitute perhaps the most important single problem of peace."[15] Doctrines and policies were only words; what was Peking actually doing that constituted a danger to the peace? Rusk would point firmly to Vietnam.

The insoluble core of this dilemma was the fact of American commitment: if the other side did not give up, how was the United States going to bring home those 200,000 men? Bringing them home without at least some sort of formal agreement would constitute an unthinkable humiliation. No one can get to be a senator without enough political realism to know that the President of the United States would never just turn around and say he was wrong and let it go at that. Circumstances might force him to turn around, but he would never freely embrace such a failure. The senators on the Foreign Relations Committee did not know how to get around this hard reality, and yet were increasingly desperate that some way be found to do so. They feared that each step of escalation would inevitably lead to another, that China would eventually enter the war, that the United States would consider itself forced to use nuclear weapons, and that the world would be engulfed in a third, and final, global war. At one point Senator Joseph Clark of Pennsylvania broke off a line of questioning which seemed to be leading nowhere and told Rusk:

> Well, I am prepared to leave the whole subject with the observation that I would hope very much that we are going to stop escalating this war

any further. I think it was about a year ago that you told me—and I don't think I am revealing any confidences because I think you have said it publicly—that we have lots of wiggle room. I think we are running out of wiggle room. I think we are coming pretty close to the point of no return, and personally I am scared to death we are on our way to nuclear World War Three.[16]

This danger was cited again and again. A majority of senators on the committee felt it was not only possible but even likely that the North Vietnamese army and the Vietcong would continue to elude destruction, that Johnson would be under increasing pressure to pursue them further and further, beginning with forays into Cambodia and Laos and eventually leading to an outright invasion of North Vietnam. They remembered General Douglas MacArthur's assurances in the late fall of 1950 that the Chinese would not enter the Korean War even if MacArthur marched all the way to the Yalu River, and what had happened when he did. The North Vietnamese might simply retreat in the face of American advances until U.S. and Chinese troops would again be facing each other across a border. No one doubted Johnson was fully aware of these dangers, but they also knew he would be under terrific pressure to take any step that might avoid an American defeat. He had already taken many steps, after all, that he had once rejected as extreme.

Concern that the war in Vietnam might expand to include China was not confined to members of the Foreign Relations Committee. General James M. Gavin, a former ambassador now working with a Boston firm, also emphasized the danger of Chinese intervention in a long letter published by *Harper's* magazine in January, 1966. Gavin was not necessarily opposed to the war, but he very much doubted the administration could achieve its apparent aims with the 200,000 American troops in Vietnam at the turn of the year. It seemed clear to him that either those objectives were not going to be won, or that major troop increases were going to be necessary. Since the administration did not seem to be saying anything about the problem, Gavin decided to do so. His proposal was a simple one:

Today we have sufficient force in South Vietnam to hold several enclaves on the coast, where sea and air power can be made fully effective. By enclaves I suggest Camranh Bay, Danang and similar areas where

American bases are being established. However, we are stretching these resources beyond reason in our endeavors to secure the entire country of South Vietnam from Vietcong penetration. This situation, of course, is caused by the growing Vietcong strength. The time has come, therefore, when we simply have to make up our mind what we want to do and then provide the resources necessary to do it.[17]

Official response to Gavin's enclave proposal was angry and immediate. He was deliberately misunderstood to have suggested something akin to fortified redoubts, and then attacked as a military nitwit for wanting to pull American troops back into a series of Dien Bien Phus where they would be sitting ducks for the enemy. After the letter became public Gavin was invited to a Pentagon meeting with Secretary McNamara, Cyrus Vance, and General Wheeler, who made it clear they did not appreciate his public suggestions. On February 3 in New York, Taylor denounced Gavin's plan, without naming him, as guaranteeing "a crushing defeat of international proportions."[18] The attack by Taylor, an old friend, hit hard; in Boston Gavin held a press conference in which he implied he was bitterly sorry for ever writing the *Harper's* letter in the first place. He said he had only been trying to point out a simple military fact: American forces in Vietnam were insufficient to do the job we apparently intended to do.

This, of course, was no secret to the administration and was the reason for the vehemence of the attack on Gavin. The administration understood that in counterguerrilla war you lose if you do not win, and that Gavin's proposal, by foreclosing a victory, guaranteed a defeat. At the same time, however, the administration did not want a lot of public discussion about what it would take to actually win. Officials had leaked military proposals for doubling U.S. troops in Vietnam to 400,000 men, and then increasing them still further to 600,000 by the end of 1968. Public reaction was not encouraging, especially in light of informed skepticism that even 600,000 men could win the war. Gavin, in his letter, had suggested that quadrupling U.S. forces would probably bring in Chinese "volunteers" or lead to the resumption of fighting in Korea. The administration had, in fact, already decided on a continued troop buildup and carried out its plans; by the middle of 1968 troop levels would reach 549,000. In early 1966, however, officials were not prepared to say just how many more troops they were going to send, for obvious reasons. The situation was a curious one: those who understood Gavin's point were generally in favor of the war and knew the logic of the situation would demand more troops. As a result they said nothing about the disparity between our goals and the size of the army we had sent to achieve them, knowing that more troops would be forced to follow. Those congressmen who opposed the war did not fully comprehend the open-ended nature of Johnson's commitment. Each troop increase came as a surprise, and they allowed themselves to hope each would be the last. Johnson was, in fact, sending the troops his strategy would require without ever admitting just what that strategy was. Gavin's attempt to blow the whistle on this procedure alerted a lot of people to the nature of the military problem we were undertaking, but it failed to force the government into a public admission of what it was really planning to do.

General Matthew B. Ridgway, a former Army Chief of Staff, commander of U.S. forces during the Korean War, and a sponsor within the military of both Gavin and Taylor, eventually entered the enclave debate on Gavin's side with an article in *Look* magazine which was both too little and too late to prevent the escalation Gavin had implied was coming. In the article, "Pull-out, All-out or Stand Fast in Vietnam?," Ridgway warned that there was no easy route to victory through air power and agreed with Gavin that the Chinese would not allow the United States to win simply by increasing its forces on the ground. They were as committed to North Vietnam as we were to the South, he said:

> We should be wary of experts who feel they can correctly interpret Chinese intentions and can predict how they will react to any move of ours. We know what the Chinese are capable of in Southeast Asia. This is the knowledge that should guide us in appraising our strategy.[19]

Ridgway's eminence shifted public opinion another degree toward doubt about official policy, but it did not halt the steady drift toward an ever-larger war. After days of well-publicized "disappointment" with Hanoi's response to his peace offensive, Johnson ordered the bombing to resume on January 31. In a televised statement he said, "Now the world knows more clearly than ever who insists on aggression and who works for peace."[20] In a press conference which immediately followed Johnson's statement, Rusk implied that from now on the other side could expect only war and more war:

It is possible that one of the obstacles to peace has been a failure on the part of Hanoi to understand that the United States will in fact meet its commitment. . . . If they are relying upon domestic differences among us to save their cause, they must understand that that will not occur.[21]

Rusk was right up to a point. A number of senators continued to oppose the war, demonstrations were held in New York and Washington protesting resumption of the bombing, and new protest groups were forming, but the majority of the country was prepared to go along with the President. It would have agreed in essence with Governor Nelson Rockefeller, who said in New York, "My personal feeling is that in this moment of crisis we all ought to support the President. He is the man who had all the information and knowledge of what we are up against."[22]

When the bombing had begun in February, 1965, just one year before, the vast majority of the Senate and the House of Representatives publicly supported the step, perhaps feeling that the question would soon be moot since Hanoi would be forced to back down. Early in 1966, however, the mood was somewhat different. Dissident senators remained powerless to influence the course of the war, but they continued to direct public attention at the dangers and inconsistencies of official policy.

The fifteen senators who had written to President Johnson on January 27 met again on Tuesday, February 1, the day after the end of the thirty-seven-day bombing halt, and decided to urge the Senate Foreign Relations Committee to hold public hearings on the war. On Thursday, February 3, the committee's nineteen members met and voted sixteen to three to begin hearings on the following day. At the White House, Johnson made immediate plans for what amounted to a public relations counterattack. One official has related that everything was quiet when he left the White House for lunch at about 12:30 Thursday; when he returned there was chaos. Johnson had decided on the inspiration of the moment to fly to Honolulu for a meeting with Nguyen Cao Ky and other South Vietnamese officials in an attempt to distract public attention from the Fulbright hearings. In the confusion as they made hurried plans for the impromptu conference, White House officials forgot to inform the South Vietnamese ambassador to the United States until late Thursday night.[23]

The President's announcement of the conference on Friday, February 4, his departure on Saturday, his welcoming speech for Ky on Sunday (in which he made a slighting reference to "special pleaders who counsel retreat"[24]), and his final speech summing up the three-day conference on Monday succeeded in capturing headlines from the Fulbright committee up to a point. The first hearing, with foreign aid chief David E. Bell on Friday, was obscured, but subsequent hearings were followed on national television all the more closely for the sense of crisis created by Johnson's sudden trip. In his speech on Monday, February 7, the President had made his determination clear: "We are brothers in arms. We will not tire. We will not flag. We intend to work with you, to fight with you in defeating the Communist aggressor."[25] The effect of this ringing declaration was to focus attention on those senators who nevertheless insisted on challenging the assumptions behind Johnson's "absolute resolve" to see the war through.

It was well known in Washington that William Fulbright and Lyndon Johnson had once been close friends and that Johnson, asked his opinion on foreign policy matters while he had been majority leader of the Senate, would often say, "See Bill. He's my Secretary of State."[26] Fulbright's concern with Johnson's handling of foreign policy sharpened after the President sent 24,000 U.S. troops to the Dominican Republic in April, 1965, and then fumbled in search of an adequate explanation, insisting first that the operation was designed only to save American lives, later that it was necessary to prevent another Cuba in the Caribbean. The list of Communists cited by the President as proof of this danger turned out to include several children and even some individuals who had died before the crisis began. In July, 1965, the Senate Foreign Relations Committee held secret hearings on the intervention which disturbed Fulbright even more. On September 15 he sent the President a copy of a speech attacking the intervention, which he delivered on the Senate floor later that afternoon. Johnson responded indirectly through Senator Thomas Dodd, who bitterly attacked Fulbright for "an undiscriminating infatuation"[27] with radical movements, and by columnist William S. White, who charged him with a lack of self-restraint. Both Dodd and White were known to be intimates of the President and their assaults were assumed to reflect the President's thinking. The result of Fulbright's speech was an open break between the two men. Fulbright was pointedly removed from the White House invitation list on occasions when the chairman of the Senate Foreign

Relations Committee would normally have been included as a matter of course. In December, the air force refused a routine request for a jet to take a congressional delegation headed by Fulbright to Australia. On February 2, White again attacked Fulbright, this time pointing out his record on civil rights votes (which reflected the anti-Negro bias of his Arkansas constituency) and suggesting that Fulbright's lack of commitment to victory in Vietnam reflected a fundamental lack of interest in Asians because of their color. When General Gavin appeared before the Foreign Relations Committee on Tuesday, February 8, the air of drama was partly caused by the sense that these hearings represented a struggle between Fulbright and the President.

The hearings, technically held to consider an official administration request for an additional $415 million in economic aid, $275 million of it for South Vietnam, were held on six separate days and represented the most intense public consideration of the war in Vietnam up to that time. Rusk had appeared on January 28 and Bell on February 4. Gavin testified on February 8, former U.S. ambassador to the Soviet Union George F. Kennan on February 10, Maxwell Taylor on February 17, and Rusk, for a second time, on February 18. The all-day hearings, attended by the full Foreign Relations Committee as well as a large number of spectators, were televised live and brought face to face those who supported and those who opposed the war in Vietnam. Fulbright's purpose was primarily educational; he made no attempt to propose an alternative policy, but simply subjected existing policy to a penetrating, sometimes caustic analysis which it had previously escaped. In his State of the Union speech on January 12, 1966, Johnson had described the history of the war in terms that were fanciful to say the least:

> Not too many years ago Vietnam was a peaceful, if troubled, land. In the North was an independent Communist government. In the South a people struggled to build a nation with the friendly help of the United States. . . . There were some in South Vietnam who wished to force Communist rule on their own people. But their progress was slight. Their hope of success was dim. Then, little more than six years ago, North Vietnam decided on conquest and from that day to this, soldiers and supplies have moved from North to South in a swelling stream that swallowed the remnants of revolution in aggression.[28]

Fulbright's purpose was to replace this historical fantasy with a more exact sense of what had happened in Southeast Asia.

The first two hearings following President Johnson's return from Honolulu raised a number of doubts about the wisdom of attempting to halt Communism, if that were the true American purpose in Vietnam. General Gavin and George F. Kennan were hardly doves in the usual sense of the term, but both found it hard to see what the U.S. could hope to gain that would justify the enormous cost of the war. Gavin, appearing on Tuesday, February 8, told the committee he had written his *Harper's* letter the previous November because he feared the United States was gradually moving toward the initiation of urban bombing in an attempt to break the will of the North Vietnamese. Experience had shown it wouldn't work, he said; it would intensify the war immeasurably, without improving the American position in the slightest.

Gavin also pointed out that fighting China in Southeast Asia was senseless. China's war-making capacity was largely centered in Manchuria; if war with China were necessary, the proper place for it, from the American point of view, would be Manchuria. In response to a series of questions by Fulbright, Gavin told the committee of a U.S. Army study of the feasibility of intervention in Vietnam at the time of the French defeat at Dien Bien Phu in 1954:

> We considered the advisability of entering the Hanoi delta, and as I recall, to be precise, we talked about the need for some eight divisions, plus some 35 engineer battalions; we anticipated the supply [problems] would be very great, medical and so on, and there was some significance to Hainan Island if we were going to go into the Delta and so on. We gave it quite thorough consideration. . . . We finally decided, when we were all through, what we were talking about doing was going to war with Red China under conditions that were appallingly disadvantageous.[29]

The problem of China remained paramount. Gavin made it clear that the United States could not invade North Vietnam without bringing in China, could not fight China without the use of nuclear weapons, could not hope to win without occupying large parts of the country, and could not occupy the country without bringing in Russia, which would naturally want to occupy those areas along her own borders. The number of U.S. troops necessary for such a war would be in the millions; the devastation caused by nuclear weapons would be "beyond understanding";[30] the problems of reconstruction would be "appalling."[31] Gavin felt distinctly uneasy in his role as critic of the government and of the military, but at the same time he was obviously troubled by the direction in which he felt events were drifting. He found it difficult to express himself at times; occasionally his syntax broke down completely. Again and again, however, his concern came through clearly: the war did not make sense, control of events was slipping out of our hands, the possibilities for tragedy were immense. He felt the administration had lost its sense of proportion about the conflict; it was apparently considering the commitment of half a million troops, perhaps even more, at a total cost of $25 billion a year. Gavin couldn't see the sense in it; South Vietnam just wasn't that important.

On Thursday Kennan spoke to the same point, suggesting that "if we were not already involved as we are today in Vietnam, I would know of no reason why we should wish to become so involved and I could think of several reasons why we should wish not to."[32] He dismissed the notion that Vietnam, of itself, was militarily, economically, or geographically significant. He warned that the other side was not going to give up, and that a serious attempt to "win" the war would undoubtedly bring in the Chinese. Furthermore, the war was damaging our relations with Russia and, even worse, Japan, a country that was of indisputable significance in the world. Kennan doubted the United States had anything to gain from "the spectacle of Americans inflicting grievous injury on the lives of a poor and helpless people, and particularly a people of different race and color."[33] American insistence that its prestige was at stake in Vietnam was hardly likely to impress Europeans who had abandoned whole empires since World War II, he said. All the talk of America's commitment to Vietnam, Kennan said, left him

> a little bewildered. I would like to know what that commitment really consists of, and how and when it was incurred. . . . If we did not incur such an obligation in any formal way, then I think we should not be inventing it for ourselves and assuring ourselves that we are bound by it today. But if we did incur it, then I do fail to understand how it was possible to enter any such commitment otherwise than through the constitutional processes which were meant to come into play when even commitments of lesser import than this were undertaken.[34]

The testimony of Gavin and Kennan emphasized that China was the key to the war in Vietnam. Without reference to China, the U.S. government would never have been able to argue plausibly that U.S. interests were at stake in Vietnam. The danger to which Gavin and Kennan pointed, however, was not China's involvement in Vietnam, but the chance that our escalation of the war might cause her to become involved. Chinese influence in Hanoi was far less than American influence in Saigon. Listening to their testimony, as millions did throughout the country, it was hard to believe that the war was other than a purely Vietnamese situation. Until the United States intervened, there were only Vietnamese fighting Vietnamese. Increased intervention might bring in Chinese troops to counter the American troops, but so far the North Vietnamese were prepared, by themselves, to take on both the South Vietnamese and the Americans. In short, the worst had not yet happened, but might.

On Thursday and Friday of the following week, General Taylor and Secretary Rusk attempted to defend the administration's position on the war. Taylor, who had been U.S. ambassador to Saigon and who had favored military action since the beginning of President Kennedy's term in office, appeared as an independent witness but was correctly understood to be arguing the administration's case. He insisted that the United States was fighting a limited war for limited ends, that current strategy would be successful, and that the alternatives of all-out war or precipitate withdrawal were equally unacceptable. The importance of the war, he said, lay in the fact that it was a test of the Communist strategy of wars of national liberation: if Hanoi won, similar wars would spring up elsewhere around the world; if the United States won, peace might be expected in the underdeveloped world. Was the war important? "An easy and incomplete answer would be that it must be important to us since it is considered so by the other side."[35]

Taylor pointed out that total losses of the Vietcong and North Vietnamese during the first six weeks of 1966 indicated an average monthly loss of 17,000 men. He carefully avoided saying how many men the North Vietnamese might be willing to commit to the struggle, how many men the United States might need to oppose them, or how long the fighting might continue, but implied that things were coming to a head. If the enemy's current rate of losses continued throughout the year, he said, the other side would be in difficulty by 1967. Fulbright noted, however, that the total number of Vietcong had increased from 103,000 in January, 1965, to 243,000 a year later, despite the loss of 34,000 dead and 11,000 captured.

Throughout his testimony Taylor continued to point out that the American purpose in Vietnam was to persuade Hanoi to abandon its aims in South Vietnam. When worried senators tried to learn just how far the United States would go to achieve that end, Taylor became vague, assuring everyone that Russia would not enter the war if the United States tried to blockade Haiphong harbor, that China would not enter the war if more U.S. troops were sent, that Hanoi would eventually "mend its ways"[36] if the United States had the grit to persist. He suggested that the factor most likely to prolong the war would be opposition at home. In one of the sharpest exchanges of the entire series of hearings, Taylor and Senator Wayne Morse clashed over the question of public opinion.

> *Morse:* You know we are engaged in a historic debate in this country, where there are honest differences of opinion. I happen to hold to the point of view that it isn't going to be too long before the American people as a people will repudiate our war in Southeast Asia.
>
> *Taylor:* That, of course, is good news to Hanoi, Senator.
>
> *Morse:* I know that is the smear that you militarists give to those of us who have honest differences of opinion with you, but I don't intend to get down in the gutter with you and engage in that kind of debate, General.[37]

On Friday, February 18, Rusk appeared before the committee again and read a long, detailed statement supporting his earlier arguments. In essence, he said that the situation in Vietnam had to be viewed as an episode in the struggle between the United States and the Communist world since the end of the Second World War. A victory for Hanoi would be a victory for Communism and a defeat for the United States. For that reason alone it was in the vital interests of the United States to frustrate Hanoi's attempt to reunify Vietnam under its own rule. Rusk never pointed to anything concrete as a justification of the war; he never implied there was any economic or geographical reason why it made any difference who controlled South Vietnam. His arguments referred solely to intangibles: the United States was fighting in Vietnam to prevent the "other side" from starting other wars elsewhere. Our "credibility" was at stake. We had said we would defend Saigon's independence and now we had to do it. Rusk dismissed "Communist efforts to confuse the issue"[38] by suggesting it was a civil war, a matter of purely local importance to the Vietnamese. The United States sought only to preserve the situation as it had prevailed after the 1954 Geneva Accords: "If the armed attack against South Vietnam is brought to an end, peace can come very quickly."[39]

Rusk was questioned at length by members of the committee, but he refused to abandon the narrow view of the Vietnam situation he had expressed in his opening statement. It was clear most of the committee members were prepared to accept Rusk's outline of the facts of the situation, without accepting his conclusion that the outcome was important enough to justify the commitment of hundreds of thousands of troops and billions, ultimately even hundreds of billions, of dollars. Only Senator Fulbright, speaking slowly and tentatively, tried to bring in the larger questions involved. It was clear to him that Hanoi was, in fact, trying to reunify Vietnam under its control, but he was not sure the United States had any right to interfere. He referred repeatedly to the question of negotiations. He sensed that asking Hanoi to give up its "aggression" was equivalent to asking it for unconditional surrender. Rusk automatically spoke of Vietnam as two separate countries; Fulbright spoke of one. For Rusk, the 1954 Geneva Agreement was a final settlement; for Fulbright, it was a temporary thing. At one point he told Rusk that the United States should be prepared to tolerate a settlement in which all Vietnamese, including the National Liberation Front, were free to participate:

After all, Vietnam is their country. It is not our country. We do not even have the right the French did. We have no historical right. We are obviously intruders, from their point of view. We represent the old Western imperialism in their eyes. I am not questioning your motives. I think our motives are very good, as has been testified on numerous occasions. But I still think from their point of view it is their country, and however bad the people have acted, other countries have had civil wars, we had one. In my part of the country [Arkansas] we resented it for a long time. So did yours. [Rusk was from Georgia.] You can remember the feelings that were there. These are very unfortunate controversies. But what bothers me, and I know a number here, is that this is in one sense a relatively minor matter. In another sense it seems to

be the trigger that may result in a world war, and I do not want that
to happen, and that is what we are really concerned with.

Rusk: And none of us want it to happen, Mr. Chairman, but when you
say this is their country—

Fulbright: It is their country, with all its difficulties, even if they want
to be Communists. . . . Just like the Yugoslavs. I do not know why
we should object to it.

Rusk: We are making a distinction though, that is that South Vietnam
is not Hanoi's country.

Fulbright: It is not our country. It used to be one country.[40]

Throughout the hearings Fulbright had tried to bring larger issues
into the debate over the war. With George Kennan he had tried to show
that China had not been historically an aggressive nation, and that its
actions in Tibet and the northern districts of India were not clear-cut
cases of aggression, as the administration implied they were. In one
long exchange with General Taylor he tried to deal with the problem
of the morality of the war, and especially of the use of napalm, in an
attempt to show that the war was not a battle between the forces of light
and darkness, but one between two sides equally determined to kill their
opponents by any means available. Fulbright feared the creation of a
warlike mood in the country, that emotions were hardening, that
greater violence was impending.

Nothing had been settled by the time the last of the six hearings
came to an end late Friday afternoon, February 18, but the effect of
the hearings was considerable. It was clear that a majority of the
Foreign Relations Committee was deeply disturbed by the war,
doubtful of its necessity, fearful of its potentiality, uncertain what to
do about it. Fulbright and others had suggested that the differences
between the administration and the committee were largely a matter
of judgment. Both sides probably felt they had won the debate, but
the most important result was a degree of awakening in the uncom-
mitted public, which watched the hearings on live television. It was
clear that fundamental differences existed, hard to grasp exactly what
they were. Easy certainties evaporated during the hearings. It was not
so simple to choose between Gavin and Taylor, Rusk and Kennan.
On the last day Senator Morse referred again to his belief that the
question ultimately would be decided by the American people, an

unseen jury which had listened to six days of testimony but could give no early sign of its verdict.

The administration took the hearings seriously and attempted to counter their effect. On February 11, the day after Kennan's testimony, President Johnson held a news conference in which he said he did not see very much difference in their positions. "No one wants to escalate the war and no one wants to lose any more men than is necessary. No one wants to surrender and get out. At least no one admits they do. So I don't see there is any great difference of opinion."[41] On the following day Rusk defended the administration at a rally at Emory University in Atlanta, Georgia. On Wednesday, February 16, Johnson pledged in a speech in Atlantic City, that Hanoi "will never deter or defeat us"[42] while Rusk spoke in Las Vegas. On the same day Senator Russell Long of Louisiana backed the President in a surprising display of old-fashioned patriotism on the Senate floor: "I swell with pride as I see Old Glory flying from the Capitol. I pray that no other flag will fly over it. My prayer is there may never be a white flag of surrender up there."[43]

While the President had been defending his policies, and Rusk had been defending the President, and Long had been defending the Capitol, Assistant Secretary of Defense for Public Affairs Arthur Sylvester had been meeting in the Pentagon with representatives of five major veterans' groups in order to ask them to put pressure on Senator Hartke, a leader among those who had signed the January 27 letter to Johnson, to persuade him to quiet his public opposition to the war. When Sylvester's effort became known, it was abandoned. On Saturday, February 19, Senator Robert F. Kennedy suggested in New York that the NLF be admitted to a coalition government in South Vietnam, initiating a whole new round of controversy which finally evaporated after a meeting between the senator and the President on Tuesday, February 22.

Fulbright continued to brood about the situation in Vietnam through the winter and into the spring of 1966. In the past he had been concerned largely with Europe and then Russia; Asia was new to him. He read steadily in order to understand the background of the war, and the more he read the more he felt that American policies were completely out of touch with the realities of Vietnam. In April he delivered a series of lectures in honor of Christian A. Herter, Secretary of State under

Eisenhower, at Johns Hopkins University. These lectures were little noticed at first, but then caught the attention of a steadily widening public. Fulbright could not point to a single argument or fact that was the key to the war, some revelation that might suddenly change people's minds. It was clear by now that nothing would change Rusk's mind, or Johnson's, and yet, Fulbright felt, there was something deeply wrong with the war.

In the first lecture, on April 21, Fulbright said he opposed such acts of protest as burning draft cards but recognized they were the inevitable result of silence on the part of himself and others who might have been expected to speak out against the war:

> It is only when the Congress fails to challenge the Executive, when the opposition fails to oppose, when politicians join in a spurious consensus behind controversial policies, that the campuses and streets and public squares of America are likely to become the forums of a direct and disorderly democracy.[44]

He warned that the war was having a corrosive effect on the American spirit, largely because of doubt about its strict necessity and a growing desire on the part of the public and officials alike simply to smash through to a solution by the use of America's overwhelming military power. "Gradually but unmistakably," Fulbright said, "America is succumbing to that arrogance of power which has afflicted, weakened and in some cases destroyed, great nations in the past."[45]

On the following Wednesday, April 27, Fulbright delivered the second of the Herter lectures and then on Thursday he spoke to the Advertising Bureau of the American Newspaper Publishers Association meeting in the Waldorf-Astoria Hotel in New York. Earlier in the week the group had been addressed by Humphrey, who discussed the war for an hour without once mentioning the possibility of negotiations, and by Ambassador to the United Nations Arthur Goldberg. With the exception of a single outburst, the group listened with cold civility as Fulbright, in his slow, deep voice, outlined the effect of the Vietnam war on the United States, both domestically and in her foreign relations. He began with the latter, citing the cooling between Russia and America, the failure of our European allies to join us in the struggle, the worldwide concern about the administration's "undue preoccupation" with Vietnam. Then he mentioned two ways in which the war was eroding American life. The first, he said, was by deflecting spiritual and financial resources from the Great Society.

> The second and potentially most damaging is the stirring up of a war fever in the minds of our people and leaders; it is only just now getting under way, but, as the war goes on, as the casualty lists grow larger and affect more and more American homes, the fever will rise and the patience of the American people will give way to mounting demands for an expanded war, for a lightning blow that will get it over with at a stroke. The first demand might be a blockade of Haiphong; then, if that doesn't work, a strike against China; and then we will have global war.

At this point members of the audience shouted out, "No, no." Fulbright went on to cite the ways in which this war fever was beginning to reveal itself. Finally, in a sentence that, with his earlier reference to the "arrogance of power," was to cut to the heart of the way people felt about the war, Fulbright said, "America is showing some signs of that fatal presumption, that over-extension of power and mission, which brought ruin to ancient Athens, to Napoleonic France and to Nazi Germany."[46]

No major political figure ever painted a darker picture of what the war was doing to the country. These speeches caused a brief sensation; Fulbright was all but called a traitor or a madman. His warning was dismissed as an overstatement, an hysterical exaggeration of doubts naturally shared by all thoughtful men. But Fulbright's bleak vision remained after the sensible, balanced editorials were forgotten. The frustration grew, just as he had warned. Pressure increased on the President to widen the bombing. Passions deepened over the war, and Fulbright was not alone in fearing that America was losing its balance, and would choose Armageddon over humiliation.

SEVEN

Voting on the War

President Johnson's landslide defeat of Barry Goldwater in 1964 carried forty-seven new Democrats into the House of Representatives, where they provided the margin of voting strength behind Johnson's legislative successes in 1965. Early in 1966 it became apparent that these freshman Democrats, many of them from districts historically controlled by the Republicans, would be facing an uphill struggle for reelection. Poll after poll showed a steady decline in Johnson's popularity and an equally steady increase in dissatisfaction with the progress of the war. Off-year elections have traditionally meant a gain in House seats by the party out of power, but the size of the average gain depends on how far back one goes to begin averaging. Johnson, hoping to minimize the effect of a Democratic defeat in 1966, liked to cite the average loss of forty-one seats which had occurred every four years since 1890. Republican leaders preferred the thirty-three-seat loss in off-year elections since 1932, or the thirty-one-seat loss since 1946.

It was inevitable that the elections in November would be interpreted as a referendum on Johnson's presidency and, since his presidency was increasingly preoccupied with the problem of Vietnam, as an indication of public feeling about the war. From the beginning of the year it had been clear that the frustrations caused by the war in Vietnam would have an effect on the election, but it proved difficult to predict just what sort of effect. The Republican minority leaders in the House and Senate periodically criticized the administration for its lack of candor and for mismanagement, but stopped well short of opposing the war itself. They argued that the Republicans would gain from dissatisfaction over the war because most of it, statistically at any rate, was hawkish in nature and the limits placed on the military effort were the fault of Democratic doves. If there were more Republicans in Congress, it was suggested, the war would be pursued more vigorously and therefore won more quickly.

Senator Joseph S. Clark of Pennsylvania, a Democrat, insisted that the public was actually opposed to the war, whatever the polls might show. The Democrats would be hit hard, he said, because voters would identify the war with the President's party. In a press conference held in San Francisco, where he was attending a meeting on Saturday, February 26, Clark said, "The American people are turning against the escalation of this conflict. If President Johnson accepts the recommendation of General Westmoreland and Ambassador Lodge [for more troops], I believe we will lose 75 seats in Congress in the next election."[1] When Clark returned to the Senate, Humphrey told him he was hurting the party and asked why he had made such a damaging prediction. "Because I believe it," Clark answered. "I know, Joe," the Vice President said, "but you're driving the President crazy."[2]

The President's concern was twofold. In the first place he wanted to curb talk about disaffection in his own party, which could only hurt at the polls. More importantly, he wanted to disassociate the war and the elections to prevent North Vietnam from interpreting a Democratic defeat as an antiwar victory. Johnson believed Hanoi would give up only if it became convinced the United States would not, and he worked hard to keep his party in line. Throughout 1966 he derided the notion that there was any serious dispute about what to do in Vietnam and dismissed talk of a grass-roots revolt as the work of over-enthusiastic journalists and professional malcontents. He argued that Democratic congressmen could run on the record of the legislation passed during the preceding two years and challenged his critics to come up with an alternative policy for Vietnam if they thought he was doing the wrong thing.

At a press conference in Washington on Tuesday, March 22, Johnson said he had studied the results of recent polls in eighteen congressional districts across the country. In twelve of those districts the Democrats were doing even better than they had in 1964, he said. Talk of a Democratic revolt was baseless:

Some folks play politics. They give out statements. I see on the ticker about three or four handouts a day. They are usually some new press man who has been hired, or a fellow who thinks he is being paid by the column, like a stringer. He gives out these handouts and provokes fights. He puts a little twist on it. . . . There are these people who pick these figures out of the air. I heard someone the other night talking about 74 or 80 House seats. It was amusing. I wondered how much he knew about any House seat. [3]

In fact, however, the press was giving the President the benefit of the doubt. Journalists paid relatively little attention to the very real ferment at the local level of the Democratic Party, where at least one hundred candidates ran for office on peace platforms in twenty states. Major challenges were mounted in Oregon, Massachusetts, New Jersey, Washington state, New York, Connecticut, and California, and the war was a significant issue in races in Montana, Tennessee, Illinois, Michigan, and elsewhere. In Wisconsin, Democrats at a state convention in June passed a resolution calling for a cease-fire after overwhelmingly defeating by a voice vote a proposal to include a conciliatory paragraph praising Johnson for his "restraint" and his "efforts to achieve a just and honorable peace." [4] In Dearborn, Michigan, Mayor Orville Hubbard arranged for a referendum on the war. The question he placed on the ballot asked voters, "Are you in favor of an immediate ceasefire and withdrawal of United States troops from Vietnam so the Vietnamese people can settle their own problems?"[5]

Most of this activity received only glancing notice by the press, and that often hostile. At best the press seemed to share the President's public attitude that these were exercises in futility by people who were inclined to over-emote. In fact, however, the peace campaigns in 1966 were clear evidence that Vietnam was beginning to dominate, and would eventually obsess, American politics at every level. A year earlier very few politicians would have asked seriously in private the question Dearborn's mayor now insisted on asking in public. In January a number of antiwar and civil rights activists met in Chicago to create the National Conference for New Politics (NCNP), a broad coalition of individuals and groups which planned to support peace candidates or even to run their own. On Monday, February 7, the "Inside Report" column of Rowland Evans and Robert Novak described the meeting and observed:

What this amounts to is a leftist wrecking crew injecting a sinister new element into American politics. The message to liberal Democrats is clear. Take an anti-Communist foreign policy stance and we will drive you out of office—even if it means splitting the liberal vote and thus electing a Republican. Conceivably a weak-willed liberal or two will crumple.[6]

The intensity of this attack (the "sinister new element," after all, was only an appeal to voters to express themselves democratically on the war), like the derision expressed by President Johnson, reflected a fundamental doubt about the nature of public feeling on Vietnam. The one thing the administration did not want was a referendum on "peace," since who wanted to run against peace? Red-baiting was widespread in 1966, and at least partly successful. A vote for the end of the war was described by officials as a vote for Hanoi and against American boys fighting in Vietnam. The attitude of the people during this year-long debate remained something of a mystery. They disliked the war but generally seemed to believe the United States could win in a hurry if only we went all out. At the same time, however, few candidates in either party felt there was much to gain by running on a prowar platform. Strong support for the war seemed to hurt more than it helped; the people who favored it did not care very strongly, while those against it were passionate and hard-working. As an issue the war was a hornets' nest, and most candidates tried to disassociate themselves from it, which often meant disassociating themselves from the President as well. The advice of Representative Wayne Hayes, a Democrat of Ohio, was widely followed: "Keep your head down, don't get tangled up in the row over Vietnam if you want to come through the '66 election."[7]

Confusion about the best way to handle the issue of the war extended to the peace movement, which divided between those who wanted to run peace candidates and those who felt Johnson's victory on a peace platform in 1964 proved the futility of electoral politics. The movement was in a state of chaotic ferment, with a growing faction beginning to think of themselves primarily as radicals, which meant they were fighting not only for concrete goals like an end to the war, but also for something like a "revolution." The word was still being used largely as a metaphor, its violent connotations a kind of weapon in public debate, a warning that the speaker was *serious.* The first fear of radicals is always co-optation, by which they mean piecemeal reforms which might reconcile the discontented masses without basically altering their condition. The danger of co-optation is high during an election because, put simply, promises are cheap. Political campaigns don't really change anything, radicals argue, and at the same time waste the energy of people who work in them. As a result, radicals were deeply suspicious of any peace platform that did not propose an end to the war through an end to the system they felt was ultimately responsible for the war.

This ambivalence toward elections was apparent in the political activities of the Newark Community Union Project, SDS's most successful effort at organizing in Northern slums. NCUP was active in the 1965 campaign of a black militant in the State Assembly who had been denied renomination by the Democrats. His third-party effort was an organizational disaster, largely because NCUP's guilt about working in something so identified with the system as an *election* prevented them from treating the election seriously. They did not win, or even come close to winning. The dilemma that crippled them was that poor people in Newark needed things that were in the power of elected representatives to grant or withhold. If NCUP were really committed to the poor, it ought to fight for control of those public offices that affected their lives. At the same time, however, they feared that winning elections might be possible only at the cost of their radicalism.

While SDS was trying to talk itself into electoral campaigning on a limited level (Paul Booth, an SDS national officer, had been at the Chicago meeting of the "leftist wrecking crew," for example), other activists were trying to talk SDS out of it. At a rally sponsored by the National Coordinating Committee to End the War, held in Chicago on March 26 (others were held the same day in New York, Washington, Boston, and San Francisco), Staughton Lynd criticized both SDS and the May Second Movement for backing way away from direct action programs aimed at the draft. He admitted that efforts to create a broad-based resistance to the war could be attacked as utopian, "But then tell me your scenario for how running a Congressman in Berkeley and a Senator in Chicago leads on to changing American capitalism and stopping American imperialism."[8]

Despite such doubts, however, a number of peace candidates ran in 1966 with the support of both radicals and liberals. The best-organized and the most sharply focused of these campaigns was Robert Scheer's challenge of Representative Jeffrey Cohelan for the Democratic nomination in California's Seventh Congressional District, which includes the university town of Berkeley and part of Oakland. Scheer, a thirty-year-old radical who was foreign editor of *Ramparts* magazine, attacked Cohelan in a campaign based on the slogans, "Withdraw the troops. End poverty."[9]

Cohelan, first elected to the seat in 1958, was a liberal Democrat with a 95 percent rating from the Americans for Democratic Action who had consistently backed Johnson's Vietnam policy. On April 5, 1965, for example, Cohelan had given a speech on the floor of the House which blamed the war, as did the administration, on a "Communist attack which has increasingly been waged and directed from the North." He concluded in a paraphrase of Rusk, "If the Communists can be persuaded to leave their neighbors alone, then peace is possible in South Vietnam and all of Southeast Asia." Even worse from the point of view of Berkeley radicals had been Cohelan's criticism of the International Days of Protest held on October 15–16. "The war in Vietnam is most certainly a vital national issue," Cohelan said two days later. "It both deserves and demands public thought and comment. But if this comment and participation is to be constructive it must be conducted in a lawful and responsible manner." Cohelan had backed Johnson's peace campaign in 1964, yet supported the war; he had voted for the War on Poverty programs, yet his own district contained black ghettos where poverty was untouched. Cohelan himself was quiet and hard-working, the sort of representative who was conscientious in meeting quorum calls and in fulfilling his committee assignments without ever attracting much attention. He was proud of his warm relationship with the House Democratic leadership. If he worried about the war, he did not let it show. Cohelan's political history and the large number of antiwar activists in his constituency made him an obvious target.

The campaign to unseat Cohelan began only a month after he started his fourth term, in February, 1965, when a doctor in the Seventh Congressional District sent him a telegram angrily demanding that he speak out against the war. Cohelan's vague and evasive response further angered the doctor, Dan Simon, and he sent a letter to six thousand registered Democrats in the district asking them to send post cards to Cohelan if they also opposed his support for the war. Cohelan received more than a thousand cards and Simon, surprised by the response, decided to increase the pressure. In August he and others met to choose a candidate who could challenge Cohelan in the 1966 election. Scheer's name was proposed by a member of the Faculty Peace Committee at Berkeley and a campaign eventually formed around him. Despite the neat trim of his beard and his Brooks Brothers suits, Scheer was a genuine radical and a long-time opponent of the war. On a grant from the Center for the Study of Democratic Institutions Scheer had written an influential study of the origins of American involvement in Vietnam focusing on the role of counterinsurgency experts and the importance of support for Ngo Dinh Diem by New York's conservative Francis Cardinal Spellman.

Radicals on the nearly dormant Vietnam Day Committee were active in Scheer's campaign from the beginning, causing a liberal-radical split in his support which both helped and hurt him. The first split over strategy came with the decision to challenge Cohelan in the Democratic primary, rather than attempt to build a new party which would challenge him in the fall. Other disputes centered on questions of political style, radicals insisting that the issues be emphasized and the candidate relegated to the background. One such argument centered on the design for Scheer's bumper stickers: radicals wanted the slogan to be bigger than Scheer's name, liberals the opposite. The liberals won.

One of Scheer's early victories was the endorsement of the California Democratic Council (CDC), a state-wide organization of liberal Democrats headed by Simon Casady. Casady's act infuriated California Governor Edmund G. Brown, who engineered Casady's removal in retaliation. Throughout the campaign Scheer was plagued by midnight phone calls from worried VDCers who warned that the campaign was being captured by the CDC moderates, or from equally alarmed CDCers convinced the VDC was taking over. Scheer himself was often irritated by the radicals, whom he once described as "professional non-students who are either drugged on LSD or on Marxist theory." In political terms the radicals were a mixed blessing, their manpower crucial (at one point Scheer had more than a thousand students working for him), but their hostility to every sign of political professionalism self-defeating. They also drew an outpouring of red-baiting from the regular Democratic organization backing Cohelan. Despite these and other drawbacks, the liberal-radical split in Scheer's campaign gave it a fire and drive which made it formidable. The infighting was proof of its earnestness, the struggle over slogans evidence that the campaign hoped to win more than office. The liberals wanted to beat Cohelan and the radicals wanted to make a sharp departure from the politics of compromise and accommodation. The result was a campaign fought with extraordinary energy on the issues.

Cohelan quickly realized the seriousness of Scheer's campaign but publicly tried to dismiss the challenge as one prompted solely by dislike of the President. "These people really believe the President wants war," Cohelan told one reporter. "They have no idea of his anguish. They have no idea of my anguish. They don't like this big Texas swinger and that's that."[10]

Scheer and his supporters did not care whether or not Cohelan and the President agonized over the war. They simply wanted the United States, in Rusk's words, to stop doing what it was doing. Scheer often argued that the war cost more every hour than had been spent on Oakland's entire poverty program in 1965 (about $1 million). The main issue, however, was not the cost but the morality of the war. "We are asking the people of this community to act as moral men," he said. "We're going to tell them what is being done in their name and we are going to make them either take responsibility for it or repudiate it." His position was unequivocally clear. In speeches, leaflets, and ads he was quoted as saying, "The U.S. should never have gone into Vietnam, should not have stayed there and should now get out." The campaign's larger purpose was also clear. An ad published in the San Francisco *Chronicle* on June 6, the day before the primary, said, "There is one language Johnson understands—it is the language of political power. Election of Scheer would be the most effective protest against the war yet mounted in this country."

The administration agreed and actively supported Cohelan throughout the campaign. In April, Postmaster General Larry O'Brien helped organize a testimonial dinner for Cohelan, at which he received the endorsement of Senators Kennedy and Fulbright. During the campaign Cohelan made frequent use of a forty-five-second television ad in which Kennedy supported him for reelection. Johnson's interest in the outcome was also expressed more directly. On the night of the primary his press secretary, Bill Moyers, called the clerk of Alameda County three times to see how Cohelan was doing. When the votes were counted it was clear he had done barely well enough: Scheer failed to win the nomination but still received 45 percent of the votes, an indication of how widespread disaffection with the war had become. The administration naturally insisted that a miss was as good as a mile, but Cohelan himself indicated that he had received the message by moving toward the ranks of congressional doves.[11]

The political effect of the Scheer campaign was curious; it convinced Democrats who opposed the war that an effective opposition could be raised within the party, but at the same time it convinced radicals that electoral politics was a debilitating trap. Jerry Rubin, one of the founders of the VDC, was Scheer's campaign manager for a brief period, until his radical proposals (burning down a slum tenement; holding a "Marx-Jefferson Day" $100-a-plate fund-raising dinner) began to frighten off the liberals; the day after the primary Rubin was in Chicago talking with Paul Booth about a job with SDS. Scheer, too, eventually turned against electoral politics as an effective means of change.

Simon Casady, on the other hand, was further convinced by Scheer's near success that Johnson was vulnerable and that voters were prepared to turn against the war, if the issue were only presented in the right way. He joined the group that created the National Conference for New Politics and attended the first meeting of its executive council, held in New York the weekend following the California primary. On May 22 the NCNP had run an ad in the *New York Times* which said, "The killing of Americans and Vietnamese will not stop unless opponents of this war and of the bankrupt foreign policy which it reflects can turn their dissent into real political power." At a news conference held in New York's Berkshire Hotel on Sunday, June 12, Casady spoke of the NCNP's plans to raise $500,000 for peace candidates and to train one thousand volunteer workers in order to support fifty candidates in twenty states. He said the group had also established a "Committee on 1968"[12] which would actively seek a peace candidate willing to run against Johnson. One man mentioned as a possibility was Robert Kennedy, at that moment in the middle of a trip to South Africa. Kennedy promptly expressed his support for Johnson's reelection in 1968. After this beginning, however, the NCNP slipped from public sight for the rest of the 1966 campaign.

Scheer received a higher percentage of the primary vote than any other peace candidate in 1966, although one of them, Mrs. Alice Franklin Bryant, actually won a four-way race for the Democratic nomination in Washington state's First Congressional District with 35.7 percent of the vote. In New Jersey, Rutgers University professor David Frost won 11 percent of the vote in the Democratic primary for the senatorial nomination on September 13. In Massachusetts the same day, Thomas Boylston Adams was last in a three-way race with only 8 percent. President Johnson naturally preferred to emphasize the failure of peace candidates rather than their number, when the fact that there were any at all should have indicated to political observers that Johnson's consensus on the war was growing shaky.

In September, Johnson reminded a reporter that Senator Morse had predicted the war would be an issue. "Well I don't think it's a great issue with the voters and the results so far support me, not him," Johnson said. "Take that Massachusetts election. How much did Adams get? Six per cent? Eight per cent? Even those antiwar people in California couldn't win. I don't think any President in any wartime situation has generally had as clear sailing as I have had."[13]

Johnson was correct in thinking that opponents of the war had failed to find a way in which they could present their position to the voters and win, but he was wrong in concluding that he had "clear sailing" as a result. As most political observers sensed, it was Johnson himself, and not the war, which was the issue in 1966. Widespread, clearly focused, and effective opposition to the war failed to develop, but Johnson's popularity declined steadily, with only occasional interruptions whenever he took dramatic military action. One of these sudden jumps in the polls followed his decision to bomb oil-storage facilities in both Hanoi and Haiphong in a series of raids beginning June 29 and continuing through July 5. In a speech delivered on Thursday, June 30, in Omaha, Nebraska, Johnson defended the raids and his conduct of the war, while placing responsibility for it squarely on his own shoulders:

It was only 20 months ago that the people of America held a great national election and the people of 44 states of this union, including the great state of Nebraska, gave me a direction and voted me a majority for the Presidency of this country. . . . Now there are many, many, many who can recommend and advise and sometimes a few of them consent. But there is only one who has been chosen by the American people to decide.[14]

Johnson never more clearly confirmed that Vietnam was "Johnson's war." The bombings offered momentary relief for national frustration over the war, as had all previous escalations, but the inevitable effect was further disillusion with the war, and therefore with the man whose war it was. The bombing of the oil facilities had no more apparent effect on the fighting in the South than had the introduction of American troops, the beginning of the bombing, the retaliation following the Tonkin Gulf incidents, or any of the previous steps taken by Johnson or Kennedy to convince North Vietnam by the threat or use of force that it could not attain its objectives in South Vietnam. Professional politicians all seemed to agree that the 1966 elections would go well for the Democrats if the war was going well, badly if badly. Johnson's strategy, however, depended on convincing the other side to abandon its aims. Until the very moment the other side gave in it would be impossible to know the war was going well. In all probability the other side would appear the most determined when it was closest to giving in, just as Johnson himself would in 1968. Whenever Johnson escalated the war there was a brief public response, a hope that now things would finally change. But of course they never did change. The war never did "go well" and Johnson suffered accordingly.

Johnson's strategy in the 1966 elections changed repeatedly. At first, early in the year, he seemed to be aiming for a standoff by praising Congress for its legislative record and toning down all references to party. Later, in speeches at Democratic fund-raising dinners in Washington on Thursday, May 12, and in Chicago five days later, he seemed to be making a double attempt to keep his party in line and to identify support for the Democrats with support for the war and thus a demonstration of patriotic loyalty. In the Chicago speech he reminded his opponents "that there are men on the other side who know well that their only hope for success in this aggression lies in a weakening of the fiber and determination of the people of America."[15] In a passage deleted from the official *Weekly Compilation of Presidential Documents,* Johnson went on to say, "There will be some Nervous Nellies and some who will become frustrated and bothered and break ranks under the strain. And some will turn on their leaders and on their country and on their own fighting men."[16]

The temptation to sharpen the division of opinion over the war into a conflict between patriots and traitors was usually resisted by Johnson.

His critics naturally pounced on every slip, such as his reference to Nervous Nellies, but comparison of Johnson's speeches with those of some conservative Republicans and Southern Democrats reveals the difference between public irritation (such as Johnson sometimes expressed) and outright rabble-rousing of a sort that could easily have heated the country to a violent pitch. Passions became violent enough without it. In July some of Johnson's aides told reporters the President felt that an all-out loyalty campaign strategy would win the Democrats forty or fifty seats in the House of Representatives. It is difficult to determine now if that approach might have worked then, but it is clear, at any rate, that Johnson decided against trying it.

As the election approached Johnson began to plan for a last-minute cross-country campaign to districts where Democratic congressmen were in trouble. His aides quickly discovered a certain coolness toward the plan; a lot of embattled congressmen were not really sure a visit by the President would help. Johnson switched to a different strategy. A few weeks before the election he announced he would attend a meeting in Manila with officials from South Vietnam and other allies in late October, a move certain to capture headlines in the final weeks of the campaign. Johnson naturally denied that the election had anything to do with it. The communique issued by the Manila Conference and the seventeen-nation tour which followed it were both, however, long on drama and short on substance. On his way home after the conference, for example, he made a sudden visit to the U.S. military base at Cam Ranh Bay in South Vietnam where he pinned medals on proud military men, including General Westmoreland, and ended the day with a speech in a hot and crowded officer's club during which he said, "I thank you, I salute you, may the Good Lord look over you and keep you until you come home with the coonskin on the wall."[17]

More dramatic and less meaningful still was the communique issued jointly by the governments of the United States, South Vietnam, Australia, New Zealand, Thailand, the Philippines, and South Korea on October 25. The central passage read:

> Allied forces are in the Republic of Vietnam because that country is the object of aggression and its government requested support in the resistance of its people to aggression. They shall be withdrawn as the other side withdraws its forces to the North, ceases infiltration and the level

of violence thus subsides. Those forces will be withdrawn as soon as possible and not later than six months after the above conditions have been fulfilled.[18]

The pledge to withdraw within six months naturally captured the headlines, but it amounted to less of a peace gesture than at first appeared to be the case.

Back in the United States, former Vice President Richard Nixon, who had been campaigning heavily for Republican candidates, delivered a speech on Thursday, November 3, in which he criticized the Manila communique. "The adminisration's current policy resigns America and the free Asian nations to a war which could last five years and cost more casualties than Korea,"[19] he said. This prediction was not without impact since 5,700 Americans had been killed in Vietnam by the time of Nixon's speech, and 35,000 had died in Korea. Nixon had already proposed that Republican and Democratic leaders meet following the election to decide on a joint strategy for winning the war before 1968, a proposal that expressed nominal support for Johnson on Vietnam while implying criticism of the way he conducted himself. This proposal and Nixon's criticism of the Manila communique angered Johnson, who retaliated bitterly in a news conference on Friday, November 4, twice referring to Nixon as a "chronic campaigner," charging he did not know what was going on when he was Vice President and knew even less now, alluding to Nixon's disastrous campaign for the California governorship in 1962, and deriding his attempt to win the Republican presidential nomination against Barry Goldwater in 1964. Obscured in this extraordinary personal attack was a tacit admission that the Manila communique amounted to a pledge to withdraw only after complete victory over Hanoi:

> We have explained that we would pull out just as soon as the infiltration ceases. We made that statement and we set a time limit on it. Why would we want to stay there if there was no aggression, if there was no infiltration, and the violence ceased? We wouldn't want to stay there as tourists.[20]

The attack on Nixon was partly calculated, since Nixon was probably the least popular national figure in the Republican Party, and yet was a symbol of it. The President's bitterness was also the result of personal pique, however. Polls had indicated that the Democrats were going to suffer serious losses and that Johnson's presence in the final days would hurt more candidates than it would help. During his world tour following the Manila Conference, Johnson's aides told reporters of plans for the final campaign swing. When the President returned, however, he issued a brief statement on Thursday, November 3, saying he was scheduled to undergo a minor operation and that his doctor had recommended he begin to cut back on his working day. When reporters wrote that he had "canceled his tour" he was furious, denying at his Friday press conference what every political reporter in Washington knew to be fact, that there had ever been a tour to cancel.

Johnson's efforts to stem the Republican tide persisted until the final moments of the campaign. He had attempted to create a patriotic tableau with his visit to Cam Ranh Bay in October. At the Manila Conference he had made a dramatic but insubstantial peace gesture with his pledge to withdraw American troops within six months after "the violence ceased." During the final weekend before the end of the campaign he made a last attempt to convince the voting public that the price of the war would not go up indefinitely. Secretary of Defense McNamara flew to Texas, where the President was resting up for his announced operation. After conferring with the President, McNamara held a press conference in which he said the American troop buildup in Vietnam would continue during 1967, but at a slower rate than it had during 1966.

This announcement, made on Saturday, November 5, was in fact a piece of fancy numerical footwork, since McNamara's estimate was based on the 385,000 American troops projected for the end of 1966, while the actual troop level on November 5 was about 340,000. Nixon caught the true significance of McNamara's announcement immediately. During a television interview show on Sunday morning, Nixon pointed out, "All he said was that we wouldn't increase next year as much as we did this year. I interpret that to mean we'll have over 500,000 men in Vietnam next year."[21] On election day the Department of Defense quietly conceded that Nixon's guess was correct.

When the election returns were counted on Tuesday, November 8, the result was a clear setback for the Democratic Party and for President Johnson. The loss of forty-seven seats in the House, the very number gained in 1964, was substantially higher than the average off-year loss no matter how far back one went for average figures, and the

Republicans also gained three Senate seats and eight governorships. In the House, where the results were generally thought to reflect most accurately the feeling of the public, conservative forces gained about twenty votes. It was obvious to professional politicians that President Johnson no longer had the political strength to repeat his legislative successes of 1965. Richard Nixon and Michigan Governor George Romney had both emerged from the election considerably strengthened for an assault on Johnson in 1968, and Nixon accurately characterized the vote as "the sharpest rebuff of a President in a generation."[22]

A setback for the President was not necessarily a setback for his Vietnam policies, however. Reading the returns correctly was not easy. Republican leaders were careful to deny the existence of an element of war-weariness in the Republican victory. In Nixon's statement following the election he said he hoped it would be "absolutely clear to Hanoi and Peking that the new House of Representatives will be much stronger than its predecessor as a bulwark of support for a United States policy of 'no reward for aggression.' "[23]

In Dearborn, Michigan, where the war had been the subject of a direct referendum, the vote against immediate withdrawal had been 20,667 to 14,124, at least theoretically a victory for the President. At the same time one could not dismiss the fact that nearly 40 percent of the voters had rejected the leaders of both political parties, voting for an immediate end to the war. In Illinois, Senator Paul Douglas, a leading liberal for a generation, was defeated largely because so many antiwar Democrats, resenting his steadfast support of the President on Vietnam, voted for his opponent, Charles Percy. In Oregon, the defeated Democratic senatorial candidate, Robert B. Duncan, attributed Mark Hatfield's victory to discontent with the war. There was no doubt that Hatfield was opposed to the war, but Hatfield himself had considered his opposition a kind of liability. He had toned it down once the campaign got under way. Further confusing the situation was the fact that Duncan had soundly defeated an outspoken peace candidate for the Democratic nomination.

The elections of 1966 registered an indisputable discontent with the leadership of President Johnson, but failed to say anything unarguable about the war. Opponents of the war who had attempted to make it an open issue in 1966 could point to the near misses of several peace candidates, especially Robert Scheer, but the overall effect was disappointingly vague. None of the local peace campaigns made much impression nationally, and the two major parties remained trapped by the conventions of the Cold War, free to argue about the details of the war, but not about its purpose or necessity. The elections revealed a paradox at the heart of the issue of the war: given no other choice, a majority of the people would vote to fight on rather than give up, and yet this support was illusory. Offered an indirect means of repudiating the war, people would turn against it. A tiny handful of Democratic politicians drew this conclusion and began to plan accordingly for 1968. The organized peace movement, however, doubtful of elections as a means of protest, was hardly satisfied by the indirect rebuff sustained by the President in 1966. They saw the war in sharper terms, were determined that it be decisively rejected, and doubted that any politician would ever find the courage to take an unqualified stand against the war, or could win if he did.

On Saturday, November 5, ten thousand people attended a rally in New York, one of a number held around the country. They were urged to write the single word "peace" on their ballots and leave the rest blank. One large banner read, "You voted in 1964 and got Johnson—why bother?"[24]

Discontent with the war could not easily be ignored at the local level, where every politician was either supported or opposed on the question of the war, but this was not so apparent higher up. Reading the election results in the Oval Office, Johnson might miss the strong feeling in every congressional district. The important fact was not that a majority still supported the war but that a minority existed, was growing, and took the issue very seriously indeed.

Feelings over the war were rising. The President's repeated warnings that criticism of the war only encouraged Hanoi inevitably began to elicit a response. On March 4, for example, Attorney General Nicholas deB. Katzenbach announced that the Subversive Activities Control Board (SACB) was beginning legal proceedings to label the W.E.B. DuBois Clubs a Communist front. The following day the club's Brooklyn chapter attempted to hold a news conference criticizing the SACB but was prevented from doing so when club members were physically assaulted by spectators. City police watched for awhile and then arrested the victims. On March 6 the club headquarters in San Francisco was wrecked by a bomb. On April 9 the Berkeley headquarters of the

Vietnam Day Committee was also bombed. Even more alarming was an incident in Boston on March 31, when seven young opponents of the war were attacked by a mob of high school students on the steps of the South Boston District Court House where the seven had planned to burn their draft cards. Again, police stood idly by during the attack. Pictures of the bleeding victims appeared in newspapers across the country.

Emotion was rising on both sides of the issue. On Monday, November 7, the day before the election, an incident occurred at Harvard which revealed the potential for violence. Opposition to the war was nothing new on the Harvard campus, but argument had been growing steadily more heated. Students felt the war was not just an error of policy, but somehow *wrong*. In October, Norman Thomas, white-haired, frail, and nearly blind, had given a speech about the war in which he said, "If I die before this *terrible* war is ended, I will feel that my whole life's work for decency has been a failure."[25] The incident of November 7 showed that students shared Thomas's passion, but were losing his faith in the power of words alone to change the world.

On that day Secretary McNamara was to meet in an informal session with about fifty students in Quincy House, one of Harvard's residences. Learning of the visit beforehand, the Harvard chapter of SDS had proposed a debate on the war between McNamara and Robert Scheer. The Kennedy Institute of Politics, which was sponsoring McNamara's visit, declined the invitation. SDS mimeographed a series of embarrassing questions and distributed it to students who were to attend the Quincy meeting.

At about 3:30 on the afternoon of the seventh McNamara entered Quincy House. A crowd began to gather around the exits to the building while Scheer, among others, denounced McNamara and the war. "We call Khrushchev the 'Butcher of Budapest' here in the United States," said Scheer, whose speeches on the war had always been reasoned and restrained during his campaign in June. "The United States Air Force has bombed the North Vietnamese city of Vinh out of existence. I think it's time to start calling LBJ the 'Butcher of Vinh.' "[26]

At 4:30, the hour McNamara was scheduled to leave for his next appointment, a limousine pulled out of the Quincy garage and was quickly surrounded by SDS. The rear of the car was empty; organizers of the visit had planned it as a decoy.

While SDS milled around the empty limousine, McNamara was led through the Quincy basement to another gate where a station wagon was waiting for him. Just as the car was about to drive off, a small group of SDS people noticed McNamara and managed to block the car. Another crowd quickly gathered. Students pressed in around the car, began to rock it back and forth, and argued with the Secretary of Defense, who had rolled down his window. SDS leader Mike Ansara reached an agreement with McNamara for the answering of two questions. The first question from the crowd was about civilian casualties in Vietnam. McNamara, now standing outside the car, said, "I'm afraid I don't know how many civilian casualties there have been in the Vietnam conflict."

"Don't you care?" came a shout from the crowd.

The second question dealt with the alleged invasion from North Vietnam.

"The war in Vietnam didn't begin in 1957 as you said in your question," McNamara said. "It began earlier than that, in 1954, when the North Vietnamese sent down cadres to infiltrate with the refugees who were leaving North Vietnam."

"Bullshit," someone shouted.

McNamara's mood abruptly changed. "Look, I went to school at Berkeley and spent four years there doing a lot of the same things you here are doing. I was doing the same things as you are, but there were two big differences. I was *tougher,* and I was more *courteous.* And I'm still *tougher!*"

McNamara said he was leaving and Ansara asked the crowd to let him go, which it did. Like so many others, the incident at Harvard was a failed confrontation, a collision which clarified nothing. But this time it was followed by a sense of shock and horror at the barely suppressed emotional violence. Harvard had always prided itself on its readiness to consider the merits of any argument unemotionally. The McNamara incident struck many in Cambridge as little different from the street politics of Italy and Germany during the rise of Fascism. Thousands of students and faculty signed a petition apologizing to McNamara and even the SDS seemed to feel a little uneasy about what had happened. But not for long. Passions over the war were rising like an inexorable tide. That brief confrontation had better expressed the true feelings of students than all the speeches, debates, editorials, congressional hearings, and elections put together. When language fails, students were beginning to feel, only action is left.

EIGHT

Black Power

As the war in Vietnam continued it reached out to touch ever-wider areas of American life. At times Washington correspondents seemed able to write about nothing else; religious groups debated and passed resolutions attacking, supporting, or reserving judgment on the war; it seemed to show up somewhere in every speech, sermon, book review, editorial, commencement address, or private conversation. The war was argued everywhere in almost identical terms, again and again, until people never wanted to hear another word on the subject. From its beginning the war was emotionally entwined with the civil rights movement, evidence of official determination in ironic contrast to the halting federal efforts to end inequality between the races. On June 11, 1963, the day before the assassination of Medgar Evers and in the midst of a violent black-white political struggle in Birmingham, Alabama, President Kennedy pointed out the obvious inequity in asking black soldiers to defend freedoms abroad that they were denied at home. "Today we are committed to a world-wide struggle to promote and protect the rights of all who wish to be free," he said. "And when Americans are sent to Vietnam or West Berlin we do not ask for whites only."[1]

Despite obvious official inconsistencies, however, the issue of the war was handled carefully by civil rights leaders. Feelings were so passionate that a false step could destroy a reputation or discredit a cause overnight. Most major political figures expressed their doubts about the war obliquely or not at all. Both Morse and Gruening had practically been eliminated from political life by their opposition to the war. The heated reaction to Senator Fulbright's "arrogance of power" speech had forced him into a partial retreat. Walter Lippmann's columns attacking the war resulted in Washington gossip that he was growing senile. The charge of disloyalty, and even treason, faced anyone who spoke out too clearly on Vietnam. Leaders of the civil rights movement, however critical they might be in private, avoided comments in public that would arouse all the enemies of American Negroes and divert attention from black agitation for legal rights and an end to poverty.

On one occasion early in the war Martin Luther King abandoned caution and became the immediate target of a storm of abuse and criticism. Speaking at a meeting of the Southern Christian Leadership Conference held in the Virginia State College football stadium in Petersburg on July 5, 1965, King, a pacifist, said:

> I'm not going to sit by and see war escalated without saying anything about it. . . . It is worthless to talk about integration if there is no world to integrate in. I am certainly as concerned about seeing the defeat of Communism as anyone else, but we won't defeat Communism by guns or bombs or gases. We will do it by making democracy work. . . . The war in Vietnam must be stopped. There must be a negotiated settlement even with the Vietcong.[2]

Following the speech King was called by members of the administration who "explained" the President's position on the war. He found a sudden coolness on the part of previous supporters like Governor Rockefeller of New York. Later, he was convinced that this speech led the FBI to resume the tapping of his telephone. If his statement had evoked a responsive chord from more than a passionate minority, King would have continued to speak out on the subject. Instead he found near unanimity that the war was too explosive to deal with. As a result he backed away from the issue, although making no attempt to disguise his private feelings about it. It was not until eighteen months later, when the war had reached gigantic proportions and the civil rights movement had split down the center, that King again spoke out against the war, claiming that it was the major obstacle blocking domestic reform in the United States.

The civil rights movement was not unusual in its caution when dealing with the war. The issue was explosively divisive and the churches, the labor movement, universities, political clubs, and even some pacifist organizations often tried to avoid it. The alternative was generally a bruising debate producing hard feelings and, at best, a precisely worded statement soon forgotten. Most of the institutions in American society were touched only tangentially by the war, but the civil rights movement was affected directly in ways that finally made the issue impossible to ignore. Young activists, most of them college dropouts, were increasingly subject to the draft as the war continued and the number of American troops in Vietnam steadily grew. Movement workers deeply involved in the struggle for voting rights in the South, their lives often in danger, could not understand why they should be torn away from their work and sent halfway around the world in a doubtful cause. "I am not looked upon as an equal citizen in everyday life," said a black activist named John Otis Sumrall at a conference on the draft held in Chicago in December, 1966. "Why am I looked upon as an equal citizen when it comes time for me to report for induction? . . . I would feel just like the KKK over there. Denying those people freedom of choice, just like black people are denied freedom of choice in the U.S."[3]

A number of activists sought exemptions as conscientious objectors but found that their local draft boards, especially in the South, and still more especially in the case of blacks, were hard to convince. Even in New York draft boards were reluctant to grant CO status to civil rights workers. David Nolan, a veteran of several hard-fought campaigns in Virginia who was registered in New York City, was questioned about his application at a hearing on April 18, 1967. He was asked if he was not simply afraid to go to Vietnam. He said no, he had often been physically threatened, and had found a bomb on the porch of his home in Lawrenceville, Virginia, just two weeks earlier. He was then asked what he would do if personally attacked. Nothing, he said; he had been beaten by some Ku Klux Klansmen not long before and had not retaliated. A pugnacious board member asked how he knew his attackers were Klansmen. Nolan said the attack occurred at a Klan rally and his attackers were wearing Klan robes. He was classified 1A and drafted.

It was impossible for the movement to see the draft as anything other than a direct assault upon its work. The rest of America had ignored racial injustice for years, activists felt, and now the young men who were trying to do what had been left undone were being impressed into the army. Movement workers also knew that the war was costing huge sums of money desperately needed to alleviate poverty at home. Like the rest of the country, the civil rights movement had no clear position on the war when it first began to escalate, but unlike the rest of the country they could not ignore the issue. It struck too close to home. The eventual result was a generational and ideological split within the movement, an exaggerated collision between left and right, which prefigured, and to some extent even caused, the more basic division which gradually emerged in the country as a whole.

The importance of this split in the civil rights movement is hard to overstate, because of its immediate effects on the white student movement and on the Democratic Party. The party was, of course, a broad coalition of many interest groups, from Southern plantation owners to New York intellectuals. Some sections of the party were hostile to the civil rights movement and some indifferent, but the mind and heart of the party, its most committed and articulate members, felt the movement raised questions of conscience too important to avoid. If the war had touched only Vietnam, President Johnson might have retained control of his party. When it alienated the civil rights movement and starved domestic programs of funds, the party split. In the same way, the struggle within the civil rights movement was reflected in the white, middle-class student movement, where the logic of events and the example of blacks turned moderates into radicals, and radicals into revolutionaries. The war was one of those things that come along once in a generation and call entire societies into question, forcing people to choose between irreconcilables. Just as militant young blacks split with their more cautious elders, student activists turned against the Democratic Party because even its most liberal leaders refused to break completely with Johnson's policies in Vietnam. At a meeting of the Harvard Young Democrats in March, 1967, for example, Mike Kazin and another student on the club's executive committee introduced a resolution favoring immediate withdrawal from Vietnam. After it was overwhelmingly defeated, Kazin read the following statement and then walked out:

> An organization which does not take a clear position in favor of immediate and unconditional withdrawal of the American occupying army which is in Vietnam fighting the Vietnamese people cannot possibly be a vehicle for significant or radical political change in the United States.

The Young Democrats speak about working within the system, but, contrary to the usual argument, this method will yield fewer practical results than independent action outside. I will be quitting the Young Democrats to be able to devote my full time to SDS, which is the only organization on campus which I believe is seriously committed to changing American society.[4]

It is important to understand how the civil rights movement split on issues intimately connected with the war because the process was repeated endlessly, with less publicity and narrower results, throughout American society. The struggle in the movement tended to focus on the ‑ole played by Martin Luther King because his importance as a leader as undeniable. He was sensitive to the deeper contradictions in American life and the iniquity of the war, but never diluted his commitment to Christian pacifism, integration of the races, and the possibility of spiritually redeeming American society. The resentment of King, at first tentative and discreet, centered in the Student Non-Violent Coordinating Committee, which organized the first sit-ins, participated in the Freedom Rides, and then undertook a major effort to win voting rights throughout the Deep South. By the end of 1964 SNCC was in a confused, exhausted state, torn by the breakdown between whites and blacks during the Mississippi Summer Project, and drained by the organizational strain of bringing a thousand young white students into a hostile state. Perhaps more important, but less noticeable, was the gradual disillusionment of SNCC activists who had worked so hard for so little. Four years of agitation had won the right to sit at lunch counters, or to use white restrooms, or to stay in motels. Nevertheless, northern whites sometimes seemed to think these were great concessions and that seeking anything more was "pushing too far, too fast."

Three years of fighting for the right to vote had brought the registration of only a handful of Negroes, and in Mississippi political power was still a white privilege. Blacks had been beaten and killed for seeking basic rights that should have been theirs for a century. The FBI refused to protect them, the Democratic Party refused to seat them in Atlantic City, liberals told them to move slowly, conservatives told them the government could do nothing, and the white South told them never. The result was just what one would expect, a bitterness that turned them against the very society they once had sought to reform. Early in 1965 the columnists Evans and Novak began to attack SNCC for leftist tendencies, implying darkly that the organization was being infiltrated by Communists. This melodramatic view only obscured the changes that were in fact taking place. SNCC was not being infiltrated, but was changing internally as the direct result of five years of struggle.

Throughout this period SNCC had been of two minds about Martin Luther King, who was religious and respectably middle class, who lived and dressed well, who often met with high government officials, including the President, and whose politics were infused with the Christian ideal of brotherhood and reconciliation. During the huge Washington rally held in August, 1963, bitter and cynical young SNCC activists ridiculed King's later famous "I have a dream" speech. It seemed to them altogether typical that Washington's Catholic Archbishop Patrick O'Boyle, a participant in the rally, should insist on toning down a much stronger speech by SNCC's chairman, John Lewis. When King finished speaking the white liberals on the speakers' stand applauded loudly. When Lewis finished they stared blankly out over the audience. In 1965, SNCC's long-fermenting suspicion and resentment of King took on an edge of true hostility.

SNCC had been active for some time in Selma, Alabama, slowly creating local organizations which began to press for voting rights, jobs, and an end to segregation. When these attempts were violently resisted by Sheriff Jim Clark's deputies using bull whips, billy clubs and cattle prods, the local Selma groups decided to ask King's help, a move that SNCC inevitably resented. National attention was drawn to Selma when King arrived on January 8, 1965, and began leading marches to the Selma courthouse. Eventually King called for a march to the state capitol in Montgomery, fifty-two miles away, on Sunday, March 7. The march was forbidden by Alabama's Governor George Wallace, but 650 people marched anyway, although King was absent. When the group reached the Edmund Pettus Bridge on Selma's outskirts it was attacked by Clark's mounted deputies and by state troopers, who used tear gas and clubs in a brutal assault vividly reported across the country.

An emergency call for support brought four hundred clergymen to Selma for a second march along the same route, called for Tuesday, March 9. Passions had risen to a pitch just short of hysteria. King's nonviolence was not shaken then, or ever, but SNCC activists who had been beaten repeatedly over the years, who had founded the Selma movement, and who had been attacked on Sunday while King was safely out of town, were angry as they had never been angry before. A court order prohibiting the march had been issued, but King, sensing the determination around him, decided to defy the order. On the appointed day the group marched to the bridge, crossed it, came to a halt before a line of police, and then hesitated. Finally King called on the group to turn back, to go home, to be patient, to wait until the courts were on their side. Young movement activists never forgave him.

At the same time, however, the events in Selma had a pivotal effect on the push for new voting rights legislation. Before a joint session of Congress on March 15, President Johnson committed the nation to guarantee the vote:

> The Constitution says that no person shall be kept from voting because of his race or his color. We have all sworn an oath before God to support and defend that Constitution. We must now act in obedience to that oath. ... This time, on this issue, there must be no delay, no hesitation and no compromise with our purpose.[5]

He said this was a challenge the country could not fail to meet, and then, slowly emphasizing his words, he added: *"And ... we ... shall ... overcome."* The bill he introduced, probably the most effective civil rights legislation ever passed in the United States, was signed into law on August 6, setting a kind of record for legislative speed.

The voting rights bill represented a complete victory for the voting rights strategy adopted by SNCC just four years earlier. For the first time since passage of Jim Crow legislation at the turn of the century, Southern Negroes could register to vote with something approaching freedom. SNCC ought to have been elated, but its reaction was somewhat different. They were infuriated when Johnson adopted their slogan, "We shall overcome." They argued that the law was one hundred years too late and said racism was too deeply imbedded into American life to be affected by the vote. During the following year SNCC gradually abandoned its political programs and at the same time began to shrink in size. At the end of 1964 SNCC had a full-time staff of about 225 and an annual budget of $700,000. A year later the staff had dropped to 135, field workers had been taken off the payroll, Freedom Schools were closed, and SNCC began its strange retreat from the struggle it had begun. Many former SNCC staffers stayed on in Mississippi and Alabama, of course, but the organization as a whole began to wither at the very moment of its triumph.

Something similar was happening to the rest of the civil rights movement at the same time. The Selma-to-Montgomery march which finally
took place on March 21 marked a kind of end to the civil rights movement as it had existed up until that time. The movement's moral
passion had been directed at real and specific injustice, most of it in the
South. For ten years after the Montgomery bus boycott the movement
had struggled against clearly unconstitutional discrimination against
Negroes in the South. With the passage of the voting rights bill, that
struggle ended in victory, but those who had taken part in the movement had begun to realize that the problems that Negroes faced in
American life went far beyond legal discrimination.

The movement, perfectly suited to rouse a nation's conscience, was
a clumsy instrument when it came to proposing detailed legislative
programs to end poverty, reform education, create jobs, train the un-
skilled, and the like. The civil rights movement did not retreat into
inactivity, but the new programs it adopted did not lend themselves to
mass demonstrations, confrontations with the police, and emotional
calls for justice where justice had been clearly and concretely denied.
The goals of the movement necessarily changed but its highly charged
moral passion did not. Their strength in the beginning had been their
ability to see injustice where others saw only custom. Now they began
to see injustice on a broader, at times on almost a theological scale. In
these changed circumstances one wing of the movement undertook
day-to-day organizing which attracted little attention, but another
wing, small, intense, and articulate, began to describe the movement's
ultimate goal as revolution.

After the passage of the voting rights act most of SNCC's energy was
spent on internal struggles over three basic questions: reform versus
revolution, the role of whites in the movement, and the war in Vietnam.
Five years of struggle had taught SNCC that the nation, not just the
South, was racist; that it was violent, that it was willing to ignore the
Constitution, that the rich did not care about the poor. The effect of
this knowledge was crippling. Instead of making SNCC more effective,
anger made it confused and irresolute. By 1965 SNCC found it hard to
fight for things because it did not really believe America offered anything worth fighting for. The obvious way out of this impasse was
revolution, but such a course created problems of its own. Since blacks
formed only 10 percent of the U.S. population, and since the United
States was fundamentally stable, the prospects for a SNCC-led, or even

SNCC-approved, revolution were dim indeed. As a result, SNCC, like other activist groups in other eras, turned into a debating society. Less and less time was spent on community organizing, and more on arguing ideological questions with a maximum potential for dissension and a minimum for practical result.

At a meeting in Atlanta in November, 1965, where revolution, the war, and the role of whites in the movement were all heatedly argued, Bob Moses concluded that SNCC was dead or dying. Moses's basic organizing aim had always been to encourage local leadership, to convince ordinary people they could control their own lives and in that way help the oppressed to find their own liberation. In rural Mississippi he had helped Negroes to create their own movements for their own ends; he was deeply suspicious of any attempt to tell people what they ought to want, or even how they ought to go about getting what they wanted. There is a contradiction implicit in Moses's attitude, since complete reliance on local initiative would have kept him from going to Mississippi at all.

Moses was distressed by SNCC's tendency to argue rather than organize, by its steadily widening distance from the people, by the increasing harshness and futility of its rhetoric. Finally Moses walked out of the November meeting during an interminable dispute over a minor point and then came back an hour later in a strange, passionate mood. He tried to explain what he thought was going wrong. "The longer you sit here in this church and argue," he said, "the more the movement is passing you by."[6] Other SNCC members were inclined to think they *were* the movement; how could it pass them by? For Moses the principal sin of an activist was pride. He sensed the same pressures at work in himself to be a leader, to make statements, to issue manifestos, to embody the aspirations of the people, to negotiate, maneuver, deal, and compromise. The heart of the movement was the people, Moses felt, the poor sharecroppers and jobless blacks in ghettos. The "leaders" were only passing through. For awhile SNCC and the people meant the same thing by freedom, but now SNCC meant something else. SNCC would have insisted that it still represented the deepest interests of the people, but for Moses this was a cruel sophistry and a contradiction. The people might be powerless, but their humanity was sacred. *Their* aspirations were what mattered, not SNCC's notion of what they needed. What the people wanted was simple, and SNCC was growing complex. They were leaving the countryside to argue ideology in borrowed churches.

The rest of SNCC did not seem to grasp Moses's point. He abruptly gave up, left the meeting and SNCC, broke off his friendships with all whites, changed his name, and disappeared. Not even his oldest friends quite understood what had happened, but it was clear SNCC would never be the same. Moses had represented the soul of the early movement and its almost mystical faith in ordinary people leading ordinary lives. The existential focus on the immediate in people's lives, on what they felt about themselves and wanted from the world, disappeared with Moses. From that moment on SNCC became a traditional political organization, an elite cadre with its own ends, keeping its own counsel. Everything was done in the name of the people, of course, but the people did not participate.

In the wake of Moses's departure SNCC, like the rest of the country, was gradually drawn ever more deeply into the issue of the war. SNCC members had been suspicious of the war since the initial troop buildups announced by President Kennedy in the late fall of 1961. One of the principal points made by newsmen in Saigon during 1962 and 1963 had been that Diem was hated by the Vietnamese people, and that the Vietcong's revolutionary program enjoyed wide support in the Vietnamese countryside. SNCC naturally sympathized with what they saw as a rural reform movement by nonwhites. When the bombing of North Vietnam began in 1965 they, like everyone else connected with the movement, found themselves on the side of the small, backward country being bombarded by a large, industrial country.

SNCC people often commented bitterly on the way white activists had switched their concern from civil rights to the war (overlooking the black resentment that had encouraged them to do so), but at the same time they were also drawn in the same direction. Individually, SNCC people had been active in the opposition from the beginning. Moses himself took part in the Berkeley teach-in held in May, 1965, and in the Assembly of Unrepresented People in Washington in August. That summer John D. Shaw, a young movement activist who had taken part in demonstrations in McComb, Mississippi, in 1961, was killed in Vietnam. The McComb Freedom Democratic Party circulated a petition calling on young Negroes to refuse to fight in Vietnam while their families were oppressed in Mississippi. The petition cited a young white

soldier who was discharged from the army after he went on a hunger
strike and had refused to fight in Vietnam.

> Negro boys can do the same thing. We can write and ask our sons if they
> know what they are fighting for. If he answers freedom, tell him that's
> what we are fighting for here in Mississippi. And if he says Democracy
> tell him the truth—we don't know anything about Communism, social-
> ism and all that, but we do know that Negroes have caught hell here
> under this American Democracy.[7]

At its staff meeting that November, SNCC debated whether or not
to come out against the war, finally deciding not to on the ground that
it might cost the support of white Northern liberals. On January 3,
1966, however, a SNCC activist named Sammy Younge was murdered
in Tuskegee, Alabama, when he attempted to use the white restroom
at a gas station. SNCC's executive committee was meeting in Atlanta
at the time of the murder, and it immediately decided to issue a major
statement. The relationship of the war to the civil rights movement,
long a subject of private discussion by activists, was stressed in the
statement that John Lewis read to reporters in Atlanta on the afternoon
of January 6:

> The murder of Samuel Younge in Tuskegee, Alabama, is no different
> than the murder of people in Vietnam, for both Younge and the Viet-
> namese sought, and are seeking, to secure the rights guaranteed them by
> law. In each case, the United States government bears a great part of the
> responsibility for these deaths. Samuel Younge was murdered because
> United States law is not being enforced. Vietnamese are murdered be-
> cause the United States is pursuing an aggressive policy in violation of
> international law. . . . We ask: where is the draft for the freedom fight
> in the United States? We, therefore, encourage those Americans who
> prefer to use their energy in building democratic forms within this coun-
> try. We believe that work in the civil rights movement is a valid alterna-
> tive to the draft. We urge all Americans to seek this alternative, knowing
> full well that it may cost them their lives—as painfully as in Vietnam.[8]

SNCC's statement said it was "in sympathy with" and "supported"
those who were "unwilling to respond to the military draft."[9] This fell
considerably short of urging young men to refuse induction, but reporters interpreted SNCC's position as being sharper than it really was. The
headline on the front page of the *Atlanta Constitution* for January 7

read, "DEFY DRAFT CALL, SNCC CHIEF URGES." The headline on page 12 said, "SNCC LEADER AND LEGISLATOR BACK DRAFT CARD BURNINGS." The legislator was Julian Bond, a SNCC activist elected to the state legislature from Atlanta the previous fall. The legislature was predictably outraged and voted on Monday, January 9, to refuse Bond his seat. The action brought a legal battle which lasted nearly a year before the United States Supreme Court finally ruled, on December 5, 1966, that the legislature did not have the right to exclude Bond for something he had said.

Once SNCC had broken publicly with the government on the war, its drift toward radicalism was rapid. The moderate expression of "support" for Americans who preferred civil rights work to the army was followed by a stronger statement in June, jointly issued by Stokely Carmichael and Carl Oglesby of SDS, calling for an outright termination of the draft. By August, SNCC was holding demonstrations outside the Atlanta induction center which gave wide currency to the slogan, "Hell no, we won't go."[10] In October, Carmichael stated publicly that he would go to Leavenworth before he would join the army. Many SNCC activists did, in fact, refuse induction, and their example was to have an important effect on white activists a year later.

While SNCC was beginning to speak out against the war it was also grappling with the problem presented by the presence of whites in a black movement. As early as November, 1963, during a three-day meeting in Greenville, Mississippi, SNCC had debated the role of whites in the movement. Like other activist groups, SNCC had moved steadily toward the left, a tendency that put whites into an awkward position: they either resisted the tendency, which could be said to imply a lingering degree of sentimental allegiance to white society, or they encouraged the drift in order to demonstrate the depth of their commitment to the black cause. Either way, whites found themselves in an unnatural situation where their motives were easily suspect.

The Mississippi Summer Project, which threw a thousand young whites trailing clouds of publicity into the arms of several hundred uncelebrated blacks, added to black resentment of whites in the movement, which was not, after all, *their* movement. Cultural differences only made things worse. Negroes did not feel at ease around highly educated, middle-class, often breathlessly idealistic young whites. One problem was that these whites tended to be better at things that required organizational efficiency. Another was that the experiences of black activists had embittered them against whites in general, something they could not freely express around white sympathizers, for obvious reasons. Whites idealized what they felt was a unique freedom from racism on the part of blacks, and yet many young black activists, embittered by years of struggle, in fact hated whites as whites. Most important, however, was the fact that white activists simply did not comprehend the poor rural Negroes SNCC was trying to help. Confronted by their diffidence, whites tended to be brisk and overbearing, telling people to register just as other whites had told them all their lives not to register.

During the winter and early spring of 1966 a number of SNCC people, including Stokely Carmichael, worked on a position paper to be delivered at the organization's annual meeting scheduled for May 8 to 15 in Nashville, Tennessee. Carmichael had become increasingly suspicious of the influence of whites in black organizations, seeing it as a subtle attempt to keep blacks from going too far. He once said at a meeting in Atlanta he had never known a white organization he could trust. A young white activist who considered himself Carmichael's friend rose to ask, "Not one, Stokeley?"

Carmichael answered with cold precision: "No—not one."[11]

This feeling was fully expressed in the position paper that Carmichael and Bill Ware presented at the Nashville meeting attended by almost all of SNCC's 135 staff members, 25 of whom were white. Called the Vine City Project Paper on "Whites in the Movement," it associated white control of black organizations with colonialism, referred to historical white fear of violence whenever blacks began to organize, and began to ask clearly, for the first time, all but unanswerable questions:

> We have dealt stringently with the problem of "Uncle Tom," but we have not yet gotten around to Simon Legree. We must ask ourselves, who is the real villain? Uncle Tom or Simon Legree? . . . Whites are the ones who must try to raise themselves to our humanistic level. We are not, after all, the ones who are responsible for a neo-colonialism in Africa and Latin America; we are not the ones who held a people in animalistic bondage over 400 years. We reject the American dream as defined by white people and must work to construct an American reality defined by Afro-Americans.[12]

SNCC was no longer in a mood to see the problem in a Christian perspective like that of Martin Luther King, who said that history had hardened the hearts of Southern whites, and that Christian love could soften them. SNCC saw things in a harsher light. Whites either urged forgiveness and reconciliation, a position with which SNCC no longer felt any instinctive sympathy, or agreed with the emerging SNCC sense of whites as cruel and irredeemable, which naturally led one to wonder just exactly what they thought of themselves. The problem had been quiescent so long as SNCC concentrated on concrete grievances such as voting rights; when it began taking sharp ideological positions on broad issues, whites and blacks were thrown unavoidably into conflict.

The Nashville meeting was repeatedly disrupted by violent emotional outbursts. One black field secretary suggested that SNCC subsidize one hundred blacks who would study nuclear physics and then emigrate to Africa where they would supervise the construction of nuclear weapons for an attack on the United States. How could white SNCC people respond to that?

The chairman of SNCC, John Lewis, was reelected during the Nashville meeting but after Lewis said he planned to attend the White House Conference on Civil Rights scheduled for June 1–2, a second vote was called for. This time Lewis was defeated by Carmichael. One white SNCC member, Jack Minnis, was elected to a policy-making position as a concession to moderates, but in fact he ceased to play a serious role in the group's deliberations. By the end of the Nashville meeting SNCC's white members had, in effect, been expelled from the group. Carmichael's first act as SNCC's new chairman was to issue an angry statement refusing to take part in the White House conference and denouncing the war.

The fragmentation of the civil rights movement, and the alienation of a large segment from American society, was carried a major step further that June during a hastily organized, chaotic, and acrimonious three-week march through rural Mississippi. James Meredith, who in 1962 had become the first Negro to attend the University of Mississippi, returned to the state in June, 1966, vowing to walk the 220 miles from Memphis, Tennessee, to Jackson, Mississippi. On the second day of his "walk against fear," Monday, June 6, just two miles South of Hernando, Mississippi, on U.S. Highway 61, Meredith was shot and wounded in the back by a man hiding in the brush beside the road. First reports circulated by the Associated Press said Meredith had been killed. Leaders of civil rights organizations across the country immediately pledged to complete the walk and began arriving in Memphis on Tuesday.

Among those at a rally that night held in Memphis's Centenary Methodist Church were Martin Luther King, Roy Wilkins, Whitney Young, Floyd McKissick, and Stokely Carmichael, who told the audience of about a thousand, "I'm not going to beg the white man for anything I deserve. I'm going to take it."[13] That was enough for Wilkins, Young, and other moderates, who quietly abandoned the march before it got under way. When a march manifesto was released the following day calling for federal voting registrars in six hundred Southern counties and a "freedom budget" of billions to help poor Negroes, their names were missing.

The marchers, ranging in number from as few as fifty to several hundred, walked from Memphis to Grenada and then made a long detour through the Mississippi Delta counties where Negroes were often in the majority of every category except that of registered voters. From the beginning an air of suppressed violence touched the march and a running rhetorical battle was fought between the SCLC and SNCC. In Batesville on Friday night, June 11, the Reverend Ralph Abernathy of SCLC said, "If you got any notions that Negroes can solve our problems by ourselves, you got another thought coming. We welcome white people." He paused and then asked the crowd, "Ain't that right?" The crowd shouted back, "That's right!"[14] SCLC publicly welcomed white supporters who joined the march, while SNCC members disagreed, sometimes chanting, "Ho, ho, whattaya know, white folks gotta go!"[15]

In Greenwood on June 17, SNCC's violent mood began to emerge clearly. At a rally in front of the Leflore County Courthouse in Greenwood, Hosea Williams urged the crowd, "Get that vote and pin that badge on a black chest. Get that vote. . . . Whip that policeman across the head."

King, standing next to him, interjected, "He means with the vote."

"They know what he means,"[16] insisted Carmichael, who that day had been arrested for the twenty-seventh time and freed on $100 bail.

That night Carmichael transformed the movement with a phrase. "We're asking Negroes not to go to Vietnam and fight but to stay in

Greenwood and fight here," he said at a rally. "If they put one of us in jail, we're not going to pay bond to get him out. We're going up there and get him out ourselves. . . . We need black power." Then, shouting to the crowd, he asked, "What do we want?"

"Black power!" the crowd shouted back.

"*What do we want?*"

"BLACK POWER!"[17]

At a rally in front of the Sunflower County Courthouse in Indianola four days later, Abernathy asked another crowd what it wanted. "Black power!" the crowd shouted. "Say 'freedom,'" commanded Abernathy. "Freedom!" shouted the crowd.[18]

King sensed the powerful appeal in SNCC's new militance, but knew the slogan "black power" could easily unite the white 90 percent of America against the black 10 percent. In Yazoo City on the night of June 22, he spent five fruitless hours trying to persuade Carmichael to abandon the black power slogan, suggesting "black equality" as an alternative. Carmichael refused.

As a result of the march, which ended in Jackson on Sunday, June 26, black power immediately became *the* issue of the movement and sparked a continuing struggle between those with broad, militant aims and those with narrow, conventional goals, a struggle that ultimately destroyed the movement as a movement.

SNCC's move to the left was not shallow or perverse, but simply a response to what its own members had done, seen, and learned. Their growing sense of themselves as revolutionaries in a society too deeply flawed for reform had a strong effect on white activists, who went through a similar process in much the same way, for much the same reasons. A paradoxical effect of SNCC's self-transformation was that it won greater national attention at the very moment it was retreating from the field organizing with which it had begun. In 1967 SNCC's highly visible revolutionary anger was an important element in the political climate of the entire country. By the end of 1968 the group had all but disappeared.

SNCC's transformation came as the movement began to expand beyond the limits of the old South. Rioting in black Northern ghettos in the summers of 1964, 1965, and 1966 forced movement leaders to turn their attention to the far deeper and more intractable problems posed by poverty and social disintegration in the cities. The contradiction of

American devotion to freedom in Vietnam and indifference to it in Mississippi was bad enough. Still worse was the diversion of money from the war on poverty to the war in Vietnam.

In the fall of 1965 King began organizing a major campaign in Chicago, where tens of thousands of depressed Southern blacks had gone looking for the Promised Land. Instead, they found discrimination, joblessness, and physically decaying slums where families and people were relentlessly broken down. King knew that anger was building in Northern ghettos, hoped the war on poverty might begin to change the lives of the black urban masses, and was increasingly disturbed as promised funds failed to appear. "Where your heart is," he said as the Chicago movement was getting under way, "is where your money is. I fear, with the escalation of the war, a cutdown and damage to the social programs here. Do we love the war on poverty, or do we love the war in Vietnam?"[19]

The first broad initiative of the Johnson administration had been the war on poverty, an issue congenial to Johnson's populist instinct. He had supported the New Deal strongly and had proposed a number of federal programs to alleviate poverty in rural Texas when he first went to Washington. Kennedy had planned to make poverty a major issue in 1964, and after his death Johnson turned this embryonic concern into a coherent, ambitious program which he announced in his first State of the Union Message on January 8, 1964:

> This administration today, here and now, declares unconditional war on poverty in America. . . . It will not be a short or easy struggle, no single weapon or strategy will suffice, but we shall not rest until that war is won. . . . [We] must pursue poverty, pursue it wherever it exists—in city slums and small towns, in share-cropper shacks or in migrant-worker camps, on Indian reservations, among whites as well as Negroes, among the young as well as the aged, in the boom towns and in the depressed areas.[20]

This went a long way beyond Kennedy's speeches on poverty in Appalachia during the 1960 presidential campaign. Johnson had referred to virtually every major category of poverty in America, and it was not long before the poor learned about his declaration. The hopes raised so high then were to be a continuing source of anger and bitterness later. The Economic Opportunity Act of 1964 was passed by the Senate in July and by the House in August, but the first funds were not actually appropriated until October and the first program was not announced until November 25. All the while, Johnson was expanding still further his plans for broad domestic reform, announcing in a speech at the University of Michigan on May 22 that he planned to carry America "not only toward the rich society and the powerful society, but upward to the great society."[21]

It is hard to exaggerate just what a huge undertaking the war on poverty was, how high it raised hopes, or how seriously it was taken by many of Johnson's strongest and most articulate supporters. Kennedy's election had reawakened a dream of active and enlightened government, a faith in what men could do once they determined to control the conditions of their lives. Johnson, possibly the greatest legislator in American history, seemed the right man in the right place at the right time to engineer something close to a renaissance in American society. Johnson was criticized heavily from the left, of course, but his domination of the center in late 1964 was secure. There were a good many people who believed that the United States had reached one of those qualitative turning points in its history, that the combined efforts to end poverty and racial injustice might end a century-long struggle and open the way to an altogether new sort of national life.

As it was conceived and carried out, however, the war on poverty disappointed the people it was intended to help in two major ways. First, it had promised that individual programs would be run with the "maximum feasible participation" of the poor. Local political organizations were happy to have the 90–10 matching funds for community action programs, but did not like to share their control, particularly since so many programs were aimed at unresponsive, and occasionally downright oppressive, local governments.

At the annual conference of mayors in June, 1965, Sam Yorty and John F. Shelley, the mayors of Los Angeles and San Francisco, accused the Office of Economic Opportunity (OEO) and its director, Sargent Shriver, of "fostering a class struggle."[22] Robert Wagner in New York and Richard Daley in Chicago took a similar position. This, of course, was inevitable, since the problem of poverty is partly the problem of political power and OEO funds provided exactly the sort of patronage on which political organizations are built. City councilmen, state legislators, and even congressmen throughout the country took office thanks to the support of OEO-funded community groups in the following years. It could be, and was, argued that this proved the seriousness of the war on poverty, but it was not an argument likely to impress those already in power. As a result, entrenched politicians resisted "maximum feasible participation," with increasing success, and the poor in many areas reluctantly concluded that things were not, after all, going to change.

The second and more important way in which the war on poverty disappointed the poor was by raising hopes which Congress would not pay for. In its first fiscal year, during which the OEO was active for only seven months, it received $800 million. During its second year, from July, 1965, until June, 1966, it was appropriated $1.5 billion. During its third year, the administration requested $1.75 billion and Congress appropriated $1.61 billion, which actually represented a decrease in the rate of spending. At a news conference on November 22, 1966, only five months into OEO's third year, Shriver outlined the cutbacks in programs which were going to be necessary because of the low appropriation. "The poor will feel they have been shortchanged," he said. "They will feel they have been double-crossed. The poor will feel that democracy is only for the rich."[23]

The single most important cause for under-financing of the war on poverty was the steadily rising cost of the war in Vietnam. In OEO's second fiscal year the war had cost $4.7 billion. When the administration submitted its budget for fiscal 1967 it estimated that the war would cost about $10 billion. The director of the Bureau of the Budget, Charles L. Schultze, testified before the Joint Economic Committee of Congress on February 2, 1966, warning that it was difficult to predict expenditures because of the inherently uncertain situation in Vietnam:

> We face the year ahead with a substantially different set of conditions than those under which previous budgets in recent years have been formulated. The major factor, of course, is the economic impact of the conflict in Vietnam. The cost of these operations will add some $10.5 billion to federal expenditures between 1965 and 1967. . . . At the same time, the 1967 budget had to be formulated under conditions of great uncertainty. No one can honestly claim to predict with accuracy the course of future events in Vietnam. We have presented budget estimates which reflect all the costs of Vietnam operations as we can best foresee them.[24]

This was not exactly the case. In December, with the off-year elections over, McNamara admitted that the true cost of the war during fiscal 1967 would be approximately $20 billion. He blandly explained that the original low estimate was the result of an assumption, made only for purposes of budgeting, that the war would end on June 30, 1967, the last day of fiscal 1967. In fact, the cost of the war had simply been hidden for a year. The cost of the war in fiscal 1968 and fiscal 1969 continued to rise, with the inevitable results. Administration promises that the United States could afford both guns and butter were hollow. The $20 and $30 billion a year cost of the war in Vietnam inevitably put a severe financial strain on the U.S. government which could not be disguised indefinitely by bookkeeping alone. Huge deficits accumulated and eventually, in the summer of 1967, Johnson was forced to ask for a 10 percent tax surcharge to pay for the war. Conservatives in Congress, knowing they had the President at a disadvantage, insisted that he cut back social programs of every sort before they would grant him the new taxes he needed. The war on poverty was still the most important initiative in social engineering ever undertaken in the United States, but compared to the war in Vietnam it was a second thought.

As important as the actual shift in funds from this country to Southeast Asia was the shift in governmental concern. On June 4, 1965, before the war had begun to command the best efforts of everyone in the Johnson administration, the President made a speech at Howard University in Washington in which he pledged to make the final efforts necessary to guarantee American Negroes true equality. Ending the denial of legal rights was only half the problem, he said.

> For the great majority of Negro Americans—the poor, the unemployed, the uprooted and dispossessed—there is a much grimmer story. They still are another nation. Despite the court order and the laws, despite the legislative victories and the speeches, for them the walls are rising and the gulf is widening.[25]

Johnson had implicitly recognized not only the injustice, but the danger, in allowing black Americans to continue in their inferior status. His pledge to raise them to the level where they would have not merely the legal right, but a genuinely fair chance, to compete for the good things of life alongside whites was as bold a governmental initiative as any in the nation's history. He had called for a White House conference in November, later postponed, under the theme, "To Fulfill These Rights." By the time the conference opened on June 1, 1966, however, Johnson and his administration were preoccupied by the war. The poverty program never again received the sort of top-level, undivided attention that alone might have made it work. During an appearance on CBS television on April 19, shortly after returning from his world tour following the Honolulu conference, Vice President Humphrey said the war offered an opportunity "for realizing the dream of the Great Society in the great area of Asia. . . ."[26] The absurd presumption of this statement might have served as the epitaph of the war on poverty at home. For perhaps eighteen months the war on poverty was first in Johnson's mind; after that the insoluble dilemmas of the war in Vietnam demanded more, and finally all, of his attention. Even so, the war on poverty has in fact achieved far more than its critics on the left have been willing to concede, but in 1966 its successes were overshadowed by the bitter irony of the incomparably greater American effort in Vietnam. If there had been no war, activists at home might have been more tolerant of the false starts and setbacks of the war on poverty. The poor had been always with us, after all, and the human dimensions of the problem were immense. The war made such tolerance impossible.

The civil rights leaders who attended the White House conference were predictably angry. They argued that the federal government was not adequately enforcing the laws it had already passed, that Mississippi Negroes still risked violence when they tried to register and vote, that the "flexible guidelines" of the U.S. Office of Education were flexible enough to include segregation, that the FBI was not interested in crimes against blacks, that the war was using up funds which should have been spent solving domestic problems. One section of the conference passed a resolution that, "The ingenuity, energy and resources of this country must be redirected and devoted to the building of new towns [in the South] and not to villages in Vietnam."[27] A vote on a clear antiwar resolution proposed by CORE's Floyd McKissick was initially ruled out of order by the section chairman, who said, "I don't want to put that albatross around the civil rights movement."[28] When the vote was finally held, McKissick's resolution was soundly defeated by other civil rights leaders who felt they had trouble enough without antagonizing the President.

The frustrated mood of the conference participants was captured in a remark by Floyd Robertson, a forty-seven-year-old sharecropper from West Point, Mississippi, brought to the conference at a cost exceeding a quarter of his yearly income. "If the government says it's goin' to do, it ought to quit politickin' and *do,*" he said. "We poor folks need help *now.*"[29] The conference voted a resolution favoring the usual "massive" attack on social problems at a cost of "billions," but in fact the civil rights movement no longer agreed on what the problem was or what to do about it. What sort of "massive" assault did they have in mind? No one could say. The movement was too divided to offer a common solution, and the government too preoccupied.

King deliberately remained in the background of the White House conference, but he was troubled by the inability of civil rights leaders to agree on what ought to be done, and doubly concerned by the ample evidence that the war on poverty was being not only financially, but emotionally and intellectually starved to support the war in Vietnam. The fragmentation of the movement was even more apparent during the Meredith march, and the debate on black power which followed it put civil rights leaders into public and permanent opposition for the first time. The movement was threatening to break up at the very moment when it was needed most.

Early in 1966 King had moved into a third-story walkup apartment in Chicago's Lawndale slum, where 140,000 blacks lived in decaying buildings. Despite his landlord's hurry to end long-standing housing code violations, King, who tried to spend three days a week in the city, learned firsthand of the mixed anger and demoralization of urban Negroes, 7.6 percent of whom were out of work, double the national average. He told one interviewer, "There are more Negroes in Chicago than in the whole state of Mississippi and if we don't get nonviolent groups, the alternative is Watts. And, without another alternative, Watts will look like a Sunday school picnic compared to what will happen."[30]

In the South, King had grown accustomed to brutal, open resistance on the part of local sheriffs and city governments. In Chicago, Richard Daley was more subtle. He sent fifty building inspectors into the city's ghettos and made a point of other city-initiated actions to cure urban decay. The problems could not be cured so easily, of course, but Daley's approach still made it difficult for the SCLC to focus its campaign. On July 10, two weeks after the end of the Meredith march, King led 45,000 demonstrators from Chicago's Soldiers Field to City Hall to initiate a major effort to end housing discrimination. In the weeks that followed he led other marches into white neighborhoods. One of them, held on Sunday, July 31, was met by George Lincoln Rockwell, leader of the minuscule American Nazi Party, and a white mob carrying signs that read "White Power." The black marchers were chased back to the black area of Chicago under a hail of bricks and rocks.

On August 20, campaign leaders announced a march through the violently anti-Negro, all-white suburb of Cicero, just outside Chicago's city limits. The near certainty of violence resulted in a last-minute meeting on August 26 among King, Daley, the Chicago Real Estate Board, the Chicago Housing Authority, and other civic and business groups. The resulting agreement led King to cancel the August 28 march, an act that made him once again the target of militants who felt he had backed down after winning an ephemeral victory. In fact, little was accomplished by the marches, and the agreement had almost no effect on the daily lives of the black ghetto masses. That fall the Chicago movement gradually faded away, more a failure than a success.

In mid-December, exhausted, King began a two-month vacation on the island of Bimini, where there was little to do but sit and think. He finished writing a book he had started some time earlier, *Where Do We Go from Here?*, and brooded about the war in Vietnam. King had always been openly critical of the war and in mid-1966 had accepted an invitation to become cochairman of Clergy and Laymen Concerned About Vietnam. On Bimini, however, he decided the war was destroying both the movement and the country, squandering resources in a cause that was wrong. The movement as a whole had carefully avoided the issue of the war for the very good reason that it could expect to make enemies and achieve nothing. King did not underestimate this likelihood, but he decided the war could no longer be ignored or circumvented. If the United States was to resume the effort of reconstruction at home, the war in Vietnam had to be ended.

Shortly after his return, King spoke at a meeting in Los Angeles on February 25, 1967, where he opened a personal campaign against the war with an attack on its physical horror, its doubtful morality, and its devastating effect on efforts at reform in the United States:

Despite feeble protestations to the contrary, the promises of the Great Society have been shot down on the battlefield of Vietnam. . . . It is estimated that we spend $322,000 for each enemy we kill, while we spend in the so-called war on poverty in America only about $53 for each person classified as "poor." And much of that $53 goes for salaries of people who are not poor. . . . We must combine the fervor of the civil rights movement with the peace movement. We must demonstrate, teach and preach until the very foundations of our nation are shaken.[31]

The seriousness of King's pledge was made clear at a meeting of the SCLC's board in Louisville, Kentucky, on March 29 and 30, where he proposed civil disobedience as a tactic of opposition. On April 2 he told the *New York Times* in an interview that, "I made a decision to become involved as an individual, as a clergyman, as one who is greatly concerned about peace."[32] On the morning of April 4 in a news conference at the Overseas Press Club in New York he told reporters, "Honestly, if I had to confront this problem I would be a conscientious objector. I would not even serve as a chaplain."[33]

That afternoon in Riverside Church, in a long speech which was to mark a kind of turning point in the country's attitude toward the war, King spoke out more clearly and passionately against the fighting in Vietnam than had any other national figure:

As I have walked among the desperate, rejected and angry young men I have told them that Molotov cocktails and rifles would not solve their problems. . . . They asked me if our own nation wasn't using massive doses of violence to solve its problems, to bring about the changes it wanted. Their questions hit home, and I knew that I could never again raise my voice against the violence of the oppressed in the ghettos without having first spoken clearly to the greatest purveyor of violence in the world today—my own government. . . .

Somehow this madness must cease. We must stop now. . . . I speak for the poor of America who are paying the double price of smashed hopes at home and death and corruption in Vietnam. The great initiative in this war is ours. The initiative to stop it must be ours. . . .

As we [clergymen] counsel young men concerning military service we must clarify for them our nation's role in Vietnam and challenge them with the alternative of conscientious objection. . . . I recommend it to all who find the American course in Vietnam a dishonorable and unjust one. Moreover, I would encourage all ministers of draft age to give up their ministerial exemptions and seek status as conscientious objectors. . . .

Every man of human convictions must decide on the protest that best suits his convictions, but we must all protest.[34]

The response to such speeches had evolved into an invariable pattern. Like Morse in 1964, Hans Morgenthau in 1965, and Fulbright in 1966, King was criticized for having "overstated" his case against the war. Particularly resented was King's charge that the United States had become "the greatest purveyor of violence in the world today," although it was true. Things were more complicated than that, editorialists insisted; reasonable men might differ over the wisdom of the intervention, but the United States would hardly do anything without the best interests of its victims at heart. And so on. Suggestions that the war was not only unwise but morally wrong, always elicited the most passionate denials for one simple reason: if the war were *wrong*, no one had a moral right to be neutral. In a familiar tone of superior lament, the Washington *Post* typically concluded on April 6:

Dr. King has done a grave injury to those who are his natural allies in a great struggle to remove ancient abuses from our public life; and he has done an even graver injury to himself. Many who have listened to him with respect will never again accord him the same confidence. He has diminished his usefulness to his cause, to his country and to his people.

This, of course, was exactly the sort of response long predicted by moderate leaders of the civil rights movement. In the following days they firmly disassociated themselves from King, hoping to preserve their own "usefulness." King, however, had decided there was little value in a usefulness which referred only to the ease with which he could obtain appointments to see the President, whose politeness did not disguise the fact his mind was elsewhere.

The point, King felt, was whether or not the war was wrong. After watching what it was doing to the country as well as to Vietnam itself, King felt the hour had arrived to resist. If he were accused of overstating his case, well, he had been accused of pushing too far, too fast since he first went to Montgomery, Alabama, as a young minister in 1955. King's moral stature in American life was probably unparalleled. No amount of editorial "realism" could cloud what King had said or diminish its effect. His break with the administration was complete. He did not have reservations about details; he rejected the war entirely. It was wrong; it was destroying both Vietnam and the United States; one's only obligation was to stop it. The movement that King led was a political fact of major importance in American life. When he spoke in Riverside Church he was not pledging solely the efforts of the Southern Christian Leadership Conference, a group small in numbers though large in influence. He was in effect pledging heightened consciousness, a new spirit of opposition and resistance, from all those who had considered King's movement their own. The liberal wing of the Democratic Party took nothing more seriously than the long struggle for black rights. When King spoke out on the war, he said clearly what so many had long suspected: the great tide of reform in American life, so long needed and so late in coming, was being destroyed by an evil war.

NINE

From Protest to Resistance

Opponents of the war found it always difficult, and often impossible, to agree on the best way of opposing it. One reason for this dissension was the fact that the war was actually a secondary issue to many of the organizations most active in trying to end it. The dozen or so minor socialist and revolutionary groups in the United States made no secret of their primary interest in bringing down capitalism. The civil rights organizations were more concerned with injustice at home than war abroad. Student groups were worried about the draft, and were especially prone to bruising ideological struggles on points of purely theoretical interest. Traditional organizations like SANE and Americans for Democratic Action were obsessed with being "responsible," which generally meant trying to come up with an alternative Vietnam policy which might conceivably be accepted by those in power. From time to time all those groups could be coaxed into uneasy and temporary agreement on a single slogan or course of action, but most of the time they were pulling in their own directions for their own reasons.

At the heart of this anarchy was the difficulty, if not impossibility, of devising a realistic strategy for ending the war against Johnson's will. The task was obviously formidable and none of the many proposals for carrying it out received very broad support. Steve Weissman, who had been active in the Berkeley Free Speech Movement and one of those who had voted for turning back at the demonstration in October, 1965, insisted that the first obligation of the opposition was to be effective. The point was not to disassociate oneself from the war, but to end it:

The public statements of the VDC stressed the moral and personal need "to stop the war machine," "to send shock waves from Maine to California, and from the United States to all parts of the world." The individualist principle of the Nuremberg trials was perhaps the major theme of propaganda. There was little talk of how we might be effective, as if the moral and existential necessity was only to protest, and not to affect the war.[1]

Weissman proposed that the opposition be organized around a three-part anti-draft program which would end student deferments (on the ground they discriminated against the poor), would provide for conscientious objection to particular wars, and would allow draftees to perform alternate service. Weissman was far from the only person thinking about the draft, but support for the various programs was relatively narrow and no one believed they could actually deprive the United States of the army it needed to continue the war.

Staughton Lynd's fantasy of occupying the government[2] was only half-serious to begin with and appealed primarily to the revolutionary groups with tiny memberships. Later, the number of "revolutionaries" on college campuses would grow at a dizzying rate (and then disappear as quickly), but only a handful were ever to convince themselves that seizing power was a realistic objective. Congress, of course, could theoretically cut off funds for the war, but in early 1967 that seemed as remote as revolution. On March 20, for example, the Senate passed the administration's request for a supplemental appropriation of $12.2 billion for Vietnam by a vote of seventy-seven to three. After two years of steadily mounting warfare, expenditure, and casualties, only one more Senator, Gaylord Nelson of Wisconsin, was willing to join Morse and Gruening in their lonely refusal to go along with the President. In the October, 1966, issue of *Liberation*, Staughton Lynd proposed a direct action campaign against the war "because I think that this will give the Romneys and Kennedys the best chance to end it by winning in 1968." In other words, he did not know how to end it any sooner.

In the absence of a better plan, the peace movement finally reached limited agreement on another demonstration. But this time, they decided, it was going to be so huge and imposing as to attract the attention even of Lyndon Johnson. Mass demonstrations are the traditional form of popular protest, and a number of people felt that the opposition had not yet made a really serious attempt to mount a major march against the war. It is not generally recognized what sort of effort goes into a major demonstration, and this was to be the biggest of them all. The first task was a reorganization of the peace movement.

The National Coordinating Committee to End the War in Vietnam, formed during the summer of 1965 to organize broad-based opposition to the war, had sponsored nationwide demonstrations in the fall of 1965 and the spring of 1966 but, like all such organizations after a certain time, was beginning to run out of energy. In July, 1966, the Inter-University Committee for Debate on Foreign Policy, which had organized the first teach-ins, held a two-day meeting in Cleveland to discuss the possibility of forming a new organization to replace the NCC. In August, the Fifth Avenue Peace Parade Committee organized a New York march and rally on the twenty-first anniversary of the bombing of Hiroshima. The turnout was relatively small, but the demonstration further undermined the moral authority of the NCC, which had refused to take part for reasons of its own. By the end of the summer the NCC had abandoned its national role to become the Wisconsin Organizing Committee.

The peace movement was going through one of its periodic depressions, convinced that nothing could persuade Johnson of the folly of his course.

In September, 1966, a new organization called the Mobilization to End the War in Vietnam was formed to sponsor demonstrations between November 5 and 8. On the weekend of November 26, a new meeting in Cleveland was called by the Inter-University Committee to evaluate the November demonstrations and decide what should come next. No one could argue convincingly that another demonstration would have any more effect than the previous ones, but it was decided to make a major effort anyway. A new group was formed called the Spring Mobilization to End the War in Vietnam under the chairmanship of A. J. Muste, the eighty-two-year-old dean of the peace movement. The four vice chairmen were David Dellinger, editor of *Liberation;* Ed Keating, publisher of *Ramparts;* Sidney Peck, a professor at Western Reserve University; and Robert Greenblatt, a professor at Cornell who headed the Inter-University Committee. They chose Saturday, April 15, 1967, for the demonstration. In the December, 1966, issue of *Liberation,* Muste explained why another try was worth the effort:

> The feeling of letdown, of hopelessness, which overcomes at times because the Johnson war-machine grinds on, is in the final analysis something to be ashamed of. Johnson and the war machine are things to be faced, to stand up to, not to stand in awe of or cringe before. Our task is to disarm them, not to be morally and politically disarmed by them. Did we really think the job would be easy and attained at a modest price?

The Spring Mobilization immediately decided the march should be nonexclusionary, reopening all the old arguments about coalitions, united fronts, working with the Communists, and red-baiting. Muste argued that broad coalitions seeking specific ends were useful. "If you want to get the frying pan off the fire," he would say, "you've got to have a handle."[3] From the beginning the Spring Mobilization proceeded in a state of uneasy truce between warring factions whose private opinion of each other was often harsh, but who were willing to work together, up to a point, for the larger purpose of opposing the war.

The Spring Mobilization was not the first attempt to create a really broad coalition, but it was by far the most successful, eventually bringing together groups from every major political community.

Groups on the revolutionary left were among the first to join. On December 28 and 29, 1966, more than 250 members of organizations on the left met at the University of Chicago to consider a proposal by Bettina Aptheker, a leader of the Free Speech Movement, for a nationwide student strike against the war. Among the organizations represented at the meeting were the Communist Party, the Progressive Labor Party, the Socialist Workers Party, and Youth Against War and Fascism, groups with bitter rivalries dating back as far as the Stalin-Trotsky split in the 1920s. After the usual acrimony about "revisionism" and related subjects, they decided that a student strike was "not realistic at this time"[4] and voted to support the Spring Mobilization instead.

Their dissensions in Chicago were inevitably echoed within the Mobilization during debates over slogans and speakers. When the Mobilization refused to back immediate withdrawal, for example, YAWF charged that it was "beginning to echo the left wing of the State Department."[5] For most of those within the Mobilization this sort of bickering was irritating but hardly worth making a fuss over. The Reverend James Bevel, an associate of Martin Luther King in the SCLC who was named director of the Spring Mobilization in January, refused to take seriously the question of who was left of whom. "We're going to get left of Karl Marx and left of Lenin," he would say. "We're going to get way out there, up on that cross with Jesus."[6]

For SANE, however, alliance with YAWF, the Communist Party, or the Committee to Aid the NLF, which planned to march carrying the NLF flag, was out of the question. SANE conservatives argued that the revolutionary left would inevitably alienate the mainstream of American life and politics, making it easy for the administration to discredit the march. Their real objections were somewhat more visceral. They had learned that history can play tricks; the allies of today can become the pariahs of tomorrow. SANE did not share the general conviction that the McCarthy era was over. They also remembered, and still resented, the struggles of the 1930s, when the Communist Party, under direct control of the Soviet Union, infiltrated and sometimes took over a wide range of unions and activist groups.

Early in 1967 Dr. Spock, SANE's cochairman since the fall of 1963, proposed that the organization cosponsor the April 15 marches to be held in New York and San Francisco. A SANE faction led by Norman Cousins of the *Saturday Review* opposed the move because of the Mobilization's tolerance of black militants like Stokely Carmichael and groups that planned to openly support the Vietcong. Eventually a compromise was reached which allowed local SANE chapters to decide on their own whether or not to take part in the march. In California, the struggle continued right up until the week of the march. Robert Pickus, a veteran peace worker who headed SANE in northern California, held a news conference on Wednesday, April 12, in San Francisco, which came close to repeating his statement before the International Days of Protest in the fall of 1965. He publicly disassociated himself from the demonstration, criticizing organizers of the march for blaming only the United States for the war when, he felt, Ho Chi Minh was equally responsible.

On the fourteenth the *New York Times* praised Pickus for his stand and repeated his criticism of the Mobilization as one-sided. Later that day, reporters at a news conference held in New York by Reverend James Bevel asked hostile questions about Communists in the Mobilization and whether it favored a Communist victory in Vietnam. At the end of March, the House Un-American Activities Committee had released a report claiming Communist domination of the Mobilization, citing as proof the Communists who had attended the Chicago conference at the end of December. The effect of this internal dissension and external assault had been small in 1965, and was still smaller now. Behind all the charges and countercharges there was only one issue that mattered to the movement: the war.

In organizing the march the Mobilization had concentrated its efforts on numbers—one reason it had insisted on the broadest possible coalition. Peace organizations, churches, women's groups, political clubs, and universities had been contacted throughout the country. Cars, buses, and even entire trains had been organized to bring demonstrators to the two marches scheduled for New York and San Francisco, with the Mississippi River supposed to be a dividing line between the two. The purpose of the march was to show that active opposition to the war was not limited to a few radicals and political idealists, as the administration often tried to imply, but included vast numbers of ordinary Americans. If any major politician were to be persuaded to run against the war in 1968 he would first have to be convinced the opposition was broad enough to sustain a serious campaign.

The last major demonstration had been held more than a year earlier, on March 26, 1966, when protests took place in half a dozen cities. The largest had been in New York where 22,000 people had marched down Fifth Avenue from Ninety-first Street to the Central Park entrance at Seventy-second Street. At a rally in the park A. J. Muste had told the crowd, "We have had a tremendous parade and rally. Let us take a lesson from it and learn that by escalating our activity and protests we can de-escalate the war."[7] Now the entire American peace movement had made a five-month effort to mount a really major demonstration of public opposition. Peace workers often spoke with scorn of the "numbers game," but if the April 15 march were not large in numbers it would be a failure. Worse, it would actively discourage anyone from challenging President Johnson in 1968. David McReynolds, a member of the War Resisters League, wrote several weeks later:

A couple of days before the demonstration a friend and I made guesses about the possible turnout. I have 20 years of experience in organizing, attending, witnessing demonstrations. His experience is even longer. Between us we agreed that the Spring Mobilization had to turn out 50,000 people or it would be a flop. 70,000 would be a victory. 100,000 would be one of those improbable, unlikely, wonderful shots.[8]

Following the Vietnam hearings of February, 1966, by Senator Fulbright's Foreign Relations Committee, President Johnson had said he did not think he and his critics were very far apart. He was right, and remained right for nearly two more years. Elected officials were reluctant to depart from official policy by more than inches, urging "greater efforts" to get peace talks started, or an "end to escalation," or "going to the UN," or more emphasis on "the other war" of winning hearts and minds, which in Vietnam was referred to as WHAM.

The caution of public figures was the natural result of American casualties. The President and the country were increasingly hostage to the dead. The President's critics were probably as reluctant as Johnson himself to support any policy that would indicate the dead had died in vain. To turn against the war completely was not emotionally easy. The logic of the war was such that the only real alternative to war was withdrawal, at best with an agreement which would disguise the country's failure to win its original objectives, at worst with no agreement at all. If the other side would not meet our terms, we could either reduce our demands or fight on. Hanoi would not agree to Johnson's terms, and so he fought on. Once one had decided *not* to fight on, one had to accept the other side's terms, and those terms were hard. Washington and Hanoi were miles apart in 1967. Any critic of the war who broke completely with the administration would have been forced by the situation to accept terms so far from the original American goals as to constitute "giving up." The very phrases used to describe such a solution—"cut and run," "turn tail," "scuttling," "surrender"—explain the reluctance of any public figure to advocate a policy of withdrawal.

As a result, the relatively minor public differences over the war disguised a far deeper private disenchantment with the course of events. Superficial unanimity like the seventy-seven-to-three Senate vote on funding the war in March meant nothing. During an interview on educational television broadcast on February 1, 1967, Senator Mansfield alluded to this deeper discontent among senators when he said "all of them are uneasy about it [the war]. Many of them are frustrated." He estimated that a third wanted "more vigorous action," another third "would like to see an honorable conclusion brought about as quickly as possible," and the last third "would be in the middle somewhere."[9] By an "honorable solution" Mansfield's second group did not mean a military victory or anything close to it, but they found it difficult to express this directly. When Johnson said the two sides were not very far apart, he could cite only their common language as evidence. When the administration referred to an "honorable solution," it meant one in which the other side abandoned the larger part of its goal. When senators like Mansfield used the phrase, they meant a solution in which the United States quietly reduced *its* aims in the interests of compromise. In the winter of 1966–67, division over the war did not appear to be as sharp as it actually was.

On Christmas Day, 1966, the *New York Times* printed on its front page the first of fourteen news stories written in North Vietnam by Harrison Salisbury, the assistant managing editor of the *Times* and winner of a Pulitzer Prize for foreign reporting in 1955. Earlier in December, 1966, on the second and fourth and then again on the thirteenth and fourteenth, the United States had bombed a railroad complex at Yan Vien, about six miles northeast of Hanoi, and a truck park at Van Dien, about five miles to the south. Hanoi had charged the United States with bombing civilian areas in the city itself. The Defense Department categorically denied bombing civilian areas and said the charge of having bombed "Hanoi" depended on how you defined a city. It insisted the raids were outside the city limits.

In his first story Salisbury stated that Hanoi's "built-up, densely populated urban area extends for a substantial distance in all directions beyond the heavy-lined city boundaries" on a map released by the State Department. As for official denials of raids against civilian targets, Salisbury wrote:

> This correspondent is no ballistics specialist, but inspections of several damaged sites and talks with witnesses make it clear that Hanoi residents certainly believe they were bombed by United States planes, that they certainly observed United States planes overhead and that damage certainly occurred right in the center of town.

On Monday, December 26, the Defense Department admitted the probability of accidental hits in civilian areas but blamed the North Vietnamese for putting antiaircraft batteries, oil dumps, radar stations, and other military facilities "in populated areas and, indeed, sometimes on the roofs of government buildings."[10] The Department said it planned to check thoroughly another Salisbury story, published Tuesday, which reported widespread damage to the city of Nam Dinh. During fifty-one raids between June 28, 1965, and December 23, 1966, Salisbury said, 89 civilians had been killed and 405 wounded. One textile plant had been bombed nineteen times and on April 14 at 6:30 A.M., when factory workers were changing shifts, a raid killed 49 civilians and wounded another 135. On Thursday, December 29, Assistant Secretary of Defense Arthur Sylvester said he thought Salisbury's casualty figures revealed "rather precise, careful bombing"[11] since, on the average, only 1.5 civilians had been killed in each of the sixty-four raids on Nam Dinh acknowledged by the Defense Department. Despite official insistence that civilian areas had been bombed only accidentally, the administration seemed to have been caught in an outright lie. And despite official attempts to minimize civilian damage in North Vietnam, Salisbury's vivid stories brought home the horror of the air war to vast sections of the public for the first time.

The Defense Department was, of course, furious. Salisbury's stories were all painstakingly checked for errors. A great deal was made of the fact that Salisbury did not acknowledge North Vietnamese officials as the source of his statistics until a story printed in the *Times* on Thursday, December 29. The Defense Department also made available to the *Washington Post* a North Vietnamese pamphlet entitled *Report on United States War Crimes in Nam-Dinh City,* which had been distributed to foreign correspondents in Hanoi in November. Sylvester told a *Post* reporter he "found it very interesting"[12] that casualty figures in the pamphlet and the Salisbury stories matched exactly. The effect was minimal. Since Salisbury freely admitted his figures came from North Vietnamese officials, it was not surprising they matched those in the pamphlet.

More important was the overall impression of Salisbury's stories. Bomb damage in North Vietnam had been reported before, but the *Times* and Salisbury both had a recognized stature that gave his reports authority, and they appeared only a few weeks after U.S. denials that it had bombed civilian areas in North Vietnam. Sylvester tried to dismiss Salisbury as sentimental and the *Times* as disloyal when he referred to them in a Chicago speech as "Harrison Appalsbury" and "The New Hanoi *Times.*"[13] The attempt failed. After the appearance of Salisbury's stories, the suffering of the North Vietnamese became an accepted factor in argument over the war.

The weakening of confidence in the administration's word was compounded on February 4, 1967, when the *Washington Post* revealed that the December 13 and 14 bombings had not only escalated the war by attacking the city of Hanoi for the first time, but had also brought an abrupt halt to a peace initiative by the Polish government. As the story gradually emerged, it was learned that the Polish member of the International Control Commission established by the 1954 Geneva Conference had been acting as a go-between in tentative discussions of a bombing halt by Hanoi and the United States. After nearly six months of quiet maneuvering, the American ambassador to Poland, John Gronouski, was meeting with Polish officials on the terms of a possible formula for halting the bombing at the very moment raids were being conducted against Hanoi on December 13. After new raids the following day, the Poles broke off the talks and on December 30 Gronouski was informed that Hanoi was no longer interested.

When the *Post* story broke on February 4, a Saturday, White House aide Walt Rostow was meeting in Washington's Sheraton Park Hotel with about three hundred editors of college newspapers. Rostow was hissed and booed when he avoided answering a question about the *Post* story:

> This is an extremely interesting and delicate phase in what is or what might turn out to be a negotiating process. Nothing has yet happened that would justify us in saying we have a serious offer to negotiate. This is a bad time to discuss any particular negotiating track.[14]

The track foremost in Rostow's mind was not in Poland but in London, where he knew that Soviet Premier Alexei Kosygin was to arrive for an official visit the following Monday, February 6. Speculation on the possibility of peace talks had been encouraged by the remarks of the North Vietnamese Foreign Minister Nguyen Duy Trinh in an interview with the Australian journalist Wilfred Burchett on January 28. Trinh had said that only after a halt in the bombing "could there be talks."

Senator Robert Kennedy had arrived in Europe the same day and was reportedly informed in Paris later that Hanoi considered the Trinh statement important. In other words, it was suggested, Hanoi might be offering talks in return for a bombing halt. Back in the United States, Kennedy met with President Johnson as Kosygin was arriving in London. Despite vigorous administration attempts to discredit the peace initiative Kennedy was reported to be bringing back, it was widely felt that Trinh's interview, Kosygin's visit to London, and Kennedy's meeting with De Gaulle in Paris all indicated that a turning point might have been reached.

The United States had already announced a halt in the bombing in honor of Tet, the lunar new year, to extend from Wednesday, February 8, through Sunday, February 12. On Thursday, February 9, Kosygin gave an internationally televised press conference in London during which he recommended the Trinh statement as a basis for action. In effect, he seemed to be putting Moscow's diplomatic weight behind a bombing halt-and-then-negotiations formula. In Washington the same day Rusk stated the U.S. position in a press conference where he said, "We must know the military consequences of such a military action on our part. They must not expect us to stop our military action by bombing while they continue their military action by invasion."[15]

Details of the discussions between Kosygin and British Prime Minister Harold Wilson in London remained secret, but it was clear that Wilson was hopeful and that success hinged on whether or not the bombing was resumed on schedule Sunday morning. It was not, but the delay was a short one. At four o'clock Monday afternoon, February 13, Washington ordered the bombing resumed, and hopes for peace, or at least for peace talks, were dashed once again. A few days later Wilson publicly blamed Washington for the failure and said "peace was in our grasp."[16] The administration, of course, blamed Hanoi.

On March 21 the true positions of the two governments became clearer when Hanoi broadcast the text of two letters exchanged at the time of the talks in London. A letter from Johnson to Ho Chi Minh dated February 8 was moderate and reasonable in tone but included a provision that seemed the less generous the more closely it was examined:

> I am prepared to order a cessation of bombing against your country and the stopping of further augmentation of U.S. forces in South Vietnam as soon as I am assured that infiltration into South Vietnam by land and by sea has been stopped.[17]

In effect the United States was asking Hanoi to abandon its men in South Vietnam, which of course amounted to surrender. The administration pointed to the angry tone of Ho's letter dated February 15 as proof Hanoi was not really interested in peace, but most observers nevertheless noted, first, that Washington's conditions for a bombing halt had hardened considerably since the "peace offensive" one year before, and second, that Ho's letter was written after the resumption of the bombing on Monday afternoon, February 13, when the possibility of talks presumably had come to an end. It was not until several years later that it was learned Johnson's letter had also abruptly hardened the terms for a bombing halt in the middle of the London talks. American officials had given an entirely different formula to Wilson and Kosygin, only to find they had been bypassed by Johnson's letter, which was delivered directly to the North Vietnamese embassy in Moscow.

At the time the situation was confused by the usual charges and countercharges, but it was obvious the President was in a more intransigent mood than he had been during the long bombing halt thirteen months earlier. As a result many Americans were beginning to doubt their government's interest in a peaceful solution to the war, if the price was compromise. During the remainder of February, American attacks on North Vietnam were sharply escalated. U.S. artillery fired across the DMZ for the first time, U.S. warships began shelling North Vietnamese supply routes on a continuing basis, and U.S. planes began mining North Vietnamese rivers. On March 10, the first major industrial target, the iron and steel plant at Thai Nguyen, was bombed by U.S. planes. It was difficult to resist the conclusion that the United States intended to settle the war militarily.

The bombing of North Vietnam, which the United States had undertaken with such optimism in 1965 and now insisted so vehemently was necessary to the war effort, was beginning to seem a two-edged sword. It had not prevented North Vietnam from increasing its military effort in the South, it had not forced North Vietnam to the negotiating table, it was costly in both men and planes, and it was straining belief in the good will of the United States around the world. As the bombing continued into a third year, the war began to simplify into a contest between the arrogant desire of a great country to have its way and the moral determination of a small country to resist. The strong cannot torment the weak and expect to win general respect and sympathy; the bombing, the heaviest in history, began to seem cruel and vindictive. After a time it ceased to make much difference what North Vietnam had done or failed to do. The thing that mattered most was her courage. The two countries seem embodied by their leaders: Ho Chi Minh aging, fragile, and quietly determined; Lyndon Johnson large, crude, and loudly insistent. North Vietnam evacuated her cities and mobilized the countryside and endured while the United States waged war halfway around the world and enjoyed boom times at home. The contrast was morally grotesque.

In his letter to President Johnson, Ho had said, "Vietnam is situated thousands of miles from the United States. The Vietnamese people have never done any harm to the United States."[18] The administration had twenty sophisticated arguments why this made no difference, but in human terms it did. Americans did not really care who ruled South Vietnam, and they did not take much pleasure in the fact that the United States was systematically destroying North Vietnam from the air. The bombing was demoralizing, all right, but it was demoralizing Americans.

One of those watching Kosygin's televised press conference on February 9 was Robert Kennedy, at his home in Virginia. Kennedy had said little about the war since a proposal in February, 1966, to include the National Liberation Front in peace talks and in any coalition government that might result. A number of his advisers had been urging him to speak again.

Kennedy said later that Kosygin's speech had convinced him the major obstacle to peace talks was the bombing. He began working on a speech which went through a number of drafts before he finally delivered it on the Senate floor on the afternoon of Thursday, March 2. An hour before speaking Kennedy met with half a dozen reporters in his office, telling them he felt the futility of military action outweighed the possibility that his speech might end up hurting American boys by encouraging Hanoi. The heart of Kennedy's speech, a copy of which was delivered to the White House the same afternoon, was a proposal for a new, indefinite bombing halt to be coupled with a statement that the United States was prepared for peace talks to begin within the week. Kennedy cited the long bombing halt in the winter of 1965–1966 and asked why a similar initiative could not be undertaken "in this far more hopeful moment?"[19]

In substance, Kennedy's speech did not go much beyond earlier proposals for halts in the bombing, but its impact was greater than its substance. In the first place, Kennedy had the political resources to challenge Johnson in 1968. Kennedy had firmly rejected the idea, but it was clear he could, in fact, undertake such a challenge and that no sense of personal loyalty prevented him from doing so. Second, Kennedy's speech had an emotional tone which conveyed a deeper disenchantment than appeared in his relatively moderate proposals. He spoke of the war not in terms of legalisms, but in terms of human suffering:

> Certainly the bombing of North Vietnam makes the war more costly and difficult and painful for North Vietnam. It is harsh punishment indeed. But we are not in Vietnam to play the part of an avenging angel, pouring death and destruction on the roads and factories and homes of a guilty land. . . . It should be clear by now that the bombing of the North cannot bring an end to the war in the South; that, indeed, it may well be prolonging that war.[20]

That the President did not take Kennedy's speech lightly was proved by the whirlwind of official activity with which he attempted to bury it. Rusk in Washington and General Westmoreland in Saigon both released statements rejecting Kennedy's proposals, and the President first led White House reporters to Howard University for a sudden speech on civil rights and then appeared at the U.S. Office of Education to make remarks about the state of the nation's schools. His biggest effort, however, was an announcement that the Soviet Union had offered to join the United States in talks about limiting missiles. Despite all this activity, Kennedy's speech was the lead story in most newspapers the following day, and the struggle over the war began to focus on the issue that would grow to dominate and finally decide it: the bombing.

Salisbury's stories from North Vietnam at the turn of the year, the hardening of American conditions for a bombing halt, and Kennedy's new break with the administration all fed public disenchantment with the war. Two years of bombing and troop increases had achieved nothing. People who had originally decided to wait and see had waited and seen. Johnson's policy had widened the war without bringing victory any closer. The result was a broader public willingness to oppose the war, to point to administration failures for what they were, and to protest the administration's apparent plan to fight on indefinitely.

On December 29, 1966, a letter to the President signed by one hundred student leaders was released to the press. The idea for the letter had been suggested by Allard Lowenstein at the annual meeting of the National Student Association the previous August. In its final form the letter was respectful in tone but it still made clear that the war enjoyed little support on American college campuses: "Unless this conflict can be eased," the letter said, "the United States will find some of her most loyal and courageous young people choosing to go to jail rather than to bear their country's arms. . . ."[21]

On February 1, forty-two of the student leaders who had signed the letter met with Rusk in Washington but told reporters later they had left the meeting still unsatisfied. Robert Powell of the University of North Carolina, spokesman for the group, said they were particularly worried about the President's insistence on "complete surrender of the goals and ambitions of the other side."[22] The students themselves had been surprised at the ease with which they had obtained signatures to a letter that would have been considered extreme even a year earlier. The letter was only the first in a flood.

Lowenstein attended a meeting in Washington of Clergy and Laymen Concerned About Vietnam on January 31, where he recruited a number of students from Union Theological Seminary in New York for a concentrated effort to organize letters protesting the war. When they returned to New York they obtained a small, three-room office in the seminary and installed a Wide Area Telephone Service line which allowed them to make unlimited long distance telephone calls for $3,000 a month. Tight scheduling kept the phone working for at least fourteen hours a day, with East Coast calls being made during the day and West Coast calls at night. Between January and June they organized a new letter to the President signed by two hundred student body presidents, a petition to allow draftees to choose an alternative service signed by ten thousand students on nine campuses, and a letter to McNamara signed by one thousand young seminarians. Other groups arranged for at least fifteen letters signed by literally thousands of faculty members at Princeton, Yale, Cornell, the University of Michigan, Columbia, the University of Texas, and other schools. Many of them were published as full-page ads in the *New York Times* and other newspapers and at least one spread across four full pages. The effect was a public impression of spreading protest reaching every section of the country.

This new spirit of opposition quickly appeared at schools where such things had been unheard of, like Stanford University near San Francisco, where Vice President Humphrey gave a speech on February 20. A few days earlier Stanford students had decided to hold a protest walkout and a teach-in, by far the most militant demonstrations ever undertaken at the school. Two hundred and eleven faculty members signed an ad which read, "We, the undersigned members of the faculty, welcome Vice President Humphrey to Stanford, but in so doing we cannot allow our welcome to imply approval of the administration's resumption [February 13] of the bombing of North Vietnam, extending a policy which Mr. Humphrey has unequivocally endorsed."[23]

As Stanford's Memorial Auditorium was filling on the afternoon of the twentieth, three faculty members handed out leaflets urging students not to walk out, arguing, among other things, that Humphrey's bodyguards might panic and shoot anyone who stood up suddenly during his speech.

Humphrey began with a clumsy remark about visiting the "now" generation which precipitated an initial walkout of about fifty students. While more than two thousand people listened to his speech over loudspeakers outside the building, Humphrey began talking at length about the Great Society. "What about Vietnam?" a student shouted.

"I told that gentleman to ask that question," Humphrey said. "Otherwise I was afraid I'd forget to answer it."[24] There was some laughter and applause.

Then Humphrey went on to say, "If President John F. Kennedy were alive today he would be doing exactly what the Johnson administration is doing at this very hour."[25] At this point another two hundred students marched angrily out of the auditorium. When Humphrey had finished speaking he was followed more than one hundred yards to his car by a crowd of students shouting "Shame! Shame!"

Previously indifferent to the war, Stanford students began organizing protest groups which remained active long after the Vice President's visit had been forgotten. It was not what Humphrey had said, exactly, that angered them, but the fact that people were running out of patience and forbearance and credulity. It was clear that the war was not being won, that it was brutal and expensive, that the government had less time for other issues, that every student in the country was a potential victim of a bitter little quarrel in a far-away corner of the world. The incident at Stanford in February was only one of literally hundreds fed by the same doubts, frustration, and anger. None of them had much apparent effect, and yet each focused the minds of students and faculty on a single public issue. The war was fast becoming the great inescapable fact in American life. It was a nagging presence in the back of all but the dullest minds. Circumstances raised the issue with relentless frequency: are you for or against the war? Yes or no? This was not the sort of question that could be answered once and then dismissed. It had to be answered again and again, and each time more people decided they were, in the end, against it.

As the war continued other aspects of American life were brought into question. Radicals insisted that the system was at fault, not just errors in policy, and there was increasing evidence they were right. In its March, 1967, issue, the radical magazine *Ramparts* revealed that the National Student Association had been secretly funded by the Central Intelligence Agency through dummy corporations and foundations. The NSA and government officials acknowledged the truth of the report, setting off investigations which revealed in following weeks that the NSA had been far from alone. Among other organizations that had been receiving CIA money were the American Friends Service Committee (AFSC) in Philadelphia, the Congress of Cultural Freedom, which published the magazine *Encounter,* the National Council of Churches, the American Newspaper Guild, several unions, and a number of educational institutions.

The effect of these disclosures was profound. The entire country was revealed as something like an engine of the Cold War. How was one to take the anticommunist stance of *Encounter?* What was one to think of protests against the war by the National Council of Churches? What was one to conclude about AFSC programs to help the poor in Guatemala and other countries? Some officials lamely argued that the CIA had provided money to essentially liberal organizations for liberal purposes at a time when anticommunist hysteria during the McCarthy era made it impossible to provide funds openly. This was not an argument that much enhanced the word "liberal." The NSA–CIA disclosure was further proof of the invasion of American life by the military. One of the slogans of the April 15 mobilization was "End University Complicity,"[26] a result of the discovery of just how much federally funded research on university campuses was being done for the Department of Defense, often secretly. At many schools the largest single source of funds was, in effect, war and the preparation for war. Radicals argued that the CIA's secret funding proved how "repressive" American tolerance was. Petitions, letters, and peaceful demonstrations were the sort of protest the CIA would be happy to finance, since they acted as a safety valve and achieved nothing.

As the mobilization approached, the public was beginning to see the war differently. In the January 27 issue of *Life*, a World War II correspondent, Robert Sherrod, had expressed a frustrated sense that the war was monstrous and yet inevitable, a disaster about which nothing could be done:

> After nearly two months in Vietnam, I find this the most hateful war we have ever fought. Surely, we never would have got into it if we had known how deep was the well, but we are the victims of one tragic miscalculation after another. We find ourselves supporting a government of mandarins with little basis of popular support, fighting for an army that has little inclination to do its own fighting. Yet in all candor I see nothing to do except continue the course we now pursue, hoping that a merciful providence will show us a way out. We have committed our national honor. . . .

On the eve of the mobilization Sherrod's feelings were shared by many who had turned against the war slowly and reluctantly, and knew no better than he what to do about it. The slogans of the April 15 march, and the programs of the various groups sponsoring it, were far less important than this disspiriting sense that the war was endless and meaningless. The march asked its participants only to appear in public as a sign of concern. The number of Americans prepared to do so had grown enormously in only a year.

Early on the morning of Saturday, April 15, 1967, demonstrators began gathering in the vast grassy field called the Sheep's Meadow in New York's Central Park. More than one thousand students from Cornell University alone made the eight-hour trip to New York on chartered buses, arriving early. The Ethical Culture Society and other groups in Cleveland filled a special ten-car train. Other large groups came from Philadelphia, Boston, Washington, Chicago, and Detroit. A band of Sioux Indians had arrived from a reservation in South Dakota. While the Sheep's Meadow slowly filled, the U.S. Committee to Aid the NLF erected a forty-foot tower and hoisted the red, blue, and yellow flag of the Vietcong to its top. In a rocky area at the southeast corner of the Meadow, a group of seventy frightened students gathered at 11 A.M. in the midst of several hundred supporters to burn their draft cards.

At 12:30 Martin Luther King, Dr. Spock, Stokely Carmichael, the Reverend James Bevel, and other leaders formed ranks at Sixth Avenue and Central Park South and then began to march downtown toward the United Nations, about a mile and a half away. Other groups fell in behind the leaders, medical students in their long white coats, veterans in bits and pieces of uniforms, professors in their caps and gowns, an aging group marching with a large red banner of the Communist Party, the first time it had been publicly paraded in many years. Red paint was splashed on marchers at one point and steel construction rods were thrown from a half-finished building at Forty-seventh Street and Park Avenue. Along one section of Lexington Avenue, eggs and derisive shouts came from the windows of high-rise apartment buildings. Jeering counterdemonstrators in small clusters waited along the route of march.

When the leaders of the march finally reached the UN, King and five others delivered a note of formal protest to Dr. Ralph Bunche in his office on the thirty-eighth floor of the UN's main office building. The meeting was brief and formal. The leaders then returned to speak to the mass of people crowding into UN Plaza on Forty-seventh Street and extending down First Avenue to Forty-second Street. King repeated much of what he had said at Riverside Church ten days earlier, then urged college students to spend the summer organizing opposition to the war. Bevel spoke about civil rights. Carmichael attacked the war, the administration, and the draft. Dr. Spock, increasingly irritated by SANE's caution, urged the antiwar movement to focus its attention on the war, not ideological differences with those who ought to be allies. "If we allow ourselves to be split," he said, "we will be chewed up, fragment by fragment, because we have powerful and relentless enemies."[27]

The speeches continued for a good part of the afternoon while marchers drifted off and were replaced by others still arriving. When it began to rain heavily about 5 o'clock, crowds of demonstrators were still waiting to start out in Central Park. By 6:30 the speakers platform had been dismantled and the vast crowd had left the plaza. Large numbers of marchers gave up along the route and others, wet and cold, continued to trickle into the plaza long after the demonstration was officially over.

Peace activists who had been to every major demonstration in fifty years had never seen anything like the great flood of people who marched in New York that day, a stupendous mass that could have swallowed the crowds that filled football stadiums, a simply incredible number of people filling a huge area in midtown Manhattan. How many had there been, exactly? More than ever before, certainly; more than had been expected, and more, as it turned out, than officials were willing to admit.

Organizers of the march, elated throughout the day and even a little awestruck at the unprecedented turnout, were outraged when they heard news reports quoting the New York Police Department's estimate of 125,000 demonstrators. The headline in Sunday morning's *New York Times* said only 100,000 had marched, although the story in the paper quoted the police estimate as "100,000–125,000." Later that day King held a news conference to give his own estimate of 300,000 to 400,000, and other march organizers thought the true figure might have been as much as 500,000. In San Francisco, official estimates ranged between 20,000 and 40,000, although marchers more than filled the 65,000-seat Kezar Stadium in Golden Gate Park. The under-estimates were the result of mixed hostility and preconception. Until that moment no one, in the government, in journalism, or in the peace movement itself, had realized the extent to which disenchantment with the war had spread. Whatever the real number of marchers on April 15, it was by far the largest demonstration in American history up until that time. The administration would have to say something.

The response was quick in coming: the administration dismissed the number of marchers, pointing to the 200 million citizens who had stayed home. This obviously missed the point. Supporters of the war were prepared to answer yes to certain questions put to them by poll takers, but that was the limit of their commitment to the issue. Although less numerous, opponents were willing to work, march, contribute money, and even go to jail. In November, 1969, when another antiwar demonstration, quite likely the largest of them all, was held in Washington, President Nixon gave a speech over television before the demonstration in which he asked Americans to send him letters and telegrams of support, a relatively easy and inexpensive gesture; about 100,000 Americans sent such letters, while at least three times that number actually *went* to Washington and marched for hours on a bitterly cold day. And yet the polls showed a majority of the country supported Nixon. The same paradox was apparent at the April, 1967, demonstration. The polls showed public support for the war; the demonstration proved how shallow that support was.

The most sustained effort to discredit the march was made by Dean Rusk the following day. During the National Broadcasting Company's Sunday morning show, "Meet the Press," Lawrence E. Spivack raised the subject: "We had huge demonstrations again yesterday. Do you think these demonstrations are having an effect in North Vietnam? Do you think that they are prolonging the war in any way?" Rusk answered:

> Well, these have been called "huge." I suppose they are large, but remember, we have a population of almost 200 million people and those who speak for the 200 million Americans are the President and the Congress on these issues. We have in our constitutional system an opportunity for lawful and peaceful expression. I am concerned, Mr. Spivack, that the authorities in Hanoi may misunderstand this sort of thing and that the net effect of these demonstrations will be to prolong the war and not to shorten it. You see, if we heard that 100,000 people were marching in Hanoi for peace, we would draw very important conclusions from it. Now we don't know whether Hanoi is sufficiently sophisticated to understand that this is not the way the American people come to their decisions and that these demonstrations will not affect the conduct of the war.[28]

Rusk's position was a strange one. Was he saying that the constitutional rights of protest were empty and irrelevant? That a similar march in Hanoi would be meaningful only because it would be illegal? That the American peace movement would have to break the law if it wanted to be effective?

Just over a week later General Westmoreland, in the United States for meetings with the President, the Secretary of Defense, and the Joint

Chiefs of Staff, also attempted to imply that the peace movement in America was helping Hanoi. At the annual luncheon of the Associated Press during the convention of the American Newspaper Publishers Association, held in the Waldorf-Astoria on Monday, April 24, while fifty demonstrators marched in a picket line on Park Avenue, General Westmoreland said U.S. forces were defeating the North Vietnamese and Vietcong at every turn.

> And yet, despite staggering combat losses, he clings to the belief that he will defeat us. And through a clever combination of psychological and political warfare, both here and abroad, he has gained support which gives him hope that he can win politically that which he cannot accomplish militarily. . . . [U.S. troops] are dismayed, and so am I, by recent unpatriotic acts here at home. Regrettably, I see signs of success in that world arena which [the enemy] cannot match on the battlefield. He does not understand that American democracy is founded on debate, and he sees every protest as evidence of crumbling morale and diminishing resolve. Thus, discouraged by repeated military defeats but encouraged by what he believes to be popular opposition to our effort in Vietnam, he is determined to continue his aggression from the North. This, inevitably, will cost lives. . . .[29]

Like Rusk, Westmoreland was not making himself altogether clear on this subject. Did he mean to say that antiwar demonstrations would have no effect on official resolve? Or were the North Vietnamese in fact right in thinking that American disenchantment with the war would eventually lead to an American withdrawal?

The administration's attempt to blame the length of the war on those opposed to fighting it at all released a storm of outrage focused on a side issue rather than the war itself. In fact, the choice facing the country was a harder one than the President's elected opponents were yet willing publicly to acknowledge: the war had to be won or lost. Congress would have gone along with the President if he had decided to pursue an unequivocal military victory, despite the very considerable risk of war with China, and it would have accepted a compromise solution to the war, but it was not prepared to do the only thing the President found it easy to do, and that was to accept the idea of an endless war. Johnson often referred to the number of Americans killed in car accidents in an average week, apparently hoping the country would learn to accept the weekly dead and wounded in Vietnam with similar indifference. The cost of the war and the levying of troops to fight it by conscription, as well as the actual casualties, however, all ruled out a strategy based on patience. As early as 1960, North Vietnamese leaders had said they would win because the United States did not like long, inconclusive wars. They had been right. Eventually an administration, headed by either Johnson or his successor, would have to put the country on a war footing and ignore the risks of decisive escalation, or abandon its aims. There was no middle way.

The demonstration in New York City on April 15 had two important effects which strengthened the antiwar movement in seemingly contradictory ways: the first was to prove that opposition to the war was far broader than public opinion polls had seemed to show, thus encouraging insurgent political campaigns in 1968; and the second was to convince a large segment of the movement that simply *demonstrating* their opposition was not enough.

Following the draft-card burnings in the fall of 1965, opposition to the draft had faded into the background. As far back as April, 1961, during a conference on the draft at Oberlin College, Peter Irons, a member of the Student Peace Union, had proposed a mass demonstration of opposition to the draft by having students publicly turn in their draft cards. The idea was often revived after the expansion of the war in 1965, but students did not seem ready for such a radical act, and activist groups generally were cautious about confronting the federal government so directly. At its convention in Kewadin, Michigan, in June, 1965, SDS had decided against concentrating on the war in Vietnam in favor of "stopping the seventh war from now"[30] by fundamentally changing American society.

Nevertheless, SDS members continued to worry about the war and draft, especially since political activists were in the age group most likely to be called, but the various campaigns SDS considered never went beyond the discussion stage. On October 16, 1965, the *Chicago Sun-Times*, apparently on the basis of preliminary SDS proposals which it had obtained, published an exaggerated story saying that SDS was planning a massive nationwide anti-draft campaign. Talk of investigations by Washington threw the SDS national office into a panic, and Paul Booth flew to the capital. On October 20, 1965, he held a news conference in the National Press Club. "The commitment of SDS, and of the whole generation we represent, is clear: we are anxious to build villages; we refuse to burn them," he said. "We are anxious to help and change our country; we refuse to destroy someone else's country."[31]

Booth's use of the word "refuse" was misleading, however. SDS was committed only to supporting conscientious objectors. The SDS national office submitted to its members a proposal for a mild anti-draft campaign but results of the referendum were inconclusive. For a while SDS considered urging students not to participate in the Selective Service System examinations scheduled for May 14 and 21 and June 3, 1966, but at its National Council at Antioch in April it finally decided only to pass out leaflets at the examinations. At a second National Council in June, held in Ann Arbor, Michigan, Carl Oglesby and Stokely Carmichael drafted a joint statement calling for outright abolition of the draft, but SDS itself again avoided taking a stand on the subject, as it did during the national convention at Clear Lake, Iowa, in August.

One reason for this caution was an overblown fear of what the federal government might do in response. In the past SDS had confronted state and local governments in situations where the federal government, at least theoretically, had been either neutral or on SDS's side. Opposition to the war was inevitably leading it into confrontation with power in Washington, and SDS feared the government would act with all the energy and dispatch.so notably lacking when, for example, civil rights workers were attacked in the South. It did not strike them as impossible that dozens of arrests might occur in a single night. It was only gradually that SDS realized repression would not be swift and heavy, and found confidence in their ability to survive it when it came.

Elsewhere, students opposed to the war on moral grounds, a small but growing number, began to move toward principled refusal to take part in it. In July, 1966, eight members of the Yale University SDS, impatient with the group's caution, independently decided to start planning a mass turn-in of draft cards the following November 16 along the lines of Irons's 1961 proposal. The plan led to a meeting of forty or fifty activists in Des Moines, Iowa, on August 25 and 26. Most of the argument centered on the question of official repression, which everyone expected to be severe, and on a tactical matter. Some favored single, dramatic events like the card turn-in proposed by the Yale students; others supported slow, steady organizing of the sort used by SNCC in the countryside of Alabama and Mississippi. In the end the group failed to support the November 16 proposal, but those who had been present carried the idea away with them. One of them, Tom Bell, returned to Cornell University that fall determined to organize opposition to the draft.

Bell decided against approaching any of the established activist groups at Cornell with a draft-resistance proposal, figuring the only result would be endless argument and a shallow commitment by those eventually persuaded to take part. He wanted people who would be personally committed to resisting the draft, not a group that had talked itself into a position it did not really feel. He began with three other people who felt more or less as he did. When they had come to an understanding of what they planned to do, they began talking to others. The group expanded slowly, first to seven members, and then to fifteen. At each stage they thoroughly discussed the questions involved in draft resistance. Should one totally refuse to cooperate with the Selective Service System, or was it morally permissible to comply with the regulations necessary to obtain a deferment as a conscientious objector? Should one go to jail, inspiring others to resist by example, or remain free, and organize? Was leaving the country a kind of escape? Was draft resistance a moral act, or primarily political? Was one refusing to associate with an immoral war, or trying to stop it? The Cornell group rejected the idea of going to Canada and gradually moved in the direction of going to jail after a long meeting with Ralph DiGia of the War Resisters League, who had been to jail years before and quieted some of the fears of the Cornell group by saying what jail had meant to him.

The Cornell group had reached a position favoring total noncooperation with the Selective Service System but had not yet agreed how to make their decision public when one member, Bruce Dancis, decided to act on his own. On December 14, 1966, he publicly burned his draft card outside a Cornell building where faculty members were discussing the question of the draft. More than three hundred students watched him do it, and the effect on the school was immediate and profound.

On March 2, 1967, five other members of the Cornell group issued a formal call proposing that at least five hundred students pledge to burn their draft cards in New York on April 15 as part of the Spring Mobilization. The idea was that students afraid to act alone would be prepared to burn their cards as part of a large group. If five hundred students failed to agree, the pledge would be nonbinding. The Cornell group's call marked the beginning of an entirely new stage in the opposition to the war. They did not simply protest official policy, but disassociated themselves entirely from the government, and, if need be, the country that sanctioned its policy:

> The armies of the United States have, through conscription, already oppressed or destroyed the lives and consciences of millions of Americans and Vietnamese. We have argued and demonstrated to stop this destruction. We have not succeeded. Murderers do not respond to reason. Powerful resistance is now demanded: radical, illegal, unpleasant and sustained.[32]

Cornell was not the only center of concern with the draft in the winter of 1966–1967. A Chicago group held a "We won't go" conference on December 4 attended by more than five hundred people, and the SDS finally committed itself to an anti-draft program at its Berkeley National Council during the same month. SDS issued two buttons, "Resist" and "Not With My Life You Don't," and its new spirit was captured in a report of the National Council by the SDS national secretary, Greg Calvert, entitled "From Protest to Resistance." The following month, in January, 1967, the still-embryonic anti-draft movement was given a further impetus by the publication in *New Left Notes,* the SDS newsletter, of an official memorandum called "Channeling" which had been sent to local draft boards by the Selective Service System in 1965. Discovered by an SDS member, Peter Henig, the document described in detail how the "club of induction" was used to manipulate young men into desired channels, such as teaching, defense work, graduate school, and so on.

Adopting anti-draft resolutions and actually refusing to go were two different things, however. The first draft-card burner to be prosecuted, David Miller, had been convicted and given a suspended sentence in March, 1966, contingent upon Miller's acceptance of a new card. This he would not do. On April 6, 1967, Miller was sentenced to two and a half years in federal prison and carried from the courtroom when he refused to walk. Federal Judge Harold Tyler, Jr., said he understood Miller's position but added, "I must be concerned for the thousands of our men in Vietnam, many of whom, I am sure, are just as opposed to this war, philosophically, as you are."[33]

It must be remembered that Miller's crime was solely that of burning his draft card, a small square of cardboard, the destruction of which in no way hindered, although it symbolically defied, the Selective Service System. Burning a draft card in the spring of 1967 seemed like a sure way of going to jail. The Cornell pledge, circulated on college campuses throughout the country, made slow progress. By the end of March only 90 students had signed the pledge; by the eve of the demonstration the number was still only 120.

That night about sixty signers and supporters met in a loft on Fourteenth Street in New York City to decide what they should do. The executive committee of the Spring Mobilization, concerned about the defection of moderate groups like SANE, was opposed to the draft-card burning and had been quietly attempting to talk the Cornell group out of the idea. After a long debate, Bruce Dancis got up and asked the group directly, "How many will burn their cards if fifty do it at the same time?"[34] He counted the raised hands: there were fifty-seven.

The following day about seventy students gathered in the center of a large group of supporters and spectators at the southeast corner of the Sheep's Meadow at 11 A.M. At first they were frightened and secretive, avoiding reporters and burning their cards almost furtively. Gradually, however, their mood relaxed. A young man stood in the center of the group with a coffee can in which the cards were burned; one by one, then more quickly, the cards were passed up through the crowd to the young man and dropped into the flames. Others began coming forward spontaneously from the crowd, including a young man in a Special Forces uniform named Gary Rader.

In all, more than 175 cards were burned, and the group was suffused with a triumphant spirit of pride and defiance. Their opposition to the war had become total in a single gesture. For the first time a means of opposing the war was also, at least in theory, a means that could end it. If enough young men refused to fight, the war would be over. Hardly anyone felt such massive resistance was really possible, but the threat was nonetheless real. At the same time, draft resistance imposed a kind of sanction on the country, since it meant that young men would have their lives torn by agonized indecision or interrupted, perhaps even destroyed, by prison. Those refusing to cooperate with the Selective Service System could not be dismissed as hippies, shirkers, or deluded "peaceniks." They were often the best students with the deepest moral convictions. If their refusal to fight could not actually starve the armed forces of manpower, it could still alienate the best of a generation. The Resistance added dramatically to the "cost" of the war, touching thousands of lives for the first time. Officials in the administration had often suggested that students opposed the war because they were afraid to fight, an argument refuted by the willingness of young men to go to jail for their beliefs.

While the Cornell group was burning its draft cards in New York, a separate organization calling itself "The Resistance" was formally announced in San Francisco. In a speech in Kezar Stadium, David Harris, until recently the student body president at Stanford University, issued a call for a nationwide card turn-in to be held the following October 16. A leaflet handed out by the group Harris and three others had founded was calm but determined:

> We of the Resistance feel that we can no longer passively acquiesce to the Selective Service System by accepting its deferments. The American military system depends upon students, those opposed to war, and those with anti-Vietnam war politics wrangling for the respective deferments. Those opposed to the war are dealt with quietly, individually and on the government's terms. . . . While those who are most opposed to the war have been silenced, the system that provides the personnel for war crimes continues to function smoothly. . . . We do not seek jail, but we do this because as individuals we know of no justifiable alternative and we believe in time many other American men will also choose to resist the crimes done in their names.[35]

Harris, a brilliant speaker who conveyed an existential intensity in his refusal to be part of the war, captured the new mood beginning to spread through the country. He and others were beyond arguing; they no longer even bothered to list their objections to the war, as if its immorality were a given. While liberals like Arthur Schlesinger, Jr., proposed that the war be deescalated, Harris and others were saying that it was wrong, that it ought to be ended immediately, and that a man of conscience could have nothing to do with it. By their example they posed a painful question for every draft-age young man with doubts about the war. One either accepted complicity in the crime, or went to jail. After three years of war, some of its most brutal moments broadcast routinely on television, it was impossible to ignore the cost in human suffering which the war imposed on Vietnamese and young Americans alike. Harris put the question squarely: take part and be a murderer, or resist.

The call of the Resistance went out at the right moment. Groups sprang up across the country to organize the October 16 turn-in and the idea of the Resistance spread to include those too old for the draft. In the fall of 1964 a group in New York, consciously imitating a public statement by 121 French intellectuals during the Algerian War, had circulated a "Declaration of Conscience Against the War in Vietnam." Eventually signed by four thousand people, the Declaration was delivered to the White House during the Assembly of Unrepresented People in August, 1965.

In the spring and summer of 1967 a number of new statements were drafted and circulated and then abandoned for one reason or another. One that drew on several predecessors and achieved wide circulation was "A Call to Resist Illegitimate Authority," drafted by two Fellows at the Institute for Policy Studies in Washington, D.C., Marcus Raskin and Arthur Waskow. In September, their statement, pledging support for draft resisters and thus an act that constituted a federal crime, was published in the *New York Review of Books* and the *New Republic*. Several signers of the "Call" decided that a public pledge of support was not enough; they conceived a plan to collect the cards turned in around the country on October 16 and to deliver them to the Justice Department on October 20, the day before a major demonstration at the Pentagon already announced by the Mobilization.

On October 16, turn-ins were held in a number of cities, but the largest ceremony took place in Boston's Arlington Street Church, where 4,000 people gathered to watch 50 young men burn their cards and another 250 hand in theirs to the Reverend William Sloane Coffin, Jr. A number of speeches were given, including one by a former SDS officer, Nick Egleson, alluding to ideological differences within the Resistance which eventually were to split it. The mood of the Resistance was best expressed, however, by Michael Ferber. In a speech marked by passionate idealism, despair, and fatalism, Ferber warned his audience not to expect too much from their willingness to go to jail:

> Let us not be deceived. The sun will rise tomorrow as it does every day, and when we get out of bed the world will be in pretty much the same

mess it is in today. American bombers will continue to drop incendiary bombs on the Vietnamese people and American soldiers will continue to "pacify" their villages. The ghettos will continue to be rotten places to live in. Black and Mexican farm workers will continue to get miserable wages. America's schools will continue to cripple the minds and hearts of its pupils. And the American Selective Service System will continue to send young men out to the slaughter. . . .

Let us make sure we are ready to work hard and long with each other in the months to come, working to make it difficult and politically dangerous for the government to prosecute us, working to help anyone and everyone to find ways of avoiding the draft, to help disrupt the workings of the draft and the armed forces until the war is over.[36]

More than one thousand cards were turned in on October 16 during ceremonies held in eighteen cities. On October 20, Dr. Spock, Mitchell Goodman, Marcus Raskin, and Arthur Waskow formally accepted the cards at a rally held in front of the Department of Justice in Washington. One by one, young men came forward with draft cards, sometimes their own, more often a bundle of those collected four days earlier. Sounding like the chairmen of state delegations answering formal roll calls at national conventions, they gave their names, said where they were from, and called out the number of cards as they dropped them into a briefcase held by William Sloane Coffin. Television cameras recorded it all:

"John Sanna, Buffalo Resistance. I only got my own card, I'll add it to New York."

"Lenny Heller, California Resistance, 298 cards."

"Michael Ferber, from Boston Resistance. I bring from the Arlington Street Church 237 cards."

"Paul O'Brien, Chicago Resistance. I've got 45 cards and a few assorted words of welcome for Federal marshalls and the like."[37]

When the briefcase was full Coffin and the others entered the building and met with Assistant Deputy Attorney General John R. McDonough in a conference room. McDonough politely offered the group coffee and they awkwardly accepted. The nervous secretary who poured it out created a clatter of cups and saucers. After the coffee had been served everyone in the delegation made a statement. When they were finished McDonough also read a statement, concluding, "Dr. Coffin, am I being tendered something?"

"*Tendered* something?" Coffin asked, confused.

"Yes," said McDonough, "*tendered* something."

Coffin then handed the briefcase to McDonough, but he refused to accept it. Coffin put it down on the table and Arthur Waskow suddenly burst out, "*What!?* Ever since I was a *kid* I was brought up to respect the law in the United States. Here you have just read this statement alleging that we are guilty of crimes for which we offer you proof! And you [he slammed his hand down on the briefcase], the number three man in the Justice Department, refuse to accept the evidence! Where, man, is your oath of office? I demand a response!"

Coffin brought the meeting to a close and the group returned to the crowd of about five hundred waiting outside. Coffin told the group about McDonough's refusal to accept the cards, saying it "truly says something about its [the government's] own convictions—that it doesn't have enough morality on its side to carry through with such a moral confrontation."[38]

In the beginning those who turned in their draft cards fully expected immediate arrest, as did signers of the "Call to Resist Illegitimate Authority." The Justice Department, uncertain how to respond to an unprecedented challenge, instead sent the cards back to local boards, which then contacted the man in question and threatened him with conscription if he did not take back his card. If he refused to accept it and then refused induction, his case was turned over to the local U.S. Attorney. Cases were treated very differently in different parts of the country. In some areas only a small percentage of those who refused induction were actively prosecuted; in others, Minneapolis, for example, virtually every resister was quickly arrested and brought to trial.

In the case of adult supporters of the Resistance, technically guilty of counseling, aiding, and abetting evasion of the draft, the Justice Department was even more circumspect. On January 8, 1968, five of those involved—Coffin, Ferber, Spock, Goodman, and Raskin—were indicted in Boston on charges of conspiring to violate the Selective Service Act. Hundreds of others who publicly sided with the "Boston Five," technically as guilty as they, were never prosecuted.

In spite of the Justice Department's relatively cautious response, the Resistance clearly marked a qualitative change in the opposition to the war. Once content merely to note publicly their "concern," large numbers of people were increasingly ready to demonstrate in public, and even to break the law, in order to stop the war or to disassociate themselves from it decisively. In 1965 and 1966 marches drew up to 25,000 people. In the April, 1967, march, at least 250,000 took part, and perhaps even twice that many. In the fall of 1965, a handful of young men, less than a dozen, publicly burned their draft cards. In the spring of 1967, 175 took the same step. That October more than 1,100 handed in their cards, thus providing authorities with the evidence necessary to prosecute. Many members of Congress were pugnaciously prepared to crush this challenge with brute force, imposing maximum sentences on anyone who dared to resist the law. Others, however, including members of the Justice Department itself, sensed the enormous social cost implicit in any attempt to stamp out opposition to the war with the courts.

A new spirit of determination had entered the antiwar movement. In a report on the Chicago Area Draft Resistance in the summer of 1967, Gary Rader, first brought into the peace movement in April at the Sheep's Meadow, had said: "We call ourselves CADRE. We speak of squads, escalation, campaigns. The terminology is no accident—it fits our attitude. We are no longer interested in merely protesting the war; we are out to stop it."[39]

TEN

Breakdown

For all the bitter argument over the war, it remained strangely distant, a far-away struggle on the periphery of American life. Business boomed. Few families had lost sons, and there was no rationing. The killing all took place on television, between commercials, and the government insisted there was money enough for both guns and butter. Even after President Johnson finally asked Congress for a 10 percent tax surcharge, the first request for new sources of money directly linked to Vietnam, the fighting itself remained remote. Specialists in a number of fields, especially economists worried about inflation, budget deficits, and the international strength of the dollar, knew that the true price of the war was a great deal higher than officially admitted, and that it would inevitably reveal itself. For the most part, however, the war had been conducted with apparent impunity. Calling a halt to the war in August, 1967, when Johnson made his appeal for a tax surcharge, would have exacted a more immediate price in national humiliation, in wrecked careers, in lingering recriminations about a "stab in the back." The average American, and even the average senator or representative, instinctively felt that the cost of abruptly ending the war was far greater than the cost of continuing it.

The problem facing the antiwar movement was to make the war more costly than a change in policy, painful as that would be, to impose a sanction on the country for continuation of the war. The usual sanction of war, of course, is death and destruction, and there was sentiment, and even rudimentary planning among some small revolutionary groups, for literally "bringing the war home."[1] Beginning in

1967, fire bombings, and occasional dynamite bombings, were directed at military targets such as ROTC offices and local draft boards, especially in the San Francisco Bay area. Most of the movement, however, was opposed to violence for reasons of principle and realism: violence was the problem, not the solution, they felt, and besides, the other side had all the guns. More widely considered were proposals for massive civil disobedience like the VDC's attempt to halt troop trains in Berkeley and the attempt to push through police lines by the Assembly of Unrepresented People in Washington, both in the summer of 1965. Tax refusal, an idea supported by the War Resisters League, the Committee for Non-Violent Action, and other established pacifist groups, at least theoretically offered a way to limit the government's ability to wage war, but it never caught on as a means of protest.

Nevertheless, the war did exact an ever-growing cost which convinced increasing numbers of ordinary citizens and of legislators that the United States could not afford it. The numbers of dead and wounded mounted. Equally important, Johnson's refusal to insist on special taxes to finance the war until August, 1967, had resulted in massive deficit spending which brought on inflation. The inflation, combined with military expenditures overseas, caused a worsening balance of payments that ultimately threatened not only the value of the dollar but the entire system of international payments established at the end of World War II. By 1967, New York's financial community and the interests it represented were seriously worried about the war. They did not doubt the wisdom of opposing Communism, but they began seriously to wonder if Vietnam offered the right place, at the right time, at the right price.

A group called Business Executives Move for Peace (BEM), headed by Henry Niles of Baltimore, was the only group from the business community actively to oppose the war, but the discontent it revealed went far beyond its members. On May 28, 1967, BEM placed an ad in the *New York Times* opposing the war on practical grounds. That September it met in Washington and drafted a letter to President Johnson urging an immediate and unconditional bombing halt. These and other actions, moderate and limited as they were, nevertheless represented a major loss of support for the war in the community that had backed it at first with the fewest reservations.

Equally significant was the opposition of Marriner S. Eccles, who had been chairman of the Federal Reserve Board under Presidents Roosevelt and Truman. Eccles was one of the few public figures who favored immediate withdrawal at a time when that was considered to be unthinkable. In a widely reprinted speech delivered to the Commonwealth Club in San Francisco on August 11, 1967, Eccles cited not only the immediate costs of the war, such as rising wage settlements, prices, and interest rates, but also the war's hidden costs. Between 1965 and 1967, he said, veterans' benefits had cost a total of $13 billion, and the sum was rising. In 1965 alone the Veterans Administration had spent $1.4 billion in new construction. The United States was paying $30 billion a year for the war right now, compared to a total of $12.5 billion for all "Great Society" programs, and it would continue to pay billions of dollars a year for it long after the shooting stopped. Eccles was perhaps most alarmed by the nation's $26 billion in short-term international debts, which it was committed to redeem in gold although it had less than half that amount in reserve. A run on the dollar, Eccles knew, could even spark a worldwide depression.

Unlike most businessmen alarmed by the course of events, Eccles was active in opposing the war. Besides his membership in Business Executives Move for Peace, he had sponsored the call, formally issued in April, 1967, of Negotiations Now, a group seeking a million signatures on a stop-the-bombing petition. The fact that it had been organized by liberals like Joseph L. Rauh, Arthur Schlesinger, Jr., and John Kenneth Galbraith, and was being supported by establishment figures like Eccles, brought it under attack by the New Left. Writing in the Washington *Free Press* of July 21, 1967, Sheila Ryan dismissed Negotiations Now as an establishment attempt to undercut the radical peace movement. She singled out Eccles, claiming that his firm, the Utah Mining and Construction Company, was building military bases, including one in Thailand, was engaged in mining uranium for nuclear weapons, and had an interest in an open-pit mining operation in Peru. Eccles certainly was not on the side of the National Liberation Front, she said, and therefore had to be on the side of President Johnson and the imperialists.

The significance of Ryan's attack was not so much what it revealed about Negotiations Now (which the President, at any rate, did not consider to be on his side), as what it revealed about the divisions in the country. Ryan and the New Left had gone beyond simple opposition to the war. They argued that America had become an imperial power, and that wars like the one in Vietnam were an inevitable part of the imperial system. Closely examined, the argument was basically the old Marxist analysis of the relationship between war and capitalism superficially updated. One of the curious effects of the war was the way in which the once anti-ideological, existentialist New Left adopted the revolutionary theory of the old left in a matter of months in 1967 and early 1968. With the exception of a new emphasis on the Third World and the black "colony" within the United States, the analysis of the New Left was largely traditional and entirely borrowed. In any case, the New Left no longer wanted allies like Eccles. Until her final paragraphs, in fact, it almost seemed that Sheila Ryan opposed Eccles, Rauh, Schlesinger, and Galbraith more passionately than she did the war. The liberals, who were the first targets of this widened assault by the New Left, were the first to sense the breakup of the old coalitions in American politics.

The New Left's rejection of the establishment had all the bitterness of a break in the family, since young activists generally came from the same privileged background as those they attacked. Their passion elicited an equal anger on the part of union members, World War II veterans, and small-town Americans, who saw draft resistance and antiwar demonstrations as little short of treason. In New York following the Spring Mobilization on April 15, the Veterans of Foreign Wars organized a "Loyalty Day Parade" for Saturday, April 29, to demonstrate that the majority of the country supported the President and "our boys" in Vietnam. Organizers predicted 100,000 people would join the two marches in Manhattan and Brooklyn. In fact, only 7,500 people took part. They did not really know or care much about the war, but they knew they didn't like the pampered college kids who opposed it. The emotional tone of the march was expressed by one sign which read, "One country, one flag. Love it or leave it."[2]

Embarrassed by the poor showing, a wider coalition of patriotic organizations sponsored a second march on May 13. A large percentage of the 20,000 people who turned out were union members, traditionally Democrats and part of the liberal coalition that had dominated American politics since 1932. Marvin Garson, one of the leaders of the Free Speech Movement and a radical who had always assumed that "the workers" were the most oppressed, and therefore the most progressive, members of American society, was angered by the crude patriotism of the "March to Support Our Boys in Vietnam." In his column for the *Berkeley Barb* of May 19–25, he wrote:

> The most popular chant was: "What do you want?" "Victory!" "When do you want it?" "Now!" . . . The next time some $3.90 an hour AFL type workers go on strike for a 50 cent raise, I'll remember the day they chanted "Burn Hanoi, not our flag" and so help me I'll cross their fucking picket line.

What he felt about them, of course, was nothing on what they felt about him. Almost every society seems to live with suspicion and contempt between ordinary people leading complacently ordinary lives and the politically, intellectually, and culturally "advanced" elements of the population. The war in Vietnam brought these two classes, always vaguely hostile, to the verge of collision. Opposition to the war seemed to center on university campuses and in the big cities. The President's strongest support came from traditionalists—farmers, veterans, Southern churchgoers, the best-paid workers, small businessmen. The differences between these two classes went far beyond foreign policy and reached deep into the American past, but the war encouraged and focused their mutual animosity.

In 1967, the strains in American society fully revealed themselves. The war was not the cause of divisions between old and young, or black and white, or the country and the city, but it isolated and exaggerated them. The violence in Vietnam seemed to elicit a similar air of violence in the United States, an appetite for extremes: people felt that history was accelerating, time was running out, great issues were reaching a point of final decision. Cultural war between old and young is a permanent fact of life, but during 1967 this war suddenly spread and deepened with the intensity of a new children's crusade. Differences in style were less a matter of self-definition than weapons for assault. In the spring and summer of 1967 the hippies balanced awkwardly between millenarianism and nihilism, unsure whether they most wanted to create a new world, or destroy the old.

The hippie movement spread rapidly in response to the war in Vietnam but the cultural rebellion at the movement's heart was something much older, the latest manifestation of a century-long resistance to philistinism in American life and art. The hippies' most immediate ancestors were members of a small group of students at Columbia University at the end of the Second World War. The central figures of the movement were Jack Kerouac, a French-Canadian who had come to Columbia on a football scholarship; Allen Ginsberg, the son of a high school teacher (and poet) in Paterson, New Jersey; and William Burroughs, a writer and wanderer with an instinct for extremes. Ginsberg had a friend named Herbert Huncke, a small-time thief and heroin addict who used the word *beat* to describe his own spiritual exhaustion. Kerouac liked the word's evocation of victimization, physical weariness, and the beatific. In 1948 he used it in a novel based on a trip to the West Coast two years earlier with another friend, Neal Cassady. *On the Road* was written in a breathless, endless, ecstatic style inspired by a forty-page sentence in a letter from Cassady. Kerouac completed the book in only three weeks, writing it without revision on a single roll of teletype paper provided by another friend from Columbia, Lucien Carr, who worked in the New York office of United Press International. The book was not published until 1957, but it captured the new mood of a tiny group in New York and San Francisco in rebellion against what Ginsberg was later to call the "shutdown" of the late 1940s and 1950s.

At a time when World War II veterans were desperately trying to catch up in the postwar commercial hustle, while the Cold War was closing down over American life and politics and the long boom was beginning, when giant corporations offered security at the price of bored conformity, when the New Criticism implied that art was analytic, and the suburbs were draining the cities and the universities were blossoming graduate schools, the beats turned their backs on the confident, self-promoting America of the technicians and the Jaycees. Emotionally, culturally, intellectually, artistically, and morally they rejected the complacent "opportunities" of American life. They wrote chaotic poems, studied Eastern philosophy, lived in bleak, near-empty apartments, moved on when the mood struck them, let their hair grow long and even began to wear beards at a time when most Americans were relentlessly clean-shaven. They also smoked marijuana and sometimes slept with members of their own sex, the only aspect of their lives about which they were sometimes silent.

In all of these things they were much like other artistic minorities in other ages, but they nonetheless caught the United States totally by surprise. Their very existence offered a challenge to the prissiness, narrowness, and timidity of what was being promoted as the American Way of Life. At the end of the Second World War the United States was the world's greatest economic and military power, but it was fearful of the Communist world in a way that it had never feared Hitler. The country was dominated by vast and yet timid public and private institutions which threatened to drain the country of its juices. The appearance of the beats shattered a kind of spell, reminding people that this vast new future did not have to be entered in the spirit of a frightened child, or of a slave.

In 1953 Ginsberg moved to San Francisco and found an apartment around the corner from the City Lights Bookstore, run by a poet named Lawrence Ferlinghetti. The following year Ginsberg abruptly quit his job as a market researcher and began writing poems. In 1955 he arranged a poetry reading for a friend who was opening an art gallery on Fillmore Street in the heart of San Francisco's black ghetto. Ginsberg, the last poet on the program, read a new poem he had been working on called *Howl,* an incandescent vision of the decaying world and human poverty he saw around him. Whenever he would finish reading a particularly powerful line with especially passionate intensity, a small, tight man in the dim and smoky room, Kerouac would punctuate it with "Yeah!" or "So there!" or "Correct!" When the reading was over, Kerouac told him, "Ginsberg, this poem 'Howl' will make you famous in San Francisco."

"No," said the poet Kenneth Rexroth, "this poem will make you famous from bridge to bridge."[3]

Rexroth was right. City Lights published *Howl* in 1956 and it became the most widely read poem since T.S. Eliot's *The Wasteland.* The following year Kerouac's *On the Road* was published, and the beats, previously a silent, unnoticed defection from American life, suddenly became a highly visible public movement, the subject of articles in *Life,* denunciation in Congress, and emulation on every campus. Within a year or two most colleges had coffee shops, a folk singer or two, and a small group of students who wore blue jeans, lumber jackets, and beards. Everyone told them they were mortgaging their futures for these little freedoms, but that, of course, was just the point.

Throughout the early 1960s, in uneasy tandem with the civil rights movement and the birth of a new radicalism in politics, the beats' notion of life and culture began to spread, reaching the young most easily, but not the young alone. At first its principal elements were traditionally bohemian, with an emphasis on abandoning the formal patterns of ordinary life. Gradually however, a new element appeared that eventually overwhelmed all the others—a quest for spiritual and mystical intensity which bypassed traditional religious disciplines with the aid of drugs.

Lysergic Acid Diethylamide 25, commonly abbreviated as LSD, is a synthetic drug known as a hallucinogen for its hallucination-inducing properties. In the 1950s clinical psychologists and other researchers began exploring its peculiar qualities, intrigued by its effects on perception and consciousness, which sometimes included intense visionary experiences with interesting similarities to the mental states traditionally described by mystics: timelessness, selflessness, a sense that the world is fundamentally one. One of these early experiments was undertaken at Stanford University in California in 1958 where a young writer from Oregon named Ken Kesey was a graduate student. He volunteered as a subject, took the drug under laboratory conditions, and felt himself carried out of himself, beyond all the old limits of consciousness. At that time he was pretty much like other young writers, intense, to a degree chaotic, not altogether sure if he was primarily interested in art or in life. His brief experiment with LSD was only an episode.

Another experiment was being conducted at Harvard University by two members of the faculty, Timothy Leary and Richard Alpert. Ginsberg, who had been experimenting with drugs for years, met Leary in 1960 and found him in the grip of a passionate and naive enthusiasm for the possibilities of LSD and other hallucinogens like mescaline and psilocybin. Leary felt that a lot of the world's problems could be solved by a kind of instant spiritual revolution based on LSD. He felt there was a realistic chance that American establishment liberals like Arthur Schlesinger and even John F. Kennedy might try it, with far-reaching effects. If the preoccupation with self and the competitiveness that self entailed could be eliminated, the world might be redeemed.

Leary's ideas were premature, to say the least. His experiments began to attract attention after he and Alpert astounded the scientific community with an article in the May, 1962, issue of the *Bulletin of Atomic Scientists,* in which they warned that the Russians might accompany any nuclear attack on the United States with steps to contaminate the water supply of great cities with LSD. Because of LSD's incredible potency—a gallon might turn a sizable reservoir psychoactive—such a plan would not be out of the question. The best defense, Leary and Alpert suggested, was to have the population try LSD first.

That December a Harvard dean publicly accused Leary of conducting dangerous experiments with unprepared undergraduates. Leary denied the charge but was fired by the university in April, 1963. Alpert lost his appointment a month later. A brief attempt to continue their experiments in Mexico with a new organization called the International Foundation for Internal Freedom (IF–IF) ended in the middle of June. Later that month Leary moved into a sixty-room mansion on a large estate in Millbrook, New York, where he headed a new group called the Castalia Foundation. Like Ginsberg, Leary was at first interested in the mystical properties of LSD and the idea that it could lead to domestic tranquility and world peace by introducing fiercely competitive and acquisitive Americans to large inner realities. The notion that LSD had a redemptive potential spread quickly, giving its proponents a messianic sense of mission.

Perhaps the most serious of the new messiahs was Ginsberg himself, who had returned from a long stay in India no longer a poet alone, but also a spiritual teacher. When the Hell's Angels attacked peace marchers in Berkeley in October, 1965, Ginsberg took it upon himself to reconcile the two groups. Before a second march scheduled for November, Ginsberg and Ken Kesey paid an official visit to Ralph ("Sonny") Barger, the president of the Oakland Angels. Ginsberg arrived armed only with LSD, a text of the *Prajna Paramita Sutra,* and a faith in the power of love. The combination apparently worked. On the afternoon before the march Barger released an official statement at a news conference:

> Although we have stated our intention to counter-demonstrate at this despicable, un-American activity, we believe that in the interest of public safety and the protection of the good name of Oakland, we would not justify the VDC by our presence . . . because our patriotic concern for what these people are doing to a great nation may provoke us into violent acts. . . .[4]

Despite Barger's belligerent tone the Angels had in fact reversed their position on peace marchers and hippies, whom they, like the rest of the country, tended to see as more or less the same. Following the meeting with Ginsberg the Angels abandoned their hostility toward hippies and peace activists and occasionally even acted as movement bodyguards.[5] At the rally Ginsberg suggested the movement ought to adopt a politics of gentleness. In a speech later reprinted as "How to Make a March/ Spectacle," Ginsberg proposed that "Masses of flowers—a visual spectacle—can be used to set up barricades, to present to Hell's Angels, police, politicians, and press and spectators, whenever needed, or at parade's end. . . ."[6]

For Ginsberg, drugs were a means to enlightenment, and enlightenment to peace. During the fall of 1965 he won a $6,000 Guggenheim Poetry Fellowship which he decided to use for a tour of the nation's college campuses. Students were vaguely aware of the fact that Ginsberg had once (in 1957) taken off his clothes during a poetry reading, were curious to see one of the first and most celebrated of the beatniks, and turned out in large numbers wherever he went during his five-month tour. Ginsberg's message was one of love, mysticism, and a vague bisexualism. The students had expected someone wild and found someone calm, who advised them to look at things deeply and to stay out of the army. "Make it inconvenient for them to take you," he suggested. "Tell them you love them, tell them you slept with me."[7]

Ginsberg carried his emphasis on LSD as a redemptive drug to Washington the following spring, when he testified before a Senate subcommittee including Senators Jacob Javits and Edward Kennedy, both decidedly skeptical, on June 15, 1966. Ginsberg tried to soften LSD's often lurid reputation, suggested that the failures of society made LSD attractive, and urged the senators to sponsor a major investigation of the drug's potential rather than repressive legislation. He mentioned that under the influence of LSD in a lonely cove along the coast of Big Sur in California he had once prayed for the "tranquil health" of President Johnson.

Later that year Ginsberg carried his case even further in a speech delivered in Boston's Arlington Street Church on November 12:

> Abruptly then, I will make a first proposal: on one level symbolic, but to be taken as literally as possible, it may shock some and delight others —That everybody who hears my voice, directly or indirectly, try the chemical LSD at least once; every man woman and child American in

good health over the age of 14—that, if necessary, we have a mass emotional nervous breakdown in these States once and for all; that we see bankers laughing in their revolving doors with strange staring eyes. . . . I propose, then, that everybody including the President and his and our vast hordes of generals, executives, judges and legislators of these states go to nature, find a kindly teacher or Indian peyote chief or guru guide and assay their consciousness with LSD. Then, I prophesy, we will all have seen some ray of glory of vastness beyond our conditioned social selves, beyond our government, beyond America even, that will unite us into a peaceable community.[8]

There was a pietistic side to many of those who justified LSD in this manner. Ginsberg could hardly be charged with overcaution or preciousness, but the early academic researchers who stressed clinical conditions could be. Even at Millbrook the drug was surrounded with a kind of hollow solemnity, a studied and religious air, as if one took LSD in the spirit of a communicant. On the East Coast LSD was a serious matter; those who experimented with it were inclined to be heavy and academic. They read Aldous Huxley's accounts of early experiences with hallucinogens. They read Eastern philosophy. They were articulate and relentlessly spiritual.

On the West Coast, however, things proceeded along a somewhat different path. By the time Ken Kesey was finishing his second novel, *Sometimes a Great Notion,* in 1964, he had lost his appetite for pursuing a conventional literary career and was returning to his early interest in drugs. He wanted to explore the nature of the present and its potential emotional intensity. He was curious about the mind's limits, the spirit's tolerance, and the body's endurance. That spring he bought a 1939 International Harvester school bus for $1,500. It already contained beds, a refrigerator, and a water system. Kesey added a fantastic array of sound equipment: speakers, microphones, electrical musical instruments, a variety of special apparatus for altering sound by introducing time lags, and so on. On the rear of the bus he hung a sign reading, "Caution: Weird Load," and on the front, in place of the destination sign, the word "Further."[9]

With a group he called the Merry Pranksters, including Kerouac's old friend Neal Cassady as driver, Kesey headed for New York, where his new book was about to be published. On the way back the bus stopped off in Millbrook, where Kesey was expecting an historic encounter with Leary and the Castalia group. The eastern intellectuals at Millbrook were ill at ease with Kesey's loud, flamboyant, reckless psychedelic gang, who in turn found the Millbrook people dull, restrained, and timid. The meeting was a disappointment to both Kesey and Leary, and yet both were changed by it. Kesey immediately plunged further in the direction his instincts were already leading him and Leary, dropping the last trace of old academic habits of mind, shortly followed.

In Millbrook, LSD was taken in a spirit of deliberation, with expert supervision in a quiet atmosphere and a calm mood, reflecting Leary's spiritual emphasis on "set and setting." In this manner the "dangers" of LSD were thought to be minimized. Kesey reversed these priorities. Instead of approaching new and presumably expanded states of consciousness cautiously, he would do it recklessly, with all limits and safeguards abandoned at once, exaggerating the dangers in a setting which would heighten hallucinatory effects to phantasmagoria. The difference was like that between medieval scholastic philosophers, who approached God through thousand-page commentaries on Augustine and Aristotle, and the half-demented hermits who simply plunged naked into the wilderness.

Back in California, Kesey began to plan the ultimate psychic debauch. He obtained a ballroom in San Jose, forty miles south of San Francisco, and installed an elaborate sound and lighting system which could deafen and blind. The first of Kesey's "acid tests" was held on December 4, 1965. It was designed as a rite of passage, an explosive leap into the future of such intensity that every sense and state of mind would be distorted beyond all previous limits. The effect was just as planned: a staggering subjective experience that made the rest of life seem pale. Six weeks later, a gigantic three-day Tripps Festival was held at the Longshoreman's Hall in San Francisco between January 21 and 23, 1966. On the last day of the festival, Kesey, facing jail as a result of two previous drug arrests, decided to go into hiding in Mexico, but the scene he abandoned was far different from the one he had found.

San Francisco had been the West Coast home of the beats since the early 1950s, but in 1960 the movement began to reach college and even high school students. The beats had originally settled in the North Beach district of San Francisco. When they inevitably attracted publicity, the area was quickly placed on the tourist route and the old coffee shops were gradually surrounded by topless nightclubs. In 1960, Bob Stubbs opened a new coffee shop called The Blue Unicorn on Hayes Street in the Haight-Ashbury district, named after the conjunction of two streets at its center. The old bohemians and the radical activists across the Bay in Berkeley merged uneasily in the new street culture of Haight-Ashbury, or Hashbury as it was sometimes called. Both elements were theoretically allies, since they shared the same establishment enemies, but the relationship was nervous and fragile. In the public mind beatniks and peaceniks were the same; in the same room their differences verged on animosity.

The younger imitators of the beats were called hippies (just as younger hippies, borrowing from the same vernacular, would be called teeny-boppers; cultural styles have an interesting tendency to begin with men and women in their late twenties and early thirties and then drop down through the generations until they reach the twelve-year-olds, at which point they have been so simplified as to be meaningless and the style dies). By the time Kesey left for Mexico the hippies had attracted attention as something more than a purely local phenomenon. On the first day of 1966, two brothers, Ron and Jay Thelin, opened a store on Haight Street selling drug-related paraphernalia called the Psychedelic Shop. San Francisco's notion of psychedelic was far from Leary's at Millbrook; the hippies were Kesey's spiritual children, and the revolution they intended to make was both undefined and total.

While Kesey was in Mexico he began to rethink his position on LSD, seeing it only as a way of opening the door to new modes of perception. Eventually, he felt, one would have to face that future without LSD's help. In September, he returned to California but continued to elude the police, making a well-publicized appearance at a friend's writing class at Stanford on October 1, 1966, and another at the "Love Festival" held on October 6 to celebrate the day California's new anti-LSD law went into effect. He gave an interview to a reporter from the San Francisco *Chronicle* and another to a San Francisco television station in which he said, "I intend to stay in this country as a fugitive and as salt in J. Edgar Hoover's wounds."[10]

The interview was broadcast on Friday, October 20, the same day the FBI recaptured Kesey. He was quickly released on bail and held a final festival with all the usual electronic equipment and ear-shattering music, but without LSD, a new experiment which he called the acid test graduation. The hippies, still approaching those limits Kesey had gone beyond, turned on him as a traitor and Kesey, always ahead of his time, graduated alone.

After a period of legal delay and confusion, Kesey began serving a six-month sentence in June, 1967. He got out of jail again in November and went back to Oregon. Meanwhile, San Francisco, quicker to take things up than to put them down, was pursuing Kesey's goal of totality in cultural and psychedelic rebellion.

The hippie phenomenon did not really attract broad national attention until Saturday, January 14, 1967, when Ginsberg and others held a huge "Gathering of the Tribes" in San Francisco's Golden Gate Park. More than 20,000 people showed up at the "Human Be-In," held on the park's Polo Field, mystifying reporters who did not know quite what to call it, since it was not a "demonstration," exactly, nor a "rally," and yet was clearly more than a simple festival. Among the speakers were Jerry Rubin, who was beginning to see culturally alienated kids as the most promising constituency for an American revolution, and Timothy Leary, who had abandoned the last traces of his academic life at Harvard and was cultivating in their place a natural talent for media promotion which at times verged on medicine-show hucksterism.

Dressed entirely in white and carrying a daffodil, Leary spoke for the regulation seven minutes, having been specifically denied prophet status, with its thirty-minute time limit, by the be-in's organizers. Leary had set out to proselytize for LSD, using a message with deliberately religious overtones. "Turn onto the scene," he said. "Tune into what is happening and drop out—of high school, college and grad school, junior executive, senior executive—and follow me, the hard way."[11]

Leary was already considered something of a fraud by the genuine spiritual leaders of the hippie movement, but his expulsion from Harvard in 1962 and a thirty-year jail sentence imposed in Texas for possession of marijuana in 1966 had given him a national audience. His message of turn on, tune in, and drop out reached people who would never know the meaning of the word hallucinogen.

The be-in turned a regional style into a national movement: flowers, long hair, mysticism, unstructured life, freedom, music, love, and drugs, the heart of what came to be called "the counterculture," were adopted in theory, if not in rigorous practice, by kids across America almost overnight. On March 22, 1967, the San Francisco *Chronicle* reported in a banner front-page headline local predictions that 100,000 or more kids would swarm into the Haight-Ashbury district that summer. *Newsweek* and later other magazines picked up the story and, by a complex process in which national media helped spread the hippie mystique by reporting it, the country gradually discovered, and in a sense embraced, the notion that a new kind of revolution was at work. The invasion of San Francisco never quite took place as predicted, although 300 or more teenagers arrived in the Haight-Ashbury district weekly during the height of the summer. There was something attractive in the passionate innocence of young boys and girls with flowers in their hair, convinced that all conflicts could be solved by "flower power." Social critics had been writing about the timidity and complacency and conformity of American children for at least a decade. The new freedom in clothes, ideals, behavior, and social concern seemed a healthy change. The hippies were credited with a social conscience that was a good deal more specific than the one they had, and yet the vagueness of their rebellion made it seem all the more total. They were rejecting "the American Way of Life," itself a political cliché rather than a cultural fact, which made it correspondingly easy to see their rebellion as a step on the road to salvation, or disaster. If friends of the movement did not inquire too closely into its "program," enemies found in it a threat to whatever they held most sácred, whether it was the right to private property or the importance of rigorous grading in school. There are genuine distinctions between right and left in the United States, between liberal and conservative, between old ways and new ones in American life; the hippie movement fuzzed them all. There is nothing more heated than an argument that is undefined, and the argument over the hippies was unfocused and unlimited and as a result conducted with great heat and occasional violence. Local ordinances were passed against bare feet, schools expelled students with long hair, and radio stations refused to play the new San Francisco music called acid rock. In some areas tough kids from white ghettos declared a kind of open season on hippies and the police were never much restrained by the exercise of flower power.

The element in the hippie movement that received the most immediate and lasting attention was the use of drugs. It was quickly apparent that drugs involved a good deal more than giggling teenagers passing around marijuana on summer evenings. LSD had always appeared vaguely sinister to those who didn't use it, if only for the mystical force of its hallucinatory powers. The outlawing of LSD in California in October, 1966, was followed by similar legislation elsewhere. As concern about the use of drugs spread during 1967, medical writers reported the rising incidence of LSD-induced psychosis and, still more alarming, preliminary findings that LSD could cause genetic defects and might even result in leukemia by a process of cell breakdown which was, ironically, not unlike that caused by radiation. It was bad enough that drugs were dangerous, worse that kids did not much care if they were. One hippie told an interviewer:

> LSD might shorten your life, like ten years, but like ten years is meaningless to us. What is happening is that you don't draw on experience necessarily any more but people are living more and more in the present. Under acid, twenty seconds ago can be history. . . . Everything is instant. What went down before doesn't really matter. When you're really stoned, it's now.[12]

One did not have to be a Southern fundamentalist to sense the element of nihilism in this attitude. One response to it, reasonably enough, was an attempt to understand why young people found the immediacy, dangers and all, of acid preferable to American life in mid-century. The answers most frequently given were, abstractly, all those things that had created an American crisis of the self and spirit in mid-1967: the war in Vietnam, the persistence of poverty, the prevalence of racism, the obsession with materialism, boring education, boring jobs. Attempts to explain the hippie movement were never conducted honestly, both sides using the facts as weapons in the larger political struggles which were joined most sharply over the war. Did kids really take LSD in 1967 because of the war? The kids in question were anywhere from thirteen to twenty and most of them couldn't have named the premier of North Vietnam, or explained how Harry Truman got us into the war, or Lyndon Johnson ought to get us out. But in another sense the war did have something to do with the reasons people took LSD. Even Fulbright and Robert Kennedy and Arthur Schlesinger felt the war's fearsome potential; a sense of inexorably widening war had diffused throughout the country; bad enough now, the war would get worse. War was the future of every young man, a war his elders fought over bitterly, a war that was poisoning American life. It is easy to make too much of emotional atmospherics in a time of political struggle; only a handful truly care about the details or the outcome. And yet an irreconcilable conflict on a major point must inevitably reach out to touch the rest of life. "You may not be interested in politics," SDS people sometimes said, "but politics is interested in you." The hippies were a reflection, exaggerated and distorted by the emotions of the time, of a larger crisis in American life which has since subsided but is not dead. The fact of Vietnam cannot be suppressed; the questions it raised, even if unanswered, cannot be ignored. In 1967 the hippies *thought* they were rebelling against an American reality in which Vietnam was a principal fact, and those who vaguely sympathized, like those who recoiled, thought so, too.

LSD was only the beginning. Kids began to use, and the public began to read about, other drugs even more clearly dangerous. A kind of drug hysteria touched the country. A rumor that banana peels could be smoked like marijuana, with similar results, swept the country. Tests showed it tasted awful and had no effect. Another drug called "68" or "sex juice"[13] by credulous reporters was identified by the Food and Drug Administration as concentrated oil of peppermint. Other new drugs turned out to be more serious.

In the March, 1967, issue of *The BDAC Bulletin,* the publication of the Food and Drug Administration's Bureau of Drug Abuse Control (BDAC), the bureau reported, "We have also heard rumors of the use of STP, the motor additive, as a hallucinogen. What are the hipsters in your area using?" In fact, the STP that people were putting in their mouths was not the STP others put in their cars. The BDAC apparently did not think STP would turn out to be anything more worrisome than the smoking of bananas, which had already been shown to be harmless. However, STP—the initials were said to stand for Serenity, Tranquility, and Peace—was a potent hallucinogen the effects of which were said to last twice as long as those of LSD. The drug's nature was completely unknown. Apparently produced in private laboratories, the STP appeared early in 1967, was well known in Berkeley in April, and reached New York later that spring. The secrecy of its ingredients was supposed to circumvent the law, since legislators presumably could not outlaw what they could not identify. One California rumor said that STP contained 300 micrograms of LSD, 30 milligrams of psilocybin, and 60 milligrams of cocaine. Other rumors suggested it was chemically related to a secret military nerve gas called BZ. In August, STP was finally identified as an experimental drug called "dom" which had been developed by the Dow Chemical Company. Dow had sent specimens of the drug to the FDA and other institutions for experiments in treating mental illness. It was never learned how the drug entered the hippie pharmacopeia, where it flourished briefly and then quickly faded in importance.

The most significant of the new drugs was not actually new at all. This was methamphetamine hydrochloride or "speed," one of the family of amphetamines prescribed by doctors for such purposes as diet control. The usual prescribed dosage was between five and thirty milligrams a day. Hippies at first used amphetamines in the form of pills, but during 1967 the practice of intravenous injection began to spread. The effect was an instant "rush" of hyperactivity and euphoria. Heavy users would inject 100-to-300-milligram doses every couple of hours for as long as six days straight without eating or sleeping. The physical effect on the user was catastrophic, leaving him drained of all physical and emotional resources. In addition, prolonged use could cause paranoia and profound dejection. A common sight at rock concerts became gaunt young men shaking with a wild frenzy for hours, "speeding" until they collapsed. Jeff Jasen, a reporter for the *Berkeley Barb* who had come from Oregon, went home in the spring of 1967 and described the Seattle drug scene in the *Barb* of June 23–29:

> The foundation of the local hip scene is built precariously upon the abundance of methedrine [one of the trade names for amphetamine]. Many of the hips are pseudo-teenie bopper speed freaks who turn on to a needle even before they try sex. Most localities have been doing speed for about 18 months. A series of busts put the screws on a previously profitable acid [which forced people to] look for other means of tripping. Speed was the easiest to get. Now most trippers aren't satisfied unless they've got a size 27 spike in their veins. That is, if they have any veins left.

The drug scene in San Francisco was no better. In June a free clinic was opened to provide hippies with medical care. By September it had treated more than ten thousand people for bad trips, venereal disease, malnutrition, respiratory ailments, and serum hepatitis, spread by infected needles. Haight-Ashbury publicity attracted not only kids bored with life at home, but winos, shakedown artists, Hell's Angels, and their imitators, professional drug dealers, and more than a few psychotics passing as free-spirited hippies.

In May a girl stabbed a man to death in front of Tracy's Doughnut Shop. In June a man walking along the street was shot and wounded by someone in a passing car. One young drug dealer, twenty-five-year-old John Carter, known as "Shob," was robbed of $2,600 and shot to death. For some reason his murderer also cut off one of his arms. Another dealer, a Negro named William Thomas (or Powell, depending) and known as "Superspade" was found inside a sleeping bag at the bottom of a cliff across San Francisco Bay. He had been stabbed in the chest and shot through the head. Probably the best-known of these violent incidents occurred in New York early in October when Linda Fitzpatrick, a girl from Greenwich, Connecticut, and her boyfriend, James ("Groovy") Hutchinson, were discovered in a cellar in the East Village. They had been beaten to death with a brick.

Very few flower children came to ends as brutal as these, but many were just as final. Kids began turning up dead from drugs, one of them in San Francisco killed when he shot up "methedrine" that turned out to be Drano, a caustic used to eat through the sludge in stopped-up plumbing. When the use of heroin began to spread, as it did, deaths caused by acute reactions to the drug were common. More common still were beatings and rapes. Girls quickly discovered that there were ten boys on the streets of Haight-Ashbury for every girl, with predictable results. Most common of all were confrontations with the law, sometimes ending in substantial prison sentences.

Compared to heroin, marijuana was a harmless diversion, but officials nevertheless opposed it violently. Henry L. Giordano, commissioner of the Federal Narcotics Bureau, considered the spread of marijuana "just another effort to break down our whole American system."[14] Giordano believed that 80 percent of heroin addicts "began" with marijuana and he therefore treated the two drugs as equally dangerous. The seven thousand marijuana arrests made by his bureau in 1964 had more than doubled to fifteen thousand in 1966, he told the House Appropriations Committee on February 8, 1967. The Federal Narcotics Control Act of 1956 provided for a mandatory two-to-ten year sentence for a first conviction of possession of marijuana, five-to-

twenty for a second, and ten-to-forty for a third. The arbitrary injustice
of these provisions was simply staggering, especially since federal authorities were well aware that every marijuana study had shown it to
be less of a social problem than alchohol.

State laws varied widely. In Colorado, a second conviction of selling
marijuana to persons under twenty-five years of age was a capital crime.
Leary's thirty-year Texas sentence in 1966 was evidence of the purely
vindictive way in which drug laws were enforced. Another typically
vindictive case was the twenty-year sentence given to Kerrigan Gray,
a student at Everett Junior College in Seattle in May, 1965. The state
prosecutor had sought *two* twenty-year sentences to run consecutively.
Harsh sentences like these were an assertion of authority by established
society. Prosecutors and judges alike saw the use of illicit drugs as a
challenge to be firmly suppressed. In Washington, D.C., the first person
to be tried under a law banning LSD, nineteen-year-old Raymond M.
Frank, was sentenced to a year in jail on May 12, 1967. General Sessions
Judge Charles W. Hallek told him:

> Unfortunately for you, this is the first case to be prosecuted and you must
> be the example. . . . This involvement of young people with LSD,
> marijuana and other dangerous drugs has become almost the thing to do
> these days. It must be stopped. Far too many young people in this
> community have the feeling that nothing is going to be done about this
> type of activity. I am making it clear that decent people in this society
> are not going to put up with it. I am serving notice that we are not going
> to tolerate such activity.[15]

When experiments with hallucinogens first began in the 1950s and
1960s, they had been undertaken with a tentative and religious air.
Leary's early emphasis on "set and setting" stressed the spiritual possibilities of LSD. He and other experimenters began with the attitude
first expressed by Aldous Huxley in *The Doors of Perception*. Huxley,
who had been experimenting with mescaline, suggested that the mystical sense of timelessness, selflessness, and oneness experienced under
the influence of certain drugs, or naturally in a traditional mystic state,
were actually real qualities of the real world. Drugs simply removed the
intellectual and spiritual inhibitions which prevented one from perceiv-
ing reality in a naked form. Hallucinogens, then, were a philosophical
tool.

Gradually, however, there was a shift in the focus of interest from spiritual to immediate physical experience. In an interview with *Playboy* published in September, 1962, Leary made it clear there was more to LSD than spiritual discovery and enrichment.

> *Playboy:* We've heard that some women who ordinarily have difficulty achieving orgasm find themselves capable of multiple orgasms under LSD. Is that true?
>
> *Leary:* In a carefully prepared, loving LSD session, a woman will inevitably have several hundred orgasms.
>
> *Playboy:* Several *hundred?*
>
> *Leary:* Yes. Several hundred.

Despite the fact that Leary's claim was totally fanciful (like most drugs, LSD is an anti-aphrodisiac), it was widely believed. The drug movement slowly but steadily shifted its goal from enlightenment to ecstasy. LSD wasn't taken under laboratory conditions, but wherever and whenever the mood struck. Wild concoctions were put together using cocaine, LSD, speed, mescaline, psilocybin, and other drugs. Even Kesey had grown uneasy at the excesses of kids prepared to shoot up anything for a high, from grain alcohol to ice-water.

Lisa Bieberman, who had been part of the Cambridge group that included Leary and Alpert in 1962, watched the transformation of the drug movement with dismay. She felt Leary and others had perverted, commercialized, and ultimately trivialized LSD. In an article in the August 5, 1967, issue of the *New Republic* she described her difficulties publishing a bimonthly newsletter called *Psychedelic Information Center:*

> The collected back issues are a catalogue of frauds and failures. I finally had to change my editorial policy because I came to realize that I did readers a disservice to report on things like the Neo-American Church, the League for Spiritual Discovery [a group Leary founded], the psychedelic shops and so on, as if they were to be taken seriously. Most of the psychedelic projects I reported have flopped, even though the more obvious losers were screened out before printing. Those that remain are a caricature of the psychedelic vision, a mockery of the idealism of youth. ... If the utopian vision of 1962 was too good to be true, it does not follow that what came out of it had to be this bad.

The psychedelic movement's decline in seriousness was matched by a growth in size. By 1967, when the movement was a thinly disguised form of ecstatic nihilism, college kids were routinely using marijuana. On every campus there existed a drug scene which involved more potent drugs. In numbers the experimenters were undoubtedly few, but the drugs they used make an impressive list: besides the usual LSD, mescaline, hashish, opium, cocaine, speed, heroin, and psilocybin, kids were trying amyl nitrate, glue fumes, freon gas, nitrous oxide, and ether. Early reports that LSD might cause birth defects and cancer were apparently unfounded, but the effects of intensive drug use were bad enough without them. Every big-city hospital reported numbers of kids being admitted with drug-induced psychosis, some of whom recovered quickly, and some of whom did not. Most came through a period of drug use physically intact, but they did not always find it easy to pick up their lives again.

The number of kids joining the drug culture was probably exaggerated equally by those who led and those who deplored it, just as far fewer activists were turning into radicals than was hoped on the left or feared in the center. Nevertheless, a kind of confusion, demoralization and free-floating animosity was emerging in American life. Drugs were only a symptom of a deeper boredom and unease. If the kids experimenting with drugs were divided between those looking for God and those looking for oblivion, they were united in their rejection of traditional American values and ways of living. Frank Zappa, leader of a rock group called the Mothers of Invention, felt this rejection was part of a larger cultural revolution centering on the new music:

> The only real loyalty that exists in the American teenager today is to his music. He doesn't give an actual damn about his country or his mother or his government or his religion. He has more actual patriotism in terms of how he feels about his music than in anything else.[16]

The spread of drugs and flower children throughout 1967 convinced many people that the spiritual and moral strength of the country were disintegrating. The riots which physically damaged and emotionally shocked a dozen cities that summer, and nearly destroyed Newark and Detroit, raised the possibility that the country was on the verge of an internal breakdown.

The Harlem riot in the summer of 1964 had been followed a year later by the far larger and more serious uprising in the Watts section of Los Angeles. Serious disturbances occurred in several midwestern cities in the summer of 1966, but nothing had prepared the country for the size and violence of the urban riots which began in Newark on Thursday, July 13, and in Detroit ten days later. The governor of New Jersey, Richard J. Hughes, had called out the National Guard to restore order on Friday, July 14, saying, "The line between the jungle and the law might as well be drawn here as any place in America."[17]

During the five days of rioting in Newark, 26 people were killed, 1,200 were injured, and 1,300 were arrested. More than $10 million worth of damage was reported. Despite Hughes's statement and dozens of others like it from officials throughout the country, it was clear that the riots were the product of something more than willful lawlessness. Its problems overshadowed by those of New York City across the river, Newark was a major city divided between a prosperous downtown business community and a surrounding plain of decaying black and white ghettos. Overcrowded schools, decrepit housing, hospitals with beds in the hallways, a lack of jobs all made Newark a classic example of what would soon be called the crisis of the cities. For years black leaders had been warning that the discontents of Negroes in the South were nothing compared to the anger and despair in the big-city waste-lands of the North. The arson and looting in Newark, they insisted, were an inarticulate cry of rage at inhuman conditions the people had not created and could not overcome. On Saturday, July 22, during a hastily called National Conference on Black Power held in Newark, LeRoi Jones, a poet, playwright, and militant community organizer, told reporters that the problem was black oppression:

> We black citizens of Newark, New Jersey, declare at this point that the unrest among black citizens cannot be characterized as a "riot" or as a "criminal action" on the part of black citizens. . . . We understand that this unrest was a rebellion against the forces of oppression, brutality and legalized evil that exist within the city of Newark and that we citizens have the right to rebel against an oppressive, illiterate governmental structure that does not even represent our will. . . . We will rule Newark or no one will! We will govern ourselves or no one will![18]

The following day, July 23, rioting began in Detroit. With huge areas of the central city in flames, Michigan's Governor George Romney called out 1,500 National Guardsmen and then formally requested federal aid. President Johnson stalled until Monday, when Detroit officials reported 731 fires throughout the city. The First Airborne Division was sent in to reinforce the National Guardsmen. Johnson followed the lead of the New Jersey governor in treating the riot as a simple matter of anarchy versus law and order. "Pillage, looting, murder and arson have nothing to do with civil rights," he said. "We will not tolerate lawlessness. We will not endure violence. It matters not by whom it is done or under what slogan or banner. It will not be tolerated."[19]

That night in Cambridge, Maryland, H. Rap Brown, elected the new chairman of SNCC in May, told a crowd not to hold back. "But don't tear down your own stuff," he said. "When you tear down the white man, brother, you are hitting him in the money. Don't love him to death. Shoot him to death."[20]

The President insisted rioting could have no political aspect and Brown insisted it was entirely political. The truth was a mixture of both. Black militants called the riots "rebellions," but in fact they were chaotic and directionless. The accounts of sniping, reported and accepted as fact until the riots were well over, were eventually shown to have been groundless. In Newark, especially, where overwhelmingly white and relatively untrained National Guardsmen had been firing their weapons more or less at will, most sniping incidents had actually involved police and guardsmen shooting at each other, or at figments of their imaginations. There was plenty of bitter discontent in the ghettos of Newark and Detroit, but those who took part in the arson and looting were far from pursuing consciously political goals. Their motives were vaguer than that, the result of frustration and hopelessness and anger which had no specific cause, but grew out of the totality of their condition.

Part of that bitter, reckless mood was the result of the failure of Johnson's war on poverty, the readiest explanation of which was the cost of the war in Vietnam. By the fall of 1967, the war on poverty was badly faltering, attacked in Congress, resented by many state and local officials, starved of the President's interest. Johnson was beginning to lose his control over Congress, which, still cautious in dealing with the war, expressed its independence with regard to the President's other programs. On July 20, three days after the rioting ended in Newark and three days before it began in Detroit, the House of Representatives defeated by 207 to 176 a bill that would have provided $40 million in matching grants to cities over a two-year period for the extermination of rats.

Debate on the bill was limited to heavy-handed humor about a "rat bureaucracy" and "rat patronage" and "a high commissioner of rats." "What a monstrosity of a bill," said Representative James A. Haley, a Democrat from Florida. "Let's buy a lot of cats and turn them loose." Representative Delbert L. Latta, a Republican of Ohio, said the program ought to be entirely local. "Putting out a little bit of rat poison," he said, "is not too much to ask."[21]

In the ghettos, of course, these light-hearted jokes did not strike anyone as funny. The defeat of the bill was evidence not so much of hard-heartedness as of the distance between the world of legislators and the urban poor. The ferocity of the riots in Newark and Detroit caught the country by surprise solely because they knew so little about the lives of the black poor. One week after the defeat of the bill Johnson was on television again to appeal for a national "day of prayer for reconciliation" and to report that he was appointing a special Advisory Commission on Civil Disorders. "We have endured a week such as no nation should live through,"[22] he said.

In the wake of the rioting there was a great deal of public talk about new programs to end poverty, but it was clear that a vast new commitment of federal money, initiative, and energy was simply out of the question. All three were fully absorbed by Vietnam. If the money had been there, Congress would not have approved it. Feelings were running too high. At the peak of the Detroit rioting the Republican Coordinating Committee had attacked Johnson for refusing to act with adequate resolution and force. "We are rapidly approaching a state of anarchy and the President has totally failed to recognize the problem," the committee said in a statement. "Worse, he has vetoed legislation and opposed other legislation designed to re-establish peace and order within the country."[23] They were referring to Johnson's veto of a 1966 bill that would have widened police powers in the District of Columbia, and to a bill, opposed by Attorney General Ramsey Clark, making it a crime to cross state lines with intent to incite a riot.

Frustrated by the endless war in Vietnam, which could not be won decisively without risking a much worse war with China, Congress was not about to walk softly at home. This anger would take several years to express itself fully, but the broad outlines of a social policy based on repression were already apparent the week after the riots.

On the left, the riots were seen as the opening skirmish in a new, violent phase of the movement. Phil Hutchins of SNCC told a group in Washington on July 30 that one of the things "that makes Newark important is that it begins to make the concept of urban guerrilla warfare a realistic principle."[24] Activists in the South had been toying with the idea of guerrilla war since the early 1960s, basing their arguments not so much on its prospects for success, which were zero, as on the futility of any other approach. The movement's willingness to talk about revolutionary violence did not blind it to the realities. In Mississippi, Alabama, and other Deep-South states, black violence would have been instantly and overwhelmingly suppressed.

The result of this impasse, in which the movement found itself emotionally drawn toward an unworkable strategy, was a steady escalation in the movement's use of rhetorical violence and a gradual withdrawal from its concrete field programs, which were seen as half-measures. Rap Brown's allegedly inflammatory speech in Cambridge (for which he was indicted on July 25 and arrested the following day) expressed SNCC's mood in the summer of 1967: seething with inward violence, but well aware of who had all the guns. SNCC was committed to revolution by force of arms and Brown's constant exhortation to every crowd was "get you some guns," but it was clear that a serious attempt to pursue political goals by violence would be suicidal.

Nevertheless, the movement's commitment to revolution was now irreversible. On the West Coast a white Berkeley radical named Bob Avakian announced the formation of a new group early in August called the Student Organizing Committee, which, he said, would raise money to help arm black revolutionaries. In an interview with the Los Angeles *Free Press* published on August 18, Brown further refined SNCC's analysis of the proper role of whites in the movement:

Free Press: What about whites who hate America's racism, who identify with the black revolution, but who have a hard time organizing with other whites? . . . Do you see anything that people like that could do in the struggle against racism and imperialism?

Brown: There is very little I can see them doing at this point except fighting along with us in the only way they can—by helping to arm us. They can provide us with donated arms, or they can just give us money to buy the guns we need.

In the Chicago headquarters of Students for a Democratic Society that summer and fall, the possibility of urban guerrilla warfare was under constant discussion. It was even decided, in a tentative sort of way, to begin organizing material support for black militants in the next uprising, whenever it should occur. SDS had sponsored an Economic and Research Action Project in Newark for several years and felt its commitment was being critically tested in the wake of the Newark riot. Eric Mann, a leader of SDS active in Newark, even approached a black militant there that fall to propose SDS support for a new uprising. The blacks, however, had had enough one-sided violence. Mann was told the notion was preposterous.

Nevertheless, white students who considered themselves revolutionaries began to think seriously about political violence in the wake of the Newark and Detroit riots. With a few exceptions, their thinking remained on an entirely theoretical level, but it signaled the end of the civil rights movement as it had once been. A generation that had come to political activism with hope for reform had, in effect, dropped out of politics. Their defection was another element in what reasonably appeared to be a real breakdown in the United States.

The final element in any assessment of public feeling about the war in the fall of 1967 was an uneasy sense that what the United States was doing in Vietnam was wrong. There had been no lack of passionate partisans willing to call the war genocide since the day it began; the difference in late 1967 was that ordinary people were beginning to lose faith in their own government's sense of justice and proportion. In its January, 1967, issue *Ramparts* had published a twenty-four-page story on "The Children of Vietnam" which included sixteen pages of color photographs of war-wounded children. The missing limbs, the scar tissue from napalm burns, the puzzled eyes were eloquent testimony that the war was costing the South Vietnamese more than they could ever hope to gain by victory. On April 7, *Life* published twelve pages of pictures by Lee Lockwood showing the damage caused by the U.S. bombing campaign in North Vietnam. The Defense Department might insist that bombing was directed solely at military targets and conducted with surgical precision; Lockwood's pictures showed ordinary cities smashed flat.

That same month the *New Yorker* devoted most of an issue to Jonathan Schell's long report on the pacification program, "The Village of Ben Suc." In this case pacification simply meant the forced evacuation of an entire village and the obliteration of everything left behind. No one argued in these articles, or dozens of others like them, that the United States was committing genocide or any other sort of deliberate war crime (that would come later), but it gradually became apparent that the sheer size of American military efforts was physically wrecking Vietnam. The vast resources of American technology were turning whole sections of the country into moonscape, black, lifeless, crater-pocked deserts where no one could move and live. Even the self-imposed limits of the war, such as a ban on outright invasion of the North, implied a kind of cruelty. The American government never admitted it in so many words, of course, but the bombing campaign was designed to *hurt* so much that Hanoi would simply give up.

The bland inhumanity of American military technology was captured well by an aviation writer named Frank Harvey. In 1966 he had gone to Vietnam for *Flying* magazine with few doubts about the American right to be there. Gradually he had sensed that American military power was largely irrelevant to the political nature of the war and thus amounted to a pointless atrocity. His long report, *Air War—Vietnam,* was expanded into a paperback published by Bantam in July, 1967, and reviewed prominently in the *New York Review of Books.* In a typical passage, Harvey explained that U.S. Navy pilots were introduced to the war from Dixie Station off South Vietnam, where they flew missions over the Mekong Delta before moving up to Yankee Station off North Vietnam:

> He learns how it feels to drop bombs on human beings and watch huts go up in a boil of orange flame when his aluminum napalm tanks tumble into them. He gets hardened to pressing the firing button and cutting people down like little cloth dummies, as they sprint frantically under him. He gets his sword bloodied for the rougher things to come.[25]

Harvey wrote about the defoliation program which used C-123 transports built by Fairchild-Hiller to spread eleven-thousand-pound loads of 2, 4, 5-T, a defoliant later banned after it appeared the substance could cause birth defects. Each mission cost well over $5,000 and would destroy three hundred acres of rice within three to five days, or an equal area of jungle within five to six weeks. The crews flew two missions a day, six days a week, and the motto over their Ready Room door read, "Only you can prevent forests."[26]

Harvey wrote about "Puff, the Magic Dragon," the ancient DC-3s, each outfitted with three electrically operated rapid-fire machine guns which could pour six thousand 7.62-millimeter bullets over the landscape each minute. At night they found their targets with the aid of million-candlepower magnesium flares. (The military once actually toyed with the idea of orbiting a huge reflector around the earth in such a fashion that it would shine perpetual sunlight on Vietnam, thus ending the nightly activities of the Vietcong.)

Among other military gadgets used by the United States in Vietnam were red haze photos taken by RF-4C Phantom jets. Vietcong cooking fires would appear on the film as a white dot with a tail. Processed immediately after return of the plane, the photos were passed onto the artillery, which would determine the map position of the fires and zero in with artillery fire. One did not have to be a pacifist to wonder how the photos determined that cooking fires were *Vietcong* cooking fires, or if the whole process was really fair. The Vietcong, for example, had been using tunnels since the beginning of the war. The United States would drop napalm on tunnel openings, creating fires that would suck up all the oxygen from the tunnels in seconds, leaving whoever happened to be inside to die of asphyxiation. Other accounts told of the "harassment and interdiction" artillery fire sent into certain areas at random intervals throughout the night, and the "free-fire zones" which the Government of Vietnam had placed off-limits to all its citizens. Anyone in the zone was fair game. In a later *New Yorker* article, "The Military Half," Jonathan Schell brilliantly described the way air force pilots in light planes would roam vast areas of countryside looking for "Vietcong." Whenever one was sighted, plowing a field or planting rice or hovering in the tree line at the edge of a paddy, jets would be called in to finish him off. It did not take correspondents in Vietnam long to discover that the Vietcong insurgency came from the people, that the regime in Saigon felt no hesitation about authorizing attacks on the people, and that the United States complied. It was easy to wonder if any nation, for any reason, could have the right to intrude with such technology into a civil conflict in a backward country halfway around the world.

A television reporter named Desmond Smith told of a military briefing he had attended in an article published in the *Nation* of June 12, 1967. The briefing officer had described the 365 air raids, 300 B-52 raids, millions of artillery shells, and millions of propaganda leaflets used in one operation on the Bong Son Plain. When he was finished, he asked:

> "Well, do you correspondents have any questions."
>
> "Well, only one. According to your handout, all you captured so far in Operation Pershing is 30 hand grenades, four rounds of larger caliber ammunition, three tons of rice and three tons of salt."
>
> "Sir?"
>
> "It appears that you've levelled virtually every enemy village and hamlet, killed or driven more than 50,000 peasants off the land with your fire power. My question is, how do you intend to go about winning the hearts and minds of these people?"
>
> "I'm afraid you'll have to take that up with the S.5, Sir, but jeeze, it's a real good question."

Winning hearts and minds was a joke referred to by reporters and officers alike as "WHAM."[27] The theory of the military was simple and direct: "Get them by the balls and their hearts and minds will follow." Such a strategy, however, was nothing more than military terror. Inevitably, as the war dragged on, it began to seem a tragic waste which would never solve anything. Young Americans who went to Vietnam were horrified by what they saw, the casual killing and destruction, the unbridgeable gulf between the Vietnamese and the Americans who insisted officially that they were fighting only for the right to go home. What right did the United States have to insist that the government of Vietnam should be of this or that sort? On March 27, 1967, the Akron (Ohio) *Beacon-Journal* published a long letter sent to his family by a local boy.

> Today a buddy of mine called "la dai" ("Come here") into a hut and an old man came out of the bomb shelter. My buddy told the old man to get away from the hut and since we have to move quickly on a sweep, just threw a hand grenade into the shelter. As he pulled the pin the old

man got excited and started jabbering and running toward my buddy and the hut. A GI, not understanding, stopped the old man with a football tackle just as my buddy threw the hand grenade into the shelter. (There is a four second delay on a hand grenade.) After he threw it, and was running for cover (during this four second delay), we all heard a baby crying from inside the shelter! There was nothing we could do. After the explosion we found the mother, two children (ages about six and 12, boy and girl) and an almost newborn baby. That is what the old man was trying to tell us! The shelter was small and narrow. They were all huddled together. The three of us dragged out the bodies onto the floor of the hut. It was horrible! The children's fragile bodies were torn apart, literally mutilated. We looked at each other and burned the hut. The old man was just whimpering in disbelief outside the burning hut. We walked away and left him there.

Cruelest of all the American weapons used in Vietnam was napalm. The military insisted that nothing else was so effective against an entrenched enemy, and in this the military was probably right, but napalm was also used against villages, and the victims were not only soldiers. In theory only the Vietcong lived in the free-fire zones where napalm was routinely dropped; civilians had all been warned to move away and if they failed to do so, well, they were to blame for the consequences. This bland legalism was too frail to justify the reality of human suffering, the women and children hideously burned, dying in prolonged agony or scarred for life. In the January, 1967, issue of the *Ladies' Home Journal,* a woman's magazine with no history of social activism, Martha Gellhorn wrote that, "It's time to talk of the Vietnam casualties nobody dares talk about: the wounded boys and girls. . . .

In the children's ward of the Qui Nhon province hospital I saw for the first time what napalm does. A child of seven, the size of our four-year-olds, lay in the cot by the door. Napalm had burned his face and back and one hand. The burned skin looked like swollen, raw meat; the fingers of his hand were stretched out, burned rigid. A scrap of cheesecloth covered him, for weight is intolerable, but so is air. His grandfather, an emaciated old man half blind with cataracts, was tending the child. A week ago, napalm bombs were dropped on their hamlet. The old man carried his grandson to the nearest town; from there they were flown by helicopter to the hospital. All week, the little boy cried with pain, but now he was better. He had stopped crying. He was only twisting his body, as if trying to dodge his incomprehensible torture. . . .

My interpreter questioned the old man, who said that many had been killed by the fire and many more burned, as well as their houses and orchards and livestock and the few possessions they had worked all their lives to collect. Destitute, homeless, sick with weariness and despair, he watched every move of the small, racked body of his grandson. Vietcong guerrillas had passed through their hamlet in April the old man said, but were long since gone. Late in August, napalm bombs fell from the sky. . . .

A housewife from New Jersey, the mother of six, had adopted three Vietnamese children under the Foster Parents Plan, and visited South Vietnam to learn how Vietnamese children were living. Why? "I am a Christian. . . . These kids don't ask to come into the world—and what a world we give them. . . . Before I went to Saigon, I had heard and read that napalm melts the flesh, and I thought that's nonsense, because I can put a roast in the oven and the fat will melt but the meat stays there. Well, I went and saw these children burned by napalm, and it is absolutely true. The chemical reaction of this napalm does melt the flesh, and the flesh runs right down their faces onto their chests and it sits there and grows there. . . . These children can't turn their heads, they were so thick with flesh. . . . And when gangrene sets in, they cut off their hands or fingers or their feet; the only things they cannot cut off is their head. . . ."

One could quote endlessly from this and similar articles, many of which reached a wide audience. The charter of the International Military Tribunal that conducted the trials of German war criminals at Nuremberg had specified "wanton destruction of cities, towns or villages" and "inhumane acts committed against any civilian population" as "crimes coming within the jurisdiction of the Tribunal for which there shall be individual responsibility." The use of napalm against women and children was certainly "inhumane," and the bombing of villages because they fell within an arbitrary grid on military maps was certainly "wanton." Pictures of napalm-burned children, chins fused to necks, skin flaking off in blackened chunks, legs and arms twisted grotesquely by scar tissue, were reprinted on antiwar leaflets, and the opposition to the war began to focus on napalm as the cruelest, most indiscriminate, and most characteristic example of America's failure to comprehend the nature of a political war.

Since the napalm used in Vietnam was all manufactured by the Dow Chemical Company, antiwar groups on dozens of campuses in 1967 began to protest visits by Dow recruiters who came to interview job applicants. In a typical demonstration, the SDS at Harvard blockaded a Dow recruiter for nearly twelve hours on October 25, 1967, while pickets marched outside with signs reading "Dow shalt not kill" and "Napalm is Johnson's baby powder." [28] An SDS leaflet insisted that moral issues raised by the war superseded the rights of Dow to recruit or of students to seek jobs with the company. "Unobstructed freedom to recruit implies a tacit acceptance of Dow's right to use Americans to aid in the killing of the Vietnamese," the leaflet said. "Students who deny Dow the freedom to recruit are denying Dow the freedom to kill. A war of genocide is at issue."[29] The university naturally did not agree, and a number of students were put on probation or "admonished" for their part in the demonstration, but such official reprimands hardly settled the deeper question at issue.

In the fall of 1967 the number of people convinced beyond doubt that the war was militarily hopeless or morally unjustified was far smaller than the number uneasily wondering if it would ever solve anything, or ever end. The number of people who opposed the war was far smaller than the number worried about its effect on the emotional climate of the United States. This huge, uneasy public probably would have preferred to forget the whole business, but they were not allowed to forget. It was slowly becoming apparent that the war was exacting a cost, not one of the usual sort, perhaps, since the United States was far too large, distant, and powerful to be threatened by North Vietnam, but a cost of a subtler kind.

The vast public which had been ready to let the President act as he thought best in the summer of 1964, supporting him when he bombed North Vietnam and supporting him when he promised no wider war, was beginning to turn away, wondering if the country could really afford the war. It was worried by the alienation of its children, the violence in the cities, the bitterness between the races, and the fearsome questions raised by the sort of war we had chosen to fight. It was hard to avoid a certain sick feeling of doubt about the nature of a country that could cause so much suffering and destruction, to itself, to its friends, and to its enemy, in a cause it could not even define.

ELEVEN

The Fall Offensive

During the fall of 1967 the mood of that broad range of activists who referred to themselves as The Movement underwent a sea change. They blamed their failures on themselves, argued that a politics that feared violence was self-defeating, and sought to harden themselves for an escalating struggle. A moment of crisis had been reached which demanded something more than futile moral witness. Years of growing opposition to the war had, it seemed, achieved nothing. Teach-ins, rallies, petitions, insurgent political campaigns, draft resistance, and demonstrations had been maligned, ridiculed, distorted, or simply ignored by the government. Activists were sick with hatred for the bureaucrats who made war with such aloof impunity, and with self-loathing for their own failure to stop them, or interrupt them, or even disturb for a moment their cool equanimity.

The main intellectual effort of the movement that fall was to find a way to fight. Those opposed to the war were no longer trying to express a position on the war, to literally *demonstrate* a point of view, but to end it. Traditional protest politics grant a certain moral legitimacy to the government by the very fact that the government is being appealed to, petitioned, *asked* to do something. The movement no longer granted the government anything by the fall of 1967. If this was not altogether revolutionary, still, it represented a new relationship between those in control of the country and those who felt its policies at home and abroad were equally evil. In April the movement had flooded the streets of New York with people opposed to the war. The administration simply cited all those who had stayed home, a classic instance of adding apples and oranges. The true comparison ought to have been with the numbers of people willing to march in support of the war. The two pro-administration marches in New York in late April and early May indicated that the President's principal sources of support were a huge mass of relatively indifferent citizens willing to let him have his way, and a small professional establishment which found it hard to face the implications of admitting a mistake in Vietnam.

This fact struck the movement as being of signal importance. The government did not really care if it had popular support, activists decided, since peaceful opposition in no way limited its freedom of action. If the government was to be stopped from what it was doing, then, the means had to be military in nature. The movement had no illusions that the government could be seized, but hoped it could be impeded, distracted, divided, confused, and weakened, not by speech but by action. When the movement began organizing for the fall of 1967, its leaders were less interested in the number of people who would take part than in the lengths to which they would go.

The Resistance was certainly the clearest, and probably the most important expression of this new militance, but there were others as well that promised a price in domestic unrest for continuation of the war. Four major demonstrations were held, varying in size from a few hundred to perhaps 75,000, which differed from earlier actions in their militance. Meetings of demonstrators and police had ended in violence before, but now activists expected, planned for, and in a handful of cases even provoked violence. It is important to remember how tentative and symbolic these efforts were; the faintest attempt to push through a police line was sure to result in club-swinging. Occasionally windows were broken, or bottles thrown from the depths of a crowd. In most cases the violence of demonstrators was entirely theatrical, consisting of masses of young men and women pushing, running, waving flags at the end of poles, and shouting slogans.

Even this gesture of militance, however, was enough to create a permanent split in what had been the peace movement. Middle-class, middle-aged, and traditionally liberal elements played almost no part in the four major street actions of the fall of 1967, marking the end of a long transition from liberals to radicals, and from old to young. When the focus of movement activity shifted from civil rights to the war, and from the war as a failure of policy to the war as a symptom of a sick and cruel society, older white and black elements gradually fell to the side. They found it hard to share the passion of the young, who were redefining themselves as Marxist-Leninist revolutionaries, and they found it harder still to march beside young men and women seriously preparing for resistance, barricades, and violence. Opposition to the war in the fall of 1967 was wider than ever, and yet the range of those who took an active part in demonstrations was dramatically narrower than it had been even six months earlier.

The acceptance of violence as not only inevitable but necessary was the result of years of failure. The practice of nonviolence in the early movement had been founded on two principles, one theological, the other purely practical. As a practical matter, the movement's passive resistance in the South did more to discredit the Southern racism, and the violence that defended it, than all the argument about rights and wrongs. The theological principle behind nonviolence was the Christian belief that suffering is never in vain, that sacrifice is redeemed, that a Christian witness of love would touch the hearts of oppressors and soften them. Martin Luther King never lost this faith, but the nonviolence of much of the rest of the movement did not run so deep. When they became angry they wanted to hit back, and when their witness was ignored they wanted to avenge themselves on the indifferent.

David Nolan, a draft resister facing prison in late 1967, reluctantly concluded that his gesture would probably be futile. "Perhaps three years ago," he wrote, "when there seemed to be such hope of changing America, I would have felt differently about prison than I do now. But I think we have reached the point where suffering is unredeemed, where America is tired of having its moral weaknesses pointed out, and where these actions do not have much effect."[1] Nevertheless, Nolan refused to go into the army.

In some ways the movement was near a point of despair. Activists did not know how to stop the war and yet they felt the effort was necessary, whatever the cost. In their eyes the war was wrong, a crime, murder. Many felt that what the United States was doing in Vietnam was as bad as the killing of the Jews by the Germans. Their attitude was not flexible on this point. Opposing Hitler obviously would have meant prison and probably death, and yet opposition, clearly, would have been the only morally defensible position. One might realistically shrink from a futile gesture in such a situation, but one could hardly argue that silence and evasion were the nobler course. Movement activists felt that militant opposition to the war was morally necessary *even if it didn't work.* Failure was bad enough, but to do nothing worse.

From the beginning, student involvement in the movement centered on the notion of commitment, the willingness to support one's beliefs with one's body. Students who registered voters in rural Mississippi towns during the summer of 1964 were risking their lives, but they had no choice; to shrink from the risk would have been to surrender to injustice. In December, 1964, Mario Savio had spoken of one's obligation to act, regardless of consequences, at certain moments. A time comes, he said, "when the operation of the machine becomes so odious, makes you so sick at heart, that you can't take part; you can't even tacitly take part, and you've got to put your bodies upon the gears and upon the wheels, upon the levers, upon all the apparatus and you've got to make it stop."[2]

The arguments had all been simplified by the fall of 1967: the war was evil and nothing could justify it. The movement was shrinking back to those who had no doubts or qualifications, and were willing to put their bodies in the way of the machine.

The new mood of militance rose up from the movement spontaneously, presenting the movement's leaders with unexpected and delicate problems. These leaders were not leaders at all, in the usual sense. They were simply at the organizational apex of the double-handful of more or less permanent groups which worked out the practical details of demonstrations. If they misjudged the mood of their "followers," a demonstration might be attended by . . . nobody at all. The New York demonstration in March, 1966, had attracted 25,000 people. A year later roughly the same groups, working just as hard, brought out ten times as many.

On May 20 and 21, leaders of the regional groups that made up the National Mobilization Committee, exhilarated by their altogether unanticipated success in April, met in Washington to make tentative plans for a still larger demonstration in the capital on Saturday, October 21, 1967. This time, they decided, they would bring out *one million people* (the very hugeness of the number seemed in itself a blow against the state) to demonstrate unmistakably that the American people were against the war. The plan was audacious and yet plausible. The war expanded steadily without approaching an end; the cost was rising, the draft growing. If the war seemed a kind of snowballing madness in April, how would it appear in October? A million people? Why not?

The movement's nominal leaders had, however, badly misjudged the situation. The mood of their principal supporters was changing; they did not want to express a position, to differ respectfully in the traditional manner of a loyal opposition, but to struggle, to fight, to resist, finally to destroy what they considered an evil policy and government. An attempt was made to divide the militants from that less passionate mass of citizenry who would inevitably make up the majority of any really huge demonstration. The attempt succeeded only partially. The final turnout in October was to be far smaller than the April march, only 50,000 to 75,000 people. And yet, in subtle ways, these would have a still greater effect, and those who stayed home were not inactive.

While the first vague plans of the National Mobilization Committee were being considered for the October demonstration on the East Coast, leaders of the Resistance in California, working independently, were planning for a new nationwide draft-card turn-in for Monday, October 16. When they realized the fortuitous proximity of the two dates, it occurred to them that the separate demonstrations might be joined loosely in an entire week of antiwar actions between October 16 and 21. On June 29 about twenty people sat in at the Oakland Induction Center, with surprising success. Press coverage was wide and vaguely sympathetic, and the smooth functioning of the center was interrupted, if not quite halted. Early in July, Steve Hamilton of the California Resistance wrote Norma Becker of the Fifth Avenue Peace Parade Committee, perhaps the largest of the East Coast groups, with a suggestion:

> How about declaring National Draft Resistance week, Oct. 16–21 and closing down many of the major induction centers across the country for the entire week? I know that it could be done at the Oakland Center which serves Northern Calif., Oregon and half of Nevada. As mild as the demonstration on June 29th was, they didn't resist arrest, and as small a number as there was they still gummed up the works for quite a while. You need only 15 people at a time to block the doors and with several hundred people ready to take their places they would have to tell the guys who showed up for induction to go home by the middle of the day. For

the first time we would be doing something that borders on more than symbolic protest.[3]

Planning on the two coasts followed much the same pattern, with Jerry Rubin, asked by David Dellinger of the National Mobilization Committee to be project director for the Washington march, acting as a point of glancing contact between the two. Rubin, with his talent for organizing protests with a certain aesthetic bite, suggested that the October 21 demonstration be held not at the Capitol, but at the Pentagon, the heart and brain of the war machine. The card turn-in on the sixteenth, the attempts to close down induction centers on following days, and the demonstration at the Pentagon would thus all focus on the growing militarization of American society.

The California group, calling itself the Stop the Draft Committee, met on September 14 and quickly divided on the question of nonviolence. Should protestors passively sit in at the induction center and "gum up the works"? Or should they militantly attempt to close down the center in a literal sense? The Resistance, with its emphasis on the individual moral act, favored a physically gentler but morally stronger series of actions showing the government it could not have its way without jailing its citizens. The SDS, expressing the angrier mood of the free-floating radical community in Berkeley, in effect favored a second-front strategy: the United States would have to fight at home, too, if it were going to continue the war abroad.

In the East a similar split quickly developed between traditional liberals who wanted to mount a huge protest, and younger radicals, who insisted some attempt be made actually to close down the Pentagon. The latter felt that passive protest conceded to the government a right to act as it saw fit. Radicals might not be strong enough to block or even occupy the building, but a gesture in that direction would draw the lines more sharply. The first issue of *The Mobilizer,* published on September 1, expressed a militant tone. "We will fill the hallways and block the entrances," it said. "Thousands of people will disrupt the center of the American war machine. In the name of humanity we will call the warmakers to task."[4]

A thousand copies of the issue were distributed at the National Conference for New Politics held in Chicago the first weekend in September, raising an immediate outcry from the more traditional elements represented in the National Mobilization Committee. Union organizers and liberal Democrats were hardly going to invade the Pentagon, even if the Pentagon would allow them to do so, and many had reservations about phrases like "the American war machine." The steering committee planning the Pentagon demonstration voted to suppress the first issue of *The Mobilizer* and a second, leading with a calmer version of demonstration plans written by Sidney Peck, was quickly printed.

Nevertheless, the demonstration clearly would go farther than earlier protests. The range of participants at the New York press conference announcing the demonstration on August 28 made this unmistakable. Among them were the Reverend Thomas Hayes of the Episcopal Peace Fellowship, Abbie Hoffman and Jerry Rubin, Carl Davidson of SDS, Dick Gregory, and H. Rap Brown. The last, who had been urging blacks to get guns, was asked by a reporter if he planned to bring one. "I would be unwise to say I'm going there with a gun because you all took my gun last time," he said, referring to an incident that summer. "I may bring a bomb, sucker."[5] Reverend Hayes tried to mute the contradictions between these irreconcilables:

> Individuals will act on their consciences and in their own personal styles. Not all people will take part in the massive sit-in at the Pentagon, and we are not asking people to come to Washington solely on this basis. Those who do not block the Pentagon will surround it in a massive peace-in of picketing, vigiling, music, drama, and rallies.[6]

Reservations about still another demonstration had been expressed by the SDS at its convention in June, where a resolution was passed regretting "the decision of the National Mobilization Committee to call for a march on Washington in October. We feel that these large demonstrations—which are just public expressions of belief—can have no significant effect on American policy in Vietnam. Further, they delude many participants into thinking that the 'democratic' process in America functions in a meaningful way."[7]

As the date of the demonstration approached, however, the attitude of SDS changed. Plans for a sit-in actually closing down the Pentagon were something more than "an expression of belief." The chances for a peaceful demonstration seemed increasingly remote when the government threatened to withhold a march permit if the Mobilization Committee did not agree to certain restrictions on the time and route of march. When the demonstration actually took place, tens of thousands of moderates who had marched in April stayed home, and several hundred SDS people were in the militant vanguard.

Eventually the Mobilization Committee resolved these strategic disputes by failing to choose among them. The demonstration would begin with a rally at the Lincoln Memorial, would march across the Potomac River on the Arlington Memorial Bridge and proceed to the North Parking Lot of the Pentagon where a second rally would be held. At four o'clock, with only an hour or so of daylight remaining, the demonstration would culminate with a nonviolent sit-in where those inclined would be arrested for civil disobedience. Everyone would be welcome to go as far as he liked, and assured he would not be forced into something for which he was not prepared.

In California a similar compromise was reached in planning for Stop the Draft Week. The Resistance, the War Resisters League, and other pacifist groups held a peaceful sit-in at the induction center at 5 A.M. on Monday, October 16. After the group refused to leave, police quietly and efficiently arrested 123 people. At noon the same day the Resistance held a rally on the steps of the Federal Building in San Francisco where 160 draft cards were turned in. It was a traditional protest, heavy on moral witness, eloquent, little more than an inconvenience to authorities.

The following day the militants took over. More than three thousand demonstrators surrounded the induction center by 6 A.M., were warned by police to move, and then were assaulted. No other word applies. Twenty-five people were arrested during the next thirty minutes and, in a pattern of violence that was becoming increasingly familiar as angry protestors collided with police, at least twenty were injured. The violence, not altogether unexpected, was still a shock. Demonstrators, reporters, and bystanders were clubbed indiscriminately, and attempts to resist goaded the police to inevitable excess. By 9 A.M. the induction center had been cleared, buses of inductees began to arrive, and the center went about its business normally.

That night a meeting was held to decide what to do. Plans for a march on City Hall to protest police brutality, or on the office of the chancellor of the University of California (for reasons no one could quite define), were proposed, debated, and finally rejected in favor of another sit-in Thursday morning, where ninety-seven people were arrested. By Friday it was again the militants' turn and this time an incredible ten thousand people showed up, many of them wearing motorcycle helmets and carrying shields. When the police attacked, the demonstrators retreated, blocking streets as they went. Benches, potted trees, garbage cans, even cars, trucks, and buses were pushed into barricades, cutting off access to the induction center for three hours. Whenever police attacked a barricade, demonstrators melted away and reappeared elsewhere.

For one brief morning opponents of the war felt they had the upper hand, that the government was powerless and could be resisted, that the war could be *stopped*. The effect on the movement throughout the country was electric. On Wednesday night, when the new mobile tactics had only just begun to emerge in reality after years of discussion, Jerry Rubin called the *Berkeley Barb* from New York, saying, "The whole atmosphere here has been changed by what's happening at the Oakland induction center. People here have been inspired by it. Everybody's talking about it."[8]

Overnight the Oakland street battle became movement legend. Like guerrillas in Cuba, Vietnam, and Algeria, American radicals could tactically outwit and outmaneuver the police. Attacked, they would fade away; seeing an opportunity, attack. Defiance of the government would encourage the timid. Clumsy retaliation by authorities would only win sympathizers. In an escalating process, the struggle would grow sharper, lines clearer, the movement larger, the government more repressive, until the bloated American empire would collapse of its own unsupported weight.

It was a heady, improbable, in retrospect incredible dream, and yet frustrated student radicals saw in it their first glimpse of hope. Years of political argument and failed protest had convinced them the war was no mistake, not a miscalculation in policy, but the inevitable result of the American system. But how to overthrow the system? Traditional two-party elections simply swallowed radical campaigns. The American ruling class knew its own interests and could hardly be touched by moral appeal. No mass of demonstrators, however large, could actually occupy the seat of government so long as it was defended by the war machine. The solution, radicals argued and perhaps believed, was guerrilla war, adapted to the urban realities of the United States.

In theory, at least, there was a certain rough logic in this analysis. It broke down completely, however, on the rock-like fact that however much Americans might turn against the war, they were not about to overthrow the system to end it. The system might be tough on the Vietnamese in the immediate instance, but it was good to most Americans and the United States was, in point of simple fact, totally lacking in genuine revolutionary potential. One of the organizers of Monday's nonviolent demonstration, Roy Kepler, felt the "success" of the mobile tactics had been overrated. At the end of the week he said:

> Eight or ten thousand people on Friday, milling through the streets and blocking intersections in a mix of "self-defense" and "militant" styles, were little more successful than the 123 of Monday in terms of the amount of time that they prevented access to the Induction Center. But has anyone asked himself what might have been possible Monday (or any other day of the week) if instead of 123 people there had been 500 or 1000 or more people ready to undertake disciplined nonviolent action backed up by the readiness both to absorb any violence on the part of police and to accept arrest and imprisonment?[9]

Kepler was undoubtedly right in the tactical sense, but he had failed to detect a broader shift in the mood of the activists. The appeal of the new mobile tactics was not simply the possibility that they would succeed where nonviolence had failed, but also the opportunity that militance offered of literally striking back at the indifferent society that had ignored them for so long. They wanted to win, of course, but even more than that they wanted to fight. They were in a mood for revolutionary daring and their new plans promised a quick end to the social peace. No government allows itself to be overthrown; if the revolutionary enthusiasts mounted an effort beyond a certain size, blood would flow. The promise of domestic violence alarmed a large class of people opposed to the war but unwilling to resist it in the streets. Many of those who would not wreck the country to end the war were even less willing to wreck the country to win it. If the war meant chaos at home, they wanted the war to end.

There were two main thrusts of activity at the demonstration in Washington on Saturday, October 21. The first was a traditional rally with traditional speeches at the Lincoln Memorial, followed by a mass march across the Arlington Memorial Bridge to the Pentagon in Virginia, where a second rally was held, with more speeches. The speech-making was a good deal more militant than it had been in the past—at the Lincoln Memorial, John Lewis, the former chairman of SNCC, asked for a moment's silence in memory of Che Guevara, the Cuban revolutionary killed in Bolivia two weeks earlier; at the Pentagon, Carl Davidson said draft boards would burn—but the rallies themselves were orderly, a "protest" in the familiar mode of "dissidents" express-ing an alternate point of view to the public at large and the powers that be. The second main thrust of activity was much smaller, involving four to five thousand people at the very most, who attempted to blockade the Pentagon and, briefly, actually invaded its very halls.

Just after crossing the bridge Saturday afternoon, perhaps a thou-sand SDS people and New York radicals loosely organized as the Revolutionary Contingent broke from the main body of marchers, moved at a run through the woods between the Potomac and the Pentagon, made a brief feint toward federal troops stationed to the north and left of the Pentagon, were turned back, and then, with greater determination, felled a fence by the North Parking Lot and streamed across the mall to the main steps of the Pentagon. A line of Military Police was pushed back sufficiently to let a body of protestors occupy part of the Pentagon Plaza before the main entrance. The MPs quickly reestablished their line, cutting off the group in the plaza from the larger group occupying the steps and the mall. Between the two areas was a fifteen-foot-high wall which Tom Bell, the SDS organizer from Cornell who had been instrumental in arranging the April 15 card-burning in the Sheep's Meadow, managed to scale. For the rest of the day, using a bullhorn, he maintained contact between the two groups of protestors in the plaza and on the steps.

Some restraining ropes which had been captured by the demonstra-tors were now used to allow people on the mall to scale the wall where Bell stood with his bullhorn, thus strengthening, but not by much, the group on the plaza. At about this time, too, a small group, twenty-five at most, pushed past half a dozen MPs guarding a side entrance to the Pentagon itself, disappearing down the corridors within, where they were quickly arrested by federal marshals.

This initial series of rushes was to establish a beachhead of sorts which was to remain, with some erosion, for the following thirty-two hours, until shortly after midnight Sunday. Thorn Dreyer, a writer for an underground newspaper called *The Rag* published in Austin, Texas, described the situation at this point in the day:

> The Pentagon had set up a neat little game for us. We were to be allowed to go to a certain place at which a line would be drawn. If we wanted to be civilly disobedient, we would walk across that line, go limp, and nice cops would drag us off to the "jails" that had been set up nearby. . . . They were going to let us do our thing and our thing would be the same old liberal bullshit. We hadn't played it the way it had been set up for us. We were moving and were in a real position of strength. There were battles, advances, new fronts opening on all sides.[10]

The rest of the demonstration was a gradual whittling down of these original salients. At about 6:30 Saturday evening, as dusk began to fall, someone in the mall lit his draft card and held it aloft. Others quickly followed, tiny flames in the darkness spreading out through the crowd. Tom Bell on the wall remembered the difficulty in persuading even fifty or sixty young men to burn their cards just six months earlier.

At midnight, after reporters had left and things were thought to be quieting down for the night (the official permit ran until midnight Sunday), soldiers and federal marshals began to clear the plaza in a deliberate, brutal manner. Soldiers would inch forward until their toes were literally under the crossed legs of sitting demonstrators, then federal marshals would reach through the line of soldiers and grab the protestors. They were eager with their clubs and the worst victims, according to every witness, were women. The scene at times was one of pure horror, women beaten senseless and then dragged off into the dark with bloody, broken faces. No one moved or got up to leave despite the violence, and the marshals and soldiers slowly worked their way through the crowd.

Members of the Revolutionary Contingent, most of them back in the crowd, shouted out to "fight back,"[11] but the SDS, sensing this was turning into a static, losing battle, the very antithesis of the Oakland mobile tactics, urged people to leave if they wanted to. Cathy Wilkerson of the Washington chapter of SDS called out over a bullhorn, "Many people are talking about leaving. The government says they'll let us go peacefully, if we leave now. Don't you back-row militants prevent the front row from leaving."[12]

Sidney Peck of the Mobilization Committee borrowed the SDS bullhorn and called on officials to stop the arrests until someone in authority could be found. The official permit allowed them to remain; the clearing action was illegal. This appeal struck most of the demonstrators, SDS and Revolutionary Contingent alike, as a liberal cop-out, a reaffirmation of the old, accommodating relationship between "dissidents" and "officials," but it apparently worked. Shortly afterward, the clearing operation stopped.

In the following weeks Movement legend would grow around the militance at the beginning of the demonstration, the running surprise attack which had captured the steps and the plaza. All night long, too, the demonstrators had appealed directly to the troops, like Trotsky in 1917. Three soldiers were even said to have dropped their rifles and joined the protestors, but the Pentagon denied it and the protestors had no proof. The crowd shouted "Join us," appealed individually to soldiers, offering them flowers, food, and cigarettes, told them *they* weren't the enemy, but rather the officers and government officials responsible for so much suffering in Vietnam. Glossed by the Movement were other, uglier incidents in which protestors taunted and cursed soldiers, sometimes even hitting or spitting at them. Still, at its height, the appeal to the soldiers was moving and effective. While the clearing operation was going on Saturday night, Gary Rader spoke to the troops with a bullhorn, his voice eerily blending with the orders of officers:

> My name is Gary Rader. I'm twenty-three years Company B hold your line. Nobody comes, nobody goes I want to tell you what led me to up to that Company hold your line what led me up to that decision nobody comes, nobody goes we will be heard.[13]

During the night the numbers of demonstrators dwindled to a few hundred, on Sunday built slowly back to perhaps two thousand. It was a long, exhausting day of boredom and speeches, some of them brilliant and impassioned, most dull and familiar, none paid more than passing attention. The demonstrators held on as dark came Sunday night and the midnight deadline approached. An official voice came over a public address system an hour or so before the demonstration was to end:

> The demonstration in which you are participating ends at midnight. The two-day permit which was agreed to by leaders of the demonstration and GSA [the General Services Administration, which had negotiated details

with the Mobilization Committee] expires at that time. All demonstrators must depart from the Pentagon grounds at midnight. All persons who wish to leave voluntarily can board buses on the Mall. Those demonstrators who do not leave voluntarily by midnight will be arrested and taken to a federal detention center.[14]

The message was repeated several times, but only thirty-four protestors of the hundreds still there decided to leave. A few minutes past midnight the arrests began; this time there was no violence. The demonstration ended to largely unfavorable comment in the press emphasizing unkempt youths cursing soldiers, supporting the Vietcong, insulting the flag, and so on. Few journalists wondered in print why ordinary American kids, however dirty and long-haired, refused to move when marshals were beating up their friends, why they charged the Pentagon in the first place and then stayed where they were for nearly a day and a half, why they insisted on being arrested in the end, when they could have walked away. The President's wife said she had been appalled by all the trash the demonstrators left behind.

For the movement the demonstration was a mixed success, encouraging for the evidence it gave of spreading militance, dispiriting for the ease with which officials had contained their most determined forays. The era of orderly dissent was over, it seemed, but revolutionary resistance was still hardly more than a dream. Perhaps three soldiers really did join the demonstrators, the first of a potential wave, but thousands did not. The struggle had been carried to a new level, but the war continued. The President pointedly ignored the challenge to his power and afterwards praised the restraint of marshals and troops. The administration, which, after all, determined who and how many would die in Vietnam, was apparently unreachable.

For the revolutionaries, however, this continuing impotence was offset by the anger spreading across college campuses. Official violence was ending what little room still remained for compromise and understanding between the movement and the establishment. The brutal clubbing of women at the Pentagon created a reservoir of anger which the revolutionaries planned to tap for a broader, deeper assault on things as they were.

At Harvard a week after the Pentagon, SDS held a rally where Jared Israel said the Pentagon was not the only American institution dominated by the Enemy:

They're right here on campus. Cop violence isn't any disruption of the "normal" process in America. It's just the other face the rulers are forced to show when the people become too militant. As you listen to these girls tell you how cops beat them over the head, remember that those cops are much less guilty than "educated" [Nathan] Pusey [the President of Harvard] or "nice guy" Dean [Fred] Glimp. Don't be fooled because they make refined dinner conversation, or because they know something about art. They are the rulers—they are the *real* enemy. And we've got to attack them, right here.[15]

The usual consequence of a major demonstration against the war was a period of organizational exhaustion, strategic confusion, and relative quiescence. Every march was followed by a sense of letdown: so much attempted, so little gained. Nothing more than an offhand remark by the Secretary of State, an earnest appeal for compromise by Hanoi from the President, newspaper appeals calling for negotiations, new bombing targets in North Vietnam, more troops in the South: the pattern was always the same. The situation always seemed most hopeless after the greatest efforts. Then gradually movement spirits would revive, anger would supplant inertia, some new plan would strike a responsive chord, and the effort would be resumed.

Things were different, however, following the demonstration at the Pentagon. The direct challenge to American power had ended the long agony of quiet, restrained, and futile opposition. It is one thing to urge wisdom on a mistaken man, emotionally quite another to assault an evil system. The Pentagon marked the end of the old ambivalence: now there were two sides, one right, one wrong. They were hopelessly mismatched, of course, but a sense of the quickening potential for upheaval in American society gave the movement new determination. Later an element of despair would emerge in the insistence that the struggle in America was ultimate, a choice between revolution and reaction; it did not leave much room for hope. But now the movement was eager to act. In the weeks immediately following the Pentagon, the movement attacked the war twice again, experimenting with its new street tactics, sharpening the divisions in America with simplified rhetoric, insisting there could be no middle ground.

When Dean Rusk came to New York to address the Foreign Policy Association on November 14 at the Hilton Hotel, the Fifth Avenue

Peace Parade Committee hurriedly organized a demonstration to protest outside. In the past, relations with the New York Police Department had always been cordial, if cool, but this time there was no cooperation whatever. Parade permits were withheld until shortly before the demonstration, and then narrowly construed. Committee marshals were harassed when they tried to keep order outside the hotel, the crowd was ordered from areas it had been permitted to occupy and was edged toward violent confrontation.

A large proportion of the two or three thousand demonstrators welcomed the tension. About two hundred members of the SDS chapter at Columbia University, a chapter that had been moving steadily toward militance over the previous eighteen months, were determined to follow the Oakland example. A leaflet was distributed which read:

> Using mobile tactics, the people in Oakland closed down the induction center and surrounding area for over three hours. Then the National Guard was called. So the people split. They held a victory march back to Berkeley; the Guard had nothing to do. Good guerrilla tactics! Take a stand only when superiority in numbers and tactical position are yours.[16]

The first demonstrators began gathering across the street from the Hilton at Sixth Avenue and Fifty-third Street about 5 P.M. At 6:10 a group of students from Brooklyn College pushed through the barricades and was immediately turned back by club-swinging police. At about the same time, Columbia SDS met a few blocks away at Seventh Avenue and Fifty-first Street and marched uptown stopping limousines and Cadillacs. A second group of about fifty started at Sixth Avenue and Fifty-seventh Street, moved south to Fifty-third and then east to Fifth Avenue, blocking traffic along the way.

About 6:30 the main demonstration began to disintegrate when mounted police forced a crowd back against a ledge. A line of police standing on the ledge then attacked the crowd from the rear and for a few minutes there was something close to hysteria, people facing clubs from behind and rearing horses ahead, crowding in on each other, covering their heads, shouting, trying to force a way free to either side. A young man with a bullhorn appeared at this point to recruit people for the more militant street actions spreading out from the hotel. "It's a simple guerrilla tactic," he said. "Hit the enemy where they're weakest. You'll never get anywhere with all those cops here."[17]

Police blocked demonstrators heading east toward Fifth Avenue, deflecting them south the half-mile to Times Square where they stopped traffic, surrounded the Armed Forces Recruiting Station in the middle of the square, and broke windows. The Allied Chemical Tower news sign flashed a message: "Demonstrators picket Secretary of State Rusk." The crowd cheered. A second message said, "Johnson says U.S. peace offer shows who is interested."[18] The crowd shouted, "Bullshit! Bullshit!"[19]

The crowd then moved east to Bryant Park, where a man with a bullhorn shouted, "We're not demonstrating against Rusk. We are demonstrating against the Foreign Policy Association. We're demonstrating against the American establishment, against the liberal fascists."[20] Rapidly dwindling, the crowd continued east toward the United Nations, then cut back through midtown Manhattan to the Hilton, and finally dispersed. Rusk neither saw nor heard them. He had slipped into the hotel through a garage entrance before the first demonstrators arrived, and left the same way at 10:45, after most of them were gone.

One final attempt was made in New York that fall to find a practical and effective way to fight against and actually hinder the American war effort. Where the Resistance attempted to limit manpower for the army by encouraging principled draft refusal, other activists argued it would be easier and more effective to assault the machinery of the draft itself. About a week after the Pentagon, a group of New York activists formed a Stop the Draft Committee which included Eric Weinberger of the Fifth Avenue Peace Parade Committee, Lenny Brody of the Resistance, Syd Stapleton of the New York Student Mobilization Committee Against the War, and Linda Morse of the National Student Mobilization Committee, with Art Goldberg, a veteran of the Free Speech Movement, handling press relations.

On Thursday, November 30, a formal press conference was held in the Penn Garden Hotel announcing a five-day attempt, from December 4 to 8, to close down the Whitehall Street Induction Center. David McReynolds of the War Resisters League said "at least fifty people" would attempt to block the entrance to the induction center and Dr. Spock, who had resigned his cochairmanship of SANE in order to work with the National Conference for New Politics, said this was another attempt to force a legal confrontation with the federal government over the draft. "But the government is not likely to prosecute us," he said, referring to the card turn-in at the Justice Department the weekend of the Pentagon demonstration. "Its bankruptcy in the moral sense is proved by its refusal to move against those of us who have placed ourselves between the young people and the draft."[21]

The week of demonstrations was to begin Monday with a card turn-in at the Church of St. John the Evangelist in Brooklyn, a sit-in on Tuesday, and then escalating street actions following the Oakland model through the rest of the week. In this way the committee, like the planners of the Pentagon demonstration, hoped to provide a wide range of possible actions allowing people to involve themselves as deeply as they liked, but no deeper. The Saturday before Anti-Draft Week, the California Resistance leader David Harris warned the New York committee that mobile tactics had been much less successful in Oakland than was being supposed. People had been arrested, the induction center had continued to function despite interruptions, and the moral clarity of the confrontation—a huge and impersonal war machine opposed by young men with no other weapon than moral conviction—had been blurred by the violence and confusion. Harris's arguments were rejected; moral witness was no longer enough for most activists. They wanted to strike directly and physically at the enemy.

It was still dark at 5:30 on Tuesday morning, December 5, when demonstrators began gathering outside the massive, red-brick, nine-story induction center built in 1886. It was immediately apparent that the Police Department was in complete control of the situation. The narrow, wandering streets surrounding the building were lined with heavy wooden barricades, and more than 2,500 patrolmen were on hand to ensure that inductees would be able to enter and leave the building. David McReynolds was on a platform, silhouetted by television lights, using a bullhorn to tell demonstrators that there were two groups, those who wanted to march in a legal picket line and those who wanted to commit civil disobedience and be arrested.

Dr. Spock and Mitchell Goodman, who had helped organize the "Call to Resist Illegitimate Authority," arrived shortly before 6 A.M. and joined the group planning to commit civil disobedience. After several awkward minutes standing in the frigid dark chatting with newsmen, Dr. Spock asked Goodman, "What are we supposed to do?"

"Well," said Goodman, "I don't really know, but we are supposed to get through here [he pointed to a barricade] to that place on the sidewalk. The only one who really knows is David McReynolds." They waited another few minutes.

"Well, we can't just stand here," said Spock. "This is foolish."[22]

He got down onto his hands and knees on the cold concrete and attempted to crawl under a barricade, but the solid mass of policemen refused to give way, and he butted with his head in vain. Finally Spock and others were allowed to cross the barricade and sit briefly on the steps of the induction center before they were arrested, removed to paddy wagons, and driven away. By the time the sun was up, 264 people had been arrested, not all of them as gently as Dr. Spock. One young man had been dragged to a paddy wagon by his hair. Policemen shouted "Help him up!"[23] while they punched and kicked him. Despite the sit-in, the usual 250 young men entered the building, got into the main elevator beneath the legend "The Security of World Peace Starts Here," and were duly inducted into the United States Army.

The demonstrations of the following three days were fueled by a sense of the futility of traditional protests like Tuesday's sit-in. Details for the demonstration, the civil disobedience, and the arrests had been worked out in meetings at Gracie Mansion, the official residence of the mayor, John Lindsay. The specious air of such carefully planned, non-violent scenarios convinced radicals the government did not just tolerate, but actually welcomed passive resistance. The only way genuinely to oppose the government, they argued, was to fight it. Spock could go to jail every day for the rest of his life without blocking the induction of a single draftee. The point was to cut off the flow of soldiers and stop the war, not simply cleanse oneself of moral complicity.

Before dawn on Wednesday morning, December 6, about 2,500 demonstrators gathered in Battery Park in lower Manhattan, a short distance from Whitehall Street and the induction center. They divided themselves into three columns and set out for the center, but 5,000 New York police found no difficulty in turning them back. One of the columns, led by Linda Morse, was quickly named "The Lost Battalion" because it became confused in the net of streets around the induction center. Every time her column tried to approach the center it was blocked by police barricades and finally, lost and dispirited, the column allowed itself to be led back to Battery Park. By 9 A.M. all three columns had returned without having disrupted, or even reached, the induction center.

The mood of the returned crowd was angry as speakers proposed one plan after another. Syd Stapleton said there were too many cops and not enough demonstrators. "I learned a long time ago that when there are more cops than demonstrators you can't do a thing without getting hurt," he said through a bullhorn. The crowd shouted back, "No, no," "Let's go to Wall Street," "On to the Waldorf," "We can't stop now."[24]

Eric Weinberger suggested a march uptown to City Hall, and about four hundred demonstrators immediately set out. Blocked by police from marching up Broadway, the group shifted to the west and proceeded up Church Street. On Park Row near City Hall they blocked traffic and then split again, with a small group marching up to the Waldorf-Astoria Hotel at Park Avenue and Fiftieth Street, where Dean Rusk was speaking at a luncheon meeting of the National Association of Manufacturers. Fifteen police from the Tactical Patrol Force broke up their brief demonstration outside the hotel at 1:15 P.M., and a final group marched on to the United Nations and there dissolved. Inside the Waldorf, Rusk told the manufacturers,

> I cannot tell you how much longer it may take to achieve peace in Vietnam . . . [but] the situation in South Vietnam is not a stalemate. And what has been done by the splendid Americans who are there has already yielded dividends of historic significance. Behind the shield which we have helped to provide, a new Asia is arising.[25]

That night about three hundred activists met at Columbia University to plan the next day's actions. Linda Morse publicly criticized herself for timidity in failing to storm one lightly defended police barricade. Steve Cagan, who had been a member of the group that had marched up to City Hall and then the Waldorf, proposed that a number of mobile forays spread out from Battery Park. The following morning about five hundred people gathered in Battery Park for the third straight day. At 6:30 Cagan announced over a bullhorn that four secret sites had been chosen by activist leaders as targets for demonstrators. To prevent police from being there to meet them, he said, the destinations would be whispered from one person to the next. He left the platform, joined the crowd, and began whispering the secret targets. The second "demonstrator" he approached was a plainclothes policeman who immediately arrested him.

There was a brief running battle with police as the demonstrators set out, and police stayed with them most of the way. At 8:15 they were met by police in Times Square and later that morning police hauled off 170 demonstrators from a park near the United Nations despite the fact police officials had given them permission to gather there.

Activists met still again that night, and on Friday, December 8, the final day of Anti-Draft Week, confused directions led five hundred protestors to a federal office at Irving Place and Sixteenth Street, rather than the New York headquarters of the Selective Service on Forty-second Street. Ordered to disperse from the area, the crowd refused and was attacked by police. Trapped against an iron fence surrounding Washington Irving High School, demonstrators had nowhere to run, and police simply drove a wedge into the crowd, with clubs flying. About half of the day's 140 arrests were made during those few violent minutes, and when the struggle was over blood stained the sidewalk in a dozen places in front of the school. Remnants of the crowd moved to Union Square, where Fred Halstead of the Socialist Labor Party urged them to go home and begin organizing a really *big* demonstration.

Angry shouts of "No, no"[26] drowned him out. When Sid Davidoff, a top assistant to Mayor Lindsay, worked his way toward the front of the crowd in Union Square, people shouted, "Cop, cop." "No," said Davidoff, "Mayor's assistant." A girl standing beside him, referring to the colored lapel button which identified him to police, shouted, "Then take off your button, take your chances!"[27]

A final group of about one hundred reached Times Square at 1 P.M., and another seventy-five were arrested at Rockefeller Plaza, where they had gone to protest outside the offices of the Dow Chemical Company. By mid-afternoon it was all over. Four days of determined street action had resulted in 581 arrests, dozens of split scalps, and a helpless feeling close to despair, but no discernible interruption in the stream of young men who daily passed through the Whitehall Street Induction Center on their way to Vietnam. After Wednesday, the protestors had even abandoned the attempt to reach the heavily defended building. By that time even a wild run through Manhattan seemed like a victory against the government.

In one sense the movement was exhausted at the end of 1967. Militant demonstrations in California, Washington, and New York had resulted in well over a thousand arrests without having any appreciable effect on the government. Other demonstrations not mentioned here, like a huge and bloody anti-draft protest at the University of Wisconsin in November, were turning thousands of students into self-conscious revolutionaries, but nothing had occurred that would have suggested to an objective observer that revolution was any closer. In one sense the movement had tried harder and achieved less than ever before. There was no shortage of men for the war; Congress had not moved beyond the old expressions of "concern"; no conventional politician believed the President could be seriously challenged in 1968; and the movement itself, more angry and frustrated than ever, had failed to find a successful form of protest. The government had ignored speeches, petitions, and rallies for years; now they ignored direct assault, and even turned it to their own benefit by branding the movement as extremist. No one who had witnessed the futile efforts of demonstrators in New York in December, outnumbered at every turn by police, had much hope that the government could physically be prevented from continuing the war.

Despite this, young activists were in a mood of near elation. It had been hard enough a few years earlier to get five thousand marchers willing to ask publicly for negotiations. Now at least fifty thousand had marched to the Pentagon, and some of them had even defied openly the federal marshals and troops sent to guard the building. Several thousand activists in Oakland, and an equal number in New York, had actually defied the police day after day in spite of violence and arrests.

In that part of the movement called the New Left there were two basic strategic attitudes toward the new militance. Marvin Garson, an activist since the Free Speech Movement, had written after Stop the Draft Week that the moment had come for action that might "require us to take a few casualties."[28] Two weeks later he explained he was not taking a military view of protest politics, attempting to pit the movement's strength against the government's with force the deciding factor, but rather advocating a change in the atmosphere of the entire country:

> We are engaged, basically, in street theater rather than insurrection. Our barricades and shields and coke bottles, their tear gas and fire hoses and bayonets, function less as real weapons than as stage props. The refrain of our play is that if you need conscription to have an army, then you will need an army to have conscription. The moral of our play is that you cannot have imperialistic war abroad and social peace at home.[29]

Garson did not say, but meant, that the movement was in effect still *protesting*, that is, making an appeal to the society at large, but adding a believable threat to the appeal. He recognized the movement's inability to *force* an end to the war; it could only promise that the war would exact a price.

Jerry Rubin took a different view, arguing that the movement had the capacity to bring down the system by a gadfly warfare which would push the country to the brink of a nervous breakdown:

> This system lives by murdering in Vietnam, exploiting the world, and killing black people at home; and we say to hell with middle class "security" and phony status games, we are going to screw up this society. And we can do it too. . . . The goal? A massive white revolutionary youth movement which, working in parallel cooperation with the rebellions in the black communities, could seriously disrupt this country, and thus be an internal catalyst for a breakdown of the American ability and will to fight guerrillas overseas. Thus defeated abroad by peasant revolutionaries, and disrupted within by blacks and whites, the empire of the United States will find itself faced with rebellions from fifteen different directions.[30]

Rubin was a little vague about just what blacks and whites were going to *do*, exactly, but this was less significant, for the moment, than the promise of disruption that his appeal embodied. The fact that blacks and young whites could not actually bring down, or take over, the American government was less important than the increasingly real possibility that they might actually try.

This point was not lost on mainstream political figures. In New York City, Joseph L. Rauh, a leader of Americans for Democratic Action and a long-time liberal who had been torn between his support for Johnson's domestic programs and his doubts about the war, told a Democratic group on November 16 that unless a peace candidate ran in 1968, "the rioting at the Pentagon will look like a panty-waist tea party. . . . We've got to turn this horrible frustration from the streets to the ballot box."[31]

TWELVE

"You Can't Beat Somebody with Nobody"

When Staughton Lynd advocated an anti-draft movement in early 1966, he said one of its purposes would be to clear the way for "the Romneys and the Kennedys" in 1968. He wasn't the only opponent of the war who expected the ultimate public struggle over the war to occur in the next presidential election, but there was little agreement on how such an antiwar campaign ought to be waged or who ought to lead it. While movement radicals attempted to escalate their opposition in the streets throughout 1967, three separate political efforts were slowly being organized to oppose Johnson at the polls the following year. One of them was an incubus within the President's own party, a second centered on the notion of a radical third party, and the last, in many ways the most promising, proposed an antiwar candidate and campaign by the Republicans.

In the 1964 presidential election the Republican organization created by Barry Goldwater was shattered, and the moderate wing of the party, which had been so hesitant and ineffective in its attempts to prevent Goldwater's nomination, determined not to repeat their earlier mistake. They had been too slow to organize in 1964; as things turned out they were too quick in 1968. Led by Nelson Rockefeller, the governor of New York, the moderate Republicans united behind George Romney, the governor of Michigan, who had refused to support Goldwater four years earlier. Romney, an earnest, likable, handsome Mormon, turned out to be a clumsy campaigner who found it impossible to oppose the President effectively on the one issue that really counted. Romney had no natural talent for answering hard questions, and Vietnam was the hardest question of all. This failure was only partly his own doing, however. Like all presidential candidates, Romney was to some extent a captive of his party, and his party, eager to oppose Johnson himself, was unwilling for reasons of history and ideology to oppose Johnson's war. Romney thus found himself trapped between two unpalatable extremes: he could advocate an all-out military effort to win the war, and to hell with the risk, or he could propose a realistic compromise which would very likely be repudiated by his own party. The middle ground was already occupied by the President, who insisted the United States would have to grind on until the other side was willing to abandon its aims.

Romney waffled on the issue of Vietnam for more than a year, sometimes damning the war as a foolish, futile mistake and then, in the same speech, insisting we had to win it. A man with strong, clear feelings on many issues, he appeared to the public as a fuzzy thinker who could never make up his mind. In the end he was destroyed as a candidate by his failure to find a consistent position on the war which offered a realistic way to end the agony. It is worth taking a close look at Romney's erratic shifts from hawk to dove and back again because his difficulties were shared by all the men who wanted to run against Johnson in 1968.

We have already seen how Romney suddenly reversed himself on the war during the summer of 1965, withdrawing the reservations he had expressed at a governors' conference in July after the President flew all fifty governors to Washington for a special briefing. Romney quickly realized that if he continued to oppose the war he would oppose it alone and, in the vernacular of the time, he climbed aboard with a statement of support for the President.

In the wake of this episode Romney and nine other governors from both parties were flown to South Vietnam for an official tour in early November, 1965. At the end of four days of military briefings, talks with embassy officials, and field trips to civil action projects, military bases, and the U.S. Aircraft Carrier Ticonderoga, the governors, Romney included, backed U.S. policy. It is difficult to see what else he or they could have done. On certain courses of action there is no turning back, and war, without question, is one of them. By the time Romney arrived in Saigon on Friday, November 5, well over 150,000 American troops had been committed to the war. Far more sophisticated observers than he assumed American military might would crush the Vietcong. It was relatively easy to argue that the U.S. ought to fight harder, impossible to propose giving up the fight altogether. American boys were dying, and one either supported the President or, by failing to do so, opened oneself to charges of helping the enemy, hardly the sort of position to be embraced by a man with an eye on the presidency.

Romney never found a way around this impasse. As the war ground on, the American involvement steadily grew, and the prospect of an end to the fighting, much less a victory, seemed as distant as ever, Romney tried to find a safe way to express, and thus embody, dissatisfaction with the war. Every effort ran afoul of the fact this was a *war*, American boys were *dying*, and if we didn't win, the other side would. On April 7, 1967, a week before the great antiwar march in New York, Romney gave a long-awaited Vietnam speech at a dinner commemorating the 150th anniversary of the *Hartford* (Connecticut) *Times*. For some time Romney, having stumbled, retreated, and reversed himself so often, had refused to answer questions about the war altogether. This speech, the result of weeks of effort and consultations with a wide range of Republicans, from Rockefeller to Senators Hugh Scott of Pennsylvania, Edward Brooke of Massachusetts, and Jacob Javits of New York, was intended to end the ambiguity of Romney's position on the war and the doubts that his ambiguity had raised about his candidacy. If he were going to run for President the following year, after all, he could hardly ignore the war. He needed a position his party could accept, but which would also allow him the freedom he needed to attack the President.

Romney's plane arrived from Detroit in mid-afternoon during a light snowfall. He was evasive with reporters who met him at the airport, refusing to discuss Vietnam and saying that the speech would answer all their questions about where he stood. As it turned out, the speech clarified nothing except the difficulty any Republican found in moving to the left of the President on the war. Romney categorically ruled out the possibility of unilateral withdrawal, warned of the dangers implicit in further escalation, wished we had never gotten involved, suggested Johnson be more frank about his purposes, criticized him for allowing us to be bogged down, said the U.S. should not take on the pacification program, and, finally, called for a military victory. Romney rhetorically directed his remarks at North Vietnam, but reached more immediately those antiwar leaders who still hoped a Republican might oppose the war.

> The Hanoi leaders may be holding out in the desperate hope that America will tire of the struggle, that our purpose will falter, that disillusionment and discord here at home will somehow induce us to abandon our friends and dishonor our commitments by pulling back or pulling out. That is a false hope and I for one will not contribute to it. . . . For what it is worth, I would like to tell them right now that here is one Republican I can speak for who will not settle on their terms under any circumstances.[1]

This naturally was interpreted as a virtual endorsement of official Vietnam policy, and before the day was over the White House spokesman, George Christian, issued a statement saying Romney "deserves the gratitude of the American people for maintaining our great tradition that politics stops at the water's edge."[2]

Romney eventually realized his position was no position at all, and he tangled with the issue again. Tangle is a word often used in this context but in Romney's case it is especially apt. The war was a political thicket so dense and forbidding, so filled with dangerous surprises, that one ran the most serious risks with the most casual comments. Romney plunged into the thicket again and again, but always seemed to emerge, bewildered and bleeding, at the same point: we just *had* to win.

In Washington on Wednesday, August 16, Romney said that American involvement in the war was self-defeating, since, "The more we do, the less they [the South Vietnamese] do." A moment later he said something critical of bombing policy. Did this mean, a reporter asked, that Romney disagreed with Representative Gerald Ford, the House minority leader, who had recently attacked limitations on the bombing? No, it did not, Romney said. "Ford is not asking for an escalation but for more effective bombing. I don't think bombing is the answer, and I don't think he thinks bombing is the answer, but if there's góing to be bombing, we should bomb in a more effective way."[3]

This was Cold Comfort Farm for opponents of the war, and yet the opposition continued to hope that Romney's fogged perception of the war would eventually clear. He was an unmistakably honest, feeling man. The difficulties were that he could never quite clarify all the issues in his own mind, and that he shrank from necessary collisions. If he was going to oppose the war he would have to oppose those who supported it, and that included men in his own party.

Four days after his remarks in Washington, Romney, sitting with reporters on the porch of the Grand Hotel on Mackinac Island in Michigan, said he thought the American people wanted an end to the war by "a reasonably early date." A Romney administration would not repudiate the commitments of its predecessors, he said, but still there might be "important differences in emphasis and approach and analysis." So far so good. The reporters wanted to know what he meant by "reasonably early."

"Not five years or ten years or fifteen years,"[4] Romney said.

The reporters pressed. Romney finally said he meant less than five years; that is, before August, 1972. As things turned out, that would have been an achievement, but at the time five years sounded like forever and raised as many questions as it answered. Did he plan to *win* the war within five years? If so, how? And if not, why take five years?

Part of Romney's problem was that he had gone on record about the war too early. As he slowly grew more critical of the war, he had to explain away that early support without discrediting his own powers of judgment. In an attempt to explain why he was critical now, in 1967, Romney told a Detroit television newsman on August 31 that the briefings he and nine other governors had received during their November, 1965, trip to Vietnam had been shallow, misleading, and self-serving. "I just had the greatest brainwashing that anyone can get when you go over to Vietnam," he said, "not only by the generals, but also by the diplomatic corps over there, and they do a very thorough job."[5] Romney was not the first public official to have discovered that this was the case, but he was the first to have publicly admitted he had been taken in. The admission finished him as a candidate.

All the doubts his faltering public statements had raised focused on the one word "brainwashing" after the interview was broadcast on September 3. The word implied certain things about the administration and the war that raised huge questions. Were all reports from Saigon a dishonest sham? Was the President deliberately deceiving the whole country? People were not yet generally ready to reach such conclusions and so turned on Romney instead, attacking him as unfit for the presidency. Either his brainwashing charge was an irresponsible slander, or by his own admission he had been deceived.

Romney fought on, now with a double burden. The day after he formally declared his candidacy in Michigan on Saturday, November 18, Romney appeared on CBS's Sunday interview show "Face the Nation" and charged that all our troubles stemmed from Johnson's "colossal mistake" of running *against* the war in 1964.

> You'll recall that when Dean Acheson indicated that our area of concern didn't extend as far as Matsu and Quemoy and Korea, that the Korean War started right after that. In the campaign of 1964 the President of this country indicated that he wasn't going to send any American boys to Asia. He wasn't going to bomb anything. We were going to stay out. The Asian boys ought to fight for their land. Now, it was right after that that North Vietnam intensified its activities in South Vietnam with a view to knocking it out. And I want to submit that it's entirely possible that those statements made in the 1964 campaign had an effect on Vietnam and what we've had to'do there—and what the South Vietnamese have had to face—just as it did in Korea.[6]

This statement was a sudden and erratic shift in position. In the first place, it was factually wrong, but more importantly it represented an attack on himself, as well. It was precisely on the issue of the war, after all, that Romney had refused to support Goldwater in 1964. Johnson's position then had been his, too. Worse still, the statement implied the American commitment to Saigon was crucial, leaving Romney with the old fatal choice between supporting Johnson's conduct of the war or proposing a greater military effort to win it. Romney was now lost in the Vietnam thicket and never emerged again. After weeks of hard but futile campaigning in New Hampshire, he dropped out of the race at the end of February, 1968, less than two weeks before the primary scheduled for Tuesday, March 12.

The antiwar forces that might have gathered behind his candidacy in 1967 had long since turned elsewhere. Things would have been a good deal easier for Romney if other Republican leaders had not sent him constant public signals that they would not tolerate a no-win, we-were-wrong position on the war. Senator Hugh Scott, for example, said on Monday, October 9, 1967, "The war in Vietnam is not, and must not become, a political issue. . . . It would be wrong for the loyal opposition so to misconceive its role as to become a 'peace at any price' party."[7] Scott, of course, was misusing the word "loyal," but he was right in his warning that Vietnam could not be considered as a routine "political" issue. Romney's major failure had been exactly that. Instead of addressing the issue on its merits he had tried to find a political route around it. The result was a public floundering which destroyed him.

Scott was not the only man who did not want to see the war become an issue in 1968, but the fact remained that the war was not only *an* issue, but *the* issue. Romney's failure indicated the one undeniable success of the opposition. Its efforts, so ineffective in the short run, had nevertheless precipitated a public crisis in which the war simply could not be ignored. People were sick to death of the endless argument over the nature and necessity of the American commitment to South Vietnam. They were worried about its effects on the young. They had begun to see that, rich as the United States was, it was not rich enough to have both guns and butter, as Humphrey had promised in the summer of 1965. It was apparent that much of the rest of the world, and particularly our European allies, thought the United States was half demented on the subject of Vietnam. People were growing uneasy with the brutal vision of a great nation bombing, shelling, defoliating, burning, gassing, and literally plowing under a small, backward nation with one-tenth its population. The Congress refused to approve a tax surcharge to pay for the war unless there were corresponding cuts in domestic spending. England had been forced to devalue the pound, and the dollar itself was under attack as the result of American inflation and a steadily growing balance of payments deficit. Every young man reaching the age of eighteen was directly threatened by the draft, and many of them were going to jail rather than Vietnam. Police were being called in to put down campus disturbances growing out of the war, and neither the President himself nor his closest advisers could appear in public without being the focus of massive protest.

Worst of all was the possibility that the war might slip entirely out of control. So respectable a figure as the Democratic majority leader in the Senate, Mike Mansfield of Montana, had warned of the danger in escalation. "Who will say," he asked in July, "that a third world war is not already incubating in the ever-deepening and expanding struggle in Southeast Asia?"[8] An election that failed to focus on Vietnam would be an evasion and a fraud.

By the time Romney began to grapple with the issue of the war, Staughton Lynd and the movement he represented had lost faith in the

Romneys and the Kennedys. Partly as a result of radical campaigns in 1966, and of political waffling in 1967, they were even losing faith in the whole process of electoral politics. Nevertheless, movement radicals in 1967 made a serious effort to organize a radical third-party campaign against Johnson and the war in 1968. Washington reporters and major party leaders never took this attempt seriously, arguing that third-party, one-issue campaigns historically went nowhere. Look at Henry Wallace in 1948, or Teddy Roosevelt in 1916, they said. How could Martin Luther King, the most frequently named possibility to head a third-party effort, expect to do any better, or as well?

King himself, who hoped Johnson would not run unopposed on the war in 1968, shared this assessment. When the National Conference for New Politics, which had supported antiwar candidates in 1966, began talking publicly about a King campaign shortly after the antiwar march in April, 1967, King held a press conference in Atlanta to say he would not be a candidate.

Nevertheless, for a variety of reasons, discussion of a radical third party continued. *Somebody* was going to run against Johnson and the war, after all, if only the perennial candidate of the Socialist Workers Party. Dissatisfaction with the war was indisputably widespread and therefore *somebody* was going to receive all those antiwar votes, not to mention the money and volunteers that an issue of this magnitude would elicit. There were sound practical reasons for a third-party campaign even if King, not to mention a lesser figure, could not be expected to win. An unequivocal antiwar campaign would, to begin with, create a middle ground for moderate opponents of the war. It might encourage a major Democrat to oppose Johnson for the nomination and, if it demonstrated strength, might even make Johnson himself cautious in Vietnam by convincing him he was losing support at home. Less often mentioned, but still a conscious consideration, was the possibility a right-wing Republican might be nominated, the war might take a turn for the worse, the public might shift decisively toward peace, and, faced with a clear choice in the privacy of the voting booth on election day, voters all over the country might . . . even . . . Who could say?

Robert Scheer's congressional campaign in 1966 had surprised everyone by its professionalism and its near success. A quarter of a million people, at the least, had marched in New York in April. Nixon and Ronald Reagan, the governor of California, seemed the most likely beneficiaries of a Romney failure. At a minimum, a third-party campaign alone in its opposition to the war would bring money and manpower into the movement. With any luck, activists across the country told each other during the spring and summer of 1967, it might achieve a great deal more than that.

This hopefulness was unfounded, for, as it turned out, the movement was very nearly dead. It retained a potential for huge public spasms of anger and frustration, but its ability to think clearly, organize, and appeal to a broad segment of the population was almost at an end. The strengths of the movement in its early days had been passion and simplicity: the passion that led them to act, even at great personal risk, and the simplicity that allowed them to pursue one clear goal at a time. By 1967 much of this passion had twisted in on itself, transforming the early idealism into a bitter alienation. The goals of the early movement —an end to legal segregation, the guarantee of voting rights—had largely been achieved. More complex issues had been raised in their wake, which resisted the weapons of moral witness. How could civil disobedience end the deterioration of housing in Harlem? How could prayer on city hall steps teach black children to read, or give black men jobs?

The movement, in short, was angry, confused, and divided. It no longer agreed on methods, leaders, or goals, and years of sometimes violent, always disappointing struggle had infected it with a destructive element of political spleen. In the beginning, movement activists had found that their efforts placed them outside the mainstream of American life, but their isolation was only an incidental result of their politics. By 1967 this isolation had become the substance of their politics: they were largely incapable of taking any position that implied reconciliation with the rest of the country. They were willing enough to overthrow the established order, no longer willing to win it over.

This transformation was partly ideological, of course. The movement had moved steadily to the left since its beginning, and much of it believed that nothing short of fundamental economic and political change could end poverty, racism, and imperialism in the United States. The movement was isolated because it was totally opposed to the system as it existed. At the same time, however, there was a strong emotional element in the movement's transformation into an alienated minority. It had always viewed things in moral terms and as a result gradually began to consider those responsible for racism and the war as criminals. Its alienation was thus also an instinctive refusal to have anything to do with the evils it opposed. The two most conspicuous, if not the numerically largest or most effective, wings of the movement —black militants and white radicals—did not speak for every activist willing to work for peace in Vietnam and justice at home, but they spoke in a way that drowned out the others. The rhetorical militance of their speech, their revolutionary daring at the Pentagon, their bitter refusal to take part in what they considered to be a corrupt and criminal society, all contributed to the sense of crisis in late 1967, but these were far from useful attributes for an election campaign.

The terrible impasse at which the movement would soon find itself first revealed itself clearly on Labor Day weekend, 1967, when representatives of 372 left-wing and old activist groups met in Chicago under the auspices of the National Conference for New Politics. The organizers of the group hoped the five-day conference would bring all factions of the movement together behind a common political strategy for 1968. Instead, it revealed that the dominant emotion of the movement had become anger, its characteristic tone shrill, and its revolutionary politics theatrical and quixotic. For years the movement had found it increasingly difficult to criticize publicly anyone angry about the right issues. They had enemies enough, they felt, without attacking each other. At the Palmer House in Chicago, the issues were finally obscured by the anger.

The conference broke down almost immediately over two basic demands by the Black Caucus, which in theory represented the three hundred or so black delegates (out of a total of about two thousand), but in fact consisted of an ad hoc group of old civil rights activists, poverty workers, freelance revolutionaries, and people who had wandered in off the Chicago streets. The leader of the Black Caucus was Carlos Russell, a former poverty worker in Brooklyn who had come to Chicago to write a report on the conference for the Episcopal Church. He was chosen by what the caucus called "African consensus," that is, by some means other than election.

On Friday, September 1, the Black Caucus drew up a thirteen-point resolution which it then presented to the steering committee of the conference. The thirteen points covered a wide range of issues which touched on the presidential election in only the broadest and most theoretical way. As a practical matter, accepting the thirteen points would have precluded automatically the possibility of cooperation with any significant political movement in the United States. Point 5, for example, called on the conference to "condemn the imperialistic Zionist war"[9] of June. (During an opening ceremony in the Chicago Coliseum the previous night, Dick Gregory, the black comedian, told the audience, "Every Jew in America over thirty years old knows another Jew that hates niggers. Well, it's even, baby."[10]) Point 3 required "total and unquestionable [sic?] support to all national people's liberation wars." Point 11, widely reported by the press, stated:

> We strongly suggest that white civilizing committees be established immediately in all white communities to civilize and humanize the savage and beast-like character that runs rampant throughout America, as exemplified by George Lincoln Rockwells and Lyndon Baines Johnsons.[11]

The Black Caucus said all black delegates would leave the conference forthwith if the thirteen points were not accepted "in toto, with no changes in content or wording, by 12:30 tomorrow afternoon."[12]

It is not easy to explain why the Black Caucus proceeded in this way. There is some evidence that leaders of the caucus were looking for an excuse to pull out of the conference and join another Black People's Convention taking place across town. If the conference turned down their demand, as the caucus apparently expected it to do, and no wonder, the caucus would be able to shift the blame for their departure, and the presumed failure of the conference, on to the white delegates. This theory has a certain devious elegance, but fails to explain the pugnacious tone of the thirteen points or the contumacious spirit in which they were written and presented. They seemed better designed to sever than to create lines of communication to white organizations. In that case, why did they submit them?

Because the civil rights movement had called into question the entire history of black and white in America in the most general and abstract way. Blacks were not angry solely about things as they were in late 1967, but about four hundred years of oppression, violence, and injustice. In a technical sense, perhaps, black people might be free now that the legal basis of black suppression had been ended, but as a matter of sociological fact they remained the victims of history controlled by whites. Black unemployment, the breakdown of black families, the mortality rate of black infants and the rats in black slums, the overwhelmingly black population of the nation's prisons, the inability to read and write of black children, the disproportionate number of black soldiers killed in Vietnam, every deprivation and indignity and injustice suffered by the black community, in short, was the fault of white people. Black activists, increasingly conscious of their history as they struggled to transcend it, had grown steadily angrier at the very historical moment when the fate of black people was finally becoming complicated, a question of economics and the techniques of social change, and not simply a question of good and evil, white iniquity and black victimization. The thirteen points were a manifestation of all the bile and fury that had built up during the bitter struggles of the civil rights movement.

That, at any rate, was the sort of explanation offered in the wake of the conference in an attempt to mitigate the bitterness that had been revealed and aroused. The civil rights movement, after all, had been a unique and necessary undertaking, and white activists were hardly eager to exacerbate hostility between the races. During the conference itself the best response to the thirteen points probably would have been a point-by-point refutation honestly and openly challenging the thirteen points on political and intellectual grounds.

This, however, was the one thing white groups found it impossible to do. Instead, white delegates used the Black Caucus's peremptory demand as an occasion for what can only be called a twenty-four-hour orgy of self-laceration and guilt. Instead of just rejecting the thirteen points as out of order, white activists argued they ought to be accepted in a general, uncritical sort of way, as a gesture of brotherly solidarity quite independent of whatever the points might literally say. The Southern Student Organizing Committee distributed a leaflet Friday night arguing in favor of acceptance. "Think in radical terms rather than worrying about particular white interest groups [i.e., Jews]," the leaflet said. "Don't try to change specifics of the resolution—that's completely missing the point. Let's vote with the spirit of it. Learn, baby, learn!"[13]

What was the point that arguing the specifics would have missed? "This is a critical turning point in the movement," said Edwin Greer of the American Independence Movement in Connecticut. "It's an offer from our black brothers and sisters to work with us."[14] The same point was made a little differently by Bert Garskoff, a teacher at Michigan

State University and chairman of the NCNP's Committee on Resolutions. "We are just a little tail on the end of a very powerful black panther," he said. "And I want to be on the end of that tail—if they'll let me."[15]

On Saturday, September 2, delegates to the conference voted three to one to accept the thirteen points. At this point things become still more complicated. On Sunday the Black Caucus was briefly captured by the Communist Party and the W.E.B. DuBois Clubs, which were controlled by the Communists. At their urging, the Black Caucus presented the conference with a new demand for 50 percent of the votes, obviously a controlling percentage, and half the positions on all conference committees. The purpose of the Communists was twofold. First, control of the conference by the Black Caucus would have meant control by the Communists once-removed, since they, for the time being at any rate, secretly controlled the caucus. A second reason was that majority sentiment at the conference appeared to favor local community organizing, a movement catchword, rather than an antiwar campaign in the 1968 election. If no third-party effort were mounted, the only antiwar candidate would be run by the Socialist Workers Party, the organ of Trotskyism. The Communists were not about to allow all those antiwar votes, not to mention the publicity, money, and volunteers, to go to Trotskyists. If the Black Caucus had 50 percent of the conference votes, some kind of third-party effort backed by the Communists would obviously be approved. Hence their maneuver.

Little of this was apparent to the rest of the delegates at the time, however, and a new bout of self-lacerating debate preceded the voting on the new Black Caucus demand. Again, feeling was overwhelmingly in favor of granting what had been asked. In the White Radical Caucus, manned by veterans of the Vietnam Summer program but led by the more radical and articulate SDS, only one white student, David Simpson of the University of Georgia, said he would oppose the demand. "I know it's all irrelevant and meaningless," he said. "I'm just not going to vote for it because it's such a sick thing. I just don't want any part of such a sick thing."[16]

By this time the demand really did make little difference. Simon Casady, a cochairman of the committee that had organized the conference, assumed the blacks were simply angling for control of the NCNP treasury. "I guess what they're asking is to let them hold our wallet,"

Casady said to Warren Hinckle, editor of *Ramparts* magazine, "and we might as well let them."

"Especially since there's nothing in it," said Hinckle.[17]

Martin Peretz of Harvard University, a principal backer of the conference, had already walked out twice, and traditional sources of political funds could hardly survive acceptance of the thirteen points, much less surrender of the entire organization to a faction controlled by the Communist Party. Militants considered a loss of liberal funds as a sign of independence and revolutionary integrity, which it perhaps was, and the beginning of a truly relevant *radical* movement to transform America, which in this case it certainly wasn't. It was the beginning of the end for the NCNP.

While the 50-percent demand was being prepared by the Black Caucus Sunday afternoon, James Forman, minister of international affairs for SNCC, was demonstrating to the conference at large what control by the caucus would probably mean. As chairman of that session, he read a long resolution dealing with the Ivory Coast, of all places, and then called for a vote. "All in favor say aye."

Shouts of "aye" from the floor.

"All right, the ayes have it."

"Point of order," shouted a blonde girl in the audience. Forman tried to ignore her but she persisted. "Point of order! Point of order! You haven't called for the nays."

"There's no points of order here," said Forman. This brought shouts of "Dictator," "Is this a dictatorship?" and so forth. "That's right," said Forman, "and I'm the dictator."

More shouts. "Point of order! Point of order!" insisted the blonde girl.

Finally, after several dozen whites stalked from the room, Forman backed down, trying to pass off the episode as a joke. "Jesus Christ, man," he said, "we just can't have any fun."[18]

Nevertheless, the conference voted Sunday night to grant the Black Caucus's demand for effective control. The organized bullying of whites by blacks was supplemented by intimidation on a smaller scale. Blacks who were little more than Chicago street hoodlums invaded the conference and buttonholed white delegates for the fare "back to Mississippi"[19] or demanded they buy tickets to a blacks-only dance. The Mississippi Freedom Democratic Party was robbed of its funds for the trip home. A hippie who had hitchhiked to the conference from California watched a black youth selling newspapers walk up to a white radical, spit on his jacket, and demand, "Buy this if you want to help my people." "Sure, sure," said the white radical, who pulled out a coin and bought the offered paper.[20] The conference was indeed a turning point in the movement, as Edwin Greer had said, but it hardly marked a new era of black-white trust and cooperation, as he had argued.

What, meanwhile, had happened to the original plans for a movement antiwar campaign against Johnson in 1968? On Saturday night plans for a major effort to create a full-scale third party were decisively voted down. A proposal for a third ticket—that is, presidential and vice-presidential candidates who would run against the war without attempting to create a permanent party—was barely defeated 13,519 to 13,517. (A complicated system of weighted voting had been devised to reflect the strength of the various organizations participating in the conference.) The NCNP, it was decided, would concentrate on local organizing. Members of the California group and the White Radical Caucus proposed an alternative which would encourage local organizing but allow electoral efforts as well. Support for this move, known as the California compromise, was the result of efforts centering in Berkeley for the creation and official recognition of a third party called the Peace and Freedom Party, the most recent result of the organizational thrust begun by Scheer's congressional campaign in 1966 and Jerry Rubin's campaign for mayor of Berkeley early in 1967.

Although the issue had theoretically been settled by the voting Saturday night, the California compromise was proposed in a complex form by the Black Caucus on Sunday night and passed by an exhausted and thoroughly confused conference. The Communists were thus assured of an alternative to a Trotskyist on the ballot; radicals were assured there would be no middle-of-the-road electoral cop-out; delegates from California were assured they could support the Peace and Freedom Party if they were of a mind; and liberals were assured that if they wanted to oppose Johnson effectively in 1968, they were going to have to look outside the movement.

Before the conference adjourned it created two twelve-man organizing committees, each half black, to coordinate local organizing and electoral activities. The NCNP was already in debt for the Chicago conference, however, had no prospects of new funds, and was so confused in its purposes as to be virtually powerless. It quickly sank into impotent obscurity. Many individuals and organizations went on to do useful work elsewhere, of course, but that was the last time so many political trends—black militants and white radicals, liberal reformers and left-wing revolutionaries, church groups and Communist cadre, pacifists and would-be guerrillas—met to consider a common course of action. If they had succeeded in reaching useful agreement, they truly would have been a movement. Instead, they only confirmed their own bitter division.

Marvin Garson probably summed up the disaster best. "Does anyone still remember," he asked,

> the daily leaflets and rallies of the Free Speech Movement, which gave the rank and file a pound of solid fact and reasoning for every ounce of rhetoric? The FSM operated under the principle that any bit of dishonesty or opportunism, however innocuous it might seem at the moment, would grow like a cancer until it killed the movement. . . . The NCNP did not suddenly falsify what had been an honest movement; the style of the movement had been disintegrating for years. Still, it came as a shock to me to listen to the press conference that the new board held as the convention was breaking up. They had boxed themselves in so thoroughly that there was hardly a single question they could answer honestly. . . . [21]

There was a third-party campaign in 1968, after all, but it was headed by George Wallace and General Curtis LeMay, who had once recommended bombing the North Vietnamese back to the Stone Age. Wallace received thirteen million votes and at one point looked as if he might throw the election into the House of Representatives, which was more hawkish on the war than Lyndon Johnson. Everything considered, the debacle at the Palmer House was probably the luckiest thing that happened to the peace movement in 1967. If the spleen that the movement vented on itself had been released during the election instead, the opposition to the war might have been seriously discredited. As it was, the movement's refusal to take part in the election left room for those who were against the war and determined to give Americans a chance to vote for peace.

By September, 1967, then, it was already clear that there would be no major antiwar third party opposing the President in 1968, and that Romney was incapable of articulating an alternative to current policy on the war. This led to the incredible possibility that Johnson might actually run as the *peace* candidate, since the only position on the war open to a Republican with a chance of winning his party's nomination would be an appeal for more war, rather than less. The consensus of Washington political columnists that fall was that Johnson had every reason to smile because no Republican could get to his left on the war, no radical third party could win, even if one should emerge, and no other Democrat could win the nomination because all the rules and precedents said an incumbent President could not be denied his party's nomination if he wanted it.

It would not only be difficult for the Democrats to nominate someone else, it was argued, but self-defeating to try, since a serious attempt would only strengthen the presumably prowar Republicans by dividing the Democrats. As early as March, 1967, Walter Lippmann had observed that "the opposition to President Johnson [on the war] has its active center in his own party." The practical effect was political immobilization of the forces opposed to the war:

> A Johnson-Kennedy fight for the nomination would split the Democrats and assure the victory of the Republicans. Not only that: it would certainly favor, even if it did not assure, the nomination and election of a right-wing Republican, perhaps Nixon, perhaps Reagan. For if the Republicans are sure to win, right-wing politicians who control the party machinery will feel they have nothing to fear if they nominate a man they really like.[22]

Nothing happened to change Lippmann's analysis and, in fact, things turned out pretty much as he had foreseen. Despite all the practical considerations urging caution on dissident Democrats, however, they began searching for a way to oppose Johnson's war policies by challenging him directly in 1968, not because the prospect of victory, either in Chicago or in the election itself, seemed likely, but because the importance of the issue demanded it.

Antiwar campaigns in 1966 had largely failed, but often by narrow margins which encouraged many of those who had attempted or supported them. By late 1967 two major foci of antiwar sentiment within the Democratic Party had emerged in the Reform Democratic movement in New York City and in the left wing of the Democratic Party in California. In March, 1967, the California Democratic Council, a coalition to the left of the party's leader, Jesse Unruh, formally decided to run an antiwar slate of delegates in the June, 1968, primary if nothing had been done to bring the war to a close within six months, that is, by September, 1967. Open opposition to Johnson by the CDC's leader, Simon Casady, cost him his position but he remained influential and the CDC did not back down from its position.

In New York on April 23, 1967, Alex J. Rosenberg, the Democratic leader of the Sixty-fifth Assembly District, warned in a speech to the Ansonia Independent Democrats that Johnson's policy in Vietnam was costing him the support of his own party. "We helped to elect this administration because it promised peace," he said. "We did not intentionally elect a vice president to walk arm in arm with either Marshall Ky or Lester Maddox."[23]

Two weeks later the general committee of the Committee for Democratic Voters, the official arm of the entire Reform Democratic movement in New York, passed a resolution by a vote of sixty-one to fourteen that " . . . the war in Vietnam is alienating a sufficient number of Democratic voters to cause the defeat of local and state, as well as national Democratic candidates [i.e., the President himself] in next year's Presidential election."[24] The group had rejected resolutions supporting the war and pledged an effort "to work for the nomination in 1968 of a candidate other than Lyndon Johnson." When a group of Reform leaders later that year told Edwin Weisl, a friend of Johnson and the party's national committeeman from New York, that they could not support the President, Weisl replied, "Well, we simply must tell everyone that Johnson is a man of peace."[25]

The opposition to Johnson seemed to take a major step forward when the Americans for Democratic Action voted on May 20 to support "that candidate of either party, who offers a genuine hope for restraint in the conduct of the war in Vietnam and for its peaceful resolution on honorable terms."[26] The "honorable terms" proviso stopped well short of open opposition to the war itself, but the threat to back a Republican was serious, serious enough, at any rate, to draw a sharp and effective counterattack from forces within the ADA loyal to the President. Gus Tyler, the political officer of the International Ladies Garment Workers Union, sent a letter to the ADA board opposing a blank-check promise of support for even a "reactionary Republican isolationist against a liberal Democrat because the former promises peace."[27]

Unions provided much of the ADA's funds, and Tyler's letter got a quick reaction. The ADA inserted the word "liberal" before "candidate" in the original resolution, thus negating much of its force. The split within the Democratic Party that this seemingly minor episode revealed was to continue up until the election itself. Unions, probably the largest block within the Democratic coalition created by Roosevelt in the 1930s, were not about to oppose a President who represented their interests so effectively solely because of a war halfway around the world. If they shared the frustration with the war's lack of progress, they most emphatically did not share liberal doubts about the militant anticommunism which the war represented. Not all unions took this position, of course, but the establishment labor movement, most particularly the leadership of the AFL-CIO, was behind the goals of the war 100 percent.

It was thus clear from the beginning that any attempt to oppose Johnson's renomination would split and weaken the party as badly as Lippmann had predicted. Gerald Hill, who had replaced Casady at the head of the California Democratic Council, addressed this problem directly in June in a speech to Democratic leaders from the East Coast:

> CDC has been told that its opposition is divisive—to the Democratic Party and the nation. That's nonsense! The *war* is dividing my party. The *war* has turned the hopes for a massive war on poverty into prolonged frustration. The *war* has divorced America from advancement of civil rights and economic opportunity for all Americans. And the *war* is killing peasants and young Americans in Southeast Asia.[28]

Fear of splitting the party was not easily quieted, however. In September, Daniel Patrick Moynihan conceded Hill's point in a speech to the ADA, saying the opposition was probably "correct in holding that the war has brought stalemate to government efforts on behalf of Negroes at home, but they are wrong, I would think, in their proposed solution, which is for the government to get out of Vietnam."[29] The national honor had been committed too deeply. An electoral attempt to end the war would only help the Republicans, who would make things worse.

The split in the party, however, could not be suppressed, ignored, or papered over with carefully worded resolutions. On June 3, 1967, for example, Robert Kennedy appeared at a Democratic fund-raising dinner in New York with President Johnson. Kennedy praised the President without restraint as a man who "has poured out his own strength to renew the strength of the country." Outside the Americana Hotel, a number of Reform Democrats, including City Councilman Theodore Weiss, were among the 1,400 demonstrators protesting the war. "Many of us within the party have been vocally opposed to the President's policy," Weiss said. "Suddenly we're asked to participate in a 'Salute to Johnson.' This is asking too much of us."[30]

Liberal antiwar Democrats in New York and California and, as the year progressed, half a dozen points in between, were hardly the whole of the party, but they did embody important sources of potential support for any attempt to unseat the President. The vast majority of party officials and of those who led the various organized blocks within the party either agreed with the President or were too conscious of his power to be drawn into an effort to oppose him for reasons that had moral and intellectual force, but the most dismal prospects. They expected Johnson to defend himself and did not see how he could be defeated or what was to be gained in a practical political sense even if he were. The man who finally decided it had to be attempted, and could even be achieved, was a long-time activist named Allard Lowenstein, then little known to the public but with a certain following among student groups and liberal Democrats.

Lowenstein had been president of the National Student Association during the 1950s, the last before the CIA began funding it as a weapon in the Cold War. He had been active in a wide range of causes, literally risking his life in South West Africa, Spain, and Mississippi, where he had been an organizer working with SNCC in the early 1960s. A friend of Norman Thomas and a supporter of Adlai Stevenson in 1952 and 1956, Lowenstein had been extremely hostile to the first signs of a turn toward Marxism-Leninism within SNCC. He opposed the movement's rapprochement with the old left, and especially its willingness to work even with the American Communist Party. His completely unsuccessful efforts to head off that development earned him a lasting reputation in activist circles as a red-baiter and liberal apologist.

The increasingly fierce enmity of movement radicals did not end his effectiveness with liberal elements of the student movement, however, and his natural political gifts made him a formidable figure. He was a tireless organizer and a spellbinding speaker who could inspire the most

diffident audience. He would characteristically begin with a lofty philosophical explanation of what had to be done, outline a broad strategy,
describe the tactics that would be necessary, and then conclude by
saying, Here's what you do when you leave the meeting. He could make
anything seem possible and he had the imagination in early 1967 to see
that Johnson's formidable powers as leader of the party and nation
would count for nothing on election day. Johnson was wedded to the
war, Lowenstein felt, and ending the war therefore meant defeating
Johnson.

Lowenstein's first approach, in March, 1967, was to investigate with
Norman Thomas the possibilities of a third-party campaign to be led
by Martin Luther King. He abandoned this notion later that spring as
a result not so much of King's disclaimer in April as of the growing
evidence that a serious effort could be mounted within the Democratic
Party itself. In June, Lowenstein met in Washington with other peace
activists in the conference room of the Friends Committee on legislation. With him, among others, were Curtis Gans, a staff worker for the
ADA, Bella Abzug of Women Strike for Peace, Ed Schwartz of the
National Student Association, and two professors active with the Inter-
University Committee for a Public Hearing on Vietnam, the group
responsible for the teach-ins of 1965.

The problem faced by the group in attempting to organize opposition
to the President's renomination was twofold. First, a nationwide organization had to be created based on antiwar sentiment, rather than on
the special interests of traditional blocks within the Democratic Party.
Opposition to the war, relatively recent in conventional political terms,
was present in every section of the party, while dominant in few. In
effect, a parallel party structure had to be created on this issue alone.
Second, a major public figure had to be persuaded to run against
Johnson, a huge task considering the widespread assumption that the
attempt would ultimately fail. Johnson was not a man known to treat
disloyalty lightly, and the political future of anyone who challenged
him and lost would be dim indeed. Lowenstein, who sometimes seemed
to know everybody everywhere, said he would find a candidate.

At this early stage Lowenstein did not expect to persuade someone
to run until the first few primaries had already proved the existence of
a powerful opposition to the war within the party. Even without a
candidate, the primaries were already certain to reveal at least some-

thing of the antiwar sentiment that existed. A nationwide network of groups calling themselves Citizens for Kennedy-Fulbright in '68 (later, Fulbright's name was dropped from the group's title) had already begun to organize and was planning to run Kennedy slates in New Hampshire and other primary states. In July, the governor of Wisconsin signed a new primary law which would put every recognized candidate's name on the ballot unless he specifically declared he would not be a candidate, thus guaranteeing Johnson would be on the ballot. The primary law also allowed a voter to write in no if he opposed those listed on the ballot. The head of the local Citizens for Kennedy-Fulbright, a University of Wisconsin graduate student named Kenneth McKay, said the group would organize a "vote no for President" campaign against Johnson if Kennedy kept his name off the ballot. With these and other primary possibilities for demonstrating opposition to the President, Lowenstein hoped to persuade someone to oppose Johnson at the convention in August.

Lowenstein's early efforts quickly became known within the party, of course, and opposition to the "dump-Johnson movement," as it was being called by mid-summer, was organized by Joseph L. Rauh. Rauh was convinced the movement would fail to unseat Johnson, and might even disguise the true extent of peace sentiment within the party. His proposed alternative, outlined in a fifteen-page memorandum sent to three hundred liberal Democrats over the weekend of July 29–30, was to organize an antiwar block within the convention itself which would fight for a peace plank based on the formula of Negotiations Now, which was collecting petition signatures opposing the war. Basically, Rauh said, the plank would call for a bombing halt and peace negotiations among all parties to the war, including the National Liberation Front.

"The three present political drives of the peace movement [that is, plans for a third party, to dump Johnson, or to draft Kennedy] all seem calculated to produce the least possible show of strength and are thus more likely to further the cause of escalation than to bring peace," he wrote.[31] The Party's Platform Committee would have 110 members; only 11 would be necessary to file a minority report requiring the issue to be debated on the floor of the convention where the peace block could most effectively make its strength felt. Expanding on his argument later that summer, he wrote,

An incumbent President is hard enough to beat for nomination by his own party; without a rival candidate it is impossible. Just as the Kennedy-Fulbright draft will fail to produce delegates because Kennedy will repudiate it in most dramatic form, so any other similar effort in behalf of anti-Johnson delegates will fail because responsible people inside the Democratic Party will not allow their names to be connected with a drive against a Democratic President, and especially so hopeless a drive. . . . If the effort can be made on the peace issue and the peace issue alone without any personal overtones of any sort, there are very real possibilities of success.[32]

Rauh's was essentially a counsel of despair, and the effect of his proposal was ultimately the opposite of what he had intended. If the dump-Johnson movement might fail, what, after all, would even complete success of the peace plank effort mean? The party's platform, as painful experience had proved already, was not binding on the President. Johnson had chosen to break his own promises made during the 1964 election; how would he react to an uncongenial peace plank forced on him during the 1968 election? Nevertheless, Rauh had pinpointed the main problem faced by Lowenstein. Eventually, and the sooner the better, he had to have a major candidate who offered a plausible alternative to Johnson.

Lowenstein first approached Kennedy, by all odds the Democrat with the greatest personal resources and the best chance of challenging Johnson effectively. Kennedy had no love for the President but shared the general belief that an anti-Johnson campaign would inevitably fail and in the process split the party, which would be unlikely to repay his disruptive efforts with the nomination in 1972, or any other year. Kennedy, a close friend of Robert McNamara, had no illusions about the possibility of quick military success in Vietnam. He was disturbed by the war's effect on the country, felt Johnson was hopelessly trapped by his own war policy, and was genuinely alarmed by the prospect of further escalation. Some of his young senate staff members were in favor of an attempt to challenge the President, and one of them, Adam Walinsky, had submitted a memorandum proposing just such a challenge as early as the day after the mid-term elections in 1966.

The conflict in Kennedy's mind throughout 1967 reflected the two opposing sides of his character, moral intensity and political realism. On the one hand, he recognized the importance of the issue of the war in its broadest terms, and on the other, he was pessimistic about his chances of winning. If he couldn't win, why make the attempt? On the night of the New York mayoral primary in 1965, Kennedy had visited the campaign headquarters of Representative William Fitts Ryan, a Democratic candidate who was soundly defeated. Kennedy was surprised and repelled by the happy mood of the crowd, which felt a moral victory had been won by Ryan's campaign even if he had failed to capture the nomination. "My God," Kennedy said, "you'd think they'd won."[33]

The conflict in Kennedy's mind was a real and continuing one, however, and he continued to waver. On August 4, Lowenstein, recently returned from a trip to South Vietnam, flew out to California on the same plane with Kennedy, who was going to a fund-raising dinner organized by Jesse Unruh. The two sat together for several hours and Lowenstein explained what he was doing. "Who's your candidate?" Kennedy asked. "You need a movement before you can get a candidate,"[34] Lowenstein said. He said he was going to talk to members of the California Democratic Council who were planning to oppose Johnson. Kennedy said they were a disruptive element within the party, the sort of people who used to picket him when he was Attorney General, allies for nothing but failure.

"If you really think the CDC people are so bad," Lowenstein answered, "why don't you say so to the reporters who meet us when the plane gets in?"[35]

Kennedy, however, was not ready to write off potential supporters. When the reporters asked him what he thought of the CDC's plans for an anti-Johnson slate, he side-stepped, saying, "That's a matter for the people of California to decide for themselves."[36]

That month Lowenstein's efforts to create a movement began to jell. Within a day or two of the trip to California, Lowenstein met in his New York apartment with Curtis Gans and several student leaders he had recruited at the National Student Association convention the year before to run a letter-writing campaign. At the meeting, David Hawk, a student at the Union Theological Seminary, suggested that the peace movement ought to concentrate on the Resistance. Lowenstein dismissed the suggestion. "The only thing left to do," he said, "is to unseat Lyndon Johnson."[37] The students were disbelieving at first, then agreed to join his movement.

On Monday, August 14, Lowenstein addressed the National Student Association meeting at the University of Maryland and proposed creation of a group called "Non-Partisans Against the President." "This Congress," he said, "can be a launching pad for a decision to make 1968 the year when students help change a society almost everyone agrees is headed for disaster."[38] The potential of student volunteers in politics was not then as apparent to party officials as it later became, but Lowenstein realized that students were passionately opposed to the war, were in an activist mood, and could provide the manpower for a nationwide campaign short on funds.

The suggestion bore immediate fruit. Sam Brown, a student at the Harvard Divinity School, received a standing ovation and 90 percent of the votes of some 550 student leaders when he announced on Tuesday, August 30, the creation of a dump-Johnson group to be called Alternative Candidate Task Force, or ACT '68. The group proposed an effort to recruit a Republican candidate if no Democrat proved willing to run, but within two weeks, failing to find money to continue, the organization dissolved. This failure was more apparent than real, since its leaders then joined Lowenstein's group and became the nucleus of the student volunteers who were ultimately to have a decisive effect on the outcome of the New Hampshire primary.

With this beginning, Lowenstein and Curtis Gans created the National Conference of Concerned Democrats in Washington on September 1, and, traveling incessantly, spent the next three months organizing the peace factions in state and local Democratic parties across the country. He or Gans met with groups in Oregon, California, Wisconsin, Massachusetts, New Hampshire, Michigan, Indiana, New York, and elsewhere, convincing each it was not alone and creating the core of a national organization which could promise funds and volunteers for any candidate willing to challenge the President. On Wednesday, October 18, this new organization was publicly announced in a press conference held in New York. The three cochairmen of the group were Lowenstein, Gerald Hill of the California Democratic Council, and Donald Peterson of the Concerned Wisconsin Democrats. Lowenstein finally had a movement, but he still lacked a candidate.

His first choice, Kennedy, continued to waver. On Saturday, September 23, Lowenstein was in Washington for a meeting of the ADA national board which, still torn between opposition to the war and what

John Kenneth Galbraith called its "long standing commitment to political realities,"[39] decisively rejected a resolution opposing Johnson's renomination. That night Lowenstein joined a number of others for dinner at Kennedy's home at Hickory Hill outside Washington. Discussion of the presidential election became an informal debate on whether or not Kennedy ought to run. Lowenstein and Jack Newfield, a former activist and a writer, argued that he should. Arthur Schlesinger and James Loeb, a newspaper publisher, argued that he should not. At one point Schlesinger suggested that Rauh's peace plank proposal ought to be pursued. "You're a historian, Arthur," Kennedy said. "When was the last time millions of people rallied behind a plank?"[40] Kennedy agreed that the only effective opposition to the war would be opposition to the President, but he still would not agree to run.

After that night Lowenstein gave up hope that Kennedy would soon decide to enter the race, although he continued to feel Kennedy would be the logical man to oppose Johnson at the convention. A week later, on Saturday, September 30, Lowenstein flew to Pittsburgh to meet with twenty-four leaders of Citizens for Kennedy committees from eleven states. He urged them to support the soon-to-be-announced Conference of Concerned Democrats and to retain an open mind about possible candidates, since, he insisted, Kennedy would not run.

"Some people think we have to name a candidate now," he said. "I believe there is much time to make a decision." The group agreed to support Lowenstein's coalition but would not give up hope for a race by Kennedy. "It would be the absolute death of this movement if we tried to fight Johnson with nobody," said Eugene S. Daniell, Jr., head of the Citizens for Kennedy committee in New Hampshire. "Lowenstein is asking us to commit suicide."[41]

Lowenstein did not plan to run nobody, of course. He knew only that Kennedy was paralyzed by indecision, and that someone else would have to lead the movement Lowenstein had created.

Throughout the fall of 1967 Lowenstein continued to meet regularly with other possible candidates. James Gavin, who had earned a certain antiwar reputation with his letter to *Harper's* magazine proposing an enclave strategy in 1966, felt Johnson could not be defeated by a member of his own party and retained illusions about his own chances of winning the Republican nomination. Senator George McGovern agreed someone ought to run but said he faced a tough reelection campaign in South Dakota and couldn't make the effort himself. When the Conference of Concerned Democrats was announced in New York, four names were cited of the sort of people who might run, all of them senators: McGovern, Vance Hartke of Indiana, Frank Church of Idaho, and Eugene McCarthy of Minnesota.

Lowenstein had first approached McCarthy at the beginning of September, but McCarthy had suggested Kennedy would be the logical man to run against the President. McCarthy, however, had been seriously considering the idea on his own for nearly nine months. On March 22, 1967, he had dinner in New York with several former supporters of Adlai Stevenson who felt it was possible Johnson might not run and were not admirers of Kennedy. McCarthy talked at length about the war and Johnson's leadership, saying he thought nothing would alter the President's policy except a direct challenge at the polls. He himself, McCarthy said, might even decide to run against him. When his hosts later attempted to follow up this conversation with practical steps, however, McCarthy seemed to have cooled. He suggested they wait and see how things developed.

Like Kennedy, McCarthy was worried that a race against the President would attract so little support it would be no challenge at all; would, in failing dismally, in effect endorse the President's policy. But unlike Kennedy, McCarthy felt that the importance of the issues might demand an attempt, anyway. He was not opposed to the war as an effort to prevent a Communist victory in South Vietnam, but as an overcommitment of American power which was hardening lines throughout the world, strengthening the presidency and eroding the powers of the Senate, turning the United States into an excessively military power, and, finally, tearing apart the United States itself.

As a member of the Senate Foreign Relations Committee he attended a hearing on Thursday, August 17, where the Under Secretary of State, Nicholas deB. Katzenbach, argued that the Senate's Tonkin Gulf resolution was a "functional equivalent" to a declaration of war. Johnson had not exceeded the limits of the authority granted him just three years earlier; in fact, he had not even approached those limits. Closely questioned by committee members, Katzenbach at one point responded in a tone of voice near a shout, "didn't that resolution authorize the President to use the Armed Forces of the United States in whatever way was necessary? Didn't it? What could a declaration of war have done that would have given the President more authority and a clearer voice of Congress than that did?"

McCarthy walked out of the hearing angrily. In the corridor outside he ran into E. W. Kenworthy, a reporter for the *New York Times,* and said, "This is the wildest testimony I ever heard. There is no limit to what he says the President could do. There is only one thing to do— take it to the country."[42]

A second event also impressed itself keenly on McCarthy's mind. On Thursday, October 12, Dean Rusk held a long press conference in which he defended the war as directly involving the most vital American interests. We were not fighting simply to defend Saigon, he said, but to halt the spread of Communism throughout Asia.

> Let me say, as solemnly as I can, that those who would place in question the credibility of the pledged word of the United States under our mutual security treaties would subject this nation to mortal danger. . . . Within the next decade or two there will be a billion Chinese on the mainland, armed with nuclear weapons, with no certainty about what their attitude toward the rest of Asia will be.[43]

This struck McCarthy not as a justification of the war in Vietnam, but as a direct refutation of all previous explanations of the war. In a Senate speech on October 16, he attacked Rusk for relying on the "ancient fear of the Yellow Peril," said the war "may well be a costly exercise in futility"[44] and asked how a complete victory in South Vietnam, even if that were possible, could end the alleged threat posed by Chinese Communism. Katzenbach's testimony seemed to McCarthy a dangerous usurpation of power, and Rusk's *apologia* a sign the administration was losing its mental balance.

McCarthy did not decide suddenly or all at once that he would run against Johnson. He continued to say someone ought to do it, and if no one else would, well, he might. He traveled widely on speaking engagements and everywhere found evidence of Lowenstein's movement and of an almost desperate frustration, especially among students, over the steady escalation of the war. People wanted to oppose the war, to make themselves heard, and so far the only forum was the streets; the only active leaders, radicals and revolutionaries; the only method that seemed to attract attention, violence.

On October 20, after six weeks of active discussions with doves in the

Senate and dissident party leaders across the country, McCarthy was in Los Angeles at the invitation of the California Democratic Council. Gerald Hill had written to Kennedy, McGovern, Church, and McCarthy in August, but only McCarthy had responded with more than a cool letter of acknowledgment. The others seemed as far from a commitment as ever. In a conversation that morning with Hill, Lowenstein, and two other men over breakfast in McCarthy's hotel room, McCarthy asked a series of practical questions about money, volunteers, the position of the labor unions, and so on. Finally he told Lowenstein and Hill, "You fellows have been talking about three or four names. I guess you can cut it down to one."[45]

In the weeks immediately following it quickly became something of an open secret that the dump-Johnson movement finally had a candidate to oppose the President. The groups organized by Lowenstein issued public calls for McCarthy to run, and McCarthy himself was met by cheering crowds in many cities, by professionally printed signs saying "McCarthy for President," and by local party leaders who told him they would support him.

Kennedy continued to insist he would not run, but altered his commitment to Johnson by saying he would support the Democratic nominee in 1968, not that he would specifically support Johnson. At Marymount College in Tarrytown, New York, on Saturday, November 18, Kennedy said a McCarthy campaign would be a "healthy influence" on the party, and added, "It would allow Americans to take out their frustration in talk instead of violence." Then, as he sometimes did to show how divided opinion was on the war, he took an informal poll of his audience, asking how many favored withdrawal, how many more of the same, and how many escalation of the bombing. When the last group was in the majority, Kennedy said, "All of you who put your hands up, what are you doing to a lot of innocent people? Hundreds and thousands of people in Vietnam are being killed on our responsibility. You've got to think of the implications to your own conscience."[46]

Just so, and yet Kennedy still inisted he would not run. If he had changed his mind at any time right up to the moment of McCarthy's formal announcement, McCarthy almost certainly would have stepped aside. But Kennedy did not change his mind, and on Thursday, November 30, in the Caucus Room of the Senate in Washington,

McCarthy announced that he would challenge the President in the primaries.

> My decision to challenge the President's position, and the administra-
> tion's position, has been strengthened by recent announcements out of
> the administration—the evident intention to intensify the war in Viet-
> nam and, on the other hand, the absence of any positive indications or
> suggestions for a compromise or for a negotiated political settlement. I
> am concerned that the administration seems to have set no limits to the
> price that it is willing to pay for a military victory.

He summarized at length the cost of the war: the death and destruction in both halves of Vietnam, well over 100,000 American casualties
including 15,000 dead, an expenditure of at least $30 billion a year, the
slow starvation of domestic programs in order to pay for the war, the
reduction of foreign aid outside of Vietnam, and the rise in inflation at
home. "In addition," McCarthy said,

> there is growing evidence of a deepening moral crisis in America; discon-
> tent and frustration, and a disposition to take extra-legal—if not illegal
> —action to manifest protest. I am hopeful that this challenge I am
> making . . . may alleviate to at least some degree this sense of political
> helplessness, and restore to many people a belief in the processes of
> American politics and of American government. On the college cam-
> puses . . . and among adult thoughtful Americans it may counter the
> growing sense of alienation from politics which I think is currently
> reflected in a tendency to withdraw from political action and talk of
> non-partisan efforts; to become cynical and make threats for third parties
> or other irregular political movements.[47]

The incredible, then, would not happen: Johnson would not run as
a peace candidate. He and his war would be directly challenged and the
country would decide at the polls if it wanted to see the last of both.
In the days following McCarthy's announcement, major Democratic
Party leaders would dismiss his candidacy as an exercise in political
futility, a narrow political effort supported only by radicals and political
dissidents, a spoiling operation motivated solely by venom. McCarthy's
motives were inevitably questioned viciously, but in fact he had decided
to run for precisely those reasons outlined in his announcement speech.
The crisis that had divided the country, that had persuaded Lowenstein
to attempt the impossible, that had fueled the movement Lowenstein

organized, also persuaded McCarthy to expose his career to ruin. He was no more convinced than Kennedy that a race against Johnson could be successful; he only knew that the crisis demanded it. This issue could not be passed over in silence. Somebody had to take it to the people, and no one else had been willing.

THIRTEEN

The Defeat of Lyndon Johnson

At the press conference where Eugene McCarthy announced his plans to run against Johnson in at least three primaries, he was asked by a reporter if he was, in fact, committing political suicide. "I don't think it will be a case of suicide," McCarthy answered. "It might be an execution."[1]

This gloomy view was widely shared. McCarthy had been assured he would have the support he needed to take his case to the people, but he also knew enough about the realities of presidential politics, and presidential power, to know that his chances were slim indeed. The Democratic National Committee, with its financial resources and strong ties to every state committee, was completely dominated by the President. A large percentage of the delegates to the convention had already been chosen by party officials loyal to the President. Those delegates still to be chosen in the primary states were first of all professional politicians, which meant they wanted above all to elect a Democrat in November, 1968. As a result, McCarthy's opponent was not so much the President as the party itself. To unseat the President he would have to defeat the thousands of local party officials who supported him, or enough of them, at any rate, to instill a cautioning political fear in the rest. Johnson probably had few illusions about his own popularity but he was confident of the strength of his position within the party. On Saturday, December 2, he addressed party officials from six Southern and border states meeting in Charleston, West Virginia, through a telephone hookup. He dismissed his challenger without naming him:

We haven't had our primaries. We haven't had our convention. So there's really no way of guessing who the candidate might be. But I do want to say this: I fully intend to support him. [Loud laughter.] I believe we already have several volunteers for next year's ticket. In general, I like to stay out of these internal party matters.[2]

The President's confidence seemed fully justified. At the Democratic convention in 1960, McCarthy had urged the party not to abandon Adlai Stevenson with an eloquent speech which earned McCarthy a reputation as a man with formidable oratorical gifts. He was also a man of great intellectual and emotional complexity, however, and whatever inspired him in 1960 proved entirely absent in the fitful, disorganized campaign which slowly unfolded in late 1967 and early 1968.

While Johnson was speaking to the party in West Virginia, McCarthy was making his first campaign appearance at a meeting in Chicago of the National Conference of Concerned Democrats. Fifteen hundred Conference members and supporters filled the auditorium of the Hilton Hotel and as many more watched the meeting on closed-circuit television from a large room in the basement. McCarthy was late, and Allard Lowenstein began a speech to keep the crowd from growing restless. All accounts of the speech later agreed that it was a ringing challenge to battle, harshly attacking the war and the President.

McCarthy arrived while Lowenstein was still speaking, listened backstage with growing anger at what he considered an exercise in irresponsible demagoguery, and finally grew so openly furious that his aides and Lowenstein's friends joined and practically dragged Lowenstein from the podium. When McCarthy came on stage the crowd was in a heightened, exhilarated mood, ready for a speech that would express its long frustration. McCarthy denied it to them. His voice was calm, reasoned, restrained, professorial. He was deliberate to the point of political diffidence, saying at one point, "I am prepared to be your candidate."[3] The crowd wanted a champion; McCarthy presented himself with all the boldness of a sacrificial lamb.

The effect was shattering not only on the people who listened in a new agony of dammed emotion, but on the entire peace movement throughout the country which had waited so long for some way of striking back at the man who ran the country. I. F. Stone in his *Weekly* of December 11 said that he would support McCarthy, but only because he had no alternative.

He has wit, charm and grace. But he seems to lack heart and guts. This
may seem a strange thing to say of the only Democrat willing to step out
and challenge Johnson for the nomination. Unfortunately, it seems to be
true. Watching him at the press conference here at which he launched
his candidacy, one began to wonder why he was running at all. A certain
cynicism and defeatism seem basic to the man. This is no way to embark
on a fight. His hero, Adlai, was a Hamlet. McCarthy gives one the uneasy
feeling that he doesn't really give a damn.

Reporters who had accompanied McCarthy on a six-day tour of New
York, Massachusetts, Illinois, Michigan, and Minnesota between
November 9 and 13 were struck by his coolness, by his offhand manner
in answering serious questions, and by a wit so precious and aloof as
to seem almost contemptuous of his audience. On January 12,
McCarthy received an unusually tumultuous reaction from six thousand students and faculty members at the University of California in
Los Angeles which *New York Times* reporter E. W. Kenworthy said
"was probably to be explained by the fact that Senator McCarthy spoke
with a subdued but almost tangible fervor lacking in previous
speeches."⁴ Almost tangible? This was a faint fervor indeed, and, with
exceptions that only further disheartened his supporters by their rarity,
McCarthy's fervor was to remain faint throughout the campaign.
McCarthy acknowledged this in January, saying, with characteristic
understatement, "I'm not much of a projection man."⁵

More important than his public restraint, however, was his refusal
to undertake the hard political work of appealing directly to those
delegates and party officials who would ultimately make up the body
of the convention. One December morning, a Kennedy aide in New
York noticed McCarthy breakfasting *alone* at the Plaza Hotel. The aide
was stunned. Running for President was not simply a matter of allowing your name to be placed on the ballot, making speeches, and answering the questions of reporters from time to time. It was an all-day,
all-week, never-ending effort to make your case in high and low terms
to the men who were, after all, being asked to risk their political lives
in a contest that would reserve no mercy for losers.

Publicly McCarthy was a lackadaisical campaigner, often cutting
speeches short or refusing to appear altogether for no better reason than
an indifferent mood, but he was even worse privately. He would not
spend the necessary hours on the phone to potential supporters, would

not schedule the endless and equally necessary private meetings with local officials as he traveled around the country, would not even speak fully and openly with staff members trying to organize his campaign and write his speeches. He simply offered himself. Here I am, he said in effect. You know what I stand for, let your conscience be your guide. He implied then and later that his loftiness was really high-mindedness, but in fact it represented a political and emotional withdrawal from the nature of the contest he had entered. Almost everyone who had anything to do with his campaign agreed that he was, as a candidate, impossible. He simply would not fight.

This was most immediately apparent to the party leaders whose calls were not returned, who were unable to see him or waited in hotel corridors while the candidate discussed poetry with Robert Lowell, or were told he was tired and had gone to bed at 10:30 at night, an hour when the private work of politics, after public appearances, would normally begin. There is no question that Johnson, whatever his private intentions at that point about running, considered McCarthy a faint threat at the turn of the year because everything Johnson learned publicly and privately told him McCarthy not only had not, but would not, appeal forcefully to the party, which alone could grant or withhold its nomination. Anti-Johnson elements in the party would support McCarthy, of course, because they had no alternative, but the great majority of hard-headedly political party workers would remain loyal to the President because *they* had no alternative. Pessimism about McCarthy's chances was not based on illusions about the President's popularity, but on the unmistakably weak and fitful nature of McCarthy's campaign.

Part of the problem was that McCarthy was necessarily running a one-issue campaign. The war was not the only issue that interested him, but it was the only issue that justified his decision to run. He recognized that people can only vote for a man, not an issue, and offered his name and person as a focus for what amounted to a referendum on the war. In an interview with the Catholic magazine *America* published on December 16, 1967, he argued that his proper role was not to arouse sentiment against the war, but to offer the opposition which already existed a means of expression:

> I really think the whole issue of Vietnam is kind of beyond debate now. Most of the facts and the kind of intellectual judgments people are going

to make about Vietnam really have been made. . . . It becomes almost a matter of will at that point. Do you want to take a chance on some kind of de-escalation, on an easing up with some form of less violent effort? Or do you think the way to do it is to intensify the military action? . . . I think this choice is something you have to kind of personalize in a campaign.

The nature of McCarthy's campaign as a one-issue referendum only partially accounts for its early weakness, however. Equally important was the fact that McCarthy withheld some vital part of himself, remaining aloof from his own fate in a way that is not easy to explain. In a sense he ran precisely because he expected to lose. He felt that no other major politician would make a similar sacrifice, he felt the challenge ought to be made for larger reasons, and he committed himself with a private sense of personal doom. Everything indicated that this would be his last campaign. He was a Catholic and took his religion seriously; when he offered himself as a candidate, martyrdom could not have been far from his mind. But at the same time McCarthy was a proud man; he took no pleasure in the prospect of crushing personal defeat. The best explanation for McCarthy's distance from his own campaign seems to be that an element of moral seriousness made him run, and that an element of spiritual pride kept him from trying to win.

The political feebleness of McCarthy's campaign during its early weeks, obvious to anyone who knew how to count delegates, was to have important effects. In the first place, it prompted a continuing "reassessment" by Kennedy, who knew so well how this sort of thing ought to be done. Still torn between the desire to run himself and the caution that said it couldn't be done even by an adept, Kennedy began to share the agonized frustration of all those who opposed Johnson and saw the one chance to force a change in policy going down the drain. Moreover, Kennedy knew he could still run because McCarthy was making so little progress in the one place where it ultimately counted, within the party itself.

The second effect was still more important. McCarthy had nothing going for him but public sentiment on one issue. When his name on the ballot in New Hampshire and Wisconsin brought out a huge, and until the last minute unexpected vote, it meant only one thing: whatever Johnson's tactical strength within the party, he had lost the people. Given a choice, the people would reject him. It was the very practical hopelessness of McCarthy's campaign that made his relative success loom large, that cast all predictions into doubt, that finally convinced Kennedy to run, and that, in the end, revealed Johnson's weakness with the people and shattered his control of the party.

Even McCarthy's quiet style helped: it made a vote against the President seem moderate and reasonable, rather than divisive and disloyal. For the rest, Johnson's poor showing in New Hampshire, so much weaker than originally predicted that it took on the significance of an outright defeat, was the result of circumstances and of tactical blunders by the men who ran his write-in campaign. The major circumstance was, of course, the Tet offensive, which began on January 30 and dramatically contradicted the official optimism about progress in Vietnam. "One is almost embarrassed to be the messenger of such bad news," McCarthy said in the last week of February. "The situation is so obvious: the optimism of the military men was unfounded, pacification is not working, political stability is further away than ever. It's distressing that the situation had to deteriorate so far before the country woke up."[6]

The first blunder of the men who ran Johnson's campaign had been over-confidence. In the middle of December, while McCarthy was still making up his mind whether he should add New Hampshire to the primaries he had already pledged to enter, the President's supporters were predicting that McCarthy could get no more than 5 percent of the vote. A month later they were willing to concede 15 percent, but that still would have given the President a five-to-one victory. His supporters argued that New Hampshire was a conservative state, hawkish on the war, but this turned out to be a source of weakness rather than strength.

Since the events of 1968 were dominated by Vietnam, it is worth taking a fairly close look at the situation in which the President found himself at the first of the year. Even before the Tet offensive, the United States was making painfully slow progress in Vietnam, if it could be said to be making any progress at all. The President's seemingly centrist position of no wider war and no surrender was in fact a formula for endless public frustration. The reasoning behind the President's position was coherent enough, but it was politically untenable.

Winning the war decisively would have meant the destruction of North Vietnam's war-making potential, but this was impossible so long as the North Vietnamese could retreat across a line—any line—beyond which they would not be followed on the ground. So long as the North Vietnamese army survived on the ground it could continue to cross whatever line marked the border of its sanctuary and attack U.S. troops —from Laos and Cambodia, from North Vietnam if those two countries were invaded and occupied, from China if Johnson took the next step and invaded North Vietnam. The dilemma of the President's position was that he might inflict pain on the North Vietnamese that no sensible regime would volunteer to endure, but if they unsensibly endured it anyway, there was nothing he could do about it. An invasion of North Vietnam almost certainly would have meant war with China, and an attempt to crush North Vietnam with nuclear weapons would have at least risked nuclear retaliation by Russia or China. Even if there was no retaliation and a nuclear bombing campaign was a "success," the wickedness of such an act would have fundamentally changed relationships throughout the world.

The war would continue, in other words, as long as the North Vietnamese chose to continue it. The promise of no wider war was a promise of war without end. By coupling it with a promise of "no surrender," the President in effect foreclosed any way out of the impasse he had created. If taking steps to end the war without a "signal from Hanoi" meant "surrender," and if North Vietnam refused to send the signal, and if the United States could not take decisive military action for the reasons already mentioned, then it had no alternative but to plod on endlessly with things as they were. Obviously not every voter clearly understood that this was the case, but the general drift of things was clear enough: a vote for Johnson was a vote for more of the same.

McCarthy's solution to this impasse was brilliantly simple: he replaced the word "surrender" with what he called a "political solution" and let the voters draw their own conclusions. The only sort of "political solution" then available would not have been much in return for all the lives and money and domestic struggle the war had already cost, but McCarthy did not go into details. Later, during the first two weeks of Kennedy's campaign, Kennedy would attack the war head-on as senseless, brutal, and wrong, using language with a high emotional content, sharpening the issue rather than easing and clouding it. This, too, was to have an important effect on events, but in the beginning McCarthy's approach was the more successful: he offered the voters a way out of the agony and they took it.

Faced with evidence of McCarthy's growing momentum in New Hampshire, the leaders of the Johnson write-in effort, Governor John W. King, Senator Thomas J. McIntyre, and a local New Hampshire businessman, Bernard Boutin, responded with a crude attack on McCarthy's patriotism in an ad which ran in New Hampshire newspapers on Wednesday, March 6:

> The Communists in Vietnam are watching the New Hampshire primary. They're watching to see if we at home have the same determination as our soldiers in Vietnam.
>
> To vote for weakness and indecision would not be in the best interests of our nation.
>
> We urge you to support our fighting men in Vietnam.
>
> Write-in President Johnson on your ballot on Tuesday.

A radio ad put it even more strongly: "Don't vote for fuzzy thinking and surrender."[7] A principal weakness of this approach was the fact that "supporting our fighting men" meant more of the same, with no end in sight.

McCarthy attacked the President's newspaper and radio ads adroitly, dismissing them as demagoguery too crude and obvious to be answered in detail. The same heavy-handedness was apparent in the seventy thousand pledge cards distributed to registered Democrats throughout the state by party officials. Each card had three parts, one to be filled out and sent to the President pledging to vote for him, a second to be returned to the party locally, and a third to be kept by the voter. All three parts were numbered, thus allowing the party to determine who did, and who did not, align himself with the President. McCarthy said this struck him as "not altogether inconsistent with administration policy to kind of put a brand on people. It's something they do in Texas. I would hope the voters will react against it."[8]

Added to the clumsiness of Johnson's partisans was the practical effectiveness of McCarthy's volunteers. They came to the state in huge numbers, set up local storefronts and broad canvassing operations in every major city and town, and not only converted many of the undecided but, more important, ensured that McCarthy backers actually voted on election day. The organizational core of McCarthy's national campaign never overcame its candidate's reluctance to pursue delegates with the necessary energy, but his local vote-pulling organizations were a model of citizen politics which attracted extended coverage by the media.

When the votes were counted in New Hampshire following the primary on Tuesday, March 12, McCarthy got 42 percent of the Democratic vote and twenty of the state's twenty-four delegates to the convention. His near-sweep of the delegates was the result of still another practical error by his opponents, who had allowed forty-five Johnson loyalists to put their names on the ballot, thus dividing the President's vote. When Republican crossovers were also counted, McCarthy had come within 230 votes of Johnson.

In Washington, Johnson attempted to dismiss the significance of McCarthy's success, so much greater than had seemed possible at the turn of the year, by saying the New Hampshire primary was "the only race where anybody can enter and everybody can win." Speaking at a Veterans of Foreign Wars dinner, he called New Hampshire a state "where a candidate can claim 20 per cent is a landslide and 40 per cent is a mandate and 60 per cent is unanimous."[9] James H. Rowe, Jr., a Washington lawyer who had been appointed in February to head Citizens for Johnson-Humphrey, a national group with an office next door to the Democratic National Committee headquarters in Washington, emphasized the practical difficulties of a write-in campaign. "The real answer in my view," he said, "is that the President wasn't running and wasn't on the ballot." This was true but hardly reassuring, since Johnson had decided not to run directly in any of the primaries where he was being challenged. Despite all these disclaimers, the President had suffered a stunning personal defeat, and it was clear his nomination was no longer a certainty.

The immediate effect of the New Hampshire primary was to end Kennedy's long indecision. The following day he told reporters he was "reassessing" his position and on Saturday, March 16, he finally announced he was in the race. Kennedy had obviously hoped that much of McCarthy's support would switch to him but, with a few exceptions, it did not. Instead, Kennedy was bitterly charged with opportunism, McCarthy's campaign received an immediate financial shot in the arm from anti-Kennedy people, and McCarthy himself was transformed overnight from an insurgent to a potential compromise candidate. The ill feeling that would grow between the McCarthy and Kennedy camps was so intense that not even Kennedy's assassination could reconcile the two groups. In spite of the hostility that Kennedy's last-minute candidacy aroused, however, he plunged immediately into the struggle for the nomination with a tireless pursuit of party officials and campaign appearances which focused with passionate ferocity on the President and the war. In place of McCarthy's cool analysis of the contradictions in administration policy, Kennedy made a direct attack on the horrors of the war itself, the moral ambiguity implicit in the devastation of a weak nation by the world's most powerful, the domestic programs starved of funds, the passionate divisions of the American people.

In speech after speech Kennedy placed the blame for the failure of the war and the erosion of peace at home squarely on the President, presenting the party leaders with the dilemma they had hoped to avoid. There was never any doubt about Kennedy's determination to win the nomination or the political seriousness of his efforts. He was a man with both gifts and resources. McCarthy had waited for the party to come to him; Kennedy went after the party, and made it clear every leader would eventually have to choose between him and the President. Kennedy's public language during this period is worth quoting at length for the sharpness of the line he was drawing and the bitterness of the choice that would have to be made.

On Monday, March 18, he flew to Manhattan, Kansas, for a speech before students and faculty at Kansas State University. Wildly received by a crowd of more than fourteen thousand, Kennedy attacked the war in the harshest emotional terms:

> I am concerned that, at the end of it all, there will only be more Americans killed, more of our treasure spilled out; and because of the bitterness and hatred on every side of this war, more hundreds of thousands of Vietnamese slaughtered, so that they may say, as Tacitus said of Rome: "They made a desert, and called it peace". . . . Can we ordain to ourselves the awful majesty of God—to decide what cities and villages are to be destroyed, who will live and who will die, and who will join the refugees of our creation?[10]

Three days later, at Vanderbilt University in Nashville, Tennessee, Kennedy attacked Johnson by name as personally responsible for the division of the American people. In Los Angeles that weekend, Kennedy said Johnson was "calling upon the darker impulses of the American spirit" and, in speeches throughout the state (altering "sun" to "moon," depending on the time of day), said:

Here, while the sun shines, our brave young men are dying in the swamps of Southeast Asia. Which of them might have written a poem? Which of them might have cured cancer? Which of them might have played in a World Series or given us the gift of laughter from a stage or helped build a bridge or a university? Which of them would have taught a child to read? It is our responsibility to let these men live.[11]

Kennedy did not limit his attack to the war, but spoke eloquently of the pervasive sense of breakdown in American society as well. The civil rights movement and the war on poverty, both begun with such promise, were dying for lack of spirit and money. The young who had turned to activism in a burst of idealism in the early 1960s were close to despair, on the verge of nihilism, asked to kill in Southeast Asia where once they had been called on to regenerate the world. American prosperity was becoming a sick, self-destructive indulgence, and American power heartless and oppressive. In a widely quoted speech given at a fund-raising dinner in Des Moines, Iowa, Kennedy captured a sense of America slipping out of control:

Our gross national product now soars above $800 billion a year. But that counts air pollution and cigarette advertising, and ambulances to clear our streets of carnage. It counts the special locks for our doors and jails for the people who break them. It counts the destruction of our redwoods and the loss of natural wonder to chaotic sprawl. It counts napalm and nuclear warheads and armored cars for the police to fight riots in our cities. It counts Whitman's rifle and Speck's knife, and television programs which glorify violence to sell toys to our children.[12]

How could President Johnson defend himself against such attacks? Could he explain away the dead Americans and Vietnamese by the provisions of the SEATO treaty? Could he protest that no President had the power to prevent Specks and Whitmans? Could he list all the federal programs he had introduced to halt air pollution and crime and decay in the central cities? Could he insist that eventually the North Vietnamese would see the light and desist, and Americans would be proud they had persevered, and all the money for war would be turned to the pursuits of peace, if only the people backed him and did not grow faint and trusted there was good reason for what they did not understand?

In a purely rhetorical sense, Kennedy placed Johnson in an impossible situation. McCarthy's lucid reasoning might draw counterarguments, and it would be agreed to disagree. Kennedy's assault could not be ignored or contained. His speeches expressed the deepest misgivings in people's hearts and blamed them squarely on the President and the President's war. Throughout March, Johnson spoke often in defense of the war, promising we would not back down, saying Hanoi's only hope of victory was defeatism in America. On Monday, March 18, while Kennedy was in Kansas, Johnson spoke to the National Farmers Union in Minneapolis:

> We hope to achieve an honorable peace . . . but wanting peace, praying for peace and desiring peace, as Chamberlain found out, doesn't always give you peace. . . . So long as he [Hanoi] feels that he can win something by propaganda in the country, that he can undermine the leadership, that he can bring down the government, that he can get something in the capital that he can't get from our men out there, he is going to keep on trying.[13]

His speeches were war speeches, calling on the people to stand fast, but the truth of the matter was that the people didn't give a damn for South Vietnam. Saigon for Americans was simply not Belgium for the British in 1914. There might be arguments why American interests demanded a non-Communist government in that exposed and isolated sliver of Southeast Asia, but the arguments were abstract. American honor was involved, but there was no agreement how honor might best be served. In 1968 Johnson was backed into the position of Goldwater in 1964, forced by conscience and circumstance to defend an unpopular war.

On March 10, the *New York Times* had published a report from Washington that Westmoreland had requested an additional 206,000 troops, which would demand a call-up of reserves, in order to pursue military victory in Vietnam. There had been rumors of troop increases in the wake of the Tet offensive, but 206,000 was a far higher figure than had been imagined. In the Senate, opponents of the war felt it was about to slip entirely out of control, that an invasion of North Vietnam was becoming a real and imminent possibility. Critics talked openly and seriously of the danger of war with China, the use of nuclear weapons, cataclysm. A few days earlier Fulbright had argued on the Senate floor that the Tonkin Gulf resolution had been obtained by "misrepresentation" and was "null and void."[14]

On Monday, March 11, the day after the *Times* story, Dean Rusk appeared before the Senate Foreign Relations Committee for open hearings for the first time since February, 1966. Officially, the hearings were being held to consider foreign aid, but in fact they amounted to a debate on the war. Fulbright's opening statement dramatically indicated the shift in sentiment from technical reservations about the "wisdom" of U.S. policy in Vietnam to profound moral doubts about the entire venture and the effect it was having on the United States.

> There was a time not so long ago when Americans believed that whatever else they might have to do in the world, whatever wars they might have to fight, whatever aid they might have to provide, their principal contribution to the world would be their own example as a decent and democratic society. Now, with our country beset by crises of poverty and race as we wait and arm ourselves for the annual summer of violence in our cities, with our allies alienated and our people divided by the most unpopular war in our history, the light of the American example burns dim around the world. More alarming still is the dimming of the light of optimism among the American people, especially among our youths who . . . having believed too well what they were brought up to believe in, have arisen in a kind of spiritual rebellion against what they regard as the betrayal of a traditional American value.
>
> The signs of the rebellion are all around us, not just in the hippie movement and in the emergence of an angry New Left, but in the sharp decline of applications for the Peace Corps, in the turning away of promising students from careers in government, in letters of protest against the war and troubled consciences about the draft. . . .
>
> Perhaps in purely financial terms we can afford it [the war], although I for one am far from convinced. But even if we can afford the money, can we afford the sacrifice of American lives in so dubious a cause? Can we afford the horrors which are being inflicted on the people of a poor and backward land to say nothing of our own people? Can we afford the alienation of our allies, the neglect of our own deep domestic problems and the disillusionment of our youth? Can we afford the loss of confidence in our government and institutions, the fading of hope and optimism and the betrayal of our traditional values?
>
> These, Mr. Secretary, are some of the questions that have to be put before we can return or I can return to the normal legislative activities which technically are before the committee today.[15]

Rusk's responses to these and other questions raised on Monday and Tuesday lasted for more than ten hours, but they failed to add anything to past justifications of the war. In fact, it was later noticed that whole paragraphs of his testimony were almost verbatim repetitions of the answers he had given two years earlier. Vietnam was only one of three divided countries, he said, the others being Korea and Germany; what about them? If Ho Chi Minh was such a nationalist, why did he have forty thousand men in Laos? Without the bombing, Hanoi would have no incentive for peace. A partial bombing halt would not be accepted by Hanoi "in any way, shape or form." The United States was bound by treaty to defend South Vietnam. "I don't know what would happen to the peace of the world," he said, "if it should be discovered that our treaties do not mean anything."[16] The President had not received any formal "request" for more troops, and congressional debate on the President's military plans would be carefully read by Vo Nguyen Giap in Hanoi. Did we tell Hitler the date of D-Day? Besides, it wasn't really necessary to "consult" with the Foreign Relations Committee since the President already had a pretty good idea what they thought about the war.

Rusk's only support came from undistinguished committee members like Thomas Dodd of Connecticut, who asked, "What we are really up against is a worldwide conspiracy of aggression, isn't it?"

From one point of view the nationally televised confrontation was a standoff, neither Rusk nor the administration's critics willing to give an inch, but the important point was the change in tone of the criticism. Fulbright had made it clear he was prepared actively to resist the President's policy insofar as it was in his power as chairman of the committee to do so. So similar in tone to Kennedy's campaign speeches, Fulbright's opening statement had promised an end to discreet disagreement and the beginning of open struggle.

Johnson's speeches and Rusk's dogged determination through two days of hearings were not the President's only attempts to defend himself. On a political level he and his supporters had been fighting to maintain his position, but their efforts had been essentially bureaucratic and by mid-March were proving clearly inadequate. As early as October, 1967, such peripheral organizations as the Young Democrats, normally docile, had started to turn openly against the President.

In Michigan on Saturday, October 21, the state Young Democrats voted fifty-six to twenty to oppose Johnson's renomination. In Boston three weeks later the Massachusetts College Young Democrats, a subsidiary of the national group, was only narrowly prevented by semiprofessional politicians from voting to change the group's constitution so it could support a candidate before the national Democratic convention. Nevertheless, the mood at the meeting was strongly anti-Johnson, and anyone wearing a "Negotiations Now" button was considered a conservative. When McCarthy addressed the meeting on Sunday, November 12, he was greeted by cries of "We want McCarthy" and "Run, baby, run."[17]

At the convention of the National Young Democrats in Hollywood, Florida, a week later, Johnson's name did, in fact, evoke a standing ovation, but only in response to the feeblest of defenses of the President. "We have no alternative. We don't want Ronnie Reagan, we want Lyndon Baines Johnson."[18] More important, a resolution was passed calling for a halt in the bombing. On Sunday, December 10, the Massachusetts College Young Democrats met again and this time voted 153 to 99 to endorse McCarthy's candidacy.

The opposition of Young Democrats was hardly enough to swing the party or the election, but their feelings were characteristic of the disenchantment at the liberal heart of the party. In February, the Americans for Democratic Action met again and this time voted sixty-five to forty-seven to support McCarthy after John P. Roche, an aide to the President, unsuccessfully attempted to put off a decision until May 17. "McCarthy might not even be a live candidate by then," he said. "He might have retired to a monastery or given up politics for lent."[19] Roche immediately resigned, as did a handful of union leaders—I. W. Abel of the United Steelworkers of America, Louis Stulberg of the International Ladies Garment Workers Union, and Joseph A. Beirne of the Communications Workers of America. Equally important were the much larger number who stayed on.

More significant was the President's gradual loss of control of the party in one state after another, the most important of them the two largest, New York and California. In New York, the state's national committeeman, Edwin Weisl, fought hard to maintain party loyalty to the President. In January, for example, he had arranged for the noted lawyer Louis Nizer to defend Johnson at a meeting of the Village Independent Democrats in New York. Nizer quoted from McCarthy's *America* interview in which the senator had said he would "not necessarily halt the bombing" and that the administration should have stopped at 200,000 troops. "Is this the solution to Vietnam for which we're going to desert our President?" he asked. "Vietnam may be the Rhineland of the Third World War. . . . I'm not sure it's so, but you're not sure it isn't so."[20] The club voted 129 to 26 to back McCarthy.

Kennedy's entrance into the race shifted the balance against Weisl and Johnson. After all, Kennedy was New York's senator and could claim the prerogatives of a favorite son. John J. Burns, the state chairman, endorsed Kennedy in spite of the fact that county leaders had voted overwhelmingly on February 14 to support the President. Even before Kennedy's entrance, on Monday, March 4, Weisl's own club, the Lexington Democratic Club in New York, voted 249 to 48 to back McCarthy. Throughout the state literally hundreds of McCarthy clubs were spontaneously organized and the Coalition for a Democratic Alternative, McCarthy's statewide support group, planned to wage primary battles for convention delegates in all forty-one congressional districts.

On Wednesday, March 20, Weisl sent telegrams to all sixty-two county chairmen pledging "a vigorous and forceful campaign" by the President, and the following day he convened a meeting of forty large contributors to the party to outline the campaign they would be asked to finance. Among those present were Johnson's close adviser Marvin Watson and the Postmaster General, Lawrence O'Brien, who was considered to be the President's campaign manager despite a statement in Washington the day before that he had received no such appointment and, in fact, that he had not even "been advised that the President is a candidate for re-election."[21] At the end of the meeting, Weisl told reporters, "If I were betting, I'd bet we win a third at least [of the New York delegates in a three-way Johnson-Kennedy-McCarthy race], and have a better than 50-50 chance for a majority when the chips are down."[22] If this was as far as he would go in public, what was he telling the President in private?

In California, Johnson's most important problem was the hostility of Jesse Unruh, the party's principal leader. Unruh was the nation's only major party official who had urged Kennedy to run. After Kennedy initially refused, Unruh in effect stood aloof from regular party efforts to organize a pro-Johnson slate of delegates for the June primary. When the state party met in Fresno in January, Johnson loyalists fought hard behind the scenes to maintain at least a semblance of support for the President and the war.

The state chairman, Charles Warren, had appointed an Advisory Committee to prepare position papers for the Fresno meeting, and the Foreign Policy Task Force had unexpectedly voted fifteen to ten to submit a position paper sharply critical of the President's policies in Vietnam. Learning of this, the White House asked Eugene Wyman, the state's national committeeman and a Johnson partisan, to see if Warren could somehow mitigate the sting. Warren arranged for the preparation of a second, pro-administration paper on Vietnam to be written by Professor Robert Scalapino of the University of California at Berkeley, one of the few prominent academics who consistently supported the war. Warren then quietly appointed fifteen new members to the originally thirty-five-member Foreign Policy Task Force, polled them on the two papers, and announced at the Fresno meeting that the original anti-Vietnam paper was now only a minority report. Technically then, the state party still supported the war, but this sort of maneuvering on paper hardly represented genuine political support.

Unruh had nothing against political infighting as such but felt the issue this time was overriding; the war was too important to be glossed over. "I used to dismiss the ideological liberals with the rather pat phrase that they thought victory at the polls meant defeat for principle," he said in Fresno, surprising those who had always considered him a realist before all else. "But now I say our actions and words must be judged by the human consequences, and the political consequences be damned."[23] When Kennedy finally announced in mid-March, Unruh immediately began to organize a slate of delegates to run against the Johnson and McCarthy slates already entered. The McCarthy group had collected the necessary petition signatures within hours of midnight, March 5, and filed them later in the morning on March 6, the first date permitted for filing, earning the preferred spot on the ballot. The Johnson slate, headed by state Attorney General Thomas Lynch, was filed two days later, but only after considerable infighting within the party. Former governor Edmund G. Brown, for example, had insisted that two names submitted by Los Angeles mayor Sam Yorty be dropped from the slate because Yorty had supported Reagan in the 1966 gubernatorial election. All Democratic officeholders in the state had been offered a position on the slate but many refused, including Unruh, thirty of the forty-two Democratic state assemblymen, thirteen of the twenty Democratic state senators, and four of the twenty-one

Democratic congressmen. Johnson's name, in other words, was hardly electric in California. When Kennedy's slate was filed two weeks later it included many of those who had refused a place on the President's slate, as well as wives or husbands of those who had agreed to run as pro-Johnson delegates. These latter were described as "shadow" delegates, indicating the true sentiment of nominal Johnson supporters who were prevented by law from bolting the President's slate for Kennedy's.

The erosion of Johnson's support in the California party was matched by disaffection among the voters. A Los Angeles *Times* poll in January had indicated Johnson would beat McCarthy by 63 to 18 percent of the vote, with 19 percent still undecided. In March, even before Kennedy had entered, Johnson and McCarthy were considered by professional politicians to be running neck and neck and Kennedy was generally conceded to be more popular than either. Still more indicative was the loss of support for the war even among those party regulars nominally committed to the President's renomination. In March, three hundred members of the state's Central Committee signed a telegram to Johnson saying, "In our judgment, the only action which can avert major Democratic Party losses in this state in 1968 is an immediate all-out effort to secure a nonmilitary settlement of the Vietnam war."[24] The timing and content of the telegram were an indication that their support for the President was lukewarm, at best.

Johnson's difficulties in California and New York were symptomatic of large-scale defections across the country. In Massachusetts, for example, the President had been forced by circumstances to concede to McCarthy all of the state's seventy-two convention delegates on the first ballot simply because he would not run in the state himself, Senator Edward Kennedy refused to head a pro-Johnson slate, and other possible stand-ins, including O'Brien and John W. McCormack, speaker of the House of Representatives, were considered almost certain to lose in a head-on race with McCarthy. The state Democratic chairman, Lester Hyman, waited around for weeks for final instructions from the White House. Despite repeated visits by O'Brien, no way out of the impasse was discovered, and Johnson finally allowed the March 5 deadline to pass without permitting his name, or that of a stand-in, to go on the ballot.

Hyman filed the official slate of convention delegates just four minutes before the deadline, and in Washington the following day he said

there would be no organized write-in campaign for the President because the state committee did not have the money and the national
committee would not put it up. McCormack and O'Brien both planned
to resign from the official slate rather than vote for McCarthy on the
first ballot. Hyman announced two weeks later, three days after Kennedy's official entrance, that he was switching his support from the
President to the senator from New York.

In Minnesota things were no better, despite energetic holding action
by Humphrey, including a two-hour defense of the war delivered in
December to a meeting of the state's four-hundred-member central
committee and six hundred precinct chairmen. Humphrey's efforts
failed to prevent what amounted to an insurrection at the lower levels
of the party. On Tuesday, March 5, the same day Johnson silently
admitted defeat in Massachusetts, McCarthy people packed local party
caucuses and elected enough delegates to three district conventions to
guarantee at least fifteen of the state's sixty-two delegates to the national convention. There was also a distinct possibility that McCarthy
supporters would win in two other districts, thus giving him twenty-five
of the forty delegates to be chosen in such conventions, a majority that
presumably would then go on to elect McCarthy supporters as the
twenty at-large delegates. (The remaining two places were automatically give to state officials, who were supporting the President.)

By the night of March 5, therefore, before a single primary had been
held, McCarthy was guaranteed at least 87 delegates to the national
convention, and perhaps as many as 117, far short, certainly, of the 1,312
needed to win the nomination, but early proof that a substantial
McCarthy peace block, at the very least, would be making itself felt in
the party's platform committee and on the convention floor. Similar
grass-roots efforts were taking place with some chance of success in
Connecticut, New Jersey, and other states.

The worst news of all, however, was to come from Wisconsin, where
Johnson once had felt so certain of success he had taken almost no
effective steps to secure his position. There the President's problems
began with the nature of the primary itself, which required that the
President's name be on the ballot and which allowed a crossover vote.
Romney's withdrawal in February meant Nixon would be unopposed,
thus freeing Republicans to vote in the Democratic primary. Both of
the state's Democratic senators and two of the three Democratic repre-

sentatives had remained neutral in the Johnson-McCarthy contest, not an encouraging sign, but the state chairman, Richard Cudahy, had persuaded sixty-five of the state's seventy-two county chairmen to support the President.

Despite this nucleus of organizational strength, Johnson lost ground steadily. The President's campaign was headed by Les Aspin, a former aide to McNamara in the Pentagon, who had been appointed early in February. He received almost no support from the national organization, however, until after the New Hampshire primary, when he publicly conceded that Johnson would have to be considered the underdog. Democratic Party leaders from New Jersey and Michigan were sent to the state for a last-minute effort, and visits were quickly scheduled for Humphrey, Secretary of Agriculture Orville Freeman, O'Brien, and other high administration officials. The week before the election, O'Brien made a final visit, was immediately struck by the energetic McCarthy campaign and the perfunctory, spiritless efforts on behalf of the President. He drew the inescapable conclusion. On Friday, March 29, back in New York, O'Brien called the President and told him he was going to be defeated badly.

From an entirely practical standpoint, then, Johnson's position as March drew to a close was weak and growing weaker. A *New York Times* poll of Democratic leaders in all fifty states, published on March 24, revealed that Kennedy and McCarthy between them already had 790 delegates to the national convention, a full third of the total. Johnson still had 1,725, four hundred more than he needed to win, but only the most determined sort of campaign could keep further erosion to a minimum.

In a sense, the President had already lost. He had failed to prevent exactly the sort of passionate split in the party that could only help, and would probably ensure, a Republican victory in November. The nature of the attacks mounted by McCarthy and Kennedy meant that the President would have to dispel the doubts raised by McCarthy's probing analysis of weaknesses in the President's official justification of the war, as well as the highly charged Kennedy assaults on Johnson personally. He would inevitably be on the defensive throughout the four and a half months that remained until the convention. He would have to defend a war with arguments that had barely carried one primary and were about to lose a second. He would have to defend a record of liberal legislation which only too clearly was being starved of funds and White House attention. He would have no one to blame for the division of the country but "critics" and "dissenters" who were encouraging the enemy. He would have no appeal to his party but machine loyalty. He would have nothing to promise the people except more of the same, and they had already made it plain enough they were sick at heart with what they had.

Whether Johnson could have won the nomination is open to question. That he could have won the election on such a platform, after such a struggle, at the head of an embittered party, against an opponent free to attack from a hundred directions, is still more problematic. In politics, of course, no important battle can be won without the initial decision to fight, and no one can say with confidence what would have been the result if Johnson had reached such a decision. No one had been able to determine McCarthy's strength, after all, until he actually tested himself with the people.

The difficulty in Johnson's case was that the only avenue still open to him in March was that of decisive military action. If the people would not accept more of the same, they might nevertheless support a presidential decision to win the war and be done with it. Johnson, certainly, often claimed he was subjected to far greater pressure from hawks than from doves, and there is plenty of evidence that he was right. It was later shown, for example, that many of those who had voted for McCarthy in New Hampshire had been hawks. Exactly how Johnson would have conducted and justified such a course of action is obscure, but it is clear that means and arguments would have been available if he had decided to adopt it. He had always publicly argued that a wider war was too dangerous and surrender unthinkable, that his only course was steady (albeit mounting) pressure between those two extremes, and yet the President had reversed himself once before. No law of nature prevented him from doing so again.

For all the critics in Congress and out, he was still Commander in Chief, his administration was the source of all official information about the war, and his essential freedom of action was secure until January of 1969. The previous three years had demonstrated that the President could sometimes be deflected before he acted, but that once he had actually *done* something, no effective pressure could be brought to reverse the decision. The principal issue in 1968 was the war, the result of failure in Vietnam and of the determined efforts of the opposition at home, and yet the war was the one thing over which Johnson had control. The optimism he had nurtured in late 1967 and the first few weeks of 1968 had been thrown into doubt by the enemy's Tet offensive, but this, after all, provided exactly the sort of occasion that would justify, and even demanded, a departure. Westmoreland and the Joint Chiefs of Staff had urged a vast increase in the American effort, and it was now up to the President to respond.

While the campaign had been building for the first three months of 1968, the President's principal concern had been Vietnam. It was this, in fact, which was largely responsible for his neglect of politics and the consequent weakening of his political position. The nature of the war had been that it refused to stay fixed at one level, but periodically reached a point where a clear choice was faced between greater military effort or compromise of the original purposes. All the old issues had to be reargued, the dangers weighed again, the consequences of failure reexamined, the chances of success reconsidered, and the costs balanced once more against the importance of the struggle. Johnson liked to say his resolve was firm, but it was not firm for the simple reason that he had to decide anew between more and less, and, as President, could decide either way. The Tet offensive and Westmoreland's request reopened all the old questions; only the President could answer them.

By March of 1968 the bombing and the war had become almost coterminous. In a sense the focus of debate had shifted from the war as a whole to the bombing, the North Vietnamese claiming that peace would never be possible so long as the bombing continued, and American military men insisting the war could never be won so long as the bombing was limited. After the long bombing halt in the winter of 1965–1966, President Johnson had in effect hardened his terms, insisting that the other side make some concrete military concession before he would halt the bombing again. The North Vietnamese slightly softened their position. In an interview with the Australian journalist Wilfred Burchett on January 28, 1967, the North Vietnamese foreign minister Nguyen Duy Trinh said that only after an "unconditional" halt in the bombing "could there be talks."

An attempt by the Russian and British premiers in London a week later to organize peace talks broke down when the White House insisted on reciprocity, that is, a military concession that would go beyond

Hanoi's implied promise of talks in return for a bombing halt. In a press conference in Washington on Thursday, February 2, President Johnson said "just almost any step"[25] by the other side would do. Rusk clarified the nature of the step on February 9 when he said, "We must know the military consequences of such a military action on our part. They must not expect us to stop our military action by bombing while they continue their military action by invasion."[26]

The significance of these conflicting demands went beyond the practical military consequences. Even without the bombing, American military forces on the ground in South Vietnam were in no danger of being overrun by the North Vietnamese or Vietcong. In the Congress, however, a critical block of support for the war came from hawkish senators and representatives who controlled the military committees and were convinced of the effectiveness of bombing, if only it were unlimited. The President was in fact committed to an indefinite holding action in the South. Military-minded congressmen were unwilling to accept this open-ended strategy and, in effect, insisted on an escalating bombing campaign as their price for support of the war. To accept a bombing halt without reciprocity would thus mean a tacit acceptance by the administration of an eventual compromise with the enemy, a solution to the war by political means rather than military force.

The political struggle over the war subtly shifted during 1967 from the war itself to the bombing. "Stop the bombing" signs were carried in every demonstration; newspapers shifting their position on the war would propose a bombing halt; senators turning against it pointed to the bombing as the only obstacle to peace talks. Proposals to end the war raised disturbing questions; proposals to end the bombing would have the same effect in the long run, while bypassing in the short run the explosive question of failure. The bombing thus became the symbolic focus of contention between the doves and the hawks, between those who wanted to end the war by negotiation, even if that meant "losing," and those who wanted to win it.

In August, 1967, the Senate Preparedness Investigating Subcommittee of the Committee on Armed Services, headed by John Stennis, a Democrat from Mississippi, held extensive hearings on the bombing during which one military leader after another claimed that White House limitations were critically weakening the campaign. The military had drawn up a list of 427 potential military targets in North Vietnam, of which they recommended strikes against 359. The President and McNamara, however, had authorized raids on only 302 of the recommended targets. The hearings focused on the 57 recommended targets that were still off-limits. Two days before the hearings began, on Tuesday, August 8, the President authorized strikes against some of the restricted targets in an attempt to mute the hawkish sentiment that he knew was coming. Since he continued to withhold permission to strike the most important of the restricted targets, the port area of Haiphong, his gesture was unsuccessful.

At 10:10 on the morning of Friday, August 25, McNamara appeared before the Committee and attempted to refute the testimony of military men who had already appeared. He defended the restrictions, reasserted the limited purposes of the bombing campaign, and sharply criticized the notion that bombing could significantly alter the outcome of the war. The United States, he said, had already conducted about 173,000 sorties—one raid by one plane—against North Vietnam, destroying 4,100 vehicles, 7,400 boats of varying sizes, 1,400 railroad cars and locomotives, 57 significant bridges, and 50 major rail yards, troop barracks, power plants, and storage tanks for petroleum products. About 90 percent of the attacks had been against "targets of opportunity," that is, whatever pilots came across that looked likely. The remaining 10 percent had been against some 1,900 fixed targets of varying importance from antiaircraft gun sites to steel mills. As a result, McNamara said, about 500,000 North Vietnamese were required full- or part-time to maintain transportation facilities. The North Vietnamese thus "paid a price," but it was one they could afford if they chose to do so.

McNamara's main point, hammered at insistently throughout the day, was that no conceivable amount of bombing could actually *stop* infiltration of men and supplies into the South. The United States had raided 14 of North Vietnam's 22 major power plants, representing 86 percent of the country's electrical generating capacity, for example, but their 2,000 easily dispersed diesel generators were more than enough to keep the country running. More important, North Vietnam's three major ports and rail lines to China could handle up to 14,000 tons of supplies a day even with the bombing at its present rate, and they were only being used to about 40 percent of capacity. Of their total imports, only 550 tons a day represented military supplies, and only 15 tons of supplies a day were sent South over the transportation network in Laos and Cambodia, which had a capacity of 200 tons a day. Even if the United States completely closed Haiphong, the 4,700 tons of supplies that entered the country daily through that port could be shifted to other means of transportation, including over-the-beach operations along its 400-mile coastline.

McNamara went over each of the fifty-seven targets on the restricted list, describing in detail what they were, how they were defended, and what would be the cost in pilots and aircraft of attacking them. Such raids would have little or no effect on the conduct of the war, he said; the results simply would not justify the cost. Why did the military disagree? Perhaps, he said, because of their difference in background. As a former president of Ford, he considered a plant producing thirty tires a day pretty small potatoes.

McNamara's relentlessly detailed testimony came back always to the same point. North Vietnam sent only fifteen tons of supplies a day to the South. Its import capacity was fourteen thousand tons. Even if that were halved, Hanoi would have no difficulty maintaining or even doubling its present supply effort. Nothing short of a crime of war, the use of nuclear weapons or the deliberate bombing of population centers, neither of which had ever been considered, much less recommended, by the military, would have any significant effect on Hanoi's ability to go on fighting for as long as it chose to do so. In other words, the United States had no choice but to continue the war indefinitely until the other side *decided* to stop.

Despite McNamara's detailed arguments, the committee disagreed. In a report made public on Thursday, August 31, the committee said proposals for a full or even partial bombing halt were "naive" and "foolish." Military leaders contended that Haiphong could be "closed" and the rail lines to China "interdicted." The administration's policy had demonstrably failed to end the war. "What is needed now," the committee concluded, "is the hard decision to do whatever is necessary, take the risks that have to be taken, and apply the force that is required to see the job through."[27] The President was trapped in the middle of this dispute. Immediately following the committee's report, he insisted there was no division of opinion within the administration on the bombing campaign, despite the fact McNamara and military leaders had been contradicting each other. At the same time he authorized new targets during the following weeks and then, on Friday, September 29, in a speech in San Antonio, Texas, described American terms for a bombing halt in slightly relaxed terms. "As we have told Hanoi time and time again, the heart of the matter is this: the United States is willing immediately to stop all aerial and naval bombardment of North Vietnam when this will lead promptly to productive discussion. We of course would assume that while discussions proceed, North Vietnam would not take advantage of the bombing cessation or limitation."[28] This formula contained its own imponderables—what sort of assurance was demanded that discussions would be "productive"? and what did the President mean by "take advantage"?—but the demand for an overt military concession by Hanoi had been dropped.

Three months later the North Vietnamese responded with a new formulation of their own. In a statement released on Saturday, December 30, the North Vietnamese foreign minister, Nguyen Duy Trinh, made a clear and unequivocal promise of talks in return for a bombing halt:

> The United States Government has unceasingly claimed that it wants to talk with Hanoi but has received no response. If the United States Government truly wants to talk it must, as was made clear in our statement on 28 January 1967, first of all stop unconditionally the bombing and all other acts of war against the Democratic Republic of Vietnam [North Vietnam]. After the United States has ended unconditionally the bombing and all other acts of war, the Democratic Republic of Vietnam will hold talks with the United States on questions concerned.[29]

This statement placed the President in an awkward position. The White House was immediately bombarded with requests for a bombing halt and a negotiated end to the war, but the administration was reluctant to respond. A bombing halt would decisively weaken the President's political ability to fight on in the absence of a settlement on his terms, and, having paid such a huge price in men and money over three years, he was unwilling to seek the only sort of compromise that might have been available. At the same time, however, the American and North Vietnamese positions were now so close, on paper at any rate, that a refusal to halt the bombing seemed to confirm his critics' claims that he sought a military victory and had no interest in a negotiated solution.

On Sunday, January 7, the administration's position was expressed informally by William Bundy, the Assistant Secretary of State for Far Eastern Affairs, when he said on an NBC television show, "I'm not sure that they are anywhere near the point of being ready to yield. There is no indication of when they would talk—no indication, no mention of whether they themselves would exercise any kind of restraint."[30]

The administration avoided an official reply for weeks, saying it wanted to find out what the North Vietnamese really *meant.* Finally, on Friday, February 16, more than six weeks after Trinh's statement and eighteen days after the beginning of the Tet offensive, the President gave an answer of sorts, in effect shifting the blame onto the North Vietnamese for rejecting the San Antonio formula, when in fact he was rejecting Trinh's more recent offer. "Sometimes they will change 'will' to 'would' or 'shall' to 'should' or something of that kind," Johnson said, "but the answer is all the same."[31] In fact, however, the answer was not the same. Hanoi would talk if the United States would stop the bombing. Few of those who recommended accepting this offer had any illusions about the difficulty of reaching agreement once the talks had begun, but this was only their secondary purpose. The first thing, the opposition felt, was to end the escalation, the open-ended progression toward an ever-wider war. At the very least, a bombing halt followed by negotiations would fix the war at its present level; eventually it would lead to a compromise solution, since political realities within the United States meant that it could not fight indefinitely a war that it could not promise to win. The compromise might be a painful one, but opponents of the war had long since accepted that likelihood. The effect of Trinh's statement was to sharpen the debate at a critical moment, when the President was deciding how to respond to the Tet offensive and the massive troop request from Westmoreland. There were only two choices: more war, which would succeed militarily or not at all, or less war, with at least the possibility of a negotiated solution. Political developments during the first three months of 1968 had already shown that the middle path so long taken by the President was now foreclosed.

A great deal has already been written about the debate on the war that occurred in the White House and the Pentagon in March, 1968, and it would serve no purpose to recount in detail here the endless meetings and memorandums which led to the President's decisions at the end of the month.[32] The debate centered on Westmoreland's request for 206,000 more men but gradually expanded into a reassessment of the war as a whole, since past policies clearly had failed and the military's only solution was more of the same. Clark Clifford, an influential Washington figure since the New Deal and a close adviser to Johnson, had been appointed to replace McNamara as Secretary of Defense on March 1, and his first task was to head a group asked by the President to find ways to implement Westmoreland's request for additional men.

Clifford quickly discovered that officials in the Pentagon and the White House were sharply divided over the future of the war. The military, led by the Joint Chiefs of Staff, saw the Tet offensive as an ideal occasion for decisive military efforts to win the war, for calling up reserves, and for broadly strengthening the armed forces in general. A number of civilian officials, ranging from the Assistant Secretary of Defense for Public Affairs, Phil Goulding, to Ambassador to the United Nations Arthur Goldberg, and the President's chief speechwriter, Harry McPherson, favored a shift in goals from victory to disengagement. They opposed a further escalation of the war, which would increase its cost without guaranteeing success, and favored instead a peace initiative including a total or partial bombing halt. The debate, and the shifting balance from the military hawks to the civilian doves, was reflected in successive drafts of a major speech on the war written by McPherson for delivery sometime before the April 2 Wisconsin primary. The first draft, finished on March 10, justified the 206,000-man troop request, a reserve call-up, increased taxes, and the need for national fortitude. Revised repeatedly during the following three weeks, the tone and thrust of the speech were completely reversed.

At first reluctant even to consider a bombing halt, Johnson was finally persuaded to back down by an overwhelming shift in sentiment against the war from a wide range of his closest advisers and public officials. The first and probably most important was Clifford. He had supported the war loyally since the beginning, had opposed the early bombing halts as gestures of weakness rather than strength, and had agreed with the President that success in Vietnam was vital to American interests. Now he had been persuaded by events that the American people had turned against the war, and that the fighting in Vietnam had reached a stalemate. Long days of discussion with military leaders had convinced him that Hanoi would match any American escalation and that the only sensible solution to the war would be a negotiated compromise. The time had come, he felt, for a genuine peace initiative.

Finally, an informal group of national figures including Dean Acheson, Henry Cabot Lodge, Abe Fortas, Arthur Goldberg, George Ball, Douglas Dillon, Cyrus Vance, and three former chairmen of the Joint Chiefs of Staff, among others, met in Washington on March 25 and 26. They were briefed at length on the war and then recommended strongly that the President refuse the troop request and seek negotiations. With one or two exceptions, all of these men had approved strong military measures in the past. There were other important opponents of the war as well, of course, like Paul Nitze, who threatened to resign as Deputy Secretary of Defense rather than testify in favor of administration policy before the Senate Foreign Relations Committee. So many of the President's oldest and closest advisers had turned against a military solution that the President could not resist the combined weight of their change in mind and heart. Acheson and Clifford, especially, argued that the people would not tolerate more of the same. They had supported the war for three years but had now turned against it; there was simply no realistic alternative to disengagement.

On March 28, the original troop request long since decisively rejected, Clifford met in Rusk's office with Walt Rostow, William Bundy, and McPherson to go over the speech Johnson planned to deliver over nationwide television three days later. Clifford argued for literally hours that the speech was still too warlike, did not mark a sharp enough departure from past policy, did not make the necessary gesture toward peace. "The President cannot give that speech," he said:

> It would be a disaster. What seems not to be understood is that major elements of the national constituency—the business community, the press, the churches, professional groups, college presidents, students and most of the intellectual community—have turned against this war. What the President needs is not a war speech, but a peace speech.[33]

In public the first indication of a major change in administration policy came on Friday, March 22, when the President held a press conference to tell reporters of a "few appointments that I thought you would be interested in and would give you something to do over the weekend. I want to keep all of you occupied." His approach was characteristically devious and yet futile, a transparent attempt to mask the significance of what he was about to announce, the gesture of a fading master of indirection.

First, he said, he was appointing Sargent Shriver to be the new ambassador to France. Second, he was elevating Wilbur Cohen to head the Department of Health, Education and Welfare. Third, Bert Harding would take over the poverty program in Shriver's absence. Finally, there was the matter of "filling of the expiring terms of certain members of the Joint Chiefs of Staff." General Wheeler, the President said, had agreed to stay on for an additional year. "General [Harold K.] Johnson's term expires as Chief of Staff of the Army in July, 1968. He plans to retire. He has notified us of his desire to retire. He will be succeeded by General Westmoreland."[34]

Only a month earlier, on February 17, Johnson had stoutly defended Westmoreland, called him the finest military officer he had ever known, and said he hoped his praise "could end the gossip and the rumors about General Westmoreland's future."[35] Now he praised him faintly as "a very talented and very able officer," and even went on to add, gratuitously, that Westmoreland had also been considered for the posts of Chairman of the Joint Chiefs of Staff and Commander in Chief of U.S. forces in the Pacific, both jobs of far greater substance than the one he was to receive. The dismissal of Westmoreland was a clear indication that his strategy of "search and destroy" was also being rejected after its signal failure to destroy enemy strength in South Vietnam or to prevent the Tet offensive.

At the time of the announcement, Westmoreland had been visiting his family in the Philippines. He returned immediately to Saigon, where he was asked by a reporter on his arrival at Tan Son Nhut airport if Johnson had told him of the new appointment. "Negative," said Westmoreland. "I received the information in a personal call from General Wheeler."[36]

Westmoreland's dismissal as Commander in Chief of the American forces in Vietnam was the first clear sign that the President was preparing to reverse his position on the war. He had initiated the bureaucratic decision-making process in response to Westmoreland's original request with no apparent awareness that this time it would resist the built-in pressures for escalation. He had summoned his most trusted foreign policy advisers when it became clear he was losing the support of his own administrative officials, and the advisers, with only three exceptions,[17] had themselves turned against the old policy of steadily increasing military pressure designed to break the enemy's will to fight. Nothing had happened to change the military balance; U.S. forces were still unbeatable in the conventional sense, and yet his advisers, among them some of the nation's most distinguished public servants of two decades, no longer felt the war was worth the candle.

Johnson's political advisers, as professional and well-informed as any in the country, told him the people were no longer with him and would reject him at the polls wherever he would be required to run. The *New York Times,* the *Wall Street Journal, Newsweek,* and even *Life* were all in favor of disengagement. Leaders of Congress quietly consulted during March were all opposed to a massively increased military commitment that still could not promise an end to the war. On every side the President faced opposition. The decision he reached following these weeks of debate was the inevitable one.

On Sunday, March 31, while McCarthy was campaigning against him in Wisconsin and Kennedy was returning to New York from a political trip to Arizona, President Johnson went on national television to talk about Vietnam. His speech was long and detailed, answering many minor criticisms of his Vietnam policy which had surfaced since the Tet offensive, such as charges that he had not adequately armed the South Vietnamese and their troops were outgunned in the field. The President denounced the enemy's "savage assault" on the cities of South Vietnam and described it as a shattering military defeat for the other side. He insisted on the limited nature of American goals and warned there might be more heavy fighting to come. Then he moved into the heart of the speech, over which his advisers had argued for so long.

> There is no need to delay talks that could bring an end to this long and this bloody war. Tonight, I renew the offer I made last August—to stop the bombardment of North Vietnam. We ask that talks begin promptly, that they be serious talks on the substance of peace. We assume that during those talks Hanoi will not take advantage of our restraint. We are prepared to move immediately toward peace through negotiations. So tonight, in the hope that this action will lead to early talks, I am taking the first step to de-escalate the conflict. We are reducing—substantially

reducing—the present level of hostilities. And we are doing so unilater-
ally and at once.

Tonight, I have ordered our aircraft and our naval vessels to make no
attacks on North Vietnam, except on the area north of the demilitarized
zone where the continuing enemy buildup directly threatens allied forward positions and where the movements of their troops and supplies are
closely related to that threat. . . .

When the President came to the end of the text that had been
distributed to newsmen he did not stop, but continued with a text he
had prepared on his own.

I believe we must be always mindful of this one thing, whatever the trials
and tests ahead. The ultimate strength of our country and our cause will
lie not in powerful weapons or infinite resources or boundless wealth, but
will lie in the unity of our people. . . . What we won when all of our people
united just must not now be lost in suspicion, distrust, selfishness and
politics among any of our people.

Believing this as I do, I have concluded that I should not permit the
Presidency to become involved in the partisan divisions that are develop-
ing in this political year. With America's sons in the fields far away, with
America's future under challenge right here at home, with our hopes and
the world's hopes for peace in the balance every day, I do not believe that
I should devote an hour or a day of my time to any personal partisan
causes or to any duties other than the awesome duties of this office—the
Presidency of your country.

Accordingly, I shall not seek, and I will not accept, the nomination
of my party for another term as your President. . . .[38]

The effect was instantaneous all over the country: among supporters
of McCarthy and Kennedy, jubilation; on a hundred college campuses,
spontaneous demonstrations; in millions of homes, a sense of shock,
perhaps a touch of fear, and certainly relief. Newsmen on the national
television networks were visibly stunned, uncertain what effect this
would have on the campaign or on the war.

It was hard not to feel the moment was decisive. Students from the
University of Pennsylvania, New York University, the University of
Wisconsin, Berkeley, Harvard, Columbia left their rooms, gathered
outside, marched through the streets, chanted "Peace now!" and felt a
cloud lifting from their lives. Johnson, after all, had done what he had
said he would never do. At that very moment the skies over North

Vietnam were silent after three years of almost continuous air raids. Hanoi had promised nothing except a willingness to talk; surely, then, the United States had given in, would now accept the sort of compromise it had resisted for so long?

Leaders of the Resistance on the West Coast, pacifists in New York, SDS radicals in Chicago, old leftists and liberal organizers and peace-minded clergymen all watched Johnson on television, heard him withdraw from the race and announce the end of the bombing. Looking back on it later, they remembered a confusion of elation and doubt. There was no question Johnson had been defeated, but did that mean the war would end? The United States had resisted the tide of events in Southeast Asia for twenty years; was it now finally abandoning its old policy, or simply maneuvering for advantage? The struggle over the war had gone on for so long, with so little compromise on either side, focused so intensely at the end on the issue of the bombing, that it was difficult to know immediately the exact significance of what had happened. In the first heady moments, some people thought the war was over; others insisted that nothing had changed and it would not be clear for years who was right. The major presidential candidates, McCarthy, Kennedy, and Nixon, were cautious and restrained in their first reaction. In Wisconsin one of McCarthy's principal speechwriters, Richard Goodwin, was dazed. "It took only six weeks," he said, "it was six weeks earlier than I thought."[39] Allard Lowenstein, who had done so much to defeat the President, did not seem so surprised. "Well," he said to a friend, "what did you expect?"[40]

Inside the White House, Johnson's family and a number of old friends had gathered to support him at what was not just a turning point, but the end of his long political life. Outside there was a slight rain, a wetness in the warm night between mist and a drizzle. Perhaps a hundred men and women gathered in front of the White House gates, most of them young, some of them wearing McCarthy or Kennedy buttons, a few of them angry young revolutionaries, the majority just people who were against the war. They began to sing an old civil rights song, once the theme of a broad and hopeful movement which long since had divided and turned bitter and begun to fade away. They changed one word and sang, "We have overcome. . . ."[41] They could not have said clearly whom they meant by "we," certainly not only the few who were there. There were not many in the country at that moment, in the first awed instant of realizing things would never be the same again, who would have granted their claim. *They* overcame the tired man within the White House, who had finally given in after so long? *They* overcame a government so powerful and once so fixed in its purpose and firm in its resolve? Few would have granted that claim; the event was too huge. Perhaps those who sang only half-believed it themselves, and yet it was so.

Epilogue

If Vietnam proves anything, it is that history takes a long time to happen. Johnson's speech did not end the fighting in Vietnam or the division at home. The worst moments were still ahead, and yet the partial bombing halt nevertheless marked a decisive shift in official policy from escalation to disengagement. This was not immediately conceded by the government or recognized by its opponents, but the logic of Johnson's decision created a new momentum no easier to resist than the earlier pressures toward escalation. There is a good deal of evidence that the administration did not expect Hanoi to respond to a partial bombing halt, but it did, only four days later, and the negotiations that began in Paris that spring in effect firmly committed the United States to a compromise of its original goals. Backing away from the use of military force, even tentatively and partially, at the very moment of the most sustained military challenge by the other side was a tacit admission that, militarily, the United States had gone as far as it would go. Antiwar sentiment ballooned in the wake of the bombing halt, and it was only the vast power of the office of the presidency that allowed Nixon to go on fighting what amounted to a retreat while he sought a settlement that would at least postpone the collapse of Saigon. The partial bombing halt and the beginning of negotiations did not mean a quick end to so long and bitter a conflict, as events have shown, but it did mean that eventually the United States would leave Vietnam with a negotiated compromise, or with nothing at all.

The long endgame period between March, 1968, and the final American withdrawal five years later included some of the hardest fighting in Vietnam and the sharpest division at home, the worst moments perhaps those in the spring of 1968 when assassins killed Martin Luther King and Robert F. Kennedy. It was a time of great passion and confusion. The bombing of North Vietnam was stopped partially, as we have seen, then ended altogether, then resumed in a limited way, escalated to a greater level than ever before, limited again, resumed again, and then halted permanently. In the same way the radical and antiwar movements in the United States would suddenly expand, then subside, then grow again. There were building takeovers at Columbia University three weeks after Johnson's speech, street battles in Chicago that summer, huge demonstrations in the fall of 1969, a nationwide student strike and another huge demonstration following the Kent State killings in May, 1970, and then a final spasm of determined civil disobedience in Washington a year later. At varying times there was something close to insurrection among American troops in Vietnam, and something close to guerrilla warfare in the streets of cities at home. The war didn't end in March, 1968, and neither did the opposition to the war. What ended was the American commitment to fight and win the war.

It has been the thesis of this book that the antiwar movement in the United States created the necessary conditions for the shift in official policy from escalation to disengagement. Opponents of the war often argued whether it was better to work "within the system" or in the streets, but in fact success depended on pursuing both strategies simultaneously. Without those few intellectual leaders who first opposed the war on grounds of policy or morality, there would have been no broad movement; without a movement, national division over the war would not have reached a point of crisis in 1967; and without the crisis, there would have been no effective political challenge to Johnson's power at the one moment when he had to back away from the war, or commit the country to a vastly increased effort with a dangerous potential.

There were high-level reservations about official policy from the beginning, but the effective opposition came largely from below, from a broad range of people with differing ideas and purposes who agreed only that the United States should not be fighting in Vietnam. Clark Clifford and other officials have spoken vaguely of "division" in the country as if it were a kind of disembodied public sentiment, a collective state of mind that arose spontaneously. In fact, the division was the result of deliberate political efforts to discredit the war, to organize an opposition to it, to make the opposition visible, and finally to actively resist the war in ways that had practical consequences which could not be dismissed.

In the end the government abandoned its policy because its domestic cost was too high, its chance of success in Vietnam too slim. There was little reason to fight on, every reason to find a way out. The opposition was not alone responsible for this shift in policy, but if there had been no opposition the shift would not have happened when or in the way that it did. The American departure from Vietnam was as gradual and anticlimactic as its original intervention, but, in retrospect, just as inexorable. At the height of the war Henry Cabot Lodge used to say the other side would never surrender; it would just fade away. He was right about the process, but wrong about who would go home with empty hands in the end.

Notes

CHAPTER ONE

1) Theodore H. White, *The Making of the President* (New York: Atheneum, 1965), p. 221.
2) See, for example, General Frederic H. Smith, Jr., "Nuclear Weapons and Limited War," *Air University Quarterly,* Spring, 1960; and Henry A. Kissinger, *Nuclear Weapons and Foreign Policy* (New York: Harper & Brothers, 1957).
3) *New York Times,* March 19, 1964.
4) White, *Making of the President 1964,* p. 145.
5) *New York Times,* July 17, 1964.
6) David Halberstam, *The Making of a Quagmire* (New York: Random House, 1965), p. 69.
7) Ibid., p. 73.
8) Bernard B. Fall, *The Two Viet-Nams,* 2nd rev. ed. (New York: Praeger, 1967), p. 385.
9) *New York Times,* May 15, 1964.
10) Ibid., February 22, 1964.
11) Ibid., March 1, 1964.
12) Joseph C. Goulden, *Truth is the First Casualty* (New York: Rand McNally, 1969), p. 24.
13) *New York Times,* August 3, 1964.
14) Ibid., August 4, 1964.
15) Goulden, *Truth is the First Casualty,* p. 37.
16) Committee on Foreign Relations, U. S. Senate, *Background Information Relating to Southeast Asia and Vietnam,* 3rd rev. ed. (Washington: U.S. Government Printing Office, 1967), p. 126.
17) Goulden, *Truth is the First Casualty,* p. 71.
18) Ibid.

19) Ibid., p. 75.
20) Ibid.
21) Eric F. Goldman, *The Tragedy of Lyndon Johnson* (New York: Alfred A. Knopf, 1969), pp. 236–237.
22) Ibid., p. 237.
23) Ibid., p. 253.

CHAPTER TWO

1) He carried Louisiana, Mississippi, Alabama, Georgia, South Carolina, and his native Arizona.
2) *New York Times,* July 19, 1964.
3) With two exceptions. James Farmer of CORE and John Lewis of SNCC both refused to join the others.
4) Anthony Lewis, *Portrait of a Decade* (New York: Random House, 1964), p. 125. The bill was passed by the Senate exactly one year later and signed into law by President Johnson on July 2, 1964.
5) *New York Times,* January 30, 1964.
6) Sally Belfrage, *Freedom Summer* (New York: Viking Press, 1965), p. 22.
7) *Newsweek,* July 13, 1964.
8) *The Nation,* July 27, 1964.
9) Halberstam, *Making of a Quagmire,* p. 310.
10) Howard Zinn, *SNCC—The New Abolitionists* (Boston: Beacon Press, 1965), p. 215.
11) Seymour Martin Lipset and Sheldon S. Wolin, eds., *The Berkeley Student Revolt* (Garden City, N. Y.: Doubleday Anchor, 1965), pp. 105–106.
12) Ibid., p. 106.
13) I have taken these figures from Hal Draper, *Berkeley: The New Student Revolt* (New York: Grove Press, 1965).
14) Lipset and Wolin, *Berkeley Student Revolt,* pp. 216–219.
15) Paul Good, "A Bowl of Gumbo for Curtis Bryant," *The Reporter,* December 31, 1964.
16) Michael Ferber and Staughton Lynd, *The Resistance* (Boston: Beacon Press, 1971), p. 50.

CHAPTER THREE

1) *Life,* November 27, 1964.
2) *New York Times,* December 2, 1964.
3) Rowland Evans and Robert Novak, *Lyndon B. Johnson: The Exercise of Power* (New York: New American Library, 1966), p. 538.
4) Patrick Anderson, *The President's Men* (Garden City, N. Y.: Doubleday, 1968), p. 384.
5) *New York Times,* January 5, 1965.

6) Poll by the Associated Press, published in the *New York Times,* January 7, 1965.

7) *New York Times,* February 4, 1965.

8) Ibid., January 27, 1965.

9) Ibid., February 8, 1965.

10) Ibid.

11) Ibid.

12) Ibid., February 25, 1965.

13) *New York Post,* January 17, 1969.

14) *New York Times,* February 9, 1965.

15) Haynes Johnson and Bernard M. Gwertzman, *Fulbright the Dissenter* (Garden City, N. Y.: Doubleday, 1968), p. 188.

16) Ibid., p. 214.

17) *Life,* July 30, 1965.

18) Bruce Ladd, *Crisis in Credibility* (New York: New American Library, 1968), p. 43.

19) Dick Schaap, *R.F.K.* (New York: New American Library, 1967), p. 113.

20) Evans and Novak, *Lyndon B. Johnson,* p. 551.

21) *New York Times,* July 27, 1965.

22) Ibid., July 29, 1965.

23) Ibid., July 30, 1965.

24) Richard J. Walton, *The Remnants of Power* (New York: Coward-McCann, 1968), p. 178.

25) Ibid., p. 176.

26) Ibid., p. 178.

CHAPTER FOUR

1) Jessica Mitford, *The Trial of Dr. Spock* (New York: Alfred A. Knopf, 1969), p. 13.

2) Louis Menashe and Ronald Radosh, eds., *Teach-ins: U.S.A.* (New York: Praeger, 1967), p. 14. This anthology includes almost all of the relevant material on the teach-in movement. These quotes are from the *Michigan Daily,* March 26, 1965.

3) Ibid., p. 7.

4) Arthur Waskow, "The New American Arrogance," cited in ibid., pp. 63–64.

5) Report by Dr. Everett W. Borand of the Albert Einstein College of Medicine in New York, cited in ibid., p. 332.

6) Their correspondence is included in ibid., pp. 139–145.

7) Donald Janson, *The Nation,* May 24, 1965.

8) Menashe and Radosh, *Teach-ins,* p. 170.

9) Meg Greenfield, *The Reporter,* June 3, 1965.

10) Menashe and Radosh, *Teach-ins,* p. 171.

11) Staughton Lynd's statement at Berkeley's Vietnam Day, along with 16

others, was published in James Petras et al., eds., *We Accuse* (Berkeley: Diablo Press, 1965). Lynd's statement is on pp. 153–158.

12) Ibid., p. 156.

13) Ibid., p. 148.

14) Goldman, *Tragedy of Lyndon Johnson*, p. 427.

15) Ibid., p. 457.

16) Ibid., pp. 450–451.

17) Menashe and Radosh, *Teach-ins*, pp. 204–205.

18) Ibid., p. 205.

19) Ibid., p. 206.

20) Ibid.

21) Ibid., p. 207.

CHAPTER FIVE

1) Nat Hentoff, "Review of the Press," *Village Voice*, June 24, 1965.

2) Jack Newfield, *A Prophetic Minority* (New York: New American Library, 1966), p. 191.

3) Ibid., p. 190.

4) *Liberation*, May, 1965.

5) *New York Post*, April 17, 1965.

6) *Liberation*, May and June–July, 1965. Potter delivered substantially the same speech at the Berkeley Vietnam Day, May 22, 1965 (see Chapter Four). It is reprinted in full in *We Accuse*.

7) *New York Times*, April 18, 1965.

8) *Liberation*, June–July, 1965.

9) Ibid., November, 1965.

10) Ibid.

11) Ferber and Lynd, *The Resistance*, p. 34.

12) *New York Times*, August 10, 1965.

13) Ibid., August 7 and 13, 1965.

14) Tom Wolfe, *The Electric Kool-Aid Acid Test*, (New York: Farrar, Straus and Giroux, 1968), p. 224.

15) *New York Times*, October 17, 1965. The antiwar movement quickly picked up the slogan and turned it around. At a march in New York on March 26, 1966, protestors carried signs reading, "Support our men in Vietnam—bring them home now."

16) The lone dissenter was Rep. Henry P. Smith 3rd, a Republican of New York, who said, "It [the penalty] is far too excessive for this type of misdemeanor." *New York Times*, August 11, 1965.

17) Alice Lynd, *We Won't Go* (Boston: Beacon Press, 1968), p. 33.

18) Miller was arrested in New Hampshire later that month, was given a suspended sentence on March 15, 1966, providing he obtained a new draft card. On April 6, 1967, having refused to obtain a new card, he was sentenced

to two and a half years in jail by Federal Judge Harold Tyler in the Southern District of New York.

19) *New York Times,* October 29, 1965.
20) Lynd, *We Won't Go,* p. 40.
21) *New York Times,* October 16, 1965.
22) Ibid.
23) Ibid., November 2, 1965.
24) Richard T. Stout, *People* (New York: Harper and Row, 1970), p. 44.
25) *New York Times,* October 29, 1965.
26) Renata Adler, "The Price of Peace is Confusion," *New Yorker,* December 11, 1965.
27) *Esquire,* September, 1965.
28) Stout, *People,* p. 46.
29) *New York Times,* November 28, 1965.
30) Oglesby's speech was widely reprinted. It can be found in Mitchell Cohen and Dennis Hale, eds., *The New Student Left* (Boston: Beacon Press, 1967), pp. 312–321.

CHAPTER SIX

1) *Washington Post,* February 7, 1966.
2) *New York Times,* November 20, 1965.
3) Ibid., November 30, 1965.
4) Ibid., July 14, 1965.
5) Eric Sevareid, "The Final Troubled Hours of Adlai Stevenson," *Look* November 30, 1965.
6) *New York Times,* February 25, 1965.
7) Ibid., November 16, 1965.
8) Ibid.
9) For other accounts of this episode, see Chester L. Cooper, *The Lost Crusade,* (New York: Dodd, Mead, 1970), pp. 328 ff., and Walton, *Remnants of Power, passim.*
10) *Washington Post,* January 25, 1966.
11) Eugene McCarthy, Vance Hartke, Frank E. Moss, and Quentin N. Burdick.
12) In fact, the book, with appropriate underlining, had been given to the President earlier that day by Senator Robert F. Kennedy, who was not present at the briefing.
13) *New York Times,* January 27, 1966.
14) *The Vietnam Hearings* (New York: Random House, 1966), p. 16.
15) Ibid., p. 18.
16) Ibid., p. 22.
17) The issue date and the actual publication date of magazines are two different things. The issue of *Harper's* in which Gavin's letter appeared was dated February, 1966. It was on the newsstands in mid-January.

18) *New York Times,* February 4, 1966.
19) *Look,* April 5, 1966.
20) *Washington Post,* February 1, 1966.
21) Ibid.
22) *New York Times,* February 1, 1966.
23) See Cooper, *Lost Crusade,* pp. 296 ff.
24) *Washington Post,* February 7, 1966.
25) Ibid., February 8, 1966.
26) Brock Brower, "The Roots of the Arkansas Questioner," *Life,* May 13, 1966.
27) Johnson and Gwertzman, *Fulbright the Dissenter,* p. 219.
28) *New York Times,* January 13, 1966.
29) *Vietnam Hearings,* pp. 67–69.
30) Ibid., p. 92.
31) Ibid., p. 82.
32) Ibid., p. 108.
33) Ibid., p. 112.
34) Ibid., pp. 113–114.
35) Ibid., p. 176.
36) Ibid.
37) Ibid., p. 187.
38) Ibid., p. 236.
39) Ibid., p. 248.
40) Ibid., pp. 283–284.
41) *Washington Post,* February 12, 1966.
42) Ibid., February 17, 1966.
43) Ibid.
44) *New York Times,* April 22, 1966.
45) Ibid.
46) Ibid., April 29, 1966.

CHAPTER SEVEN

1) *New York Times,* February 27, 1966.
2) Robert G. Sherrill, "Democratic Rebels in Congress," *The Nation,* October 10, 1966.
3) *New York Times,* March 23, 1966.
4) Ibid., June 12, 1966.
5) Ibid., November 1, 1966.
6) *Washington Post,* February 7, 1966.
7) Marquis Childs, *Washington Post,* February 21, 1966.
8) *Liberation,* April, 1966.
9) Unless otherwise indicated, all quotes about Scheer's campaign have been

taken from Serge Lang, *The Scheer Campaign* (San Francisco: W. A. Benjamin, Inc., 1967).

10) Andrew Kopkind, *New Republic*, June 4, 1966.

11) The Seventh Congressional District proved unforgiving, however. Despite the fact that Cohelan began to oppose the war, he was again challenged in the 1970 primary and this time unseated by a black activist, Ronald Dellums, who was elected to Congress that fall.

12) *New York Times*, June 12, 1966.

13) *Newsweek*, September 26, 1966.

14) *New York Times*, July 1, 1966.

15) Ibid., May 18, 1966.

16) Ibid.

17) Hugh Sidney, *A Very Personal Presidency* (New York: Atheneum, 1968), p. 150.

18) Cooper, *Lost Crusade*, p. 317.

19) *New York Times*, November 4, 1966.

20) Ibid., November 5, 1966.

21) Ibid., November 7, 1966.

22) Ibid., November 10, 1966.

23) Ibid.

24) Ibid., November 6, 1966.

25) Steven Kelman, *Push Comes to Shove* (Boston: Houghton Mifflin, 1970), p. 28.

26) This and the quotes immediately following are from ibid., pp. 56 ff.

CHAPTER EIGHT

1) *New York Times*, June 12, 1963.

2) William Robert Miller, *Martin Luther King* (New York: Weybright and Talley, 1968), p. 236.

3) Lynd, *We Won't Go*, p. 88.

4) Kelman, *Push Comes to Shove*, p. 71.

5) New York Times, March 16, 1965.

6) Jon Neary, *Julian Bond* (New York: Morrow, 1971), p. 143.

7) Joanne Grant, ed., *Black Protest* (New York: Fawcett World Library, 1968), pp. 415–416.

8) Neary, *Julian Bond*, pp. 90–91.

9) Ibid.

10) Ferber and Lynd, *The Resistance*, p. 33.

11) Terrence Cannon, "Riots, SNCC and the Press," *The Movement*, July, 1967; reprinted in Ethel Grodzins Romm, *The Open Conspiracy* (Harrisburg, Pa.: Stackpole, 1970), p. 18. An account of the same incident in the *New York*

Times, August 5, 1966, says Carmichael claimed he had never known a white *person* he could trust.

12) Quoted in the *New York Times* of August 5, 1966, and reprinted in full in Cohen and Hale, eds., *New Student Left,* pp. 97–108.

13) *New York Times,* June 8, 1966.

14) Ibid., June 12, 1966.

15) Paul Good, "The Meredith March," *New South,* Summer, 1966.

16) Ibid.

17) Ibid.

18) *New York Times,* June 22, 1966.

19) Margaret Long, "The Movement," *New South,* Winter, 1966.

20) *New York Times,* January 9, 1964.

21) Ibid., May 23, 1964.

22) John C. Donovan, *The Politics of Poverty* (New York: Pegasus, 1967), p. 55.

23) *New York Times,* November 23, 1966.

24) Marvin E. Gettleman and David Mermelstein, eds., *The Great Society Reader* (New York: Random House, 1967), pp. 69–70.

25) Daniel P. Moynihan, "The President and the Negro: the Moment Lost," *Commentary,* February, 1967.

26) Arthur M. Schlesinger Jr., *The Crisis of Confidence* (Boston: Houghton Mifflin, 1969), p. 156.

27) Robert Sherrill, "Bubble of Unreality," *The Nation,* June 20, 1966.

28) Ibid.

29) Ibid.

30) *New South,* Winter, 1966.

31) Miller, *Martin Luther King,* p. 266.

32) *New York Times,* April 3, 1967.

33) Miller, *Martin Luther King,* p. 267.

34) *New York Times,* April 5, 1967.

CHAPTER NINE

1) Steve Weissman, "Beyond the Moral Imperative," *Liberation,* August, 1966.

2) See Chapter Five.

3) Conversation with Eric Weinberger, Fifth Avenue Peace Parade Committee.

4) *New Republic,* April 29, 1967.

5) *New York Times,* February 26, 1967.

6) *WIN Magazine,* April 7, 1967.

7) *New York Times,* March 27, 1966.

8) *WIN Magazine,* June 16, 1967.

9) Theodore Draper, *Abuse of Power* (New York: Viking Press, 1967), p. 155.

10) *New York Times,* December 27, 1966.

11) Ibid., December 30, 1966.

12) *Washington Post*, January 1, 1967.
13) Phil G. Goulding, *Confirm or Deny* (New York: Harper and Row, 1970), p. 75.
14) *Washington Post*, February 5, 1967.
15) *New York Times*, February 10, 1967.
16) See Cooper, *Lost Crusade*, pp. 325 ff., for the best account of this episode.
17) *Department of State Bulletin*, April 10, 1967.
18) Ibid.
19) *New York Times*, March 3, 1967.
20) Ibid.
21) Ibid., December 30, 1966.
22) *Washington Post*, February 2, 1967.
23) Jay Neugeborn, "Letter from Stanford," *New Republic*, March 18, 1967.
24) *Berkeley Barb*, February 25, 1967.
25) Neugeborn, "Letter."
26) *Berkeley Barb*, April 7, 1967.
27) Paul Good, "On the March Again: New York," *The Nation*, May 1, 1967.
28) *Department of State Bulletin*, April 10, 1967.
29) *New York Times*, April 25, 1967.
30) Ferber and Lynd, *The Resistance*, p. 34.
31) Newfield, *Prophetic Minority*, p. 144.
32) Ferber and Lynd, *The Resistance*, p. 72.
33) *New York Times*, April 7, 1967.
34) Lynd, *We Won't Go*, p. 221.
35) Ferber and Lynd, *The Resistance*, p. 90.
36) Mitford, *Trial of Dr. Spock*, pp. 261–263.
37) Ibid., pp. 124–125.
38) D. Lyle, "Dr. Spock Misbehaves," *Esquire*, February, 1969.
39) *Liberation*, July, 1967.

CHAPTER TEN

1) *Berkeley Barb*, June 16, 1967, and elsewhere that summer. Later the phrase was adopted by the Weatherman faction of SDS as their strategy in the "Days of Rage," Chicago, October 8–11, 1969.
2) *New York Times*, April 30, 1967.
3) Jane Kramer, *Allen Ginsberg in America* (New York: Random House, 1969), p. 48.
4) Ibid., p. 79.
5) This truce came to an end at the Rolling Stones free concert in Altamont, California, on December 6, 1969, where the Angels, recruited as bodyguards in return for $500-worth of beer, attacked spectators at random and killed one young Negro.
6) Kramer, *Allen Ginsberg*, pp. 9–10.

7) Ibid., p. 95.

8) *Liberation*, April, 1967.

9) By far the best account of Kesey and the Merry Pranksters is Wolfe, *Electric Kool-Aid Acid Test*. For a broader account of the San Francisco hippie phenomenon see Burton H. Wolfe, *The Hippies* (New York: Signet New American Library, 1968), a book which deserved a hardcover edition, and Nicholas von Hoffman's brilliant *We are the people our parents warned us against* (Chicago: Quadrangle, 1968).

10) T. Wolfe, *Electric Kool-Aid Acid Test*, p. 367.

11) B. Wolfe, *Hippies*, p. 13.

12) *Evergreen Magazine*, October, 1967.

13) *New York Times*, August 25, 1967.

14) David Sanford, "Pot Bust at Cornell," *New Republic*, April 15, 1967.

15) *Washington Post*, May 13, 1967.

16) *New York Times*, May 28, 1967.

17) Ibid., July 15, 1967.

18) *Washington Free Press*, August 4, 1967.

19) *New York Times*, July 25, 1967.

20) Ibid., July 26, 1967.

21) Ibid., July 21, 1967.

22) Ibid., July 28, 1967.

23) Ibid., July 25, 1967.

24) *Washington Free Press*, August 20, 1967.

25) Frank Harvey, *Air War—Vietnam* (New York: Bantam, 1967), p. 2.

26) Ibid., p. 39.

27) Ted Koppell, "WHAM!" *The Nation*, June 26, 1967.

28) Lawrence E. Eichel, Kenneth W. Jost, Robert D. Luskin, and Richard M. Neustadt, *The Harvard Strike* (Boston: Houghton Mifflin, 1970), p. 37.

29) Ibid., p. 35.

CHAPTER ELEVEN

1) Lynd, *We Won't Go*, p. 157.

2) Lipset and Wolin, eds., *Berkeley Student Revolt*, p. 163.

3) Ferber and Lynd, *The Resistance*, pp. 140–141.

4) Walter Goodman, "The War in the Peace Movement," *New York Times Magazine*, December 3, 1967.

5) Norman Mailer, *The Armies of the Night* (New York: New American Library, 1968), p. 234.

6) Ibid.

7) Ferber and Lynd, *The Resistance*, p. 129.

8) *Berkeley Barb*, October 20, 1967.

9) War Resisters League Calendar, 1973.

10) Dreyer's article was included in a special edition of the Washington *Free Press*, Vol. 2, No. 18, undated (October, 1967).

11) Ibid., November 23, 1967.

12) *Berkeley Barb*, October 27, 1967.

13) *Liberation*, November, 1967.

14) Mailer, *Armies of the Night*, p. 281.

15) Kelman, *Push Comes to Shove*, p. 125.

16) Ferber and Lynd, *The Resistance*, p. 145.

17) *The Guardian*, November 25, 1967.

18) *New York Times*, November 15, 1967.

19) Ibid.

20) Ibid.

21) Ibid., December 1, 1967.

22) Lyle, "Dr. Spock Misbehaves."

23) Sally Kempton, *Village Voice*, December 14, 1967.

24) *New York Times*, December 7, 1967.

25) Ibid.

26) Ibid., December 9, 1967.

27) Kempton, *Village Voice*, December 14, 1967.

28) *Berkeley Barb*, October 20, 1967.

29) Ibid., November 3, 1967.

30) *Village Voice*, November 16, 1967. Rubin's view was to resurface 18 months later, heavily loaded with theory borrowed from Marx, Mao, and Lin Pao, as the Weatherman thesis.

31) *The Guardian*, November 25, 1967.

CHAPTER TWELVE

1) *New York Times*, April 8, 1967.

2) Ibid.

3) Ibid., August 17, 1967.

4) Ibid., August 21, 1967.

5) Ibid., September 5, 1967.

6) Ibid., November 20, 1967.

7) Ibid., October 10, 1967.

8) Ibid., July 12, 1967.

9) *Berkeley Barb*, September 12, 1967.

10) Renata Adler, "Letter from the Palmer House," *The New Yorker*, September 23, 1967.

11) *Berkeley Barb*, September 15, 1967.

12) Ibid.

13) *WIN Magazine*, September 30, 1967.

14) Ibid.

15) *The Nation*, September 25, 1967.

16) Adler, "Letter from Palmer House," *The New Yorker*, September 23, 1967.

17) Ibid.

18) *Berkeley Barb*, September 15, 1967; *New York Times*, September 4, 1967.

19) *Berkeley Barb*, September 15, 1967.

20) von Hoffman, *We are the people our parents warned us against*, p. 146.

21) *Berkeley Barb*, September 15, 1967.

22) *Newsweek*, March 13, 1967.

23) *New York Times*, April 24, 1967.

24) Ibid., May 8, 1967.

25) Arthur Herzog, *McCarthy for President* (New York: Viking Press, 1969), p. 23.

26) *New York Times*, May 21, 1967.

27) Ibid., June 13, 1967.

28) Herzog, *McCarthy*, p. 23.

29) *U.S. News and World Report*, October 9, 1967.

30) *New York Times*, June 4, 1967.

31) Ibid., August 4, 1967.

32) *War/Peace Report*, October, 1967.

33) Schaap, *R.F.K.*, p. 41.

34) Herzog, *McCarthy*, p. 21.

35) Lewis Chester, Godfrey Hodgson, and Bruce Page, *An American Melodrama* (New York: Viking Press, 1969), p. 63.

36) Ibid.,

37) Conversation with David Hawk.

38) *New York Times*, August 15, 1967.

39) Ibid., September 24, 1967.

40) Chester, Hodgson and Page, *American Melodrama*, p. 65.

41) *New York Times*, October 1, 1967.

42) Ibid., August 18, 1967.

43) Ibid., October 13, 1967.

44) Stout, *People*, p. 71.

45) Chester, Hodgson and Page, *American Melodrama*, p. 67.

46) *New York Times*, November 19, 1967.

47) Ibid., December 1, 1967. The version of this statement printed as an appendix to Eugene McCarthy, *The Year of the People* (Garden City, N. Y.: Doubleday, 1969), has been heavily edited.

CHAPTER THIRTEEN

1) *Washington Post*, December 1, 1967.

2) *New York Times*, December 3, 1967.

3) *Life*, January 19, 1968.

4) *New York Times*, January 13, 1968.

5) *New Republic*, January 27, 1968.

6) Ibid., March 6, 1968.

7) *New York Times,* March 7, 1968.

8) Ibid., February 11, 1968.

9) *Washington Post,* March 13, 1968.

10) *New York Times,* March 19, 1968.

11) Ibid., March 25, 1968.

12) Ibid., March 11, 1968.

13) Ibid., March 19, 1968.

14) Ibid., March 8, 1968.

15) Ibid., March 12, 1968.

16) Ibid.

17) *New Republic,* November 25, 1967.

18) *New York Times,* November 19, 1968.

19) *New Republic,* February 24, 1968; *New York Times,* February 11, 1968.

20) *Village Voice,* January 25, 1968.

21) *New York Times,* March 21, 1968.

22) Ibid., March 22, 1968.

23) Ibid., January 31, 1968.

24) *The Nation,* March 18, 1968.

25) *New York Times,* February 3, 1967.

26) Ibid., February 10, 1967.

27) Ibid., September 1, 1967.

28) Ibid., September 30, 1967.

29) Ibid., January 3, 1968.

30) Ibid., January 8, 1968.

31) Ibid., February 17, 1968.

32) Accounts of this reassessment can be found in Clark Clifford, *Foreign Affairs,* July, 1969; Townsend Hoopes, *The Limits of Intervention* (New York: David McKay Company, 1969); Goulding, *Confirm or Deny;* Don Oberdorfer, *Tet* (Garden City, N. Y.: Doubleday, 1971); Theodore H. White, *The Making of the President 1968* (New York: Atheneum, 1969); and Lyndon Baines Johnson, *The Vantage Point* (New York: Holt, Rinehart, and Winston, 1971).

33) Hoopes, *Limits of Intervention,* p. 219.

34) *New York Times,* March 23, 1968.

35) Ibid., February 18, 1968.

36) Ibid., March 23, 1968.

37) General Maxwell Taylor, Abe Fortas, and Robert Murphy, a senior diplomat under Presidents Truman and Eisenhower.

38) *New York Times,* April 1, 1968.

39) White, *Making of the President 1968,* p. 124.

40) Conversation with David Hawk.

41) *Washington Post,* April 1, 1968.

Index